THE NORFOLK BROADS

STALHAM STAITHE

THE
NORFOLK
BROADS

WILLIAM A. DUTT
ASSISTED BY NUMEROUS CONTRIBUTORS

WITH ILLUSTRATIONS BY
FRANK SOUTHGATE

First published by Methuen & Co 1903
Second facsimile edition 2002

ISBN 1 84114 173 9

British Library Cataloguing-in-Publication Data
A CIP record for this title is available from the British Library

HALSGROVE
Halsgrove House
Lower Moor Way
Tiverton, Devon EX16 6SS
T: 01884 243242
F: 01884 243325
sales@halsgrove.com
www.halsgrove.com

Printed and bound in Great Britain by
Bookcraft Ltd, Midsomer Norton

CONTENTS

PART I

PART II

APPENDICES

THE NORFOLK BROADS

PART I

CHAPTER I

OUTLINE OF THE HISTORY OF BROADLAND

EVEN if the general aspect of the district were not enough to indicate it, there is abundant geological evidence that the valleys of East Norfolk were formerly the bed of a large estuary or tidal waste of waters connected with the North Sea. The Icenic settlement on whose site Norwich now stands, was, at the time when the Roman galleys came up against it, situated on some elevated land near the point where the Tas, now a shrunken stream, but then a large river, discharged its waters into this great estuary. All the level marshlands stretching as far inland as Bungay in one direction and Aylsham in another, then presented a similar aspect, only on a larger scale, to that which Breydon wears to-day. The Suffolk Hundred of Lothingland, which contains the town of Lowestoft, the parish of Gorleston, and over a score other parishes, was then an island; for there was a considerable outlet at Kirkley, through which a part of the waters of the Waveney valley found its way to the sea. At Horsey, where even now only a ridge of sandhills separates the marshlands around Hickling Broad and Horsey Mere from the sea, there was another opening through which the tides ebbed and flowed. But the largest mouth of the estuary, extending from Caister to Gorleston, was about four miles wide. It was in the midst of this opening that the sandbank formed on which some fishermen established a settlement of wooden huts, which, as the inland waters decreased in area and the mouth of the estuary narrowed, grew into the town of Great Yarmouth. Connected with the valleys of the Yare, Bure, and Waveney are smaller valleys drained by the rivers Chet, Ant, and Thurne; these, with the lowlands around Fritton Lake and Ormesby, Filby, and Rollesby Broads, also formed part of the East Norfolk estuary whose entrance was called *Garienis* or *Gariensis*.

At the time of the Roman conquest of East Anglia, the highlands around this great estuary were inhabited by an Icenic tribe called the Cenomanni. This tribe soon submitted to Aulus Plautius, and although, according to Tacitus, the Iceni, led by Boadicea, rose against their conquerors and slaughtered the Roman settlers at *Camulodonum* (Colchester), it was not, in all probability, for protection from this native race that the Romans constructed their camps or stations at Caister and Burgh Castle. The conquerors, we are told, "buylded toures on the clyues of the oceean in dyverse places" where "men dredde the arryuyng and londyng of straunge men and enemyes," and it was to protect their newly acquired colony from the attacks of invaders by sea, who might easily have sailed up the estuary into the interior of the country, that the massive stronghold at Burgh and the vanished camp at Caister were built. The fact that it was considered necessary to erect these defences, is evidence that the estuary was navigable to ships large enough to cross the stormy North Sea. At Burgh and Caister the Romans probably kept their galleys moored in readiness to contest the advance of any raiding fleet; and by way of the wide channel of the Yare valley they had no difficulty in keeping in touch with the garrison they had established at *Ad Tavum* (Tasburgh) to protect their important settlement *Venta Icenorum* (Norwich). As Robberds says, in an interesting monograph on the Eastern Valleys of Norfolk, the Roman forts on either side of the mouth of the estuary were built "for defence of this very exposed part of the Saxon shore against the inroads of those formidable Northern pirates by whom it was afterwards so frequently laid waste."

At the time of the Teutonic overpowering of the Britons of Eastern England, the valleys of East Norfolk were, so far as we can ascertain, still in their estuarine state. On the highlands of *Venta Icenorum*, and near Reedham, where the New Cut now connects the Yare and Waveney, the Saxon kings of East Anglia built residences and held their courts. But the sea tides still ebbed and flowed over the oozy flats which stretched many miles inland from the coast; the wild cries of the sea and shore birds were the only voices of this watery wilderness, which seemed destined never to become the dwelling-place of man. True, here and there were little oases or islets—*holms* they were called by the Anglo-Saxons—and on one of them, in what is now the Bure valley, a hermit named Suneman is said to have established himself during the ninth century. At Ellingham, too, between Beccles and Bungay, and on the larger island tracts of Lothingland and the Flegg district, there were doubtless little colonies of Saxons; but although the sandbank on which Yarmouth was afterwards built was slowly forming at the mouth of the great estuary, the sea still claimed the valleys as its own.

Then came the Danes, whose attacks the Romans had dreaded, and the sight of their " black war-keels " struck terror into the hearts of the peace-loving Saxons. The story of Ragnar Lodbrog, whose boat is said to have been blown across the North Sea and into the Norfolk estuary, and who, after he landed at Reedham, was murdered by Bern, King Edmund's huntsman, is probably mythical; but it indicates that the monkish chroniclers saw nothing improbable in the suggestion that Lodbrog could not land until he reached the shore of the highlands at Reedham. And we know that in the ninth century the Danes often ravaged the Norfolk coast, and that the dwellers on the shores of the East Norfolk estuary suffered severely at their hands. Year after year they came, the raven banner of Inguar and Ubba flying from the mast-heads of their viking ships. They forced their way up the Bure valley and destroyed perhaps the hermitage of Suneman; in the valley of the Waveney they compelled the Saxons to take refuge in their churches, and there burnt them alive as a sacrifice to Thor and Wodin. Later, in 1004, Sweyn sailed a Danish fleet up to Norwich, which he plundered and burnt. The Flegg (Norse *flegg*, flat) Hundreds contained within the island tract to the north of the chief mouth of the estuary were wrested from their Saxon holders, and in the names which its hamlets bear to-day we have conclusive proof that there the raiders established a considerable settlement; for in Rollesby, Mautby, and other hamlets we find the Danish *by* suffixed to the names of Rollo and Malthe, who undoubtedly were viking raiders who chose the dry ground around the Flegg inlets as sites for their homesteads, because there they could moor their boats, dry their nets, and live just such lives as they had been accustomed to, in the intervals of their viking voyages, on their own wild coast. And there, near the banks of Breydon and on the marshlands bordering the lower waters of the Yare and Bure, you may to-day, if you study carefully the faces and inquire the names of some of the dwellers amid those lonesome marshes, discover descendants of those viking settlers who fished the waters of the Norfolk estuary a thousand years ago. But the period during which the Danes held the Norfolk Saxons in subjection was a comparatively brief one. Apart from the names of some of the villages, there is little in Broadland to remind us of the raiding settlers. It was, however, according to tradition, their King Canute who, on the site of Suneman's hermitage, founded the Abbey of St. Benet-at-Holm; and though there are no traces of Danish work in the scanty ruins of this once famous monastic house, it may have owed its wealth and influence in no small measure to his lavish endowments.

To go back a little in the history of the East Norfolk valleys, it may seem somewhat strange that the Romans, when they built such important stations as the camps at Burgh and Caister, did not, as they did in the Marshland district near Lynn, compel the conquered Iceni to construct banks along the coast to keep out the sea, and so reclaim some of the oozy levels daily submerged by the tides. The fact that they did not do so seems to indicate that the tidal inflow through the mouths of the estuary was far greater than upon the lowlands lying along the borders of the Wash. As a matter of fact, the gradual choking up of the entrances to the East Norfolk estuary was an entirely natural process; and, having now arrived at the period when the town of Yarmouth came into existence, it may be as well to explain how this change was brought about.

Mr. R. C. Taylor, whose *Geology of East Norfolk* was considered so reliable a work, that Lyell based upon it most of his remarks on the character of the Norfolk coast in his *Principles of Geology*, tells us that the effect of the great tidal current of the North Sea has been to undermine the high projecting portions of the coast and deposit the débris thus detached to the southward of the undermined cliffs. That this wasting process is continually going on will be admitted at once by every one who is acquainted with the cliffs between Happisburgh and Cromer. The débris of these cliffs either forms shoals a little distance from the coast, or low tracts of land along the shore. Some twenty miles of the Norfolk coast have been subjected to this erosion, which, with the assistance of innumerable land springs in the cliffs, has resulted in the total destruction of the ancient villages of Shipden, Wimpwell, and Eccles, the demolition of several manors, and of large portions of several parishes. In the winter of 1825, Taylor writes, a tract of twelve acres was suddenly detached from the Cromer cliffs; since then many landslides have occurred. " The effects of this destructive process are traced in the banks and shoals extending twenty miles to the southward, and the formation of the low flat tract between Happisburgh and Gorleston. In their progress the tidal currents possess sufficient strength and velocity to preserve a deep channel, locally called Roads, parallel with the shore; but they deposit, both on the sea and land sides of this passage, the alluvial matter with which the waters are charged."

The destruction of one part of the coast thus led to the consolidation or banking up of another, with the result that the mouth of the great estuary, once four miles wide, became so choked that only a comparatively narrow channel was left for the inrush of the tides. Against the bank formed by the set of the tides, sediment brought down from the estuary by the ebb gradually accumulated; then the wind-blown sand from the

neighbouring beach covered it; and finally the decay of
vegetable matter completed the composition of the land upon
which the town of Yarmouth stands.   The channel or Gap at
Horsey was first closed by this process, that being the northernmost of the estuary's mouths.   Then the largest entrance
became so shallow, owing to the forming of a sandy bar, that
in the reign of Edward III. the ship channel, then much farther
north than it is now, was entirely blocked.   Since then the great
difficulty has been, not to prevent the inrush of the tide, but to
preserve a deep channel for shipping.   Seven times between
1347 and 1560 the Yarmouth port authorities found it
necessary to construct new havens.   So essential was it that a
clear channel should be preserved, that every monarch from
Edward III. to Charles I. granted money for the purpose.
Between 1560 and 1650 five other havens had to be constructed,
four during that time meeting with a like fate to that which
befell those made during the previous two hundred years.   The
expense entailed by these operations is said to have amounted
to over a million pounds.   As Taylor points out, there was a
constant effort on the part of Nature to stretch a barrier across
the mouth of the estuary, so as to connect Caister and Gorleston
and shut out the sea from the inland lowlands.

The process which resulted in the closing of Horsey Gap
and the partial closing of the chief mouth of the estuary was
also seen in operation at Lowestoft.   There the débris of
the northern cliffs was heaped along the border of the low-lying
denes or dunes; and the wind-blown sand, in which the binding
maram-grass and sand sedge rooted themselves, increased the
height and stability of these natural barriers.   On this self-
reclaimed land the greater part of Old Lowestoft, or the beachmen's quarter, is built.   The mouth of the estuarine Lake
Lothing was closed by an artificial embankment about the
middle of the seventeenth century, with the object of excluding
the sea from certain lands that were subject to inundation.
This embankment was subsequently cut through for the
purpose of enlarging the harbour; but a lock at Mutford
Bridge prevents the waters of Oulton Broad and the Waveney
entering the sea by way of Lake Lothing and Lowestoft
Harbour.

But these remarks on the processes which led to the forming of the wide marshlands bordering the Broadland rivers have brought us down to times almost within the memory of living men, and it is necessary for the completion of this rough outline of the history of Broadland to go back to the days of the Norman Conquest of England.

After the Battle of Hastings was fought and won, King William had little difficulty in bringing the greater part of East Anglia into subjection.   It was only on the Isle of Ely, that natural fortress in the midst of the trackless fens, that a small body of the English, led, if we may believe the monkish chroniclers, by the dauntless Hereward, succeeded in holding out for a while against the Conqueror and his armies.   A few of the Norfolk and Suffolk men may have fled to that fenland fastness, but the rest of the inhabitants of the two easternmost counties submitted to the Normans, and saw their manors divided among the king's favourite barons.   Norwich, where Uffa, the first king of the East Angles, is supposed to have had his centre of government, was given to Ralph de Guader, who was made Earl of Norfolk.   He it was who built on the huge artificial mound on which the castle now stands a fortress which, when the earl rebelled against the king, was able to withstand a six months' siege.   Of this stronghold there are now no traces, but of the castle built by Roger Bigod in the latter part of the eleventh century the huge tower or keep remains.   This Roger Bigod, who succeeded De Guader as Earl of Norfolk, also had a share in the founding of Norwich Cathedral, and it is not unlikely that some of the Norman work still in evidence among the churches of Broadland belonged to ecclesiastical buildings he built or endowed.   His descendants also were great builders of castles and religious houses.   One of them built the massive stronghold at Bungay, choosing, as at Norwich, some existing earthworks as its site; and from that commanding position he ruled the valley of the Waveney. A Bigod, too, it was who founded Weybridge Priory, which stood near Acle Bridge, on the Bure.

Under the Normans Norwich speedily became a place of considerable importance.   In 1086 it contained 1360 burgesses; and in 1122, on the occasion of his visiting it, Henry I. granted it a charter conferring upon its citizens like privileges to those enjoyed by the citizens of London. It became the see of the great East Anglian diocese in 1094, and Herbert de Lozinga, who was then bishop, founded the church which gradually grew into a grand cathedral. By this time the river channel of the Yare valley had narrowed considerably, and the Tas was no longer navigable; but in 1075, Ralph de Guader, when he fled to Brittany after rebelling against the king, was able to take ship at Norwich; and so late as 1327 the citizens pleaded, in connection with a charge against the burgesses of Yarmouth, that Norwich was "situate on the bank of a water and arm of the sea, which extended from thence to the main ocean, upon which ships, boats, and other vessels have immemorially come to their market," and that "all foreign merchants paid all their customs at Norwich, which was the then port, and in the king's hands." [1]

Yarmouth, meanwhile, from being a small settlement of fishermen's huts on the sandy bar which had formed at the mouth of the estuary, was becoming a flourishing fishing station and busy port. A "greate store of sea-faringe men, as also of greate numbers of the fishermen of France, Flanders, and of Holland, Zealande, and of all the lowe countries," yearly visited it; and during the herring-fishing season the barons of the Cinque ports, who had been granted jurisdiction over the port, sent their bailiffs to Yarmouth to preserve order and collect tolls.[2]   Here, too, Bishop Lozinga founded a church,

[1] Blomefield's *Norfolk*.

[2] "It is chiefly from the enactments and ordinances of successive sovereigns that the early history of the English Fisheries can be traced. At the time of the Conquest a great number of maritime fiefs on the eastern coast carried on the herring fishery, and there were numerous *salinæ* in Norfolk and Suffolk. An immense number of herrings were taken in the large estuaries which at that period covered the eastern valleys. Norwich and Beccles were great rival marts for the sale of herrings. There is evidence of Norwich being a fishing town in the reign of Canute, for Alfric, Bishop of East Anglia, having bestowed his *hagh*, by Norwich (the site on which the church of St. Lawrence was afterwards erected), upon the Abbey of St. Edmundsbury, an annual ground rent was paid to that monastery of a last of herrings. The fee farm rent of thirty thousand herrings paid to Edward the Confessor on the manor of Beccles, was at the Domesday survey raised by the Conqueror to the tollage of sixty thousand, and many similar imposts are recorded in *Domesday* as paid by the villages and towns upon the shores of the estuaries."—Nall's *Chapters on the East Anglian Coast*.

now the great parish church of St. Nicholas; and in 1272
Henry III. by charter granted the townsfolk the right to call
the town " Great " Yarmouth.   Beccles in its early days had its
share in the herring fisheries, for the herring shoals made their
way up the estuary; but it was in Lowestoft that the Yarmouth
authorities had their chief rival, for at Kirkley Haven the
foreign and native fishermen could land their catches without
paying the customary dues.

So we see that soon after the Norman Conquest important
towns came into existence on the borders of the Broadland
valleys.   Norwich quickly established its claim to be considered
the chief industrial centre of East Anglia; Yarmouth soon
became the most important port; Lowestoft its chief rival;
Beccles a rising town; and Bungay a seat of one of the great
baronial families.   On many of the manors adjoining the
valleys Norman churches were erected, some of which replaced
the Saxon buildings destroyed by the Danes.   Of this Norman
work we still have good examples in the round towers at
Haddiscoe and Herringfleet, and in the doorways of Chedgrave, Aldeby, and other Broadland churches.

Between 1100 and 1240 monastic houses were founded at
Aldeby, Langley, Herringfleet, Hickling, Acle, and Bungay, the
sites chosen being close to the rivers and marshes, which
provided abundant fish and fowl for the monks and nuns.
Peaceful times ensuing, efforts were made to drain some of
the swampy lands.   The rivers were embanked, and causeways were constructed across the trackless, treacherous fens.
The causeway now known as Acle Dam was certainly in
existence in the eleventh century, for in 1101 it was found
necessary to repair it; and before 1274 the river Ant was
embanked for the protection of the lands belonging to the
flourishing Abbey of St. Benet-at-Holm.   But for centuries
there remained wide tracts of swamp, amid which the bittern,
spoonbill, avoset, and black tern nested, where thousands of
warblers swung and sung on the swaying reeds, where misleading will-o'-the-wisps flickered, and over which buzzards,
hawks, and kestrels hovered, and herons flew with slow
wing-beats to their nests in the bordering woods.   In the
shallow lakes or Broads amid these swamps large shoals of

bream provided food for the innumerable otters which haunted the sedgy shores, and hungry pike preyed on the young water-fowl which ventured out of the reed beds. Night and day the wild crying of curlews, the bleating of snipe, and the piping of redshanks were heard above the "chucking" of the reed and sedge warblers. At night the peasants who dwelt on the borders of the fens were often startled by the loud clanging of wild geese or the trumpeting of wild swans. In winter the ooze flats from which the sea receded at ebb tide were often white with wild fowl which came there to feed. On the shores and sedgy islets of the Broads were colonies of gulls, whose clamouring during the nesting season drowned the warbling and calling of all the smaller birds of the reeds and fens.

While efforts were being made to drain these fenny tracts formed by the deposit of alluvial soil from the interior of the country, the sea still tried hard at times to win back its ancient bed. The reclaimers' work closely resembled that of the old-time dwellers among the Cambridgeshire and Lincolnshire fens; and though, in course of time, it met with a like reward, it was not done without incessant toil and the encountering of disheartening difficulties. For the line of shifting sandhills which the sea and winds had reared along the East Norfolk coast was but a frail barrier against the high tides which strong westerly winds sometimes created in the North Sea; and when such tides occurred in stormy weather, the surf-scour often demolished a portion of this sandy bastion and the sea broke in upon the lowlands. Such a disaster happened in the winter of 1287. We find an account of it in the chronicles of John of Oxnead, who writes: " In 1287, in the month of December, the seventh of the Kalends of January, the 8th day of the moon, the sea, in dense darkness, began to be agitated by the violence of the wind, and in its agitation to burst through its accustomed limits, occupying towns, fields, and other places adjacent to the coast, and inundating parts which no age in past times had recorded to have been covered with sea water. For, issuing forth about the middle of the night, it suffocated or drowned men and women sleeping in their beds, with infants in their cradles, and all kinds of cattle and fresh-water fishes; and it tore up houses from their foundations with all they contained, and carried them away and threw them into the sea with irrecoverable damage. Many, when surrounded by the waters, sought a place of refuge by mounting into trees; but, benumbed by the cold, they were overtaken by the water and fell into it and were drowned. Whereby it happened that in the town of Hyckelyngge (Hickling) nine score of different sexes and ages perished in the aforesaid inundation." It was, it appears from this account, in the neighbourhood of Horsey that the sea broke in on this occasion, and it was there that a serious inroad of the sea, fortunately unattended by loss of human life, was experienced during the last decade.

Similar inundations occurred in later years, destroying in a few hours work which had taken years to accomplish; but if Stowe and a contemporary writer can be believed, the Hickling flood was nothing like so serious as those which devastated Kent, Essex, Suffolk, and Norfolk in 1607; for then, we read, thousands of men, women, and children were drowned, whole towns and villages demolished, and vast numbers of cattle and sheep destroyed. The destruction wrought at this time has undoubtedly been greatly exaggerated, but that serious damage was done is evident from the fact that in 1609 an Act of Parliament was passed " for the speedy recovery of many thousand acres of Marsh Ground and other Ground within the Counties of Norfolk and Suffolk, lately surrounded by the Rage of the sea in divers parts of the said Counties, and for the Prevention of Danger of the like surrounding here-after." The sea, we are informed by the preamble of this Act, had caused a flood which affected places as far removed from each other as Horsey and Gillingham, Caister, Oulton, and Carrow. At Yarmouth part of the Haven Bridge was destroyed, and the Haven House, in which were the " Haven man " and his son, was " carried into the marshes six miles from the Haven." Blomefield relates that " a part of the sea-shore lying between the towns of Great Yarmouth and Happisburgh, lying low, and being sand only, was lately (1607) broken down and washed away by the violence of the tides, so that the sea broke in every tide, and with every sea-wind came up the Norwich River into the very body and heart of the county of Norfolk, drowning much hard grounds, and many thousand acres of marsh, upon which great part of the wealth of the county depends, being most rich grounds, and without which the uplands, which are mostly dry and barren, cannot be husbanded ; and by means of the salt waters, the fisheries between Yarmouth and Norwich, as well in rivers and Broads, were much damaged, so that the great plenty which used to maintain many poor men was gone, and the markets badly served with fresh fish ; to remedy which there were appointed eighteen commissioners, who, according to the direction of the Act, were to stop the breaches, it being to be feared that in time to come further mischief might follow by other breaches, or enlarging of those already made, if speedy remedy be not provided, and God of His mercy stop not the same."

These inroads of the sea often nullified the Broadlanders' efforts to reclaim the swamps ; but in the fourteenth century the loss of life by flood was hardly worthy of consideration beside that caused by an outbreak, in 1349, of the terrible Black Death. Then, it may be truly said, the Angel of Death hardly for a moment ceased to cast the shadow of his wings over the eastern counties. In Norwich alone, it is recorded, over 50,000 died, in Yarmouth 7000 ; and there was no town, and scarcely a hamlet, in the marsh districts of Norfolk and Suffolk which had not cause to mourn each day its newly dead. Brought over sea by some ship from an infected continental port, the plague first attacked the coast towns ; but it soon spread along the river valleys, village being linked to village, "closer and closer every day, in one ghastly chain of death." When Bishop Bateman of Norwich, who was abroad at the time of the outbreak, landed at Yarmouth, the first news he heard was that his brother, Sir Bartholomew Bateman, whose home was at Gillingham, had fallen a victim to the dread scourge. At Bungay the prioress of the Benedictine nunnery died, and the bishop, when he hastened to Gillingham, was called upon to institute a new prioress. During the ensuing twenty days a hundred clergy were admitted to cures made vacant by death. A little later the Abbot of St. Benet-at-Holm was numbered among the victims ; and at Hickling, where was a priory founded by Theobald de Valoins, only one canon survived. Dr. Jessopp, whose careful researches among old parish rolls and other documents have enabled him to present a vivid picture of East Anglia during this terrible time, asks, "Who can adequately realise the horrors of that awful summer? In the desolate swamps through which the sluggish Bure crawls reluctantly to mingle its waters with the Yare; by the banks of the Waveney, where the little Bungay nunnery had been a refuge for the widow, the forsaken, or the devout for centuries; . . . among the ooze and sedge and chill loneliness of the Broads, where the tall reeds wave and whisper, and all else is silent—the glorious buildings with their sumptuous churches were little better than centres of contagion. From the stricken towns people fled to the monasteries, lying away there in their seclusion, lonely, favoured of God. If there was hope anywhere, it must be there. As frightened widows and orphans flocked to these havens of refuge, they carried the Black Death with them; and when they dropped death-stricken at the doors, they left the contagion behind them as their only legacy."

It is a gloomy picture, and difficult to associate with the charming hamlets, sparkling Broads, flower-spangled meadows, and bird-haunted reed beds and copses amid which sails the summer voyager on Broadland waterways. One is glad to forget it, or to remind one's self that the days have long gone by when the conditions of life in England were such as to favour the spreading of dreadful plagues. But one cannot forget that so downtrodden were the Norfolk peasantry at that time, that it is not surprising they had sunk into a state of such callous indifference that their houses were worse than modern cattle-stalls, and constituted hot-beds for the breeding of disease. As Langland says, the lords treated the husbandmen and labourers in such a way, "that us loathed the lyf." The system of forced labour was keenly resented. Although after the plague the value of the hind's labour had doubled, statutes were passed compelling him to work at the same wages he had received before it. If he fled from service and was captured, he was branded on the forehead for his "crime." So it is little wonder that the "vermin," as Froissart calls them, grew restless through brooding over their wrongs, and although Church and

State were against them, determined to strike a blow for freedom. Contemporaneously with Wat Tyler's insurrection in Kent, and Jack Straw's in Suffolk, the Norfolk rustics revolted. They appointed as their leader John Litester, a Norwich man, who led them to Norwich and afterwards through the county, where many knights and gentlemen were glad for a time to render them service so as to escape ill-treatment at their hands. No doubt they indulged in great excesses, for John Litester was not a strong man who could keep them under control, or help them to gain the ends they had in view. For a time they were masters of the situation, and it was not until Bishop Henry le Spencer collected a force and marched against them that they were overpowered and compelled to retreat. They then abandoned Norwich, which they had plundered, and fell back on North Walsham, where they encamped on a heath outside the town, and tried to make a stand. But Bishop Le Spencer vigorously attacked them, and, after a sharp battle, dispersed them and captured their leader. The slain, it is said, were buried on the battle-field, and a stone cross which stands beside the Norwich road is believed to mark the spot where they lie. The King of the Commons, as the leader styled himself, was hanged and quartered, and the quarters set up on his house at Norwich, and in London, Yarmouth, and Lynn.

Then the hinds—the men by whose labour the lords of the manors grew rich, and by whose embanking and ditching many thousand acres of the East Norfolk fens were being transformed into grazing lands—were kept in submission for over a century; but in 1549 there was another and far more serious rising in Norfolk, under the leadership of Robert Kett, a Wymondham tanner. The grievances of which the insurgents complained were very like those under which the hinds of Richard the Second's reign had laboured; but their chief cause of complaint was the frequent enclosing of the common-lands on which they had kept their geese and swine. Among them, however, were many of the men of the Broad-land marshes, and in the petition which Kett sent to the king we find it asked that " redegrounde and meadowe-grounde may be at such price as they were in the first yere of Kyng henry the VII "; that " all marshysshe that ar holden of the Kyng's majestie by ffre rent or of eny other, may be ageyn at the price they were in the first yere of King henry the VII "; and that " Ryvers may be ffre and comon to all men for fyshyng and passage." To the men of the marshes it seemed a hard thing that they should be grudged a mess of roach or bream when they and their wives and children were starving, and that they should be debarred from earning a little money by cutting and selling the wild reeds which grew by the waterside. But the king, we learn, was indignant that such a petition should be sent to him ; and after the Earl of Warwick had slain thousands of Norfolk peasants in a battle on Mousehold Heath, near Norwich, Kett and other leaders of the insurgents met with the common fate of sixteenth-century reformers.

But while the peasantry remained little better than serfs, crouching, like whipped hounds, at the feet of the lords of the manors, the towns on the borders of Broadland were becoming important centres of industry. At Norwich and Worstead a large number of Flemings had settled, and were making these places famous for their woollen manufactures ; Aylsham had become a thriving centre of linen-working ; while Yarmouth, which was still at loggerheads with Norwich and Lowestoft about port dues and privileges, was, at the end of the fourteenth century, surrounded by " a fair high wall embattled and most magnificently towered and turretted." That such extensive fortifications were constructed, testifies to Yarmouth's growing importance ; it was, in fact, the chief port on the east coast, and prosperous not only on account of its increasing fishing industry, but because its situation at the mouth of the estuary of the three principal rivers of Broadland enabled it to supply many places in the interior with imported goods. Its merchants rapidly became wealthy, and contributed considerable sums towards the enlarging and beautifying of Lozinga's Norman church, where Roger of Haddiscoe, who was prior of St. Olave's in 1370, erected a costly and elaborate rood loft, which screened the high altar from the nave. In Norwich there were several flourishing monastic houses, and the cathedral was being enlarged and adorned through the efforts of the bishops of the diocese.

The fifteenth century saw the building, on the border of the Caister marshes, of Sir John Fastolff's great brick castle Sir John was a famous soldier, and a descendant of a family which had established itself at Yarmouth in the reign of Edward I. After serving Thomas of Lancaster, second son of Henry IV., he was present at the taking of Harfleur, and became one of the governors of that town. At Agincourt, Caen, and Rouen he greatly distinguished himself, and afterwards was appointed successively governor of the Bastille, seneschal, lieutenant, and regent of Normandy, and governor of Anjou and Maine. He was a very wealthy man, possessing houses in London, Norwich, and Yarmouth, and when he built Caister Castle he made it one of the largest and finest buildings in England; but he was an old man when it was completed, and died after occupying it a few years. He was buried in the abbey church of St. Benet-at-Holm. The castle then came into the possession of the Pastons, from whom the Duke of Norfolk took it by force; but on the death of the duke they regained possession and held it until 1599, when it was sold to one of their creditors. Since then it has gradually fallen into its present ruined state; but there is enough left of its walls and towers to indicate what a fine place it was in Fastolff's day. Among the manors held by Sir John was that of Blickling, near Aylsham. He sold it to Sir Geoffry Boleyn, a wealthy Lord Mayor of London, and its manor house became an early home of the ill-fated Anne Boleyn. This house has vanished, but on its site stands the finest Jacobean house in Norfolk. Vanished, too, is that stately hall at Oxnead which Clement Paston, a distinguished naval commander of the reign of Henry VIII., built, and in which King Charles II. was sumptuously entertained; but in the hall and gardens at Blickling can be seen some of its ornamental work, and also some of that with which Sir John Fastolff adorned his Caister home.

While most of the towns on the borders of Broadland were growing fast, Lowestoft seems to have experienced many vicissitudes of fortune. These were chiefly due to its disputes with Yarmouth concerning the herring fisheries; for these disputes led to the granting and revoking of several charters. But there is little interest attaching to these sordid squabbles, and as, after the blocking up of the great Norfolk estuary, they referred only to the herrings caught at sea, they scarcely come within the scope of a book dealing with Broadland.

At the beginning of the seventeenth century most of the swamps bordering the Broadland rivers had been drained, and the marshy pastures into which they were transformed were a source of considerable profit to those who owned or hired them.   Still, here and there, there were fenny tracts where the bearded titmouse—that pretty little fen bird—abounded, and amid which, during his residence in Norfolk, Sir Thomas Browne found many of the birds mentioned in his Norfolk list.   Wild - fowl decoying had become a fruitful source of revenue to the dwellers on the shores of the Broads, where, as Sir Thomas tells us, duck, wigeon, and teal were plentiful ; and he adds that there was also a " great store of otters " among the " rivers, great broads, and carrs," and that they destroyed large quantities of fish.   King Charles I., we learn, was supplied with herons from Reedham, where there is still a herony ; and peewits were so plentiful around Horsey that cartloads of them were brought into Norwich, and the country people used their eggs in puddings.

CHAPTER II

OUTLINE OF THE HISTORY OF BROADLAND
(*continued*)

PLEASURE-SEEKERS who lived beyond the borders of East Anglia did not discover Broadland until about thirty years ago. Since then nearly all writers about the district have expressed surprise that its charms and beauties so long remained unrecognised. But Norfolk and Suffolk folk, in spite of all that has been said to the contrary, were well aware of the delights of cruising on the slow-winding, peaceful rivers, and angling and wild-fowling on the Broads. Long before the Dissolution, the abbots of St. Benet-at-Holm entertained their distinguished guests with falconry on the Cowholm marshes; and who can doubt that the monks of Langley, St. Olave's, and St. Benet's spent many days in fishing the streams which flowed beside their monasteries? That the people of Yarmouth in the seventeenth century were no more in the habit of taking their pleasures sadly than they are to-day, and that they were quite aware how much pleasure was to be enjoyed on the inland waters, is evident from an account of the proceedings at the annual inquest of the river liberties, contained in the journal of the Rev. Rowland Davies, a famous divine of his day. The bailiffs of Yarmouth, it should be explained, at an early period in the history of the town, claimed a right to levy on fishermen a small toll for permission to establish fishing stations on the lower waters of the rivers Yare, Bure, and Waveney. This right, often disputed by the riparian owners, was enforced on the annual "inquest" day. On 7th August 1689, writes the reverend diarist, "I broke fast with Mr. Bailiff England, and about nine o'clock went with him on board a wherry made in the form of a barge. As we marched, three drums were beat, and as many colours flourished before us all along the street; and as we went up the water in each of our wherries, a drum beat at the head and a colour was flourished at the stern of our boat. We were attended by over twenty other lesser boats full of people, and if the seamen were at home and dared appear, I was assured we should have had double the number, as was usual. The first boat that led the way was full of young men in white, with caps made like those of our grenadiers. After followed our boat with the king's colours on the mast; then another alike in all things, wherein was the other bailiff; after which two wherries followed each other (!), having the arms of the town for their flag, in each of which was one of the foremen, and the quest for each end of the town; they being persons sworn in the nature of a grand jury, to an inquiry into all the abuses and all the privileges of the town, and make presentments as they find occasion." Manship, the Yarmouth historian, who also gives an account of this ceremony, adds that the inquest was attended with "banners and ensigns displayed, sometimes with sound of trumpets, beating of drums, playing of fifes, and otherwhiles sweetly singing;" and that the bailiffs carried with them scales and measures to ascertain whether the fishermen's nets were of a lawful size and mesh. After crossing Breydon, one of the bailiffs' barges went up the Waveney as far as St. Olave's, while the other, by way of the Yare, reached Hardley Cross. On their return and meeting at Breydon there was "a stir in firing guns, huzzas, and drinking healths, etc.; and so we returned in the evening as we went out."

This annual inquest seems to have been a lively festival, and there is little doubt that, if it survived, it would be very popular with Yarmouth's summer visitors, for whom its gun-firing, huzzaing, and health-drinking would have a great fascination. It was looked upon as one of the most important civic events of the year. The mayors of Norwich and Yarmouth, in their state barges, met at Hardley Cross, the limit of their respective jurisdictions over the Yare. There the Norwich town clerk, standing beside the old cross on the

river bank at the mouth of the Chet, made the following proclamation:[1] "Oyez! oyez! oyez! If there be any manner
of person that will absume, purfy, implead, or prosecute any
action, suit, plaint, or plea for any offence, tresspass, or mis-
demeanour, done or committed upon the King's Majesty's
River of Wensum, let him repair unto the Right Worshipful
Mr. Mayor and the Worshipful Sheriff of the City of Norwich,
for the redress thereof, and he shall be heard. God save the
King." A similar proclamation was read by the Yarmouth
town clerk with reference to the waters below Hardley Cross,
and the barges then went down on to Breydon, where a kind
of regatta was held. Dr. Sayers, who witnessed one of these
jollifications, relates that on such occasions "all the many
pleasure boats kept on these rivers assemble; the commercial
craft (probably the wherries) is in requisition to stow spectators,
to waft music, to vend refreshments: such of the shipping as
ascends above the Yarmouth drawbridge is moored within
ken; there are sailing matches, rowing matches, and spon-
taneous evolutions of vessels of all sorts, a dance of ships,
their streamers flying and their canvas spread. It is a fair
afloat, where the voice of revelry resounds from every gliding
tent. And when the tide begins to fall, and to condense this
various fleet into the narrower waters, and the bridge and
quays and balconies and windows of Yarmouth are thronged
with innumerable spectators—and boys have climbed the
masts and rigging of the moored ships—adding to the crowd
on shore a crowd above—and the gathering boats mingle
their separate concerts in one chorus of jollity—and guns fire
—and loyalty and liberty shout with rival glee—and the
setting sun inflames the whole lake, the scene becomes sur-
passingly impressive, exhilarating, and magnificent."

But while residents in the district were beginning to
disport themselves on the Broads and rivers, strangers were

---

[1] Several attempts have been made to explain the words "absume" and "purfy"
in this proclamation. Mr. J. H. Druery, who published some interesting notes on
the ceremony, says they are Norman, "absume" a corruption of "absoudre," to
absolve, acquit, or discharge; "purfy" derived from "par-faire," to perfect or
complete. There is an old story told in Norfolk that a Norwich town clerk was once
asked what he would do if some one expressed a desire to "absume" and "purfy."
"I should tell him to go and do it," was the reply.

little impressed by East Norfolk's level lowlands and sluggish streams. Miss Celia Fiennes, an adventurous lady, who in the seventeenth century took a ride on horseback through many parts of England, entered the Waveney valley by way of Beccles. Having crossed a wooden bridge, she found herself, she writes, on low flat grounds, which were often overflowed by the river, " so that the road lay under water, which is very unsafe for strangers to pass, by reason of the holes and quicksands and loose bottom." The houses in Beccles, she observed, were built of old timber and plasterwork ; in fact, there were no good houses in the town except Sir R. Rich's and one or two others. Still the town even then ranked third in importance in Suffolk, only Ipswich and Bury being larger and more populous.

In 1722, however, Daniel Defoe gave a better account of the East Norfolk marshlands. The river Yare, he wrote, passes through the largest and richest tract of meadows in England, stretching from Norwich to Yarmouth, and extended by the marshes on the banks of the rivers Waveney and " Thyrn." On this vast tract of meadows were fed an immense number of black cattle, which not only supplied Norwich, Yarmouth, and the country adjacent with beef, but also great quantities to the London markets. It was also particularly worthy of remark, he added, that the greater part of the Scots cattle which yearly came to England was brought on to those lush marshes, where they fed eagerly and grew " monstrously fat." He was told, and had good reasons to believe, that above forty thousand of these Scots " runts " were fed in the county every year, " and most of them in the said marshes between Norwich, Beccles, and Yarmouth." The town of Yarmouth he considered better built than Norwich, and for wealth, trade, and advantage of situation " infinitely superior " to that city ; its quay was the finest in England, if not in Europe, and along it stood some " very magnificent buildings," some of the merchants' houses having the appearance of " palaces rather than the dwelling-houses of private men."

During the latter years of the eighteenth century the sea

on several occasions invaded Broadland, usually, as in the earlier centuries, in the neighbourhood of Horsey, where there have always been weak spots in the sandhills. During one of these floods a breach two hundred yards wide was made, and the salt water, "poisoning" the rivers even so far inland as Norwich, killed great quantities of fresh-water fish. After 1791, however, the sea was kept out for over a century, and the men of the marshes had some reason for believing that they would never again be troubled by any inundations worse than the ordinary rain-floods. But in the winter of 1897 the Horsey sandhills were again unable to withstand the surf scour, and, winning its way into the narrow bed of the shrunken Hundred Stream, the sea soon poured over the adjoining marshlands. Fortunately the hundred miles or so of dykes which drain these marshes were almost empty at the time, or, as an old marshman observed, no one knows "what mightn't ha' happened." For nearly three hours the sea swept in through the breach it had made, and often the waves broke on the landward side of the sandhills. Hundreds of rabbits, which had their burrows in the warren lying between the sandhills and the marshes, were drowned; and for days afterwards the gulls and hooded crows gorged themselves with the dead fish in the dykes. After the sea had gone down, nearly 200,000 tons of salt water were pumped off the Horsey marshes in about thirty hours.

But in spite of inundations the work of reclamation has for centuries gone steadily on. Acre by acre swamps have been turned into rush marshes and rush marshes into grazing grounds. Along the banks of the chief rivers "walls" have been raised to protect and preserve the reclaimed lands, and scores of steam and wind pump-mills, discharging the water out of hundreds of miles of dykes, quickly free the marshes of rain-floods. For centuries the Broadsmen have reaped an annual harvest of reeds by the riversides and around the Broads; while hundreds of wherries have sailed up and down the rivers, carrying cargoes of corn, coal, and timber between the coast and the inland towns. At the beginning of the last century another kind of craft traded between the chief towns of Broadland. These were called keels, and it was written of them about ninety years ago, that they were " in a great measure peculiar to the navigation between Norwich and Yarmouth, and are supposed to be superior to the small craft upon any other stream in England, as carrying a larger burden and being worked at a smaller expense. They have but one mast, which lets down by a windlass placed at the head, carry one large square sail, are covered close by hatches, and have a cabin superior to many coasting vessels, in which it is not unusual for the keelman and his family to live. They are never navigated by more than two men, and often by a man and his wife, or one man and a boy. The usual passage for a loaded keel is from twelve to sixteen hours; when light, they perform it in five hours. . . . This kind of craft carry grain of every sort grown in the county—flour, etc.—to Yarmouth, besides the goods manufactured at Norwich for foreign markets. In return, from Yarmouth they bring coals, grocery, ironmongery, fir-timber, wine, spirits, etc." In the Norwich Castle Museum there is a picture of one of these keels, which were larger and heavier craft than the wherries, and had their masts placed amidships.

The reference to the exporting of Norwich-manufactured goods reminds me that even at the time when the foregoing words were written, Norwich's importance as a manufacturing centre had begun to decline. How great was once that importance can be gathered from another writer's words. The Norwich travellers, he writes, have penetrated throughout Europe; " their pattern cards were exhibited in every principal town, from the frozen plains of Moscow to the milder climes of Lisbon, Seville, Naples, Rio Janeiro, and Buenos Ayres. The Russian peasant decorated himself with his sash of gaudy calimanco, and the Spanish hidalgo was sheltered under his light cloak of Norwich camlet. The introduction of Norwich articles into Spain soon made the manufacturer ample amends for the capricious turns of fashion in his own country. The taste of foreign nations was now consulted. The gravity of the Spaniard was suited in his plain but finely textured camlets; the loom was taught to imitate the handiworks of Flora, and the most garish assemblage of colours of every dye satisfied the vanity of the Bohemian and Suabian female. The great fairs of Frankfort, Leipsic, and Salerno were thronged with purchasers of these commodities. Norwich was then crowded with its looms. Every winter's evening exhibited to the traveller entering its walls the appearance of a general illumination; and from twenty miles round the village weavers resorted to it with the produce of their industry." Such a passage as this, grandiose as it is, helps to give us some idea of the scene presented by one of the chief rivers of Broadland at the time of Norwich's greatest prosperity; for it was by way of the winding Yare that the camlets, the gaudy calimancos, and the brilliant-hued cloths which delighted the eyes of the Bohemian and Suabian beauties were borne to the coast for export to foreign lands.

But early in the last century the railway came to Norfolk, and much of the carrying trade was taken out of the wherry-men's hands. Since then, the traveller has been able to cross in a few minutes wide stretches of marshland which previously were almost untraversable except by the men who lived on them and knew the winding footpaths and the mazy courses of the dykes. Still, the railway did not rob the wherrymen of all their means of livelihood; and at the present time there are, in all probability, as many wherries as ever on the Broadland rivers. It was for their convenience that, some seventy years ago, a three-mile-long canal was cut to connect the Yare at Reedham with the Waveney at Herringfleet, making it possible for them to make the voyage between Norwich and Lowestoft without sailing round by Breydon. A few years previous to the opening of this New Cut, a scheme was conceived for extending Lowestoft Harbour by cutting through the land barrier which existed between the sea and Lake Lothing; and after much opposition from the people of Yarmouth, a Bill for making Lake Lothing navigable to sea-borne vessels was carried through Parliament. On 3rd June 1831 this work was so far advanced that the sea was let into the lake; and two large yachts, the *Ruby* and *Georgiana*, each drawing about nine feet of water, passed through the newly made cutting into the new inner harbour.

The mingling of the salt water with the fresh water of the lake was attended with some curious phenomena, and a night or two after the channel was opened Lake Lothing was brilliantly phosphorescent. Its waters were thickly covered with "the bodies of pike, carp, perch, bream, roach, and dace, multitudes of which were carried into the ocean and thrown afterwards on the beach, most of them having been bitten in two by the dogfish which abound in the bay." And the "singular fact" is recorded that a twenty-pound pike containing an entire herring was picked up at the Mutford end of the lake.

The completion of a chain of waterways—Lake Lothing, Oulton Broad, Oulton Dyke, the Waveney, and Breydon —connecting Lowestoft with Yarmouth, and the fact that the Waveney was about this time connected with the Yare by the making of the New Cut, may have had something to do with what has been called the "discovery" of the Norfolk Broads. At any rate, since about 1840, pleasure-seekers' attention has been constantly turned towards Broadland. True, at first strangers only came into the district in small numbers, and as there were then few sailing craft suited to inland cruising to be hired, and there was practically no accommodation for visitors at the marshland inns, it is not surprising that many of these strangers, after enduring considerable discomfort, went away little impressed by its beauties. Even the Rev. Richard Lubbock, who knew the district well, and whose *Fauna of Norfolk* is deservedly valued by naturalists, was of opinion that the Broads and rivers had "little to interest the seeker after picturesque beauty," though he admitted that "nothing was pleasanter than a summer expedition, for a few days, to some of the larger Broads." But the strangers who visited the Broads had to do so in cabinless boats, so that there was no shelter for them when they were overtaken by rain-storms; and, perhaps, with empty stomachs and the wind against them, they found themselves miles away from village or inn. So for a while ardent anglers, gunners, and naturalists only were enthusiastic about Broadland; people who disliked "roughing it," after a day or two's discomfort, or a thorough drenching, hastened back to Norwich, Yarmouth, or Lowestoft, and said uncomplimentary things about those persons who had deluded them by speaking of the delights of the Broads.

George Borrow, perhaps, had he been so minded, could have written a book about Broadland which would have shown wherein the charm of the district lay; for he dwelt many years beside Oulton Broad, and it has been said of him that he could " draw more poetry from a wide-spreading marsh with its straggling rushes than from the most beautiful scenery, and would stand and look at it with rapture." Charles Kingsley, too, felt that the beauty of the fens was as the beauty of the sea, " of boundless expanse and freedom ": he could have done for Broadland what he did for the Cambridgeshire Fens. But it remained, so far as I can ascertain, for Mr. G. Christopher Davies to give to the world the first satisfactory description of Broadland life. True, some years before the appearance of *Norfolk Broads and Rivers*, Nall, a somewhat neglected Yarmouth historian, had said that the marshlands around Breydon presented landscapes equalling those depicted by Potter, Cuyp, Hobbima, Ruysdael, and Vanderneer; but Mr. Davies, in his accounts of his cruisings on the Yare, Bure, and Waveney and their tributaries, surprised many who were unfamiliar with the district, by telling them that Broadland had not to rely entirely on its wide vistas, quiet waters, and gorgeous sunrises and sunsets for its picturesque effects. He told them that Wroxham, Barton, and some of the smaller Broads were not, like Rockland, simply reed-fringed meres in the midst of level marshlands, beautiful only when the reeds were mirrored by the still surface of the water or the ripples sparkled in the sunlight; but that they were bordered by pleasant woodlands, whose fresh green in early summer and glorious hues in autumn made them as lovely as many of the leafy backwaters of the upper Thames. Weaving a spell of enchantment about his readers, he led them beside banks fragrant with water-mint and purple with loosestrife, where sedge warblers sang incessantly, reed buntings twittered, brilliant-hued butterflies fluttered, and

dragon - flies darted in the sunlight.   He wrote of summer
nights spent on Wroxham, Salhouse, and Hickling, when
his yacht seemed to be floating in air between two star-
spangled skies; of days passed in the company of Broadland
anglers, gunners, eel-catchers, and decoymen; of charming
waterside hamlets whose inhabitants spoke the broadest of
" broad Norfolk "; and at all times he was ready to chat
pleasantly of the myths, folk-lore, habits and customs of
the men of the marshes.   And when he had described the
indisputable charms of the upper waters of the Yare and
Bure, he even had the courage to confirm Nall's statements
about the lower reaches of those rivers—at least, to assert
that they were not without their elements of the picturesque.
In this assertion he soon had the support of Sir John
Lubbock, who, in his *Beauties of Nature*, wrote that the
Broadland streams are like " rivers wandering in the meadows
on a holiday.   They have often no natural banks, but are
bounded by dense growths of tall grasses, bulrushes, reeds,
and sedges, interspersed with the spikes of the purple loosestrife, willow-herb, hemp-agrimony, and other flowers, while
the fields are very low and protected by dykes, so that the
red cattle appear to be browsing below the level of the water.
And as the rivers take most unexpected turns, the sailing
boats often seem as if they were in the middle of the
fields."

People of all sorts and conditions, from all parts of
England, no sooner heard of these delights, than they
were anxious to enjoy them.   Oulton, Wroxham, Hickling, Ormesby were words continually in people's mouths;
and the natives of these places, realising that they were
discovered, speedily learnt how to cater for holiday folk
craving for new scenes and pleasures.   So that now there
is no lack of craft of every kind suited to the navigating
of Broadland waterways, and all through the summer the
white sails of yachts are more numerous than the black
sails of wherries on the Yare, Bure, and Waveney.   On
board the larger of these craft every possible comfort and
convenience is provided; so that " roughing it," after the
fashion of the early adventurers on the Broads, is a thing

of the past. But the visitors who content themselves with what they can see of Broadland from a yacht's deck can never become really acquainted with the Broads and Broadland life. To gain a real knowledge of these, they must, to some extent, "rough it" as the early adventurers did: trudge the river walls; associate with the eel-catchers, marshmen, reed-cutters, and Breydon gunners; explore the dykes unnavigable by yachts, and the swampy rush marshes where the lapwings and redshanks nest; spend days with the Broadsman in his punt, and nights with the eel-catcher in his house-boat; crouch among the reeds to watch the acrobatic antics of the bearded titmice, and fraternise with the wherrymen at the staithes and ferry inns. If the stranger in Broadland is unwilling to do these things, he must rest content with the outward aspect of the district and second-hand knowledge of its inner life. But there must always be many whom lack of time, opportunity, or inclination will debar from becoming intimately acquainted with the scenery, inhabitants, archæology, history, sport, and wild life of this most delightful and interesting district; and it is for such persons, as well as for the guidance and information of those who have ample time for exploration and investigation, that this book has been written.

In concluding this rough outline of the history of Broadland, it is necessary to say something about a matter which in late years has attracted much attention and excited some indignation. I refer to the action of certain riparian owners who have denied the right of the public to have access to waters which from time immemorial have been looked upon as public highways. The trouble seems to have had its origin in the Enclosure Acts and Awards, by which, some seventy years ago, some of the Broads and much of the wet marshland adjoining the Broads and rivers were allotted to neighbouring landowners. As at that time the Broads had not been "discovered" by holiday-makers and yachting folk, this allotment was permitted to be made almost without protest on the part of the public. The wherrymen were, to a certain extent, considered, and in some instances their right of way was preserved to them; but in other cases Broads were handed over, almost unconditionally, to private owners. Since the district has become a popular playground, the restrictions enforced or attempted by some of the riparian owners have been greatly resented, have led to unpleasant disputes, and occasionally not only visitors but residents in Broadland have been proceeded against for fishing in or shoot ing over certain Broads.

At the present time the public is denied access to Hoveton Great and Little Broads, Woodbastwick or Decoy Broad, Belaugh Broad, and parts of Ranworth, Filby, and Rollesby Broads. The owners of Ranworth, South Walsham, Salhouse, and Salhouse Little Broads claim the right to exclude the public, except in so far that there is a right of way to certain staithes. The fishing is preserved on the Salhouse Broads, Hickling, Horsey, Barton, Wroxham, Sutton, and Surlingham Broads, and part of South Walsham.

Until what is known as the Hickling Broad case was decided in the Supreme Courts, few attempts were made to debar the public from fishing on the Broads. In that case the riparian owners sought to take from the public all rights of sport on or passage over Hickling Broad. The decision of the Court was that " the rights of fishing and shooting were vested in the riparian owners to whom the Broad had been allotted under an Enclosure Award, but that the right of passage and navigation is in the public, and without limitation to any particular channel." It appears, however, that if the judge had been satisfied that Hickling Broad is tidal water (as it undoubtedly is) the public would have retained their sporting rights as well as those of passage and navigation; but on the evidence adduced he came to the conclusion that the Broad is not tidal. As a matter of fact, all the principal Broads are tidal; but the mistaken judgment given in the Hickling case has resulted in fishing and shooting being prohibited on several of them, and others being closed to the public. That I am justified in calling the judge's decision mistaken will be admitted by every one who has any acquaintance with Hickling; but I may quote in support of my assertion a passage from a letter sent by

Mr. Walter Rye to the press. He says that in the Hickling
case the plaintiffs argued that the regular rise and fall of
the water was "only caused by the salt tide pushing the
water up and (letting it) down, and that this, therefore,
did not prove a tide, as the water was not wholly and
regularly salt. How utterly absurd this argument was, did
not apparently strike the magistrates, who could hardly have
denied that the river Thames at Putney, which has a rise and
fall of ten feet or more, is tidal, though it does not contain
any salt water at all. It is only a question of degree—a tide
is a tide if of inches or feet, and Rigby in the Hickling case
advised me that half an inch of proved regular tide was as
good as a foot. The presence or absence of salt water has
nothing to do with proving or disproving a tide." Mr. Rye,
in answer to the statement that the public are "forcible
would-be usurpers" of the riparian owners' rights, adds that
he thinks "the boot is entirely on the other leg. . . . Bryant's
map of the county, taken in 1826, shows Walsham Staithe
(which it would hardly have done if it had been a private
one), the now improperly closed entrance to Wroxham, and
the two entrances at the ends of Hoveton Broad, through
which the trading wherries used to make their alternative
course up and down the river if the wind suited them better
than on the main river. Since then the adjoining owners
have been continually encroaching on the rights of the
public."

That the latter have a real grievance no one can deny.
How to remedy matters is not easy to decide. A Royal
Commission to inquire into the existing state of affairs, with a
view to settling all matters in dispute, has been suggested;
so, too, has the forming of a Board of Conservators endowed
with full power to regulate and control the use of all the rivers
and Broads; but at present no steps have been taken to obtain
either Commission or Board. Some hopes of a settlement
of the vexed question of public rights have been raised by
the announcement—made by the President of the British
Association at the meetings at Glasgow in 1901—that Mr.
Pullar has placed in the hands of scientists a sum sufficient
to defray the expense of a complete survey of the inland

waters of the United Kingdom.   This survey, it is said, will clear away all doubts as to which of the Broads are tidal; in fact, its announcement has led many frequenters of Broadland to believe that in the course of a few years the closed Broads will be re-opened to them.

CHAPTER III

SPRING AND SUMMER IN BROADLAND

SPRING

IN spring the natives of the district and a few enthusiasts
for cruising and wild life have Broadland almost entirely to
themselves. In this season you may row or sail for miles
along the rivers and encounter no other craft than the wherries
and here and there a solitary gun-punt, while on Hickling,
Horsey Mere, Barton, and some other Broads you may spend
days together in April and early May and scarcely see a boat
afloat or a human being. This is not surprising, for the spring
weather is far too treacherous for extended cruising, and it is
only on those few delightful days when the sun shines brightly
and the wind blows from the south or west that a few small
sailing boats are launched from the "hard" or leave for a
while their winter moorings. The nights and early morning
hours, too, are often very cold, and if one has not a snug cabin
into which to retreat at a moment's notice, the sudden rain
squalls of spring will soon drench one to the skin. Yet for the
botanist or student of wild life who goes abroad and afloat
prepared for weather changes, the spring days are far too few
and brief; for not only the uplands around the river valleys, but
the dykes, reed beds, alder and sallow carrs, ronds, and rush
marshes each day show some fresh sign of re-awakening life.
And this in spite of the fact, which I think no one who
knows the district will deny, that signs of spring are later in
revealing themselves on the lowlands of Broadland than in the
woodlands, among the cornfields, on the roadside banks, and
in gardens. Long after the blackthorn blossoms have faded,
only last year's withered reeds are mirrored by Broad and river ;

for though the "colts" may be coming up, they are hidden by the dense jungles of amber culms.

But by the time the sedge warblers are back in the reed beds, and the dykes are full of amorous frogs, there is much to tempt one to take a cruise on the rivers or a ramble along the river walls. Every marsh and swampy rond is then bright with golden clusters of marsh marigolds; on the sun-warmed sides of the walls yellow coltsfoot has pushed its way up through the clods, and purple patches of dead nettle attract the early roving bees. On the boggy lands green rushes are gradually hiding the withered growths of rush and sedge; the silken sallow catkins are sending out their yellow anthers, and the ruddy bog myrtle fills the air with its sweet, strong scent. Sunward the river is agleam with flashing ripples; elsewhere the water is as blue as the sky. As you cross the rush marshes, redshanks and peewits rise from their nesting grounds, crying plaintively; now and again a snipe is flushed, and uttering that strange bleating note which has gained it the name of "summer-lamb," betakes itself to erratic flight. In almost every dyke where there is dead sedge or gladden, moorhens are beginning to make their nests, and the loud challenge of the pugnacious cocks is heard along the riversides; while from the shores of the larger Broads comes the harsh "cark" of the coot. The reed beds are full of sedge warblers, playing the mocking-bird to sparrow, thrush, and finch; occasionally a louder, quicker "chucking" tells of the presence of a reed warbler. By the time the reed warblers—which arrive later than the sedge warblers—are heard, you may listen for the strange insect-like "reeling" of the shy little grasshopper warblers, which lurk among the scrub of sweet gale and sallow and in the lush marsh grass. On the floating rafts of broken reeds and sedges, with which the wind and tide have covered the surface of some of the creeks, those dignified and graceful little dyke-rangers, the yellow wagtails, are strutting, carefully searching for crawling insects or darting their beaks at those upon the wing. In the marsh farm gardens tits and finches are busy among the fruit-buds, and the goldfinch, which is not so rare in Norfolk as in some counties where the bird-catchers are more in evidence, is often heard singing among the apple trees.

It was on an April day, when the gorse on the Herringfleet Hills was in full blaze of bloom, that I sailed down the Waveney to St. Olave's Bridge, and moored for the night just above the old Bell Inn.   The day had been warm and cloudless —almost like a fine day at the end of May—and the night was so warm that at midnight I opened my cabin window and lay in my bunk for an hour, looking out over the river.   The moon had risen above the hills, and the old inn, the brush-topped willows, the cottages on the shore, and the masts of the wherries on the river, were clearly outlined, like Indian ink silhouettes, against a sky-background of star-speckled, slaty blue, while a shimmering lane of silvery light stretched from the cabin window to the dark shore.   Not a breath of wind stirred the dark-plumed reeds and slender willow wands, but across the sky drifted little pearly clouds and films of mist. The curved white ironwork of the bridge—beneath which the tide was ebbing—gleamed in the moonlight like a lunar rainbow.   Except for the lapping of the tide, the only sounds I heard were the crying of the redshanks on the Herringfleet marshes and the chucking of a sedge warbler, which, in the midst of a neighbouring reed-bed, was continually bursting into song.   The rower of a little gun-punt which went gliding down-stream passed under the bridge so silently that I thought he must be either the water-bailiff or some fisherman anxious to escape the bailiff's notice; the punt with its noiselessly moving oars looked like a great black water-beetle.

The morning was as fine as the night had been.   A little way above St. Olave's Bridge, a millwright was hoisting new sails on to an old wooden windmill, and all the male dwellers on the marshes for miles around—there were not a dozen of them in all—had come to assist or look on. The millman was anxious to get the mill to work, for some cattle were to be turned on to the marshes at the end of the month, and at present the dykes which his mill drained were full of flood-water.   At midday the heat of the sun was more oppressive than it often is in June, and the millwright's assistants, who seemed quite content to work all day so that they might partake of the refreshment provided by a capacious wicker-bound bottle, were glad to cast aside their coats.   The

scene was such a busy one for the lethargic lowlands, that I
stayed an hour or more watching it; but although there was
much shouting and hauling of ropes, the progress of the sail-
hoisting was remarkably slow.   An old marshman, who, like
myself, was an interested spectator, remarked that it "fared to
him as how for all their shoutin' they didn't fare to git no
forrarder; but seein' as how it wor th' fust time in his lifetime
a mill in their parts had had new sails, he reckoned as how th'
chaps what wor at work there worn't pertickler handy at it."
I noticed that a pair of moor-hens which were making a nest
in a dyke not fifty yards from the mill were quite undisturbed
by the hammering and shouting.   With the aid of my field-
glasses I could watch them dabbling about as unconcernedly
as though they were the only inhabitants of the marshes.   The
lapwings, however, seemed very restless, and were continually
rising and wheeling in the air.

As yet there were no cattle turned on to any of the marshes
of that triangular tract lying between the Yare, the Waveney,
and the New Cut; but when, after reaching Breydon and
sailing a little way up the Yare, I moored near Banham's
marsh farmstead, the old man, who has lived his life on that
lonesome tract of marshland, told me that his marshes would
be dry enough for the bullocks to come on to them at the end
of the next week.   A matter of this kind may not seem of
overwhelming interest to the stranger who chats with a Broadland marshman, but if he is wise he will not discourage the
native when he happens to be in a talkative mood; for by
listening patiently a little while he may gain much insight into
the lives and interests of the lone-living marsh folk.   Old
Banham has a quip and joke for all comers, and as, during the
greater part of the year, he has few visitors at his almost
inaccessible farmstead, he is often glad to chat with those who
come to him by way of the river or the rough marsh walls.
He it was who told the River and Haven Commissioners, when
they held a meeting at Reedham, that the reason why the
river walls were destroyed and the marshes flooded was because
the Commissioners had dydled away the sandbank which used
to stretch nearly across the mouth of Yarmouth Harbour, so
that the flood-tides swept up the rivers with double the force

and the water rose twice as high as it did when he was a boy. But though he told the Commissioners, he laughingly remarked, that his hay crop is often spoilt before he can get it up, he could not persuade them to let the harbour mouth choke up again. But he did not tell them that in the days of his boyhood the hay crop of his marshes was not worth the cutting. In those days he could go down on to the swampy marshes and collect a bushel of hornpies' (green plovers') eggs in a morning. Bird protection is a matter which does not appeal to these old marshmen; and Banham gleefully related how old Kemp, a long-legged marshman from Haddiscoe, with an empty gun so put the " fear of death " into the heart of Plum, the keeper who came to keep an eye on the egg-collectors, that Plum fled from the marshes and would never go near them again.

On that fine April morning I spent nearly two hours chatting with Banham. A hundred and sixty years, he said, his family had lived on the marshes around Breydon; but from his own appearance and that of his stalwart, fair-haired sons I should say that it is ten hundred and sixty years since his ancestors first settled there, and that they were some of those Scandinavian viking raiders who gave their names to several of the hamlets in the Flegg Hundreds. In course of conversation with him, I learnt that the herons at Reedham, where is their chief Broadland colony, had been much disturbed of late by the cutting down of some of the trees on which they nested. He told me, too, a tale of a gun. The gun was a heavy old weapon which had been used as a swivel gun on Breydon, and for five years it stood untouched in a corner of his house, no one thinking it was loaded. Then he sold it to a man, who put it to his shoulder and pulled the trigger while he was taking it home with him in the train. Fortunately, before pulling the trigger, he pushed the barrel out of the carriage window; but so great was the recoil, and so scared was the man, that he nearly went out of the other window. " That gin him a rare fright, that did ! " We spoke about the marshland windmills. He knew of only one around Breydon that retained its original wooden cogwheels. " How old are the mills ? " " Ah, that I shoun't like to say ; but I've heerd my grandfather say that they looked jist th' same in his young time as they did when he wor an' owd man ony three weeks off being a hundred."

From Banham's farmstead I sailed to Reedham, entered the New Cut, and soon reached Haddiscoe Bridge. There I landed, and strolled along the marsh dam to the village. In the plantations around the fine old Norman-towered church the fresh green of the larches pleasantly relieved the sombre foliage of the firs; green buds were opening on the brushwood of the elm trunks, though some of the oaks, in sheltered places, still retained their last year's withered leaves. A faint odour of sweetbriar lurked in some of the lanes. In the adjoining hamlet of Toft Monks I met a woodman, who pointed out a sparrow-hawk's nest in an oak tree. Until the previous day, when he saw one of the birds leaving it, he had taken it for a squirrel's drey. The Toft Monks woods were full of birds. Great tits and blue tits were busy at the buds; in a dense conifer there were half a dozen or more long-tailed tits. Jays were continually screaming, and once I heard the laugh of a green woodpecker. A few willow warblers were singing among the undergrowth of ash wands and nut bushes, and in the fences on the borders of the woods were several redstarts and whitethroats. The old woodman had a brushwood hut in the woods, where he worked all the year making hurdles and barrel hoops. A wren had a nest in a hole in the roof inside the hut, and the little bird when it flew down from its nest was in the habit of alighting on the old man's back. As I returned across Haddiscoe Dam I met Last Farman, the marshman-naturalist, who said that the marshmen had noticed that if when they cut the sets—that is, the wands or branches—of the willows, they left the smallest and youngest branches, the trees died; but if all the branches were cut off, the trees lived. He believed that when the young branches were left they drew the sap up and out of the " wounds " made where the larger sets had been cut off, and that the trees " bled to death."

A few days later, in early May, when the chestnuts and sycamores had burst into leaf, and the birches in the carrs and copses were beginning to look like large maidenhair ferns; when the wild beaked parsley was opening its white, starry flowerets, and the dark spikes of sedge by the waterside were covered with pollen; when the white scurvy grass was in bloom by the riverside and the cuckoo flowers gave another colour to the marshes, I sailed from Potter Heigham Bridge to Horsey and Hickling. The weather was colder than it had been a week or two before, when I was afloat on the Waveney; and George Applegate (whom every one who has been to Potter Heigham knows) told me it was sure to rain before the day was " out." But the swallows and warblers were back in their old haunts, and I was minded to see them there; so about half an hour after passing under the picturesque old bridge I was in the midst of that wild waste of reeds and water, Heigham Sounds. Except for two men, who seemed suspiciously anxious to keep themselves concealed among the reeds, and who, I am afraid, were on the watch for a certain rare and beautiful little bird which breeds there, the wild life and I had the whole Sounds to ourselves. A keen breeze was rustling the yellow reeds and ruffling the grey water, but at intervals gleams of sunlight broke through the clouds which were scudding inland from across the sea and the wild marshlands, and then the Sounds sparkled and flashed as with phosphorescent fire. Scores of little brown sand martins were fly-hawking over the rippling water, or resting and preening on the swaying reeds; but neither they nor the swallows could have been quite happy, for little insect life was to be seen: the may-fly was not yet abroad. The aspect of the watery wilderness through which the largest Broad is approached was more than usually primeval, and the crying of the redshanks and plovers and the bleating of the snipe only emphasized its chill loneliness. And presently darker clouds came rolling up from beyond the ragged line of Horsey sandhills and discharged a fusilade of hail, which rattled loudly among the dead reeds, and set little fountains playing all over the surface of the Sounds.

But the hailstorm was over in a few minutes, and before I had passed through the mile-and-a-half-long Old Meadow Dyke the sun was lighting up the sandhills, so that they stood out boldly and yellow against a background of sombrous cloud. The wind was much keener on the lonely mere than in the narrower Sounds, for the mere is only a few minutes' walk from the sea-shore, on which I could hear the waves beating; so, after sailing round the little islet in its midst, and disturbing some coots which were swimming well out from the shelter of the reeds, I returned to the Sounds. Then, leaving on the left the little wood in which the herons used to nest, I sailed through Whiteslea and on to Hickling. With a pale haze hiding its low shores, the waters of the Broad that morning seemed almost limitless, and the fitful wind-gusts which from time to time swept down upon me gave me little time to distinguish the mist-mantled landmarks. A great crested grebe was rocking on the slight swell the wind had set running, and let me get within about twenty yards of it; then it dived and appeared again on the shallow water beyond the channel posts. Some of the posts, I noticed, had disappeared since the previous summer, and when I landed at Hickling Staithe I learnt that they had been broken down during the winter by the pressure of drifting ice.

From Hickling I walked by way of Ingham to Stalham. The hedge banks were yellow with primroses, red campions were beginning to bloom, and the hedges seemed full of white-throats. The doors of the fine old church at Ingham were locked, and I had not time to go in search of the keys; so, after examining the scanty ruins of the priory, and listening to a nightingale which was singing near by, I rambled between primrose-decked banks to Stalham. And late in the afternoon, when the light of the setting sun gilded the reed and rush beds of Sutton Broad, I rowed down Stalham Dyke to Barton Broad, between banks heaped with sheaves of reeds and rushes; and I passed a reed-laden raft towed by one marshman, and kept from running into the bank by another man who carried a long pole. The catkins of the sweet gale on Sutton Fen looked, at a little distance, like red berries, for their colour was that of the young lily-pads; the alder scrub on the dyke banks was already in full leaf, though the alder trees were as yet almost leafless. Treading the quaking surface of the fen, I found the slender fronds of the graceful marsh fern unfolding amid golden clusters of marigold and lilac blossoms of lady's-smock. Cuckoos were calling from the copses; and just before dusk came down on Barton, a sparrow-hawk silenced all the warblers in a reed shoal by flying just above the ragged plumes of the reeds. Then the sun sank behind a bank of close-packed clouds which lay all along the western skyline, and for a few minutes the clouds were edged with smouldering fire, while the sky above them was radiant with shafts of light.

For studying the bird life of Broadland there is no time like the spring, for the birds are not so shy then as they become later on, when the holiday folk are on every Broad and waterway. True, the bird life of the district is not what it used to be—the avosets, ruffs, and black terns are gone— but in May you may see a few spoonbills on the Breydon flats, and rarely that "haunting voice of the marshlands," the booming of the bittern, is heard among the jungles of reed. Sixty years ago you might have seen half a dozen bitterns in a morning about Heigham Sounds and Hickling. But even now Broadland is the most bird-favoured district in England, and a great number of species may be seen in a day. Marsh, reed bed, alder carr, rond, river, and dyke, each has its special species, and to watch them and listen to their strange cries and varied songs is a constant delight. To note the trees, too, as they in turn unfold their leaf buds, and the wild flowers — the first marsh marigold in March and the first orchis in May — is always a pleasure to nature - loving " children of the open air." And in springtime these delights are the more enjoyed because one has grown weary of leafless trees and Broads fringed with yellow reeds and rusty blades of sedge. The silver sheen of the sallow catkins is a sign that Nature is waking from her winter sleep, and every day gives proof that she is throwing off the lethargy into which she fell when the frosts and snows came. And when the sedge warbler's song is heard and the grass-cup nests of the red- shanks are found on the rush marshes, we know that she is wide awake and will soon be decking herself with the rainbow- hued draperies of spring.

SUMMER

The footpaths along the river walls are nearly hidden by tall, drooping grasses. Many of the dykes are almost choked up with hemlocks, frogbits, and marshwort, so that open water spaces, where the "whirligigs" and "skaters" can disport themselves, are few and far between. From the marshes the shrill sound of scythe-whetting and the metallic murmur of mowing machines are heard from early morn till dusk, and a fresh fragrance—the sweet scent of new-mown hay—is in the air. Innumerable butterflies—among them handsome black and yellow swallow-tails and gorgeous red admirals—are fluttering over the meadows and along the rose-decked driftways; over the rush marshes, now pink with orchid and ragged robin, ruddy with red rattle, and flecked with a white spray of wild parsley, beautiful little burnet moths are poising on almost invisibly beating wings. Now is the time to go in search of the lovely bell-flowered buckbean, the marsh cinquefoil, the marsh thistle, and the dainty bog pimpernel; and to range the dykes for the curious aloe-like water-soldier, the insectivorous bladderwort, and the lovely flowering rush. For Broadland is now a great wild-flower garden: marsh, dyke, riverside, alder carr, and even the swampy rond and osier bed all have their brilliant blossoms, and the summer breeze is as laden with sweet scents as though

> " Nature's incense-pans had spilt,
> And shed the dews i' the air."

The nightingales are silent, but the sedge warblers, though less seen now that the new reeds are hiding last year's yellow culms, are still singing; and at intervals the strange "reeling" song of the shy grasshopper warbler is heard among the marshes. The swallows are busy midge-hawking over marsh, Broad, and river; but they have young to feed, and their dartings under the doorways of boat-houses and into the upper storeys of the windmills are more frequent than they were a few weeks ago. The swifts, too, are continually circling around the windmills and over the rivers; but sometimes they rise so high in the air as to become almost invisible. Hundreds of rooks, jackdaws, and wood pigeons are feeding on the marshes, undisturbed by the cattle grazing there; day and night the harsh challenge of the cock pheasant is heard,—for the pheasants are almost as numerous on the marshes as in the woods,—as dusk approaches the "crek-crek" of the corncrake, a bird which seems rarer now than it used to be, comes with misleading distinctness from amid the lush grass. The nights and dawns are no longer chilly, but the mists still rise from the dykes at sunset, and all day a wavering haze of pollen-laden air veils the meadows where the grass is still unmown and undulates like a grey-green sea.

The Broadland season has begun. At Oulton, Wroxham, Thorpe, Potter Heigham, and Brundall only condemned hulks are drawn up on the boat-yards; the overhauling and refitting of yachts and launches are finished, and most of the craft afloat have cruising parties on board them. Already two or three regattas have been held, and some of the racing craft display fresh prize-flags among those which indicate earlier but well-remembered successes. Broadsmen who all winter have been indistinguishable from the other men of the marshes, have donned close-fitting jerseys with yachts' names in red or white letters on them; the conversation at the riverside inns is all about yacht-racing and the victories of this or that famous winner. The wherrymen scan critically the new craft as they pass them on the rivers; the old men among them talk of the changes they have seen. Rivers and Broads wear a holiday aspect, which, if not so attractive to some as their spring freshness and loveliness, is inspiriting and not without its charm. At night, when the whispering of the reeds often suggests a coolness that is not felt, the glow of lamp-lit cabin windows lures the moths from the waterside wild flowers; music and laughter are heard above the lapping of water and the warblers' incessant songs.

Now is the time when those who come to Broadland for rest and quietude leave the more popular Broads and water-ways and explore the upper reaches and isolated Broads. There they find what they came here for. But in spite of the district's great popularity, there are hundreds of cruisers who know so little of Broadland that they believe, when they have seen the main rivers between Norwich, Yarmouth, Lowestoft, and Wroxham, and the larger Broads, that they have exhausted its delights. A few know better, and it is they who, when the main waterways are thronged with pleasure-seekers, retire on to the quieter and less accessible upper waters and tributaries, and enjoy delights to which the majority of the river-cruisers are strangers. Some pass under Beccles Bridge, and have the Waveney between Beccles and Bungay almost entirely to themselves; others cruise up the narrow Chet, and visit the old-world hamlets near which it flows; yet others retire to the upper Bure, where, around Coltishall and Aylsham, there are enough fine old churches, Elizabethan and Jacobean halls, and pretty villages to occupy delightfully the time and attention of a visitor during the whole of a long holiday. Even the upper reaches of the Ant have their regular patrons at this season, for in a neighbourhood noted for its quaint decayed towns and villages, and famous for its memorials of the Pastons, many hours can be spent pleasantly and profitably. On and around these quiet streams, which flow through remote but pleasant places, an old-world charm still lingers, and at night, when the rattle of the mowing machines is hushed and the haymakers are gone home, one can know a peace that is very much akin to

> " The silence that is in the starry sky,
> The sleep that is amongst the lonely hills."

The beauty and enchantment of a fine summer night in Broadland make a lasting impression even on the least impressionable natures. The golden glory of sunset fades into an amber afterglow, against which windmills, farmsteads, and alder carrs are seen in striking silhouette. The breeze which all day has filled white sails and set green reeds whispering, dies away. Over Broad, river, and marsh a sudden silence falls, broken only by the splash of a leaping fish, the cry of some night bird, the rustle of a vole in the hovers, or the creak of a rowlock of some belated angler's boat. The fragrance of the waterside wild flowers becomes stronger than it has been during the daytime; thousands of moths begin fluttering over river, rond, and dyke. In a copse near the river a nightjar begins churring—a weird, mysterious, haunting voice of solitude and night—and presently, like a shadow, a sombre bird-shape comes out of the gloom of the copse, and flies, now silently, now with flapping wings, along the copse border. For a few moments it circles in the open, where its widespread wings are seen against the blue of the night sky; then it vanishes, and again the strange churring, now loud, now subdued, makes the air seem vibrant and the copse haunted by some phantom of the night. When it ceases, the night seems " full of a watchful intentness"—Nature holds her breath while she waits to hear that haunting voice again.

Presently the moon rises—rises above a horizon as level as that of the sea—and is seen at first through a fretwork of down-bent leaves in a scanty reed bed. Below the reeds, in the still, clear water, is another moon, which sinks as the other rises, until it is lost in a lane of silvery light which lies across the water. On the edge of the water, where the silver sheen is broken into flakes by a jungle of reeds and sedges, creamy clusters of meadow-sweet are revealed, like little wisps of suspended mist. But there is little mist abroad, and when the moon is a little way above the reeds, its light falls so brightly on the pastures that the grazing cattle cast long black shadows on the grass. Even the nightjar casts a wavering shadow—the shadow of a shadow—and little white moths rise to the surface of the river to meet those which midge-like touch the water. Every minute something which has hitherto hidden itself in gloom is revealed by the growing light—the slender mast of a wherry which vanished when the light in its cabin was extinguished, the white wall of a cottage seen between the trunks of some bushy-headed willows, a pair of swans which come out of a reedy creek, and glide slowly and wraith-like across the river. Then a bird starts singing—not the sedge warbler, the marshman's nightingale, but a blackcap, whose mellow music sounds sweeter now that the voices of the sun-inspired songsters are hushed. For a few minutes its fluting is heard at intervals; then a plover cries like a lone, lost wanderer amid the marshes, and the blackcap goes to sleep again.

But for the stranger in Broadland such a night as this is no time for sleeping. Rather it is a time to step aboard a dinghy and row round a Broad or along a river reach, or to land for a while and stroll along the riverside or some moonlit marsh wall. On the top of the river wall what little breeze is stirring feels like the touch of velvet to the cheek, so soft, warm, and humid is it.   Here the outlook is wider : windmills, carrs, and farmsteads miles away are revealed by the moon- light.   Marvellous are the reflections in some of the dykes, where willows and sallows seem to grow downwards towards a subaqueous sky.   On clear, moonless nights the still waters reflect the stars.   So suspensive is the silence that every sound seems startlingly audible.   A hare, suddenly frightened from its form on the rond, scampers over the river wall and vanishes amid the long grass.   A vole rustles among the sedges a moment, and then enters the water with a " flop " like a dropped stone ; a louder rustle among the rushes near a sallow carr may be made by an otter seeking a feast of bream.   The silence thus broken at intervals suggests that the wild life of the waterside is wakeful and listening intently.   Often I have fancied that the eyes of unseen birds and beasts are fixed on me when I intrude upon their haunts at night, so seldom do the creatures I know are there show their fear by taking flight. For they must be able to see man when he cannot see them, and to judge whether his intrusion among them threatens danger.

A faint gleam of lamplight on the reeds, scarcely per- ceptible, so bright is the moonlight, betokens an eel-catcher in his house-boat, keeping watch over his sett.   He is seated in a little well at the stern of the boat, where he is glad to make room for a companion who will help him to while away his night vigil.   The lamp in the cabin reveals an attempt to adorn its cramped interior.   A photograph of the house-boat— the work, probably, of some cruising amateur—hangs above the empty stove, and is flanked by a couple of coloured almanacs and a print of some distinguished British generals. But there is little room for such decorations.   A double- barrelled breech-loader hangs in a pair of leather slings nailed to the roof ; eel-lines and liggers are suspended on little hooks on the walls, together with a fisherman's " oily " and a pair of marsh boots.   At the fireside end of one of the lockers, which serve the eel-catcher for seat, table, and bed, stands a little oil stove on which a kettle is boiling ; an open cupboard at the bow end of the cabin contains crockery, bottles, bread, and a jar which holds some pickled bream.   A wicker-bound water-bottle, a punt sail undergoing repair, a frying-pan, a torn copy of an illustrated weekly paper, and a pair of coloured blankets complete the inventory of the cabin's visible contents, but the lockers no doubt contain other things useful to a water-gipsy. The boat is a smack boat, so old and leaky that it will no longer keep afloat, and is drawn up on to the land near the mouth of a sluice dyke.

The eel-catcher is threading some hooks for an eel-line, but he raises his eyes from his work every few minutes to see if the approach of a wherry makes it necessary for him to lower his sett. Now and again, too, he glances towards the sallow carr where the otter is lurking, and vows to " hev that owd warmint afore long." He talks of "orters," and how he has known one to draw an eel-line out of the water and eat the eels off the hooks. But that otter, as he says, must have been a " werry hungry warmint," for otters are fonder of bream than of eels. He doubts whether they (the otters) are much scarcer than they were fifty years ago. Every year he hears of about the same number being shot or trapped. Badgers he has never seen, and does not believe there is one in Norfolk. Like most of the eel-catchers, he knows a good deal about the habits of fish and wild fowl, such knowledge being more or less essential to him; but he scarcely knows the names of a dozen of the small birds of the meadows, woods, and water-side ; "they ain't no good to him "! He has heard the boom of the bittern, and can remember the time when bitterns were not so very rare in Broadland ; but he " can't mind as he ever seed one." Eels, he says, are nothing like so plentiful as they used to be ; anyhow, nothing like such large quantities are taken in the setts as there were thirty years ago. He has worked a sett every year for nearly fifty years, so he reckons he ought to know.

Towards daybreak the air becomes perceptibly cooler, but not so much so as to cause any discomfort. Almost as soon as the eastern sky begins to brighten, some of the birds which have been silent since nightfall begin to sing ; and by the time the rosy flush of dawn has come, all Nature seems awake. The marsh folk are early abroad ; a cattle-tender is seen on one of the marsh walls, and the clinking of milk cans is heard in the neighbourhood of a marsh farm. A fresh breeze sets the reeds swaying and rustling, and some of the yachts leave their moorings and spread their white sails. Then the sharpening of scythes and the rattling of mowing machines begins again; and before the sun is very far above the horizon the air is sweet with the scent of hay. Another day for cruising along quiet waterways, for seeing pleasant rural scenes and listening to pleasant rural sounds, for restful pleasuring and reinvigorating mind and body, has begun. But the beauty, the enchantment, the "primevalness," as some one has called it, of the night cannot be forgotten.

Among the men who sail the yachts which visitors hire for summer cruising, there are some who seem to think that the chief object a visitor should have in view is to get from place to place as quickly as possible. That this is not the case should be impressed upon such men at the commencement of a cruise; for half the charm of Broadland is lost to those who let such boatmen have their own way. Time is often better spent in staying a day or two on such waters as Heigham Sounds and Barton Broad, or even in some unfrequented dyke or inlet, than in sailing along many miles of river. Nor should the voyager confine his attention to the waterways. Broadland consists of much besides Broads and rivers. There is scarcely a marsh dam or footpath, ferry road or lane, but leads to some little hamlet with an interesting church or some picturesque straw or reed thatched cottages. Sometimes it is as well to look upon a yacht as simply a sort of movable hotel, which at any time can be made a convenient centre from which a district can be explored. In this way the delights of a holiday spent at some country farm or seacoast hamlet can be added to those peculiar to voyaging in Broadland. There are times when the necessarily cramped conditions of life on a yacht grow somewhat galling, when one tires of sitting still, even though new vistas are continually opening in panoramic succession. Then it is very pleasant to step ashore for a while, ramble along the footpaths through the upland corn-fields, see the crimson blush of poppies instead of creamy clusters of meadow-sweet, and inhale the fragrance of woodbine instead of that of water-mints.

But summer in Broadland is so full of delights that it is needless to suggest them. There are pleasures to suit almost every inclination, and opportunities for the indulgence of almost every outdoor hobby. Those who care little for quiet nooks and the study of Nature find entertainment in the regattas or in occasional excursions to the thronged sands and piers of Yarmouth and Lowestoft. Artist, botanist, bird-lover, angler, entomologist, each goes his own way and enjoys himself in his own fashion. For each there is an ample field, and to each the long days seem only half long enough. Even the antiquary need not be idle, for in St. Benet's Abbey, Langley Abbey, Caister and Bungay Castles, and many of the Broadland churches, he finds plenty to keep him interested and profitably occupied. Even men who have no hobbies or special inclinations continually come upon something in Broadland that interests them, for the district is unlike any other in England. In spite of the great change which has taken place in it in what is, geologically speaking, a brief period, it is still remarkable for its primitiveness; like large heaths, or high mountain-tops, some of the Broads seem unchanged since the world was made. On and around them men live primitive lives. By studying these men some of us learn what are the essential things of life.

CHAPTER IV

AUTUMN AND WINTER IN BROADLAND

Autumn

SUMMER often lingers on into early autumn. During the last week of September and the early part of October there are still cruising yachts afloat; at Wroxham, Oulton, and Potter Heigham hardly a wherry, yacht, or launch is as yet dismantled. On those bright, warm October days, when the banded dragon-flies twitter among the withering sedges, little flocks of goldfinches flit about among the down-topped marsh thistles, and the gyrating water-beetles are as active as in July, quite a fleet of small sailing craft is seen on the rivers. The early mornings, however, are damp and misty; the spiders' cobweb-hammocks, swung up by the dykesides and among the tall yellow grasses, are weighed down with grey beads of moisture; and even at midday a ramble on some of the marshes or a visit to an alder carr means being drenched with dew. The blue haze which all day hangs over land and water is denser than it was in summer; Nature puts a thicker veil over her fading face. When the reeds rustle in the wind, it is with a crispness of sound betokening that the reed-cutters' harvest is ripening and will soon be ready for his meag and scythe. But often for days together there is scarcely breeze enough to cause a whisper among the reeds and sedges; sailing craft hardly make any headway; the heat and moisture make the air more oppressive than it was during many days in July. The marshes perhaps are steeped in sunshine, but its light and warmth are not welcomed with birds' songs. Now and again a lark soars and sings for a while, but soon drops

4

to earth again, as though it had felt in its aerial flight the chill breath of coming winter. Except for the larks and, perhaps, in the neighbourhood of a copse, hanger, or oak-bordered driftway, a cheery robin, the feathered songsters are silent; but the plovers are beginning to flock together, and often break the silence of the lonesome marshlands with their mournful cries.

Nearly all the bright-hued wild flowers which decked the riversides and dykes are gone. The tall willow-herbs have burst their long seed-pods and smothered themselves with clinging down; the hemp agrimony is faded; the dykes are full of withered water-parsnip, loosestrife, and plantain stalks; and where the flowering rush flaunted its beautiful umbels, the dingy bur-marigold is almost the only flower in bloom. But on some of the damp margins the blue eyes of forget-me-not still peer from amid the horsetails and marshworts; and although the bladderworts and the curious aloe - like water-soldiers are sunk on to the ooze, the arrowheads still pierce the floating mantle of frogbits and duckweeds. The meadow-sweet, in spite of its fragile appearance, here and there displays a cluster of blossoms, the fragrance of which seems stronger now than in summer; the mints, too, have not lost all their mauve florets, and a few yellow-rayed composite plants give a touch of bright colour to the sun-scorched river walls. The pasture marshes, on which the cattle are still browsing, are becoming tawny as heathlands with the sapless stems of grasses which sprung up after the hay was mown; but the damp rush marshes are still green. There the beautiful grass of Parnassus, whose creamy cup-shaped blossoms seem made to hold the mist-drops, is in full bloom, amid blue devil's-bits, white umbels of angelica, and a few golden marsh marigolds, which are flowering for a second time in the year.

One sadly misses the summer birds. The warblers are gone from the reed-beds, carrs, and marshes, the wagtails from the dykesides, the whitethroats from the driftway hedgerows, and the wheatears from the heaps of ooze and weeds which the marshmen have heaped up on the dyke banks; and by the middle of October the swallows, swifts, and martens have followed them. Gone, too, are the red-shanks, after spending a little time on the Breydon flats; and the black-headed gulls have abandoned their breeding haunts at Hoveton and Somerton. Other birds have come to take their places; but none of them can be to us what the warblers and whitethroats were in spring, and the red-shanks and puits in June. Flocks of fieldfares begin to arrive almost as soon as the last harvest waggon has jolted from the upland fields to the stackyard; their harsh cries are heard on the misty marshes. With them come redwings, to feed on the ruddy hawthorn berries and in the stackyards of the marsh farms. Thousands of larks, too, have come to flock and feed with the home-bred birds in the stubble and on the marshlands. Since the middle of August great numbers of goldcrests have made their marvellous oversea flight, and now the fir copses are full of them, clinging to the needles and creeping like mice about the branches. Then the bramblings are seen on the marshes near the coast. Migrant fowl are already working southward. Wigeon, or " smee," as they are known in Broadland, are to be met with on some of the Broads and riverside ronds; so too are tufted duck. A little later the " pokers " or pochards arrive— in October, when the gunner is on the alert for golden plovers, flocks of which spread themselves over the marshes, where they feed with the green plovers; and at night the homeward-bound marshman and belated wherryman hear them whistling overhead, as they flight to the uplands, seeking a change of diet in the newly sown grain. When the October gales begin to blow, seagulls visit the marshes and herring gulls are seen on some of the Broads.

So, although the summer migrants have taken flight to warmer climes, thousands and tens of thousands of other birds have come to Broadland. Marshmen working near the coast, and beachmen prowling along the seashore after the tide has ebbed, have seen some of them arrive, large and small companies of weary-winged wayfarers, some of whom had scarcely strength enough left to reach the land when they had sighted it, and most of them were glad to alight on the bushes of sea buckthorn on the sandhills and even on the sand and shingle of the beach. But the men who see them come in are fortunate to do so; most of us miss the wonderful sight of the small birds' arrival, and only see the rooks and crows, which for days together come streaming in all along the coast, over town, fishing hamlet, and sand dune. Most of the rooks, after their long journey, make for the fields and marshlands; but the grey crows, the "Kentishmen," often settle on the beach and on the Breydon flats, where they feed on the flotsam left stranded by the ebbing tide. All along the sands, where a dark stain of coal dust, crimson plocamium, and green bladderwrack marks the limit of the flood tide, you may see the footprints of that careful scavenger, the grey or hooded crow.

On these October days, when the air is heavily laden with moisture, and the sodden grass, swampy ronds, and stagnant dykes steam in the sun and exhale an odour of tide-wrack and rotting sedge, the smoke of the weed-burners' fires drifts down from the uplands, mingling with the blue, quivering haze, and streaming through the sallow wands and red-fruited hawthorns. The pungent smell of the smoke from the smouldering weed-heaps is characteristic of a Broadland autumn day. So, too, is the sight of a solitary marshman dyke-drawing; for many of the dykes are choked up with rank-growing water weeds, which must be cleared out before the rains set in and the rain-water comes pouring down from the upland field-drains and "holls." From early morning, when a dense fog hangs over the marshes, until dusk, when the fog rises again, the dyke-drawer is at work in the midst of the marshes, generally with no other companions than the rats and voles in the dyke banks and the snipe which come to feed in the hovers. Clad in a corduroy or moleskin sleeve-waistcoat or a fisherman's "gansy," corduroy trousers, in each leg of which a telescopic tuck is taken by means of a leathern strap, heavy marsh boots, and a hat like that of a Tyrolean mountaineer, there is a primitive regard only for essentials about him which is peculiarly impressive. His appearance suggests a product of Nature in her sombre moods, a man shaped by solitude and rendered apathetic by isolation. He is slow of speech, lethargic of movement, and nothing excites him. It is difficult to believe that it was by the labour of such as he the wide marshlands were reclaimed and made to provide thousands of acres of rich grazing ground for cattle.

Although there is nothing in his appearance to suggest it, he is in all probability a man with considerable responsibilities. One such man I met had something like four miles of dykes to clear, a drainage windmill to attend to, and frequently as many as two hundred "head" of cattle under his charge. The cattle—most of them fattening bullocks—necessitated his spending almost all his time on the marshes. In one week he had, with the assistance of other marshmen, to haul five bullocks out of dykes into which they had waded until they were embedded in the mud. This same marshman had a curious tale to tell about a narrow escape he had one morning, while concealed in the reeds around a marsh pool, waiting for the flighting of the fowl. He had gone down to the pool before daybreak, and had floated a pair of decoy ducks on the water. They were wooden decoys of his own making, and to increase their resemblance to real fowl he had affixed to them pairs of real mallards' wings. Just as day dawned he became aware of the presence of fowl near him, so he began to imitate the calling of a drake, an accomplishment upon which he rather prided himself. Suddenly, while he crouched among the reeds, he heard the sharp *crack, crack* of a double-barrelled breech-loader, and immediately his decoy ducks turned over in the water. In the grey misty dawnlight, another gunner, whose attention had been attracted by the marsh-man's quacking, had mistaken the decoys for real birds. The marshman's shouting so alarmed the gunner, who was lying on the side of a neighbouring marsh wall, that he nearly fainted, believing he had shot some one. " An' he pretty nigh had," said the marshman; "for I worn't more'n a couple o' yards out o' line wi' th' decoy ducks from where he lay. But a miss wor as good as a mile." Such reminiscences are frequently to be heard by the dykesides on damp October days.

The sunsets of the humid, sunny days of St. Luke's Little Summer are painted with the most gorgeous hues from Nature's palette. The low-lying clouds are edged with smouldering gold, radiant streaks of golden light flash gloriously across the heavens, and for a time after the sun has gone down feathery coral-pink cloudlets float amid the amber afterglow. Broads and rivers reflect all the vivid hues of this cloudland glory; but not for long, for the fog soon spreads over land and water, blotting out river and dyke, marsh and mere.

To be caught by such a fog in the midst of a maze of marsh dykes is an unpleasant experience. On an autumn night I had such a one on the marshes between the Acle new road and Breydon. In the afternoon I had sailed from Yarmouth to a little creek on the north-west side of the estuary, having arranged to spend the night with a friend whose house-boat was moored near a marsh farmstead called Banham's Farm. I was to have had another companion; but he had failed to put in an appearance before I left Yarmouth, and just before dusk I strolled across to the Acle road, in order to meet him should he have come to Yarmouth by a late train and started to walk to the spot where the house-boat was moored. By the time I reached the Yarmouth toll-gate night had set in; so, having seen nothing of my friend, I hastened back towards the shores of Breydon. I had not gone far before the fog came rolling across the marshes like a great cloud of white smoke, and when I turned off the Acle road I could see no object that was more than a dozen yards away from me. Still for a while I had no difficulty in finding my way, for it lay beside a marsh dyke; but when I had crossed the railway I was soon at a loss to discover my whereabouts. For the footpath was so hidden by the grass which had sprung up since the hay was mown that I soon lost sight of it, and presently I found my way barred by a wide dyke. Having nothing else to guide me, I kept to the dykeside, hoping to find a plank bridge or gate which would bring me on to the path again. But although I found a gate I could see no path, and for an hour or more I wandered amid a labyrinth of dykes, from time to time coming upon a gate which seemed familiar, because I had already passed through it once or twice in the course of my wanderings.

The fog hung about me like a wet shroud, distilling soaking, chilling moisture. It covered my clothes with an aqueous dust, and whenever I closed my eyes mist-drops trickled down my face. On every side I was shut in by an impenetrable pall of fog; yet when I looked up I could see the stars clearly. If I had been on a wide and trackless moor the stars might have helped me; but here it was impossible to walk more than a few hundred yards in any direction, for the dykes soon brought me to a standstill. Tired of trudging through the long wet grass, I stopped against a gate and listened for some sound which might guide me; but all I could hear was the clamour of the black-headed gulls on the Breydon flats, and now and again the *laka*, *laka* of a "saddle-back" or the cry of a flighting curlew. Once I thought I heard human footsteps approaching; but it was only a bullock's hooves brushing through the long grass. Even the phantasmal company of that marshland bogle, the ghostly herdsman, who when the "sea-smoke" drifted down upon the lowlands, used to drive the cattle into the morasses, would have been welcome to me; but the only mist-wraith I saw resolved itself into a gnarled sallow bush by a dykeside. It seemed as though I were fated to spend the night on the marshes, and when I thought of the snug little house-boat, where supper was awaiting me, the prospect was anything but pleasing; but help was at hand, though I knew nothing of its coming. For suddenly, when I was thinking of trying to find my way back to the railway, I heard some one shouting, apparently not far from where I was standing. At first I imagined it must be some one who, like myself, was lost on the marshes; but when I gave an answering hail there presently emerged from the fog the burly form of Banham, the marsh farmer. "A rokey night, this here," was his greeting when he saw me; and when he learnt that I had lost my way he assured me that I "warn't th' fust by a sight" that had done so on the Breydon marshes. He thought it not unlikely that his wife might have some difficulty in finding her way home, for she had gone to Yarmouth, and should have returned by nightfall. It was for her he was looking when he found me. He soon brought me on to the Breydon wall, which I followed until I saw a light flickering like a will-o'-the-wisp. It was, however, no such "fickle and deceptive flame," but a lantern which my friend had lighted and placed on the roof of his house-boat. In a few moments it had guided me into the warmth and comfort of the house-boat's cosy cabin.

But early autumn is not all lingering summer days and chill, foggy nights. During October, when the Lowestoft yacht basin is filled with trawlers instead of yachts, and the docks, both at Lowestoft and Yarmouth, are densely packed with east coast drifters and luggers from Inverness, Banff, and Kirkcaldy, all busily engaged in the autumn fishing, there are often days of lowering clouds and wild weather. Then the cruising yachts which have lingered late on the rivers disappear as if by magic, and at Oulton, Wroxham, and Potter Heigham the fleets of white-winged craft are rapidly dismantled, drawn up on to the "hard" or hauled into the boat-sheds, there to remain until next season. For the next eight months the wherrymen, reed-cutters, and eel-catchers will have the rivers and Broads to themselves, and only enthusiastic rovers—"wild, gipsy spirits," some one has called them—will admit that during these months the lives of the natives is not all labour and sorrow. But even when the storm - clouds gather over river, marsh, and lone lagoon, there are intervals when the sunlight breaks through the wind - driven, dun - coloured scud, and makes luminous the "shadow-streaks of rain." These wild October gleams and glooms, these smiles and frowns of an autumnal April, together with the boisterous buffets of the October gales, must be seen and felt by every one who wishes to really "know" Broadland; for the district is curiously susceptible, and owes much of its charm to the variability of its atmospheric environment.

These chill and gusty days, often grey with a drizzling rain, when the willow wands wave wildly, and the heavy-gaited marshmen stumble over dense clumps of toadstools and huge puff-balls which have sprung up during the warm, damp weather, are days when a striking change is wrought in the aspect of Broadland. Until they come, summer seems loth to leave us. Our native trees—the sturdy oaks, tough alders, and hardy willows—have hardly lost a leaf; only such tender aliens as the horse-chestnuts have felt the chill of the autumn winds, and strewn the copse borders and driftways with a ruddy drift of withered leaves. But the October gales send the yellow birch leaves flying far and wide, blanch or stain the petals of the late - blooming wild flowers, and bring winter close upon the heels of summer. After the gales the withered leaves fall quickly; in the quiet of the copses you may hear them distinctly, tapping against the boughs and twigs as they fall. Even more noticeable is the fall of the beech mast, which, when once it has begun to drop, comes pattering down in showers. So too do the acorns and sweet chestnut burrs; the copse footpaths are covered with a crunching carpet of them. The crimson of the hawthorn berries deepens, and the scarlet of the wild rose and bryony berries brightens; the bracken on the Herring-fleet Hills turns golden-brown. But the most vivid autumn colouring is seen in the dykes and by the dykesides, where the leaves of the slender water - pepper polygonum (*P. Hydropiper*) are afire with vermilion and gold. Amid all these signs of waning life and decay it is pleasant to see the tightly packed catkins already formed on the hazels and alders, and to notice, when the elm leaves begin to fall, the fretted edges of the twigs, where the young buds are appearing. One realises then that the old life is only making way for the new.

October sees every eel-sett spread across the rivers; for the eels, which for some weeks have been making their way down-stream in small numbers, now begin to come down in shoals, and the eel - catcher looks for good hauls when he raises his pods. On Breydon, the two or three punt - gunners who are still to be found there are afloat before daybreak, and the loud booming of their great swivel guns puts to flight the gulls, curlews, and flocks of small wading birds — stints, knots, dunlins, and ringed plovers—which feed on the oozy flats. The flight-shooter, too, looks for some sport on the Broads and such river reaches and fleets as are crossed by the wild fowls' lines of flight. But colder weather will have to set in before the fowl come in such numbers to Broadland as to pro-

vide work for the Fritton decoymen. "Ah, them 'coys!"
the old marsh and river gunners exclaim; "there 'ont
never be any quantity o' fowl for us while them 'coys
is used." But there are few decoys now compared with
the number there used to be, and in the days when they
were worked at Horsey, Woodbastwick, Ranworth, and
Barnby, as well as at Fritton, little was heard about scarcity
of fowl. Better drainage of the marshes is no doubt
accountable for the disappearance of several species which
once bred in the district; but I agree with an old Broadsman friend of mine, who reckons that it "ain't accountable
for so much as some folks 'ud hev us belaave. What gunners
want in Broadland is more room to shute in, an' th' right
sort o' weather." Given the right weather, there is plenty
of fowl.

WINTER

An enthusiast for Broadland cruising once determined
to spend a whole year on the Broads. He began his cruise
in the middle of September, and for nearly three months
all went well with him; but on 11th December his yacht
was "frozen up" on Oulton Broad, and there perforce it
stayed until 2nd February. For about ten days he remained
on board, watching the skaters disporting themselves on the
ice, and listening to a Norwegian skipper, who was on an ice-
bound lugger near by, singing "Gamle Norge" to while away
the time. On 20th December, however, he fled to London,
where, as the reports which reached him from Broadland
were unfavourable, he stayed until the middle of January.

I well remember that winter. For six weeks navigation
was impossible on the Broadland waterways. At Oulton,
Wroxham, Beccles, and many an isolated marshland staithe,
wherries lay fettered in manacles of ice. During the greater
part of that time the marshes were hidden under a white
coverlet of snow. Skaters skated from Oulton Broad to
Beccles and back for pastime; wherrymen, old and young,
lacking work to do, donned their "pattens" and played
hockey on the ice. Some of the marshland and ferry inns—

YARMOUTH FROM BREYDON

LONG BILLS

REGATTA AT ACLE

MARSHLAND NEAR BARTON

SPARROW HAWK – CALLING HER MATE

ST. OLAVES

HEIGHAM SOUNDS

ABOVE WAYFORD BRIDGE ON THE ANT

which, when the cruising season is over, rely almost entirely on the wherrymen for custom — almost might have closed their doors to the public without turning away trade. Most of the small birds—the tits, finches, and pipits—seemed to desert the district, only a few of them being seen around the marsh farmsteads and in the shelter of the carrs and thick hedgerows; the rest, no doubt, sought the neighbourhood of the towns, where food was to be found. Even the hooded crows—the grey-backed Kentishmen whose raucous *craas* are heard so often in winter by the dykesides—flocked to the Breydon flats, or, in large numbers, sought the company of the ringed plovers and sanderlings on the seashore. The winter migrants—the snow and Lapland buntings, the shore-larks, fieldfares, and redwings—came to us in great numbers, to find a chilly welcome and the hardest fare. From the middle of December until the end of January the atmospheric conditions and the outlook over the wide marshlands were arctic; when the sun shone the dazzling whiteness of the snow - clad levels was almost blinding. In the snow the footprints of starving birds, stoats, and weasels made varied patterns, and one could trace them for long distances across the flats and along the walls. Otters left behind them a spoor by which a gunner easily might have followed them to their nests or lairs. How they lived during those bitter weeks it is hard to say. Thin ice is no obstacle to their fishing, but ice two feet thick will baffle a polar bear. No doubt the coots and water - hens provided what the frozen rivers denied.

Such long spells of frosty weather are comparatively rare. As a rule, the rivers are " open " to wherries during the greater part of the winter; often there is. no hindrance to voyaging all through the year. But when a spell of cold weather accompanied by heavy snowfall sets in, some of the marsh highways and byways soon become untraversable, and the aspect of the far-spreading lowlands is suggestive of a Lapland landscape or the Siberian steppes. In a few hours I have seen the wind-driven snow heaped in drifts ten to twelve feet high on the willow-bordered dams and against the river walls, isolating the lonely homes of the marsh cattle-tenders, filling the frozen

dykes, and forming great banks against the windmills, to
which the millmen, if they would enter them, must dig their
way. To be caught in the midst of the marshes by a heavy
snowstorm is, as many a marshman and gunner can testify,
as discomforting an experience as being overtaken there by
a dense fog. Even at midday it soons becomes impossible
to discern the familiar objects which serve as landmarks;
trees, mills, cattle-sheds, and marsh homesteads are obscured
by the fast-falling flakes and the white snow-scud whirled
from the rising drifts. The footpaths across the marshes,
often hardly discernible even in fine weather, are soon
obliterated; sometimes only by observing the direction of
the wind have men been able to reach the borders of the
marshes. Such storms have been attended by tragedies,
but to no greater degree in Broadland than in other districts
in England where travellers may be worsted in a battle with
the elements.

Crouched in a corner seat of a railway carriage, journeying,
say, from Lowestoft to Norwich, and scanning through the
breath-dimmed window the lonesome marshlands stretching
away to a misty horizon, the traveller who has had no closer
acquaintance with the district may well wonder, at this
season of the year, what constitutes the charm of Broadland.
He sees the marshes tawny with withered grasses, rushes, and
sedges, a few rooks or lapwings feeding on them or wheeling
above them, leafless alders, willows, and sallows dotted here
and there by the dykesides, and occasionally he gets a glimpse
of a steely river, its surface, maybe, blurred and ruffled by an
east wind. Once or twice, perhaps, during his journey he
may observe a solitary marshman at work, or a wherry
sailing between banks fringed with yellow, grey-plumed reeds.
Little else is likely to attract his eye. If the day is drawing
to a close, and a fog gathering over the marshes, he will
see only a grey misty waste, and probably he will be glad
to turn his attention to the farmer who is talking about a
forthcoming coursing match, or the garrulous " commercial "
who is explaining to a sleepy stranger what he would do
if he were in charge of the War Office. Broadland, he
will perhaps admit, may be a delightful district in summer;

but in winter—well, every one has a right to his own opinion, and his is that a man must be born in the district to appreciate it during the winter months.

It were well if he could see some nook or corner of Broadland perhaps the following morning. A foggy evening has been succeeded by a frosty night—a "regular rimer," as the marshman calls it. The marshes are as white as if there had been a fall of snow. Every feathery reed plume, sharp sedge blade, and bending rush is coated with glistening ice-crystals; the withering leaves of the great water-docks are like diamond-dusted shields; on the dry stalks of the water-plantains, the brown marsh thistles, and the sapless stems of the willow-herbs, the frozen mist-drops hang in silvery settings and fairy-like festoons. In the carrs and copses the frost fays have been at work, gemming every pine needle, alder catkin, and slender birch twig with crystalline spray. If a bird takes flight from a bough, some of the spray falls in a powdery, scintillating shower. The hedgerow borders of the driftways, last night bare and mist-drenched, are bedecked with frost garlands, rimy tangles of bramble, sparkling arches of briar, glittering embroideries wrought by the deft fingers of the frost sprites. Down by the river a musical tinkling is heard—the tinkling of the ice-crystals on the reed stems; every breath of breeze makes music, and the bearded titmice, as they take short flights above the reeds, utter at intervals their silvery, symphonic call-notes.

A walk along one of the marsh dams, at Acle, Haddiscoe, or elsewhere, on such a day is delightful. The keenness of the air urges one to a brisk pace which sets the blood coursing through the veins; but one's progress is not so rapid that one fails to see the gleaming of the seagulls' white wings against the blue sky, the titmice creeping along the branches of the alders, and the fieldfares—the most beautiful thrushes in the world, some one has called them—which have settled on a tree, but which are gone before one has time fully to appreciate their beauty. Starlings,—large flocks of them,—linnets, larks, and pipits are seen on the marshes, flying about restlessly, for their hard fare is hard to get when the ground is frozen and everything on it is stiff with rime. A snipe—

the marshes seem full of them—is flushed from a dykeside, and flies off uttering a harsh, startling cry. In the distance, where a marshman carrying a heavy, long-barrelled muzzle-loader is the only human being in sight, a flock of golden plovers is flighting towards the uplands. In the dusk of evening strange bird-voices are heard crying in the gloom; the weird whistle of the curlew sounds across the flats, and from high overhead comes the clanging of flighting geese.

Walking is pleasanter than sailing in Broadland on such a day; but if at midday the sun shines brightly, it is worth one's while to go afloat on one of the wilder Broads and see what effect the autumn gales and frosty nights have had on the rank aquatic vegetation which surrounds it. The upland fields are colourless, the woodlands sombre, and the sandhills drear; but where the reeds and sedges are mirrored in unruffled water, the autumn hues of withering leaf and yellowing culm are, in winter, intensified. A tract of swamp bathed in sunlight glows as though aflame, a reed bed is like a field of ripe corn, and a decaying dock leaf seems stained with ruby wine. Then the reflections of the storm-torn reed plumes, leafless stems, and bleaching tufts of water-grasses are so clearly defined, that it is easy to imagine one might grasp them, so different are they to the shimmering, evanescent semblances to be seen on a breezy summer day.

Effective drainage has rendered the marshes far less likely to be inundated by rain-floods than was the case at a time well within the memory of many living Broadlanders; but even now Broadland provides the best skating to be had anywhere in England, except on the Cambridgeshire and Lincolnshire fens. When Hickling Broad is frozen, skaters have an expanse of ice compared with which the Serpentine is a mere pond; and when frosty weather sets in, marshes at St. Olave's and elsewhere are flooded with river-water, their owners being glad to earn a few pounds by providing ice on which skating can be indulged in without risk of dangerous immersion. Marsh ice, as a rule, is as clear and smooth as glass; I have skated over acres of it, through which every grass-blade below could be seen. Broad ice, on the contrary, is often of unequal thickness and quality; for until it becomes too thick to break, the Broadsmen load their boats with it for sale to the Yarmouth and Lowestoft fish-packers.   The rise and fall of the tides, too, breaks the thin ice around the edges of the Broads, and it is only when a sharp frost has continued several days that it is safe to venture on it. Even then, often there are spots where the ice remains thin or the water unfrozen; these, the Broadsmen say, mark the position of ever-flowing springs oozing up from the beds of the Broads.   Still, I have known winters when for weeks together it was possible to skate every day almost all over Oulton Broad, and I can well remember one winter when a sheep was roasted on the ice there.   That year we had skating by torchlight in various parts of Broadland, and strange and weird was the effect of the torches flickering and flaring over the Broads, while the night-flying birds, lured by the lights, piped and cried in the darkness overhead.   Occasionally there were false alarms; the ice, falling with the tide, would crack with a report like a gun, and the skaters would scurry towards the shore.   But there was little to fear; the ice, for the most part, was over a foot thick, and the cracks were dangerous only when a skater caught a skate-blade in them, and came down with a whack which made him rub his knees and elbows ruefully.   I have heard ancient natives of the neighbourhood of Berney Arms talk of the time when good skating was to be had on that part of Breydon now known as Burgh Flats.   One old man could remember how, as a boy, he skated from Berney Arms to Yarmouth to get for his mother a halfpenny-worth of yeast—a ten miles' journey, which he had to make twice, because just before he reached home he tripped over a boat's painter lying on the ice, and fell and broke the yeast bottle. In winter, some of the marsh farmsteads were, at that time, so inaccessible that there was no way of getting coal to them unless a coal-laden wherry happened to be ice-bound some-where near.

In Broadland it is only the townsman who attempts figure-skating—an artificial performance which, Dr. Emerson remarks, reminds one of the antics of the " foolish harlequin of the pantomime."   As in the case of his brother of the fens, the native skater's chief ambition is to outdistance every one else, even if in order to do so he has to sacrifice grace to speed. Some of the wherrymen and marshmen are experts on "pattens," in so far as proficiency consists of an ability to attain a great pace; the muscular development of their legs, attained by quanting the heavily laden wherries and trudging over rough marshlands, enables them to outstay most of their rivals. Skating matches, however, for some reason, are organised less frequently nowadays than they were twenty years ago; the interest in them seems to have died out, or, at any rate, is very local.

Long spells of frosty weather, welcome as they may be to the skater and gunner, are hard times for many of the marsh-men, who, now pike-snaring is made illegal and liggering is permitted only on one or two Broads, where the inhabitants of neighbouring villages possess "ancient rights," sometimes are "hard put to" to find occupation and means of livelihood. Free shooting, except on Breydon and along the foreshores, is to be had only in very restricted areas; eel-setts cannot be worked, and even if they could, it would be to little purpose when the eels have ceased "running"; picking is impossible on the ice-laid rivers and in the frozen dykes; dyke-drawing, wall-mending, and other similar marsh occupations are equally impracticable while the dykes are filled with ice and the ground is hard as iron. Open weather is anxiously awaited, so that reed-cutting may begin. Meanwhile, it is not surprising if some visitor, who during his summer voyaging happened to hint at the possibility of such a thing, receives by post a pair of bearded titmice from Broadland. For this the marshman can hardly be blamed; it is the connivance of the visitor that is reprehensible. For in winter the bearded titmice are a constant temptation to the prowling gunner. At this season, abandoning their restricted breeding haunts, flocks of these pretty little birds wander far and wide over the district, visiting most of the Broads and following the courses of the rivers. Among the yellow reeds you may see them creeping and swinging, and hear their call-notes; sometimes a dozen or more of them are visible together, and their chinging is as delightful bird-music as one can listen to. But while you are listening, maybe, the report of a gun startles you, and if you search the reed bed you find, lying on a blood-sprayed reed blade, a tiny bunch of ruffled feathers. I myself have seen such a sight; and not all the stuffed birds set up in what the marshmen call "glassen boxes" seemed worth the death of the little minstrel who a few minutes before was clashing his cymbals among the reeds.

But the death of a bearded titmouse means, perhaps, dinners for the gunner's family for a week, or a few hours' conviviality for himself at one of the marshland inns. Even if it only means the latter, I for one, knowing something of what the marshman's life is like in winter, find it hard to blame him: the cheery glow of the fire in the inn kitchen, the beer warmed in the pewter before being poured into the mug, and the congenial company assembled on the high-backed settles flanking the wide hearth, are to the marshman what to the city man is his club. Hobnobbing with other marshmen and with wherrymen from the river, listening to oft-told tales and joining in the choruses of familiar songs, he forgets for a while the icy blasts of the frozen flats, the chill grey dawns, and the days spent in solitary toiling. The rector, when he goes by the inn, may shake his head when he hears the loud-voiced merriment within; but no one knows better than he how little enjoyment the marshman can get elsewhere at this season of the year. Old George the eel-catcher, when remonstrated with in the morning, admits that he was "a bit cherry-merry" last night; but he went to the Dog and Duck to see young Zack about a pick-head, and Billy Johnson was just home, "flush" with money, from the autumn fishing. It was a cold night, he had been ice-breaking all day, the inn fire was very comforting, and one thing led to another, so maybe—well, he may have had a *drop* too much; but seeing that Billy Johnson paid, and would not take "no" for an answer, what could he do?

But the hardest winters have an end, and when open weather comes, and the rafts can be towed or quanted up and down the rivers, reed-cutting provides employment for many of the men of the marshes. And it goes on well into the spring; in fact, until the appearance of the "colts" or young

5

reeds puts a stop to the cutting.   By that time the coltsfoot
has pushed its way up through the clods on the river walls,
the marsh marigold has bloomed by the dykesides, and the
warblers have come back to the amber reed-beds and budding
carrs.

CHAPTER V

THE OLD-TIME BROADSMEN

A VOYAGER on the Broadland rivers cannot help noticing, more especially on the Bure and its tributaries, the Ant and Thurne, the little ark-like house-boats of the eel-catchers. Most of them are very ancient, dilapidated craft; some, indeed, are so leaky that they cannot be kept afloat in the creeks and inlets, and are dragged up on to the banks or ronds; but nearly all of them are tenanted during the months when the eels are "running," and their occupants usually contrive to make themselves comfortable in their cramped little cabins. In another chapter I shall have occasion to refer again to these eel-catchers: I only mention them here in order to remark that they are almost the sole survivors of the passing race of real Broadsmen.

In the "good old days," as the surviving Broadsmen call them, when no restrictions were placed upon the taking of fish and slaughtering of fowl, the Broadsman's life was a happy one. The men who lived in isolated cottages on the lonesome marshlands, and spent days and nights on the rivers and fens, were of a freedom-loving and self-reliant type. Leaving to others the waging of war, the tilling of land, the reaping of corn, they endured shivering fits of ague, scorching blaze of summer sun, and numbing blast of winter wind, because the fascination of an unfettered life had cast its spell upon them. Busy with their nets, traps, and decoys, they were content to have no part in the doings of the world which lay beyond the horizon of their familiar marshes. For their life was far from being monotonous: every season, and almost every month of the year, brought them change of occupation. They were descendants of the men to whom the barons of old who held the Broadland manors looked for fish and fowl for their tables, and whom the abbots of St. Benet-at-Holm and Langley, when they entertained courtly guests with falconry, summoned to guide those guests to the haunts of the hernshaws. They knew every rush marsh on which the plovers nested, every inlet and dyke into which the bream and roach swarmed at spawning-time, every wild fowl by its cry or flight. Often for days and nights together they heard no voices but the wild-life voices of marsh and mere; so that the "chucking" of the sedge warbler, the clanking of the coot, and the rustling of the voles and otters in the hovers became to them companionable sounds. Their methods of gaining a livelihood made them close observers of the habits of fish, bird, and beast; the knowledge of natural history that was lost when an aged Broadsman died, would, if it had been printed, have made his name famous. They were flight-shooters, punt-gunners, eel-catchers, fish-netters, reed-cutters, dyke-drawers, and cattle-tenders. Frequently one man, in the course of twelve months, would be engaged in each and all of these pursuits and occupations.

Mr. Davies, quoting from Manship's *Book of the Foundacion and Antiquitye of the Town of Gt. Yarmouthe*, gives us an interesting account of a dispute which arose between the Yarmouth bailiffs and two representatives of the notable Paston family concerning the renting of certain eel-setts on the rivers Yare, Bure, and Waveney. From this account, which is one of the earliest references to the old-time Broadsmen, we learn that in the year 1576 there were thirty-eight eel-setts or stations, hired by fishermen at a nominal rent of a penny a year. Until the bailiffs superintended the letting of these setts, there seem to have been frequent disputes among the fishermen, though it was stated that they had "an onlye custome among them, used tyme out of mynd, that yerlie, on the day of S. Margaret, every fysherman that could that daye, after rysenge, first come to anye of the said ele settes in anye of the said ryvers, and there staye and pytche a bowghe at the said ele sett, the same fysherman should have and injoye the same ele sett that yere, without yealdinge or payenge anye thinge for the same." The bailiffs, however, after persuading the fishermen to leave to them the allotment of fishing stations, seem to have been anxious to make greater profit by the letting of the setts; for Mr. Paston, who laid the fishermen's case before the Privy Council, charged the bailiffs with having conspired with a certain John Everist, one of Queen Elizabeth's ordinary yeoman of the chamber, to obtain from the queen permission to demand for the "fishing places" a rental of thirty pounds a year, which, we are told, would have resulted in the taking away of the "whole lyvenge of the poor fyshermen." This, Mr. Paston urged, would have been against the interest of the general public; for it was by the fishermen's industry that "the citie of Norwiche and the countye of Norf. and Suff. had been plentifullie provided in their kyndes of fyshe in the comon marketts, and for reasonable pryces." The fishermen appear to have won their case, but the Yarmouth bailiffs' claim to the conservancy of the rivers for ten miles upwards from Yarmouth was granted.

The best description of an old-time Broadsman that I know of is that given by the Rev. Richard Lubbock in his *Observations on the Fauna of Norfolk*. It has often been quoted; but it is so good, and so admirably summarises the Broadsmen's various occupations, that I cannot refrain from reproducing it here. "When I first visited the Broads," Mr. Lubbock writes, "I found here and there an occupant, squatted down, as the Americans would call it, on the verge of a pool, who relied almost entirely on shooting and fishing for the support of himself and family, and lived in a truly primitive manner. I particularly remember one hero of this description. 'Our Broad,' as he always called the extensive pool by which his cottage stood, was his microcosm—his world; the islands in it were his gardens of the Hesperides; its opposite extremity his *Ultima Thule*. Wherever his thoughts wandered, they could not get beyond the circle of his beloved lake; indeed, I never knew them aberrant but once, when he informed me, with a doubting air, that he had sent his wife and his two eldest children to a fair at a country village two miles off, that their ideas might expand by travel: as he sagely observed, they had never been away from 'our Broad.' I went into his house at the dinner hour, and found the whole party going to fall to most thankfully upon a roasted herring-gull, killed, of course, on ' our Broad.' His life presented no vicissitudes but an alternation of marsh employment. In winter, after his day's reed-cutting, he might be found regularly posted at nightfall, waiting for the flight of fowl, or paddling after them on the open water. With the first warm days of February he launched his fleet of trimmers, pike finding a ready sale at his own door to those who bought them to sell again in the Norwich market. As soon as the pike had spawned, and were out of season, the eels began to occupy his attention, and lapwings' eggs to be diligently sought for. In the end of April, the island in his watery domain was frequently visited for the sake of shooting the ruffs which resorted thither on their first arrival. As the days grew longer and hotter, he might be found searching, in some smaller pools near his house, for the shoals of tench as they commenced spawning. Yet a little longer, and he began marsh mowing—his gun always laid ready upon his coat, in case flappers should be met with. By the middle of August teal came to a wet corner near his cottage, snipes began to arrive, and he was often called upon to exercise his vocal powers on the curlews that passed to and fro. By the end of September good snipe-shooting was generally to be met with in his neighbourhood ; and his accurate knowledge of the marshes, his unassuming good humour and zeal in providing sport for those who employed him, made him very much sought after as a sporting guide by snipe shots and fishermen ; and his knowledge of the habits of different birds enabled him to give useful information to those who collected them."

Mr. Lubbock then goes on to say that these hardy fenmen were great supporters of an old Norfolk pastime called "camping," which required muscle and endurance of pain beyond common limits, and "somewhat resembled the *pancratium* of the ancients, but was rather more severe." This game, which seems almost to have been confined to the eastern counties, somewhat resembled Rugby football, but was far rougher, the players often receiving fatal injuries. There were no rules to prevent what would now be considered foul play ; pushing, tripping, striking, and kicking of players were permitted; and the game often ended in a free fight, in which the spectators joined. Villages were matched against villages, Hundreds against Hundreds, and counties against counties; and so long as there was an equal number of players on each side, there was no limit to the number who took part in a game. Contemporary writers maintained that it was a noble and manly sport, and remarked upon the "animated scene" presented by twenty or thirty youths, stripped to the skin, rushing "full *ding*" at each other, amid the shouting of half the population of the surrounding villages. When a large football was used, the game was called "kicking camp"; if the players wore shoes, it was known as "savage camp." It must have been a game of "savage camp" which was contested on Diss Common between teams representing Norfolk and Suffolk. There were three hundred players on each side, and when the Norfolk men came on to the field they tauntingly asked the Suffolk men whether they had brought their coffins with them! The Suffolk men, however, were victorious. Nine deaths resulted from this "game" within a fortnight. Camping fell into disrepute towards the end of the eighteenth century, on account of its frequent fatalities; but I once met an old Breydoner who was present at a match contested at Burgh Castle. It was, he believed, the last camping game ever played in Broadland. His father was one of the players, and he feared every moment that he would be killed.

But it is with the Broadsman's methods of gaining a livelihood rather than with his few pastimes that I wish to deal here. At the time when the Rev. R. Lubbock wrote his description of a typical Broadsman, the Acts of Parliament existing for the protection of wild birds were seldom enforced, and though Norwich and Yarmouth claimed jurisdiction over parts of the rivers, there were no useful regulations for the preservation of fresh-water fishes: the gunner could shoot and the fisherman net whenever and almost wherever they chose. True, so long ago as the end of the fourteenth century, it was enacted that "no manner of artificer, labourer, nor any other layman" not possessing lands to the value of £10 a year should hunt with dogs or use ferrets; and in the reign of Henry VIII. a law was passed which made it unlawful to destroy, except with the long-bow, " dukkes, mallardes, wygeons, teales, wyldgeese, and dyverse other kyndes of wyldfowle," between the end of May and the end of August; also it was by the same Act provided that between 1st March and 30th June the eggs of " byttour, heroune, shovelard, malarde, tele," and other wildfowl should not be taken.   But even if there had been a disposition to enforce the Acts, Broadland was a district in which they could be safely ignored.   No water-bailiff in silently gliding punt haunted the waterways at night, and in the daytime hid among the riverside reeds.   Under the eyes of every one who cared to watch him, the fisherman hauled in his draw-net full of roach and bream, and the gunner brought down mallard, wigeon, and teal.   I have talked with men who remembered those days,—and who themselves shouldered the heavy, long-barrelled muzzle-loaders and spread the hundred-yards-long draw-nets,—and they spoke of them as though they were the golden age of their world—the Broadland.   As one of them said to me, " We thought little then of catching a ton of roach and bream in a day, in the Beccles or Norwich rivers (the Waveney or the Yare); and we often put back three parts of our catch because we could not sell so much fish.   At the sluices of the mill-dykes we netted pike by the stone, or we caught them by means of copper-wire snares.   Then the Breydon flats were often white with fowl, and a punt-gunner could get as many as eighty at a single shot of his big swivel gun.   Now, in spite of protectin' an' presarvin' there ain't quarter the quantity of fish in the rivers nor nuthin' like sich flocks of fowl on the flats.   On Oulton Broad alone there were seven nets used regularly when the fish were in season.   And talkin' about fowl, I've seen two acres of Breydon mud-flat wholly covered with them; when they rose the whole flat seemed to rise.   Some of the gunners got a bushel skep full at a shot.   I myself have killed nineteen out of twenty-one stints at a single shot of a shoulder-gun.   Large flocks of cormorants used to come to Breydon then; but of course they worn't no good to the gunners, who only wanted fowl what would sell."

During the first half of the nineteenth century fish were so plentiful in the Broadland rivers that few people cared how they were caught, or whether they were caught at all. Bushels of roach, bream, and rudd were left to rot on the river banks, or cast on to the land for manure, because no one would buy them, and the Broadsmen did not want them for food. But the fishermen kept on netting, and generally managed to sell the best of the fish they caught. Hundred-yard draw-nets were used in the Broads and rivers, " buskin " or bushing nets about thirty yards long were spread along the borders of the reed beds, out of which the fish were driven by beating the reeds with poles, and smaller, fine-meshed nets were used in the dykes. None of these nets, however, were of such fine mesh as those used by the Breydon smelters: these were so fine as to cut the fingers of the women who mended them. Pike were not only netted, but taken on liggers or trimmers, consisting of small, tightly tied bundles of rushes, to which a short double-hooked line was attached, usually baited with a small roach.

Abundant as were the fish, extensive and indiscriminate netting eventually resulted in a very noticeable decrease in the quantity of large and fair-sized ones; and anglers, who found their " takes " gradually growing smaller, took exception to the fishermen's destructive methods. So long ago as 1857, steps were taken to regulate the netting, but with little success. Ten years later, after pressure had been put upon them, some members of the Norwich Corporation took action, and under the City of Norwich Act of 1867 certain restrictions were placed upon the fishermen. But Norwich only had jurisdiction over the Yare down to Hardley Cross; and as Yarmouth's jurisdiction over the lower waters was only nominal, the new regulations had little effect. Under cover of night the fishermen netted the forbidden waters, carrying the fish down to Yarmouth for sale or despatch to market; and though now and again some of them were proceeded against and fined, dodging the river-watchers was considered good sport, and the game went merrily on. Nor was anything effective done until about the year 1875. A well-known fish-poacher then, after a successful night's netting, carried his catch to Norwich, where it was conveyed through the streets in a hand-cart. The cart broke down, and the catch, chiefly consisting of roach and bream, fell out on to the road in the presence of a considerable number of people. This opened their eyes to the fact, hitherto ignored except by anglers, that, in spite of the regulations, immense quantities of fresh-water fish were being caught almost daily, and efforts were made to obtain an Act which would make netting illegal. The late Mr. Frank Buckland, whom the Home Secretary had instructed to report upon the state of the Norfolk Fisheries, was approached and urged to inquire into the conditions and abuses existing in connection with the Broads and rivers.

Mr. Buckland was too keenly interested in such matters to ignore such an appeal. He visited Yarmouth, Lowestoft, Norwich, and other places, and examined a large number of witnesses. He reported that not only the Broads but the rivers were extensively netted; that the fish taken were sent to inland towns and sold for a shilling a stone, or used for manure; that the rivers were usually netted at night, and tons of small fish taken during the spawning season. The Yarmouth town clerk told him that "there was no close time on the Broads, but they were fished whenever it was considered likely that a market could be found for the fish. There was no doubt that a large number of fry were thus destroyed, as the nets sometimes used in this fishing were of very small mesh. The Mayor and Corporation had no jurisdiction over the fisheries. No doubt in former years the Corporation assumed certain rights with regard to the river-fishing, but no such rights now existed." Another witness said "he frequently had seen as much as two tons of fish in the hold of one wherry; they consisted of roach, bream, perch, pike, etc., of all sizes and ages." The evidence of other witnesses proved lamentable diminution both in the size and quantity of the fish. One man stated that he had known two tons of fresh-water fish to be sold for £7, 10s. a ton—not a farthing a pound. Half these fish were thrown on to the land. One old man of ninety, who lived at Ludham, said that "formerly he could go out with his pole and tow (rod and line) and catch a rare mess of good fish in a couple of hours, and now there were hardly any left." A Lowestoft net-maker stated that the nets used by the river fishermen were of such small mesh that they would catch fish no bigger than an ordinary cedar pencil. At a meeting at Norwich, at which Mr. Buckland was present, it was resolved that legislation for the preservation of the navigable waters was urgently required; that this legislation should extend to the Broads, at least so far as to secure a close time during the spawning season; and that all netting, except for eels and smelts, should be prohibited. Mr. Buckland agreed with this resolution, and recommended that the Home Secretary should announce an annual close time (1st March to 31st May) for all fish in the Broads and rivers; that a local Board of Conservators should be given power to make by-laws as to the mesh of nets, use of liggers, cutting of weeds, etc.; and that trawling in the rivers (which had been carried on by some of the fishermen) should be put a stop to.

In 1877 the Norfolk and Suffolk Fisheries Act was passed. Under this Act certain by-laws were made, but they did not put a stop to all netting. Some persons had urged that when fish had attained the weight of $1\frac{1}{2}$ lbs. they should be taken for food; so the use of nets with a mesh measuring three inches from knot to knot was permitted. Five years later, it was discovered that with a net having a mesh slightly under three inches from knot to knot a fisherman had succeeded in taking two tons of fish during a few hours' netting. As a result of this discovery, the by-laws were altered, and netting, except for eels and smelts, was entirely prohibited. Smelt-netting was regulated, and only allowed in certain parts of the rivers. Pike snaring and spearing were made illegal.

The passing of the Norfolk and Suffolk Fisheries Act, and the Acts of 1872, 1876, and 1880 for the protection of wild birds, made it impossible for the men who had hitherto existed almost entirely upon what they shot and netted to do so any longer. Only the eel-catchers and smelt-fishers were able to earn a little money by netting at certain seasons; and in 1881 an attempt was made to do away with eel-setts, but this proved unsuccessful. The men who were thus deprived of their chief means of livelihood naturally did not at first take kindly to their altered circumstances, and for some time the water-bailiffs and police had much difficulty in dealing with those who broke the new laws. As an example of the defiant attitude adopted by some of the fishermen may be quoted the case of one fish-poacher, who, since the passing of the Fisheries Act, has paid nearly £300 in fines, and admits that he has made as much as £74 in one week by illegal fishing.

CHAPTER VI

SOME BROADLAND FOLK OF TO-DAY

NETTING, except for eels and smelts, having been made illegal, and wild-fowl shooting forbidden during certain months of the year, the men of the Broads and rivers had to turn to other occupations in order to gain a livelihood. A few of them, as I have said, continued for a while to defy the law; but the majority grumblingly submitted to the inevitable, cut up their draw-nets, and used them to keep the birds off their garden beds. Fortunately for them, there was other work to be done on the Broads, rivers, and marshes. Some of them became wherrymen; others contented themselves with eel-catching and reed and rush cutting; yet others found employment in cattle-tending, marsh-mowing, and "drawing" or clearing out the marsh dykes. And as the Broadland became increasingly popular as a holiday resort, the demand for men who could sail yachts and pleasure-wherries increased correspondingly; and during the summer months the services of some of the old netters, who were used to boat-sailing and knew every nook and corner of Broadland, were engaged by Oulton, Wroxham, Norwich, and Yarmouth yacht-letters. Instances are also recorded of fish-poachers becoming water-bailiffs, to the delight of their poaching friends and dismay of their poaching enemies; but, with one or two exceptions, these appointments did not prove entirely satisfactory to the preservation societies. So it will be seen that there was a variety of employment awaiting the men who had to abandon fish-netting, and I do not think there is a single case on record in which the passing of the Norfolk and Suffolk Fisheries Act resulted in the pinch of poverty being felt in any humble Broadland home. Of course, even now there are men who grumble at not being allowed to shoot and net wherever and whenever they please; but the majority of the natives of Broadland admit that protection and preservation of fowl and fish are desirable, and, so far as the fish are concerned, have had good results.

Among the characteristic Broadlanders whom the visitor encounters, the wherrymen are the most numerous and conspicuous. Cruise where you will, not only on the main rivers, but up the Chet to Loddon, the Thurne to Hickling, and the Ant to North Walsham, and you find that wherever your yacht can go the wherryman has gone before you. Sometimes he is alone, for the Broadland wherry—a type of craft seen nowhere else in England—is so rigged that one man can sail it; but generally he has a companion, sometimes a man or boy, sometimes his wife. Usually he is a man whose father was a wherryman before him; but occasionally he is one who has been to sea in a Yarmouth or Lowestoft trawler or drifter, and has grown tired of a rough, seafaring life. All through the year he is afloat on the rivers, carrying cargoes of coal, corn, hay, and timber between the coast ports and the inland towns and staithes, and often his only home is his cramped little cabin aft of the long wide hold. There he cooks his food over a small stove, shelters when the weather is bad and the wind against him, and sleeps when his day's voyage is done. But should the wind be favourable he often sails all night as well as all day; for a head wind or a windless day often means many hours' hard quanting—that is, pushing the wherry along by means of a long pole. Only when the rivers are ice-bound does he take a holiday, and then, leaving his wherry frozen up at some staithe or marshside mooring, he disports himself on skates or "pattens," lounges over a fire in a riverside inn, or spends his time and money at the nearest town. But should the ice on the rivers be so thin that a passage can be forced through it, he will continue his voyaging; and if his hold is empty he will often fill it with ice for sale to the fish-merchants at the nearest port.

On the upper waters of the main rivers and on the narrow tributary streams a wherry is perhaps the most awkward obstacle a yacht can encounter, for its wide hull and large sail seem to block up the whole channel. But the wherryman is an expert at getting out of such difficulties, and as he is usually patient and good-natured, a yachtsman generally does well to follow his advice. Of late years the native voyagers have had a good deal to put up with at the hands of unskilled navigators, many of whom had never sailed a boat until they came on to the Broads; but one seldom hears of a wherryman treating a stranger with incivility or refusing to assist him if he requires aid. In return for this the least a yachtsman can do is not to hinder a wherryman if he can help it, remembering that, as Mr. Davies has pointed out, the wherrymen are on the rivers on business, while the yachtsmen are there simply for pleasure. To the summer cruiser it may seem that the wherryman's life is an enviable one. He sees him daily lounging at his tiller while he sails between sunny meads musical with larks' songs. Wild flowers of every hue deck the banks by which he glides, leaping fish make rippling rings around his wherry, the fragrance of water-mint or new-mown hay is borne to him on the breeze, and at the end of his day's voyage there is a cosy inn awaiting him! But the summer voyager fails to look at the other side of the picture, to take into account the stormy winter days, when whirling snow-squalls hide the marshlands and heap high snowdrifts against the river walls; when cutting hail smites the wherryman's face and ice-coated ropes numb his hands; when the icy wind blears his eyes and the frost whitens his beard and fringes his eyelashes with beads of ice. Then the wherryman's lot is far from enviable, and few are the men, however mean their condition, who would change places with him.

The wherry is one of the most picturesque features of the Broadland waterways, rivalling the dainty yachts in shapeliness and grace of movement. Sailing closer to the wind than any other vessel afloat, and easily handled, it is just the craft for navigating these narrow winding streams. Seen from a distance, it often seems to be sailing on a sea of meadow grass and wild flowers, and to make little headway; but viewed from a river bank or yacht's deck its sailing qualities can be properly appreciated. Its curious wire-framed flag, which resembles those of the Scheveningen and Maasluis fishing boats which visit Lowestoft and Yarmouth at Christmas-time, emphasises the Dutch aspect the windmills give the marsh-lands. Wherries are as much a part of Broadland as are reed-beds and windmills.

Even more interesting than the wherrymen to the visitor, if he has time and opportunity to make their acquaintance and study their methods, are the eel-catchers, whose quaint little arks are seen on all the rivers, but more especially on the Bure and its tributaries. These men usually live in the Broadland hamlets or in isolated cottages on the borders of the marshes, and they have several means of gaining a liveli-hood; but during the summer and autumn they can be found almost every night in the neighbourhood of their house-boats, keeping watch so that their setts may not be damaged by passing yachts or wherries. In order that their method of eel-catching may be understood, it is necessary to know a little about the life-history of *Anguilla vulgaris*, the common eel.

Until lately the reproduction of this common species was a great mystery. Even now there are marshmen and fisher-men who will seriously assure you that eels are bred out of mud; not so very long ago they believed that chopped horse-hair would, if thrown into the water, turn into eels. Even the more enlightened of them will not credit the fact that the species is not viviparous: one old man, whom I know well, told me he had found young eels or elvers inside larger ones which he had cut open. The presence of worm-like parasites in the eels no doubt accounted for this confident statement. Another old man, who is a well-known eel-catcher, said, " I don't believe the elvers come out of the sea at all. I believe they are bred out of the mud. You may see thousands of them going through Mutford Lock in April, and it's my opinion they come out of the mud in Lake Lothing. I've opened a good many hundred eels in my time, and I never saw a trace of spawn in any one of them." I told him that it was the opinion of naturalists that all the eels were bred in the sea. He replied, " If all the elvers are hatched off in the sea, how is it we get eels of all sizes in ponds right away on highlands and in the middle of fields, where there are no dykes or drains to connect them with the rivers or the sea? I know eels can get out of the water and crawl about on the land, because I've seen three of them lying on a marsh and the tracks they made when they came out of a dyke; but I don't believe they can crawl across roads and fields to ponds a long way off any dyke or river." Biologists, however, are now satisfied that *Anguilla vulgaris* spawns in deep-sea water. In an interesting paper published in the *Transactions of the Norfolk and Norwich Naturalists' Society*, Mr. T. Southwell, F.Z.S., draws attention to Dr. Grassi's discoveries in the Straits of Messina, where strong local currents bring large quantities of the larvæ (*Leptocephali*) of the common eel to the surface. These larval forms, which were formerly regarded as those of certain kinds of marine fishes, gradually develop into the tiny eels or elvers which in spring swarm up from the sea into the rivers.

Until a few years ago it was generally believed that there were at least three species of eels in the Broadland rivers; indeed, some eel-catchers affirmed that there were no less than seven. But it has been discovered that the so-called broad-nosed eels, which were considered to be a distinct species, are simply barren females of *Anguilla vulgaris*. These broad-nosed eels are hardly ever taken in the setts which are spread across the rivers for the capture of the sharp-nosed or silver eels when they are "running" towards the sea. A sett consists of a close-meshed net, the bottom of which is weighted and rests on the river bed, while the top is buoyed up on the surface of the water. In this network wall one or more openings lead into circular nets or "pods." The setts are used at night when the tide is ebbing, the network wall being then, by means of ropes and blocks, raised from the river bed (where it lies during the day) so as to form an impassable obstacle to the descending swarms of eels. The latter, on finding their passage obstructed, seek an opening in the net. They find that which leads into a circular "pod," from which, when they have once entered it, funnel-shaped circles of net prevent their escape. Fifty years ago, one hundred and ten stones of eels were taken in one night at Fishley on the Bure; and Mr. Davies tells us he once met a man who had taken three hundred stones in four nights at

Hardley Cross on the Yare. Apparently eels are nothing like so plentiful now, for the existing netters consider a catch of forty stones a remarkably good one, and a ten or fifteen stones' "take" is looked upon as satisfactory. Often, however, the setts are spread night after night and only two or three eels taken. The old eel-catcher whom I have just quoted recently had such an experience. But in his case it was not lack of eels which made his night's fishing unprofitable. Unknown to him, a sunken log prevented the lower side of his sett touching the river bed, and left a passage open through which the eels continued their journey down-stream.

The eel-catchers do not rely entirely on their setts for the taking of eels. Small-meshed bow-nets are often baited and sunk in the rivers, and nets not unlike small setts are used at the sluices of the mill dykes. By the last-mentioned method seventy-four stones of eels were taken in one night out of Leathes Ham, a small pool or pond adjoining Lake Lothing. Eel-lines are often laid out in the Broads and rivers; and in the springtime eel-spearing or "picking" is extensively practised, not only in the Broads and rivers, but in the marsh dykes. The spear or pick consists of a "head" of from four to six long barbed teeth, fixed to the end of a long pole. The teeth are set so close together that when the spear is thrust into the mud an eel caught between them seldom escapes being drawn ashore or into the eel-catcher's boat. Yet another method is "bobbing" or "babbing," which is often indulged in as a pastime. A bunch of worsted-threaded worms is fastened to a line attached to a pole. Seated in a boat or by the riverside, the fisherman lowers the bunch of worms to the bed of the river, and then "bobs" it gently up and down. As soon as an eel bites into one of the worms, its teeth become entangled in the worsted, and the "angler," who feels its tugging, carefully lifts it out of the water and lets it fall into a tub which floats beside him. In some parts of Broadland it is no uncommon sight to see old men, with lanterns beside them, bobbing all night by the riverside. I had my first experience as an eel-bobber on the upper waters of the Waveney. My instructor was a marshman. He said, "When you feel a little pull at th' line jist hyst it up carefully an' drop th' worams inter th' keeler (tub). Ony you musn't be too hasty about it, or you may shake him orf and luse him. Thas how I mean," he went on, as he brought up an eel wriggling on the end of his line, and knocked it off the bab by swinging it against the inside of the tub. " See, you ha' got one tu." I had unconsciously followed his example when he raised his bab and had babbed my first eel.

But the worker of a sett looks upon bobbing as simply playing at eel-catching, and it is to him you must go if you wish to see how the eels are caught which supply the London and other markets. If possible, you should spend a night with him in his house-boat—it will not be a very costly experience—for then you can see him haul up his pods and empty them of his night's catch. You will gain some idea, too, of how such men as he spend many nights of the year, and of how comfortable and content he is in his cramped little cabin. If the night be chilly, he will probably light a fire in his stove, and the temperature of the cabin will soon become tropical; but you are not likely to run such risk as did Farmer Oak in his shepherd's hut, for the house-boats generally have a ventilator which will not wholly close, and most of the time the door will be open, so that your companion can keep an eye on his sett. And you will hear the rats rustling in the hovers, the pheasants crowing on the marshes, the fish leaping, and the water rippling along the keel of the boat—sounds which may lull you to sleep, to dream of pleasant pastures where the cattle stand knee-deep in the grass, and rivers winding between banks decked with mauve-flowered mints and yellow water-flags. If you succeed in keeping awake, you will hear from your companion much curious lore concerning the wild life of the rivers and marshes, and many strange tales about huge hauls of fish and great slaughterings of fowl. Maybe, if he be an old man, and you have won his confidence, he will entertain you with stories of old-time fish-poaching escapades, of midnight trips on the waters above Hardley Cross, which were the first to be preserved, or of smelt-netting in a certain reach near Reedham where the smelts always seem to be more plentiful and of better quality than those taken at Burgh, but where the using of a smelt-net is strictly forbidden.   Should he be in a mood for relating such reminiscences the night will seem only too brief, and when you leave the cabin in the early morning, and are greeted by the cheery little reed birds, you will feel that your novel experience has not been an unprofitable one.

Besides the eel-catchers, almost the only men who use nets in the Broadland waters are the smelt-fishers, a few of whom, during certain months of the year, spread their nets near the Burgh end of Breydon.   Formerly a good many men were engaged in smelting; but now there are not, I believe, more than twenty men and boys, though the average price they get for smelts—two shillings a score—would seem fairly remunerative.   Burgh is not easily accessible by land, so very few people have an opportunity of seeing the smelters at work. It is a lonesome place at which to moor at night.   The deserted cement works and cottages on the shore, backed by a dark belt of woods and brooded over by that grim old Roman stronghold, the so-called castle, add to its dreariness.   And the yachtsman who spends a night there need be sure that his moorings are secure, for when the tide ebbs the outrush of the waters of the Yare and Waveney is strong and rapid, and if a yacht's moorings drag, its occupants may awake to find themselves stranded on a Breydon mud-flat, or in collision with that awkward obstacle to navigation, the Breydon railway bridge.

In winter, one of the most familiar sights in Broadland is a reed-cutter at work on a Broad or by the riverside.   For the reed-cutter's harvest is a winter one, beginning about Christmas, when the blade is off the reeds, and lasting until March or April, when the appearance of the "colts" or young reeds puts a stop to the cutting.   Eel-catchers, marshmen, millmen, and the men who sail the cruising yachts, take part in this belated harvest, which comes at a time when there is little else for them to do in the daytime, and only wild fowl to be watched for at dusk and dawn.   Scythe and meag are used in cutting the reeds, and the cutter works either in a wide, flat-bottomed marsh boat, or on a plank projecting from a boat or laid flat in a cleared space among the reeds. If, however, the reeds grow in shallow water, the men put on wading-boots and work in the water. The cut reeds are laid in the boat or on a large reed-raft, and rowed, quanted, or towed to the place where they are to be stacked. There they are tied in bundles or "shooves," five of which are supposed to have an aggregate circumference of six feet, and they are sold by the fathom, a fathom of reeds being five "shooves." They are used for various purposes, such as supporting builders' plasterwork, thatching cottages, park lodges, and ornamental boat-houses, and screening young shrubs and fruit trees; but the demand for them has decreased considerably since the days when there were "scythe rights" on the reed fens and the reeds were carefully cultivated. But there are still many hundred acres of reeds in Broadland, and the cutting of them means a welcome addition to many scanty incomes. So, too, does the cutting and selling of "gladden" and a species of rush locally known as "bolder"; but turf or peat cutting, which formerly found employment for many of the marshmen, can hardly now be called a profitable business. Still, there are a few men who cut and dry the riverside hovers and the boggy surface soil of some of the swampy lands; for peat is a good and cheap substitute for coal in the hearths of the marshmen's cottage homes.

If one wishes to know the kind of life that is led by the natives of Broadland, one cannot do better than leave the rivers and Broads for a while, go and live on one of the isolated marsh-farms, and make the acquaintance of its occupier and any men whom he may have in his employ. I have in mind a typical marsh farmer, a tall, fair-haired, blue-eyed, ruddy-cheeked giant, who might have stepped out of the pages of the *Saga of Burnt Njal*. He passes his time very differently to the upland farmer, whose success or failure to make farming pay depend chiefly upon market prices and the weather. To the marsh farmer the price and progress of roots and cereals is a matter of comparative indifference: so long as he gets his hay carted and stacked without its being damaged by rain or flood, markets and

weather do not trouble him. In fact, to call him a farmer
is almost a misnomer. His occupations are almost as numerous
as those of the Rev. R. Lubbock's typical Broadsman. True,
he is a dairy-farmer—in a small way ; and he keeps pigs and
fowls ; but he is also a fisherman and wild-fowler, reed-
harvester and osier - grower. The presence of fowl on his
marshes is, during the shooting season, always a sufficient
excuse for his taking down his gun from its resting-place
above the hearth, and leaving the farmstead to his wife's care
for hours together. When the eels are "running," he sleeps
during the day, and is to be found by the riverside or at some
dyke-mouth at night, busy with a sluice-net or sett. In
winter, when he drives his cart to the nearest market-town,
it is as likely to contain mallard as to be laden with pigs and
poultry. To the larger towns, where the upland farmer sends
his milk, the marsh farmer sends his catches of eels. When
he goes down on to his rush-marshes, it is more often in the
hope of flushing snipe or finding plovers' eggs than to see
if those marshes are ready to be mown ; when he reaps
his midwinter reed-harvest, his breech-loader always lies handy
in his boat. Holding his nose between his thumb and
finger, he can imitate the call of a drake so accurately as to
bring wild duck to the flighting-ground where he is awaiting
them. He knows the cries and call-notes of the wild fowl of
the marshes as well as the upland farmer knows the cock's
shrill clarion at dawn. The frosty weather, which holds the
ploughshare fast in the furrow, brings him out of his bed long
before daybreak, grey dawn finding him crouched in a reed-
bed or on some river wall, waiting for the flighting fowl.

His lonely life on the open, level marshlands teaches him
self-reliance ; the necessity for constant effort in order to
"make both ends meet" compels him to make the most of
opportunities. He seldom spends an idle day. Shooting,
fishing, eel-netting, marsh-mowing, cattle-tending, reed-cutting
and reed - stacking, rush - cutting, dyke - drawing, and wall-
mending—these and other occupations leave him little time
for listless lounging. As a rule, he performs nearly all these
tasks unaided, but occasionally, as in the case of my Viking
friend, he engages the services of a marshman. He is learned

in the strange lore of the lonesome lowlands, where curious old customs and superstitions linger, and men live near to Nature, reading her secrets and understanding and forecasting her many moods. His speech is flavoured with quaint colloquialisms, learnt from his father and mother, who lived and died among the marshes, or from the heavy-gaited, drowsy-eyed marshmen whom, in his youthful days, he fraternised with while they worked with crome and dydle. He calls a marsh-fog a "roke"—a word which has come down to him from his Norse ancestors; he talks of fish "roudding," meaning spawning; a sudden wind-squall he describes as a "rodger's-blast"; and when he takes his dinner with him to the dykeside, he carries it in a "frail" slung on a "crome stick." Strange old saws and rockstaffs suggest themselves to him as naturally as they did to the marshlanders of a century ago. If a wart appears on his hand, he lets a "dodman" (snail) crawl over it—an infallible cure; and he never receives a piece of gold without spitting on it—for luck. He usually has some curious catch-phrase which he interjects into his conversation. In the case of one man I know this phrase is, "As the boy said." I asked him the distance from his house to a certain windmill. He replied, "About a mile an' a half over wet an' dry, as th' boy said." Apparently that boy had forestalled him in making most of his remarks and replies.

"Like master like man" is a saying which has obvious application to the marsh farmer I have mentioned and his man, "Owd Bob Owdham." Setting aside a difference in age—Owd Bob is about fifteen years older than the farmer—they are so much alike in tastes, habits, and conversation, that a stranger, even when he has spent days in their company, has difficulty in determining which is master and which is man. In the end he probably decides that Owd Bob is master, for his manner of addressing the farmer is frequently dictatorial. I overheard him thus talking to his employer: "Well, bor, yow may say what yow like, but yow ont niver make me belaave as how this ain't a sight better sleeve-weskit than th' one what yow browt home from Yarmouth last Martinmas. Bor, I woun't change wi' yow, not if yow give me yar cord britches as wool; blow me if I would! I don't belaave yow know what's gude moleskin an' what ain't, dang me if I du!" Lengthy arguments concerning the working of the farm are as frequent between Owd Bob and the farmer as between the latter and his wife, and Owd Bob generally has the " best" of them. In fact, I think he considers his age entitles him to his own way. But he is always on the alert to further his master's interests. I heard him bargaining with a thatcher about the roofing of a shed. The difference between them as to what the charge should be only amounted to half a crown; but they argued about it nearly a whole morning, and in the end Owd Bob got the thatcher to agree to his (Owd Bob's) terms. He accomplished this by threatening to " du th' job hisself."

To strangers who approach him, Owd Bob is the embodiment of reserve and taciturnity; but when he has " summed up " a man, and the result satisfies him, he gradually admits him to his confidence. He reveals himself possessed of a keen sense of humour, and an insight into the foibles of marshland humanity that makes him the delight and terror of those with whom he fraternises at the nearest alehouse. Loutish youths have such a wholesome dread of the sting which often lurks in an apparently innocent interrogation, that they avoid him as carefully as they do the village policeman; while his quickness at turning the tables on a rustic jester has made his tongue more feared than his burly master's fist. The natural gift of correct observation and deduction which serves him so well in his dealings with men, is little less useful to him when he studies the habits of the wild fowl of the marshes, concerning which he possesses a knowledge the more valuable in that it is acquired from Nature instead of from books. True, he often identifies birds by names unfamiliar to the average ornithologist; but if you ask him to show you a reed warbler's nest or a stream where you may see a kingfisher, he will soon find one for you. He lives in a thatched cottage in the midst of the marshes—lives there alone; for he is a bachelor, his only living companions being a rusty-brown retriever and a wing-clipped hooded crow.

About half a mile from the farm to which Owd Bob devotes

his time and exceptional abilities, there is a marshland staithe where wherries moor and wherrymen land to spend an hour or so at a neighbouring inn.   It is always a puzzle to me how the landlord of that inn manages to exist, for his only customers during nine months of the year are the wherrymen and the few marshmen and gunners who occasionally come to be ferried in a marsh boat across the river.   I made his acquaintance one day when he was helping Owd Bob and the farmer at their marsh-mowing, and it was he who told me that " in his young time " jack-o'-lanterns, or " lantern men," as he called them, were not infrequently seen flickering over the boggy marshes. This is a phenomenon it has never been my good fortune to see; but Lady Cranworth of Letton, in Norfolk, records, in the *Eastern Counties Magazine,* that an old horseman on the Letton estate has " seen them scores of times running about."   There is a belief among the men of the marshes that lantern men are dangerous; anyhow, the wherrymen used to be afraid of them, and would discharge guns at them to disperse them; and Lady Cranworth states that an old man's advice concerning them was this, " If the lantern man light upon you, the best thing is to throw yourself flat on your face and hold your breath."   At Syleham, a parish on the upper waters of the Waveney, will-o'-the-wisps were formerly numerous, and were known as the " Syleham lights "; but they are not seen now.   The old innkeeper had " heerd tell " of a ball of flame being seen floating across the marshes, which, when it reached the river, seemed to cling for a while to the mast of a wherry—a story I have seen in a little book dealing with the natural history and phenomena of Broadland, and which reminds one of the seamen's corposants.

It is only, as I have sufficiently emphasised, by mixing with the wherrymen, eel-catchers, reed-cutters, and marsh folk that you can attain any satisfactory knowledge of the inner life, the thoughts, beliefs, customs, and methods of the typical inhabitants of Broadland.   By simply watching them while they pursue their various callings you will not learn very much; you must gain their confidence, see them not only on the rivers and marshes and by the dykesides, but also in their humble homes.   You must not approach them with that marked condescension which is as irritating as it is ridiculous; if you do, you will find yourself vainly knocking at a closed door. But if you will help to tow a reed-raft, haul ashore a gun-punt, share a frugal meal, part with a portion of your day's angling "take" to help provide a dinner, and, above all, occasionally try to quench an apparently insatiable thirst, you will often be well rewarded. For the native of Broadland, unless he be a hired boatman or yachtsman, is, like the Romany, somewhat suspicious of the undisguised curiosity of strangers, whose interrogations only result in his displaying an amazing but entirely fictitious ignorance.

CHAPTER VII

THE YARE AND ITS BROADS

ALTHOUGH not, from the pleasure-seeker's point of view, the best of the Broadland rivers, the Yare is, and has been for many centuries, the chief Norfolk waterway, and before the days of railways it was by means of its trading wherries and keels that the largest and most important town in East Anglia was supplied with its imported goods and despatched its considerable exports to the coast. The scenery of its upper waters is in many places delightful, quaint old villages, pleasant parks, and flower-spangled meads bordering many miles of its course; but, unfortunately for the cruiser in Broadland, these upper reaches are unnavigable except to rowing boats, and yachting parties have to confine their attention to that part of the river which lies below Norwich. Yet even below the fine old cathedral city the shores and waters of the Yare are not without charm, and between Norwich and Brundall there are several spots where the loveliness of reed-mirroring reaches and wooded uplands tempts summer voyagers to linger. For it is not until Brundall is passed that the bordering marshlands are so wide that their upland bounds recede to such a distance that the cruiser cannot appreciate their beauty; above that point picturesque farms and the country homes of Norwich citizens, village church towers, and the varied foliage of birch, beech, elm, and fir are part of the landscapes of which the winding river, with its green reeds, yellow water-flags, silvery-leaved sallows, and white poplar scrub is the chief feature. And even below Brundall there is Rockland Broad, whose wild, primitive aspect has a certain charm lacking in some of the lovelier Broads, suggesting as it does the vanished meres of Fenland.

Many a pleasure-seeker, acting on the advice of a boatman whose great anxiety it is to make a speedy voyage from Norwich to Lowestoft or Yarmouth, neglects to enter his dinghey and row up the half a mile or so of dyke which leads to Rockland, and so misses seeing what is, to my mind, one of the best of the Norfolk Broads.

Norwich is not the least beautiful of the cathedral cities of England; the view of its church towers and sylvan surroundings, seen from its castle battlements or the high ground of Mousehold Heath, is very fine. Its inhabitants have called it the " City in an Orchard," and the sylvan scenery of some of its outlying parishes justifies the name. But often in summer, when a scorching sun makes the street pavements hot to the feet, and even in the quiet close and the shadow of the cathedral walls the air is oppressive, a vision of green meadows, cool woods, and breeze-rippled streams comes to lure the gazer at Norman arches, ancient quaintly gabled houses, and mediæval carvings, away from old-world relics to a world where Nature reigns supreme and speaks to her worshippers with wild-life voices like those with which she greeted men ages before they took to heaping stones on stones and shaping them into strange designs. At such times even the " City in an Orchard " seems much like other cities where men toil within walls which keep out the pure air and sunlight, and the call of the birds, the streams, and the wind among the trees becomes almost irresistible. Then it is that the man whose eyes are weary of the streets' monotonous vistas gladly leaves the stifling city and inhales the fragrance of water-mint and dew-drenched meadow grass. Lying back in the stern of a boat, which, like a sea-bird, spreads white wings to waft itself over the water, he lets his gaze rove over meadow, stream, and woodland, listens to the rustling of reeds, the singing of birds, and the rippling of water, and says to himself——

> " Oh, this life
> Is nobler than attending for a check,
> Richer than doing nothing for a bribe,
> Prouder than rustling in unpaid-for silk ! "

At no season of the year are the river reaches immediately below Norwich without beauty; but in summer, when of Whitlingham's ruined church only the tower is visible, so dense is the foliage of the wooded hills which border the river, there are few more delightful bits of scenery in Broadland. Norwich folk have for a long time made this part of the Yare one of their chief holiday resorts; the water frolics held here in the early years of the last century were so picturesque as to have provided a subject for one of the most interesting pictures in the Museum Gallery. With Crome, Cotman, Vincent, Stannard, and other famous Norwich artists, it was a favourite haunt; in the days when the Norwich school of artists flourished, much good work was done along the river banks. But the Norfolk angler, who looks upon the Yare as the best river for bream and roach fishing, seldom cares to linger on its loveliest reaches. Hastening past the long wood-crowned hill called Postwick Grove, and also, unless he be out after pike, the Wood's End Inn at Bramerton, with its pleasure gardens, he cruises on to Brundall, where, in the neighbourhood of those famous fishing centres, the Yare Hotel and Coldham Hall, he moors his boat to stakes at stem and stern, and prepares for some of the best coarse fishing to be had in England. As a rule, if he has chosen his time well, he enjoys good sport; but even if his most tempting baits fail to lure the monster fish which are known to inhabit the Brundall and Surlingham waters, he, if he be a true disciple of Walton, cannot fail to recognise compensatory circumstances. As the old *Treatyse of Fysshynge* says, he can enjoy the " swete aire of the swete savoure of the meede floures, that makyth hym hongry. He hereth the melodyous armony of foules. He seeth the yonge swannes, the heerons, ducks, cotes, and many other foules wyth their brodes, whyche me semyth better than alle the noyse of houndys, the blaste of hornys, and the scrye of foules that hunters, fawkeners, and fowlers can make." But " yf the angler take fysshe, surely thenne is there noo man merier thanne he is in his spyryte."

But the voyager to whom the waters of the Yare are new will probably, when he reaches Brundall, be indisposed to angle until he has seen Surlingham, a small reedy Broad which is best explored in a rowing boat. A long time ago, Surlingham was a fairly large Broad, but the rank luxuriance of its aquatic growths—its sedges, reeds, and swamp flowers—has reduced the open water to a few narrow channels and small pools, while the decay of this lacustrine vegetation has provided an oozy bed for creeping roots and scattered flower seeds. So that now, when the cruiser enters Birch Creek, a channel a little way above the Yare Hotel, he finds himself shut in by dense reed jungles. These occasionally afford shelter for a flight-shooter, and are frequently " beaten " by entomologists in search of the insect life which abounds in them. It is on such Broads as Surlingham, where there are alders growing just beyond the reed-beds, that the dotted footman, that peculiarly Broadland moth, should be looked for in August, and many rare beetles and hemipteræ are found among the water plants of the sedgy and reedy margins. But it is for the hymenopterist that the neighbourhood of Brundall is a " happy hunting-ground," for it was here that rare bee, *Macropis labiata*, was discovered and several other entomological prizes were first taken.

A notable feature of Surlingham is the old ice-house which stands by the waterside. During severe winters this old sharp-gabled building used often to be stored with ice gathered from the Broad. At one time ice-gathering was quite a business with the Broadsmen and marshmen, who, when they had filled their boats, emptied the ice into a wherry bound for Yarmouth or Lowestoft, to be sold to the fish-packers on the markets. At Oulton even now it is no uncommon sight during frosty weather to see old hulks and smack-boats passing through Mutford Lock and down Lake Lothing, laden with cargoes of gleaming ice from the frozen " hams " or inlets of Oulton Broad ; but the ice manufacturing and importing companies are now in the habit of lowering their prices when Broad ice is procurable, so the ice-gatherer's occupation is scarcely a remunerative one.

Surlingham Broad is one of the chief spawning-grounds of roach and bream, but the fish do not spawn here in such numbers as they did formerly. Mr. Davies states that some years ago the Broad used, for a few days in spring, to present an interesting sight. The bream and roach would swarm up into the Broad in such vast numbers that the water was "a moving mass of fish, so that it seemed as if a boat could hardly be rowed among them. On a fine hot day the backs of the huge bream could be seen breaking the surface in every direction ; and in the stillness of the night the splashings and suckings and wallowings, the shakings of the reeds as the monsters rolled through them, and the cries and twitterings of the reed sparrows, were striking in the extreme." On a moonlight night a man remarked that the Broad "reminded him of a Stilton cheese all alive with maggots"—an observation which, as Mr. Davies says, proves that the man was not the possessor of a poetical temperament. The Rev. Richard Lubbock also noticed the great shoals of bream and roach which visited this favourite spawning-ground, and remarked that almost every instant small roach were raised half out of the water by the passage of larger ones.

There is a wild-fowl decoy at Brundall, but it is seldom used, and as I shall have occasion to deal with decoying in a later chapter, I will only say here that Surlingham is no longer frequented by such large flocks of fowl in winter as it used to be. Snipe, it is true, are often fairly plentiful; but the hammering which goes on at the boat-builders' yards at Brundall drives away the fowl that settle on the Surlingham pools. The warblers, however, have less reason to fear the presence of man, and in late spring, summer, and early autumn the reed-beds are full of them. Little grebes, too, have not wholly forsaken the Broad ; in frosty weather they are often seen on the open water. But the flocks of fowl which the Breydoners put to flight when they begin firing their punt-guns in the early morning more often make for Rockland than Surlingham, though even there, in that wild waste of reeds and water, they find no sanctuary. The Rockland gunners know when and where to expect them, and, except during the close season, invariably give them a warm reception.

A little way below Surlingham Broad, on the same side of the river, is Coldham Hall. This is a very popular inn with anglers, whose other resorts on the Yare are the Yare Hotel at Brundall, the Ferry Inn at Buckenham, the Red House at Cantley, and the Ferry Inn at Reedham, at each of which boats can be hired for a day's fishing. But the angler must bring his own bait and tackle. These, however, are matters I can safely leave to my friend Mr. Rudd, who knows the Yare as well as he does London Street, Norwich. For my own part, whenever I am in the neighbourhood of Coldham Hall, I always start sooner or later for Rockland, where I am sure to find " Scientific " Fuller, one of the few men who manage to gain a livelihood much after the fashion of the old-time Broadsmen.

I once visited Fuller on a January morning when the dykes were frozen. When I started along the ferry path from Brundall a fog hung over the marshes, but it was not dense enough to hide the willows and alders beside the footpath, though it magnified some fieldfares till they looked almost as big as wood pigeons. The smooth, steely surface of the river reflected its fringing reeds, withered willow-herbs, and slender sallow wands with the faithfulness of a brightly burnished mirror. From a distant reed - bed the call-notes of some bearded titmice came like the clashing of fairy cymbals across the water ; from the misty marshes came the plaintive wailing of peewits and harsh cries of startled fieldfares. At the clanging of the Coldham ferry-bell a flock of starlings rose with a loud whirring of wings ; but a little black-capped reed bunting, which the sharp weather had not yet driven from the riverside to the farmyards, darted to and fro undisturbed among the brittle, bladeless culms.

The chief and only really navigable waterway to Rockland Broad is a dyke about a mile and a half below Coldham Hall ; but on that January morning I walked from the inn to the Broad. The road from the river soon became a narrow field path, bordered by copses which seemed full of birds. Half an hour's strolling brought me to Rockland village, an isolated hamlet with a small staithe at which the wherries moor, and a narrow channel connecting it with the Broad. With its swampy osier grounds, yellow reed - stacks, and thatched cottages, it is a typical Broadland hamlet, and the majority of its few inhabitants are more or less dependent on the Broad for a livelihood.

A man who is an excellent shot and expert fisherman cannot live any great length of time near one of the Broads or rivers without attaining something of a reputation, so it is not surprising that Fuller, who possesses both these qualities, and has spent about fifty years on and around Rockland Broad, is well known to Broadland gunners and anglers. Like most men of his type, he is more at home afloat than ashore; and though his cottage stands within a stone's-throw of the Broad, he spends most of his time in his "gun-boat." In winter he is abroad and afloat each morning before the first gleam of dawn tinges the eastern sky, so that sunrise finds him crouched in the shelter of some reed-bed, on the alert for mallard or wigeon. During the day he may be seen laying out his "liggers" or trimmers,—a mode of fishing not illegal at Rockland,—or rowing silently up and down the dykes which connect the Broad with the river, his gun beside him, ready to bring down anything from a snipe to a wild goose or swan. In the evening, when the mist begins to drift like smoke across the water, and alders and sallows assume spectral shapes in the gathering gloom, he is abroad again, on the watch for flighting fowl. Biting blast nor nipping frost, drenching rain nor whirling snow-squall, will drive him to seek the shelter of his home if there be a likelihood of an open-air vigil being rewarded : the lee side of a reed shoal or sallow carr is all the shelter the flight-shooter needs.

Fuller appeared from behind a reed stack just as I was knocking at his cottage door, and in a few minutes we were afloat in his gun-punt. In the dyke leading from the cottage to the Broad there was open water; but the Broad, in spite of two days' thaw, was partially covered with ice, through which Fuller had broken a channel for his boat early that morning. Here and there, however, there were open pools where the swans from the rivers were searching for succulent water-weeds. Over these pools we passed quickly and quietly; but for the most part ours was a rather curious progress, made by pulling the boat along with a boat-hook, or scraping our oars on the ice. Yet even this was not so strange as a method Fuller adopts when the Broad is wholly "laid" and hard frozen; for then he fixes runners on to the bottom of his punt, hoists the sail, and glides over the ice as though he were in an ice-yacht. Speaking of this reminded him of a winter when the Broad was frozen several weeks. Then

7

a number of skaters disported themselves on the frozen shallows where the swans were now feeding, and one of them, seeing Fuller skating with his gun under his arm, challenged him to shoot, while skating at full speed, a puit (black-headed gull) which was wheeling over the Broad. Fuller, like most of the Broadsmen, despises the wanton "gull-plugger"; but on this occasion, feeling his reputation to a certain extent at stake, he accepted the challenge. Holding his gun in both hands, he waited until the gull wheeled above him. He then skated after it, soon abandoning his usual stroke for that rapid run on skates which the Broadsman resorts to when he wishes to attain a considerable speed. Then his gun went quickly to his shoulder, and a moment or two later the gull dropped almost at his feet.

But gulls are "no-account" birds from the Broadsman's point of view, and Fuller's reputation rests on far more precious spoils. He has shot quite a score bitterns, several spoonbills, goosanders, smews, and not a few of the rarer kinds of duck. With a swivel gun which he occasionally uses in his little slate-coloured punt, he has made big bags of fowl; his boat, filled to overflowing with a morning's spoils, was made the subject of a picture called "The Wildfowler," the work of a well-known Broadland artist. Well acquainted with the habits of the wild fowl which frequent the Broads and marshes, he knows that, with a favouring wind, the fowl alarmed by the Breydoners will, about twenty minutes after the reports of the Breydon guns reach him, arrive at Rockland, which is distant from Breydon six or seven miles "as the crow flies." So, when he hears the big punt-guns booming on the estuary, he is soon afloat in his punt and rowing into the cover of the Rockland reeds. But he does not often use his heavy swivel gun, for when fowl are plentiful there are other gunners besides himself on the Broad, which, unlike Breydon, is not large enough to permit of the use of such guns with safety.

Two or three snipe were flushed from the swampy ground bordering the Broad; from a "wall" on which a marshman had heaped a mound of dyke-dredgings several hooded crows took wing. When we landed we found that the crows had been feeding on large brown fresh-water mussels and a dead gull. But we were in no hurry to land. On the misty Broad we could, in spite of the ice, move more silently, and so were able to approach within a few yards of a swimming grebe without alarming it. Not a breath of wind was stirring; the amber reeds and bleaching gladden were motionless; a suspensive stillness brooded around us. When a coot moved among the sedge, it seemed startled by the sound of its own movements, and became motionless again; even the voles in the hovers appeared influenced by the atmospheric lethargy, for when an oar suddenly creaked in its rowlock a couple of them dived "flop" into the water within a yard or two of our boat. The withered reeds, rushes, and sedges, star-topped angelicas, and towering brown burdocks each had a reflected counterpart in the creeks which were free of ice; a rugged alder, on which a flock of starlings settled, was as clearly outlined in the pale blue water as against the pale blue sky.

Although most of the marsh dykes were frozen, Big Sallow Dyke and Rockland Fleet, two of the channels leading from the Broad to the river, were navigable, the rise and fall of the tides having kept them open. While we rowed up the Fleet, which is the main channel used by the wherries bound for Rockland Staithe, my companion fell into a reminiscent mood. So long had been his acquaintance with the Broad, that almost every reed and gladden bed, sallow carr, creek, and dyke, reminded him of some gunning experience. In one reed jungle he had shot a bittern; near a certain sallow bush a big dog otter, with whose traces, in the shape of half-eaten bream, he had long been familiar, had made its last meal; here, a spoonbill, driven from the Breydon flats, had met with the fate from which it had fled; there, he had stood in his boat all one morning, bringing down duck almost as fast as he could load his gun. Some of his recollections were gruesome, notably those of a trip taken with two companions, one of whom, in raising his gun to aim at a heron, had shot the other dead. That, and one or two similar occurrences, had made Fuller very careful how and where he laid his gun down in his boat. Once he had been caught in such a blinding snow-squall that he could not find his way across the Broad, and had to land and trudge across the marshes to his home.

But not one in every hundred visitors in Broadland sees Rockland in winter, when the alders are white with rime and ice-crystals tinkle among the reeds. The aspect most familiar to cruisers is its summer one, when the reeds are already several feet high, the sedges have shaken off their pollen-dusted anthers, and swallows and swifts are insect-hawking over shore and water. Then there is much to tempt one to row up the Fleet, for the banks between which one's boat glides are like gardens of wild flowers. Purple spikes of loosestrife, tall willow-herbs, towering cat valerians, and creamy clusters of meadow-sweet, almost hide the snipe-haunted swamps which lie beyond them; and when the Broad is reached, such a scene is presented as gives one a fair idea of a Fenland mere in the pre-reclamation days. On almost every side the water is bordered by reeds, whose sibilant song—a whispered welcome to the summer breeze, soothing as the voice of a wind-swept cornfield—goes on unceasingly. Beyond the reeds, the land for the most part is low; even Rockland village, which is close by the waterside, is scarcely seen until the channel is entered which leads up to the staithe; so the charm of the Broad is of that subtle kind which appeals to the ear rather than the eye. The rustling reeds, the hum of insect life among the swamp flowers, the "splash" of leaping fish, the bleating of snipe, and the "slap" of the water against one's boat's side, combine to create this charm, which grows upon one rather than wanes through familiarity. And in some folks' opinion Rockland has an advantage over some of the more popular Broads, in that its being unnavigable to the larger kinds of river craft prevents its ever being so alive with humanity as are Wroxham and Oulton during the greater part of the cruising season. Its low, swampy shores, too, help to retain its primitive aspect, and there are no neighbouring heights on which villas can be built to overlook its peaceful waters.

As it is with the Broad so it is with the inhabitants of the village of Rockland. On a June day, when the green gladden was waving its long leaves, and the Broad was so covered with the white flowers of the water-crowfoot that it seemed to be ice-laid and covered with a thin coating of snow, I chatted with the rector of the parish about his parishioners, and learnt much that was interesting and surprising. He assured me that even now there were men and women in Rockland and its neighbourhood who sought the aid of "wise women" and "cunning men" when a child was lost; who would not allow their relatives to be buried on the north side of the church; and who could not be brought to reject the idea that it was unlucky to disturb the swallows which nested in the church roof. There are old people living in the village who can remember the strange circumstances which attended the burial of a reputed witch. As the hour fixed for the interment approached, a storm arose, which so increased in fury that at the time when the coffin was being borne to the church, and from the church to the grave, the bearers could scarcely keep their feet. So long as the witch's body was above ground the storm continued to rage; but the moment the coffin was lowered into the grave the storm ceased, " and there was a great calm." When, some years ago, Dr. Jessopp related his experiences among the dwellers in his delightful Arcady, and affirmed that a belief in witchcraft survived among them, there were persons who could scarcely credit his assertion. For the superstitious folk who still cherish strange old beliefs and resort to primitive means of divination are chary of speaking of such things; you may live for years among them and know little of what is going on around you. But now and again some chance remark, curious action, or inquiry into the origin of a rustic's nickname, gives you a glimpse into what lies behind a mask of taciturnity, and by patient and careful investigation you may discover how tenacious is the hold superstition has on the dwellers in out-of-the-way hamlets of Broadland.

Cruisers on the Yare and other main rivers of Broadland cannot help noticing the narrow channels or dykes which lead up to the village staithes. Some of these channels are not wide enough to allow of two wherries passing each other, and are so shallow that only small rowing and sailing boats and wherries can ascend them. Yet it is by way of these dykes that the farmers whose lands lie along the borders of the marshes send away large quantities of their corn, and receive cargoes of coal for their homes and oilcake for their stock. For centuries these dykes, which, unlike the ordinary marsh and mill dykes, are "walled" like the main rivers, have been the waterways to isolated hamlets, whose inhabitants, until a comparatively recent date, knew little of what was happening even in towns so near as Yarmouth and Norwich except what they learnt from the wherrymen. They were, and some of them still are, the tentacular arms by which the river gets in touch with out-of-the-way places; like the branch lines of the great railways, they bring remote places in touch with the centres of commerce.

One of these channels, Langley Dyke, branches off from the Yare about two and a half miles below Rockland Broad. It is bordered on one side by marshes, on the other by a small plantation of alders, poplars, and birches; and it is worth ascending (in a small boat) because it leads to the ruins of Langley Abbey. These ruins are not very interesting at first glance, but a close examination reveals that they are not so fragmentary as to be entirely uninteresting. Like several other monastic houses in Norfolk, this abbey now forms part of some farm buildings; but while many may object to its being turned to such usage, it cannot be denied that in this instance it has resulted in the preservation of interesting work which otherwise would have vanished or fallen into decay. As it is, some of the old doorways retain their original form and mouldings. A gloomy crypt, a spiral staircase, and some good arches remain almost intact; and enough of the walls is left standing to enable the antiquary to reconstruct for himself the greater part of this ancient Premonstratensian house.

The history of the abbey is unexciting. It was founded in 1198 by Sir Robert Fitz-Roger Helke, who assumed the name of De Clavering from his lordship of Clavering in Essex. He was sheriff of Norfolk and Suffolk during the third and fourth years of the reign of Richard I., and was a wealthy man who endowed the abbey with the greater part of the revenue of his estates. The first abbot and fifteen canons, for whom there was accommodation here, came from Alnwick Priory, in Northumberland, and Langley was called a "daughter of Alnwick" for that reason. Its church was a favourite burying-place with Norfolk knights and their dames, the names of some sixty of whom are given by a Norfolk historian, who concludes his list with the remark, "Good heavens! what a number of noble personages are here deposited—in hopes of a joyful resurrection" That the monastery was a rich one is shown by the same historian, who proves that it possessed nineteen Norfolk manors and land in several towns in Norfolk and Suffolk. The benefactors of the abbey were so numerous, he adds, that it "would fully employ the clergy of that day to remember (them) in their prayers." The abbey grounds extended down to the riverside, and if the river was as full of roach and bream then as it is to-day, there was plenty of fish for the refectory on fast days. No doubt the Langley monks had "big-fish" stories to tell to, and notes to compare with, their Augustinian neighbours at Herringfleet, when they rowed down to Reedham, crossed the marshes, and were ferried over the Waveney by Sireck, who kept the Herringfleet ferry. Maybe, too, they were able to catch herrings occasionally, for the herring shoals, we are told, came up the rivers a long time after the abbey was founded, and the herring fisheries were a source of considerable income to dwellers among the marshes. Fowl, too, were plentiful, and Rockland and Surlingham fowlers would often, with shoulders bent under a burden of teal and mallard, find their way to the abbey gate. They were fortunate monks who dwelt beside the waterways of Broadland.

Langley Abbey is not a "show place." When I visited it on a bright and breezy May day, I reckoned myself favoured in encountering among the ruins a charming young guide, who seemed, as no doubt she was, as much at home among them as though she had known the abbey in its prime. She it was who pointed out to me an old stone coffin which may have been that of one of those noble personages who were buried in the abbey church, and it was from her that I heard of other discoveries made within and around the crumbling walls. I remember our discussing the possibility of that old salad herb, Good King Henry (*Chenopodium Bonus-Henricus*), which grows freely among the ruins, having been introduced there by the Premonstratensians; but I forget— perhaps because my attention was too much taken up with a bright red tam-o'-shanter—what conclusion we arrived at. But I know we stood before a fine old medlar tree, which may have furnished fruit for an abbot's dessert, and that all around us were fruit trees in the full beauty of bloom; and I know how the whole mystery of life and death became more complex to me when I saw youth and beauty treading light-foot over the dust of long-dead knights and dames. And when, as the sun was sinking beyond the border of the marshes, I bade farewell to Langley's ruined shrine and made my way back to the river, a red tam-o'-shanter and a pair of laughing eyes came between me and my visions of the monks of old.

About two miles below Buckenham Ferry,—where, on account of the number of anglers who come to share in the good roach-fishing to be had in this part of the Yare, a new inn has arisen on the site of the old one so well remembered by some cruisers on the river,—is Hardley Cross, where the little river Chet branches off south-westward. This stream is generally described as navigable up to Loddon; but even small yachts often have difficulty in reaching the pleasantly situated little town, and the last time I made the voyage I found four wherries "hung up," as the wherry-men call it, one near the mouth of the river, the others a short distance below Loddon Staithe. But my little gun-punt, which, according to the Broadsmen, is a craft which can be sailed or rowed wherever there has been a heavy dew, met with no more discouraging obstacle than an occasional patch of clinging water-weeds; and it is in such a boat, or in an ordinary rowing boat, that the Chet should be navigated. And although there is little in the river or along its banks, where the scenery is simply pastoral, to arouse enthusiasm, I would encourage every one who can do so to make the voyage; for Loddon is, to my mind, a very charming little place, and a saunter through it, a game of bowls on the old green at the back of the Swan Inn, a glance at some of the pictures the inn contains, a visit to the church, and then to Chedgrave Church or the quaint old-world hamlet and Hall on Hales Green, are a sufficient recompense for any difficulties which may be encountered on the river.

Concerning Hardley Cross and its significance I have written in an earlier chapter; but before saying something more about Loddon and its neighbourhood, I would like to mention some curious information which the Rev. W. Hudson gave in a paper read to the members of the Norfolk and Norwich Archæological Society when they made a voyage down the Yare and visited Langley Abbey. He said that it was not known when a cross was first erected at the junction of the Yare and Chet, but he had discovered that a new one was put up in the year 1543. It was made, he said, of timber, and a carpenter was paid 3s. 4d. for making it. A certain Nicholas Maryes then devoted eight days to ornamenting it with a crucifix and the arms of the City of Norwich, also with a finial and other "antikke" work, for which he was paid 4s. 4d. Another artificer then received 2s. 8½d. for cleaning the embossed work; after which a certain Tuttel made a frame to set into the ground, into which frame the cross was to be morticed. It was then oiled and varnished for 1s. 4d., and some "spekyngs" were made for the feet and hands of the crucifix, and perhaps for affixing the city arms. The "spekyngs" cost 1d. each. Then a boat was hired, and two rowers conveyed the cross, with two carpenters and two labourers, to Hardley, to which place the chamberlain and sheriffs of Norwich rode on horseback to see the cross set up. This cost 3s. 6d. The only other expenses were 2d. for rowing the chamberlain from the village to the mouth of the Chet, and 6d. for a firkin of beer for the carpenters and labourers; so that the total cost of the cross erected in 1543 was 19s. 0½d. The existing cross is a stone one. It appears to have been erected in the seventeenth century, and has been restored several times by certain mayors of Norwich, whose names are on it.

Some idea of Loddon may be gathered from the fact that it is a little country town about four miles from the nearest railway station. How it is that no tentacular branch line has yet extended itself in this direction, I cannot say; but I can affirm that to all appearance the inhabitants of Loddon are quite content to remain in comparative isolation. The town is little more than a village, where the restful quietude of the average village is intensified. Business seems to be practised during the day as a preliminary pastime to that resorted to every evening on the Swan bowling-green, where the tradesmen meet in friendly rivalry so long as daylight lasts. There is an old water-mill near the staithe which is one of the three most picturesque mills of its kind in Broadland, those at Ellingham on the Waveney and Horstead on the Bure being the others. The church, said to have been built by Sir James Hobart, attorney-general to Henry VII., stands in a good open position, and is noted for its fine but mutilated font. It also contains some interesting screen panels, a curious old iron-bound alms-box, one or two good tombs, and an old painting in which are represented the church and an imposing bridge which formerly spanned the Waveney at St. Olave's. From an archæological point of view, however, the church at Chedgrave or Chetgrave, about five minutes' walk from the water-mill, on the opposite side of the river, is more interesting, for it possesses two very fine Norman doorways, one elaborately ornamented, and some good stained glass brought from Rouen Cathedral at the time of the Revolution of 1797. This church, which is a very quaint little building, has picturesque surroundings, and the view from the churchyard is a charming one.

A pleasant stroll is that from Loddon to Hales Green, a little hamlet reached by way of the Beccles road and a byroad branching off to the right, a distance of a little more than two miles. It is a stroll worth taking, not only on account of the picturesque Green with its scattered cottages and farmsteads, but because it brings the rambler to Hales Old Hall, the old home of that Attorney - General Hobart who built Loddon Church. The Green is a little bit of rural England of the past—of England as it was in the days of the highwaymen, of stage coaches and romance of the road, of almost impassable byroads, and of rural isolation. The byroad, when it reaches it, comes to an end except in so far as it is continued by a rough waggon track leading to one or two of the bordering farmsteads. I walked down this road on a June day, and found the hedges around the Green, and the thickets beside the ponds on the Green, garlanded with wild roses and exhaling the strong scent of flowering elders. On every side of the Green, but not so numerously as to break appreciably the continuity of its leafy bounds, were clusters of old cottages, unaltered in outward aspect since the day when the dwellers in them played camping matches and danced about the Maypole on the expanse of common land which lay before their doors. I fancied that if the attorney-general who once lived in the ruined Hall at the top of the Green could revisit his old home, he would find little had changed in the manor of which he was lord; and while trying, with the aid of my recollections of the rude portrait of him in Loddon Church, to picture him to myself, I stood before his crumbling Hall. It is not a place where one can " walk alone a banquet-hall deserted," and see portraits of the knights and dames who long ago feasted and pledged each other there, for the remaining portion of the house is still tenanted, and its interior has been altered to suit the convenience of its occupiers, with the result that little or nothing is left of the decorative work which once adorned it; but the old gateway remains intact, and here and there are traces of the foundations of what must once have been a stately home. On the banks of the moat are masses of crumbling masonry, and a portion of one of the courtyard walls is still standing; so, too, is the Hobarts' old barn, one of the largest in the county. But the dwellers in the Old Hall know nothing of its history. All the information I gained from them was that it is a " perishin' " place in which to live in winter, when deep snowdrifts are heaped up on the Green and icy blasts rattle the crazy casements of the rooms in which the Hobarts lived and died.

From Hardley Cross it is only about half a mile to Reedham Ferry, and a mile and a half to the waterside village of Reedham. Here the Danish chieftain Lodbrog is said to have landed when he was storm-driven in a small boat across the North Sea. According to the monkish chroniclers, Lodbrog was out hawking one day along the coast of his native land, when his hawk, in striking down at some water-fowl, fell into the sea. Hoping to save the bird's life, he launched a boat and went to its rescue. Before he could return to shore, a storm arose and carried him out to sea. After tossing helplessly about for several days, his boat was driven into the mouth of the great eastern estuary, and he landed at Reedham and was taken to the court of Edmund, King of the East Angles. Apparently the king was much impressed by his involuntary visitor, for he not only allowed him to remain at his court, but showed him such marked favour as excited the jealousy of Bern, his chief huntsman. Bern's jealousy increased when he found that Lodbrog excelled him in all field-sports; and one day, when they were out hunting together in a wood, he slew his rival and concealed his body in a thicket. The behaviour of Lodbrog's dog led to the discovery of the body, and Bern, whose guilt was proved, was sent adrift in the boat which had borne the Dane across the sea to England. As the story goes, the boat was again driven across the North Sea, and Bern landed in Denmark, where he told Inguar and Ubba, Lodbrog's sons, that King Edmund had slain their father. On hearing this the sons vowed to avenge Lodbrog's death, and during several years they made a series of raids on Eastern England, captured Edmund, and, tying him to a tree, had him shot to death by Danish bowmen.

The story of Lodbrog is probably legendary. If it has any groundwork of fact, the monkish chroniclers have undoubtedly invented a good deal that is marvellous in it to add to the fame of the canonised Edmund. Yet, as a Norfolk geologist pointed out nearly eighty years ago, the objections to it based upon the difficulty in reconciling its main incident with the present topography of the district are without weight if we accept the statement of geologists, that at the time of Lodbrog's adventures the Broadland valleys formed an arm of the sea. It has been gravely argued that it is impossible a boat should have been driven several miles up a narrow river before its occupant could effect a landing; but, as Mr. Robberds in his *Observations on the Eastern Valleys* remarks, there is " nothing very surprising or impossible in what befel this Dane, if we consider that the whole level of marshes and meadows, from the present coast up to Norwich, was at that time covered by the waters of the ocean. A vessel driven by a north-east wind into the entrance of this arm of the sea, near Caister, would be taken, equally by the direction of the gale and the current of the tide, in a straight course towards that point where Reedham now stands." And he adds further that, admitting the story to be entirely fabulous, the author of it would not have selected Reedham as the spot on which to land his shipwrecked hero " if from the form of the coast such an event had been as destitute of probability then as it would be at the present day." Even a legendary tale, he urges, must not be entirely at variance with physical conditions.

There is very little for the voyager to see at Reedham unless he is interested in bird life, in which case it is worth his while to visit the heronry in a carr not far from the church. The entrance to the New Cut, which connects the Yare with the Waveney, is seen just below the railway bridge. It provides a channel by which wherries and yachts can reach Oulton Broad, Lowestoft, Beccles, and Bungay without having to go round by Breydon and enter the Waveney there. Below the village the Yare flows between wide marshlands dotted with windmills, and, in summer, with cattle; where the only human habitations are those of the cattle-tenders and marshmen; where the heron fishes undisturbed for hours together, and a man may wander all day and hear no voices except those of sedge warblers, larks, and meadow pipits. Now and again a yellow wagtail is seen making a " dipping " flight along the dykesides, a heron utters its harsh " frank " as it flies heavily over marsh and river to the Breydon flats or its colony in the Reedham woods, or the strange laughing cry of a black-headed gull breaks the brooding silence; but save for the wild-life voices there is little for the voyager to note until he reaches Breydon, unless—as may be the case after a day's cruise down the Yare — he should happen to reach these lower waters just at the time when the sun is sinking beyond the far-off level horizon. Then it is not unlikely that he may witness one of those Broadland sunsets which are not only gorgeous but awe-inspiring and indescribable. And he will sail across Breydon, or moor for the night at Berney Arms or Burgh, conscious of having seen a spectacle than which Nature can show nothing more sublime or more calculated to make a lasting impression.

CHAPTER VIII

THE WAVENEY, FRITTON LAKE, AND OULTON BROAD

THE Waveney, although there is connected with it one of the twelve Broads each having an area of over a hundred acres, will never be so popular with pleasure-seekers as the Yare and Bure, for the scenery of its navigable waters cannot compare with that of the other two main rivers of Broadland; and though the places of interest adjoining it are rather more numerous than those of which the Yare can boast, the distances between them are considerably greater. While, however, the scenery between Breydon and Beccles is, for the most part, monotonously flat, it is possible, by landing at certain points and strolling a little way beyond the borders of the marshes, to discover villages, lanes, and woodlands almost, if not quite, as delightful as those adjoining the Bure and its tributary streams; while above Beccles there are some pleasant but little-known reaches, and in the neighbourhood of Bungay there are spots where the scenery is almost equal to that of Constable's dearly-loved Vale of Dedham. If, however, in writing of this river, I evince an interest in and affection for places which to strangers appear to possess little to commend them, I, perhaps, may be forgiven; for it was on the Waveney that I first felt the charm of Broadland life and scenery, and on its banks the greater part of my life has been spent. At a time when Wroxham, Hickling, and Rockland were only names to me, I knew many miles of the Waveney valley almost as well as I did the river reach seen from the windows of the house in which I was born; long before I saw the reed-cutters at work at Oulton, or had even seen an eel-sett, I was at home among the haymakers in the Waveney water-meadows, and the men who, from strange and wonderful seaports, brought the wherries up to Bungay Staithe.

Assuming that a yachtsman starts from Yarmouth to explore the Waveney, he sees, as soon as he has crossed Breydon and entered on the lower waters of the river, the ruins of that fine old Roman stronghold, Burgh Castle. This great camp, undoubtedly the strongest in which the Romans established themselves in the district now known as Broadland, commanded the entrance to the two chief navigable waterways up which a hostile fleet might have attempted to win its way into the heart of East Anglia. Its construction is attributed to the Roman General Publius Ostorius Scapula. It was occupied, we are told, by a cavalry force under the command of the Count of the Saxon Shore. It was in touch with other stations, at Caister, Reedham, Burgh St. Peter, Caistor, and Tasburgh, each built on a spot where, if it were unprotected, an invading force might have landed without having to traverse treacherous swamps; and it was a convenient spot for the mooring of galleys. So far as can be deduced from its extensive remains, it was protected on the north, east, and south sides by massive walls; but its west side was open to the estuary, which it overlooked from the crest of a steep slope, leading down, perhaps, to an impassable morass. Whether this stronghold is, as Spelman and Camden state, the Roman *Gariononum*, is doubtful, some antiquaries being disposed to place that important post at Burgh St. Peter or Bergh Apton, which were on the line of a vicinal road called the Portway. The lack of space on the island of Lothingland for cavalry manœuvring seems to be the chief reason for assigning elsewhere the position of the headquarters of the Stablesian Horse.

One can hardly envy the Roman soldiers whose lot it was to occupy and defend this bleak and isolate post. Newly come, maybe, from some *æstiva* overlooking the blue waters of the Mediterranean, this Burgh camp, exposed to the piercing sea-winds, which swept untempered over the wide waste of the estuary, must have seemed to them a dreary spot, and often they must have longed to return to their native land. Pacing at night outside the ramparts, or keeping watch from the top of the round towers at the angles of the camp, the sentries could scarcely help contrasting the shrill song of the wind among the reeds with its soft murmur among the long-familiar myrtle-groves; the wild cries of the sea-birds and mazy dance of the marsh fires would be a sound and a sight of dread. Men who felt no fear when brave Icenic warriors flung themselves fiercely upon them, would feel a chill at their hearts when the wraithe-like wreaths of mist drifted up from dismal Breydon. When the loud clangour of some flighting flock of unknown fowl came startlingly out of the night gloom, even the knowledge that death was the penalty of desertion would hardly keep them at their posts. Even the men who had seen seventy thousand of their countrymen slaughtered by Britons driven to frenzy by the outrages on Boadicea and her subjects, would prefer risking a like fate to what was little better than exile in a bleak, unfriendly land. But the commands of the propraetors must be obeyed, and many of the Roman horsemen not only spent long and dreary days in this isolated stronghold, but died here, and were buried in the little graveyard just beyond the walls of the camp.

Even now Burgh is a lonesome spot, and its outlook over the wide marshes often somewhat dreary. The dilapidated old cement works by the riverside have long been idle; some of the cottages in which the workmen lived are untenanted; and the smelt-fishers who net the waters below the camp are seldom seen abroad in the daytime. A dark drapery of ivy enfolds the massive ramparts which have crowned the slope for nearly two thousand years; looking upwards from the river, one sees nothing of the green or gold of the cornfields which lie beyond the slowly crumbling walls. At night the strange churring of the nightjar is often heard from the gloom of the grove which hides the church; the piping and wailing of the Breydon fowl sounds as weird to-day to belated cruisers as they did to the Roman soldiers whose dust is disturbed by the farmer's plough. On still autumn nights the falling of leaves can be heard distinctly, and wisps of the fog which, like a fleecy pall, covers the wide marshlands, drift up the slope and through the gateway of the camp, distilling rain-like drops of moisture on the stubble of the neighbouring fields. But on

8

a bright summer day the view from the camp is not unpleasing. For miles the courses of the rivers can be traced by their bordering windmills, which, with the dark-sailed wherries, white-winged yachts, and countless cattle on the marshes, help to make such a scene as is to be found nowhere else in England. From the top of Burgh church tower many churches can be seen, and on a clear day, and with a good glass, the spire of Norwich Cathedral. So, after all, there were some grounds for Bede's assertion that "by reason of woods and seas together" Burgh was "a most pleasant castle," and not an unfitting site for that small monastery which the Irish monk Furseus, brought here by Sigebert, King of the East Angles, is said to have built in the midst of the Roman camp.

The four or five miles of river between Burgh Castle and St. Olave's Bridge call for no description. They are bordered by marshes like those through which the Yare flows between Reedham and Breydon, and only botanists in search of marsh orchids, rare sedges, and other plants which "partake the nature of their fenny bed," care to land and explore the levels lying beyond the river walls. But a mile or so below the bridge, near an old windmill and a marsh cottage occupied by the millman, I often leave the river for a while and ramble across a stretch of heathland bordering the green road from Belton to Herringfleet. There, where adders sometimes lurk amid the tall, waving bracken, pretty little sand-lizards bask on the footpaths, and that curious amphibian, the natterjack, or running toad, may be seen running like a mouse among the heath and ling, the rambler seldom hears other voices than those of wailing peewits, bleating snipes, and the whinchats, which utter their strange call-notes from the tops of the gorse and bramble bushes. Beyond the heath, along the borders of the green road,—which, in spite of the neighbouring railway, is in spring and summer the haunt of innumerable sweet-singing birds, — the dainty burnet rose decks the hedgerows, and the air is fragrant with sweetbriar. Turning to the left when this road is reached, it is not far to that which leads directly from the river to Fritton Lake, the loveliest of all the inland waters of Broadland.

Fritton Lake is not a Broad as the term is understood in Norfolk, where it means the "broadening out" of a river, but is a land-locked lake almost wholly surrounded by woodlands. In the days when the entire level of the Broadland valleys was an arm of the sea, Fritton formed part of that large estuary; but the lowlands between the lake and river are now, for the most part, reclaimed, and only a narrow un-navigable dyke represents the channel through which the sea tides ebbed and flowed. Around Fritton Lake there are none of those swampy lands such as border Rockland, Barton, and Hickling, and the depth of water in the lake is far greater than that of the real Broads. Scanty fringes of reeds there are here and there, and the sedge warblers visit them as regularly as they do those around the Broads; but elsewhere the gnarled boughs of woodland trees overhang the water, and the nightingale's song and the woodpecker's laugh are as familiar here as the *chitty, chitty, cha, cha* of the little brown bird of the reeds. Pheasants are as abundant in the Fritton woods as are wild-fowl in sharp weather on the Fritton waters; woodland and waterside wild flowers here bloom side by side. And all the varied green of oak and birch, larch and fir, goes to the making of a sylvan setting for a mirror which reflects the ever-changing aspects of shore and sky.

To pleasure - seekers the waters of Fritton Lake are accessible only during the summer months; in winter they are strictly preserved, on account of the wild-fowl which flock to them and are lured into the Fritton decoys. As you row round the lake you can see the arch-shaped entrances to the tunnel-like decoys which are still used when the fowl come southward; but to gain any real knowledge of this curious method of wild-fowl capture you must accompany a decoyman when he goes down to the waterside to work his "pipes." To gain permission to do this is no easy matter, for, as the Rev. Richard Lubbock says, " *Procul, O, procul este, profani,*" is the cry of most of the men who own or have charge of decoys; yet there are means of persuasion—they will readily suggest themselves—which some of the decoymen cannot resist. That there are such men at Fritton I will not affirm, for the Fritton decoys are the property of the owners of the lake and woods, who work them for "sport" rather than profit. I will only say that decoying is no longer so mysterious a business as it used to be.

At the beginning of the last century there were a score or more places in Norfolk and Suffolk where wild-fowl decoying was carried on every winter; in Broadland alone there were, not so very long ago, decoys at Winterton, Waxham, Ranworth, Mautby, Acle, Woodbastwick, Hemsby, and Flixton, as well as at Fritton. Nearly all these decoys are now, for some reason or other, fallen into disuse, and it is at Fritton only that they are worked regularly on favourable occasions. To make clear the worker's methods, it is necessary first to describe a decoy pipe. It cosnsists of a semicircular tunnel of wire netting and network arched over a shallow dyke which curves inland from the shores of a Broad, lake, or pool. This network tunnel is the "pipe." It is usually about twenty feet wide at the mouth, narrows as it curves inland, and is about a hundred yards long. It terminates in a long bow-net not unlike the "pot" or "pod" of an eel-sett, which can be disconnected from the rest of the pipe when the fowl have been driven into it. Along both sides of the pipe reed screens are erected obliquely; behind these the decoyman conceals himself, and, through small peep-holes, made by turning thin strips of wood sideways between the reeds, scans the open water in front of the pipes, and watches the progress of the decoying. The fowl are lured by means of tame decoy ducks and a trained dog known as the "piper." The decoy ducks, which are usually birds whose plumage closely resembles that of the wild ducks, are trained by judicious feeding to answer to the low whistle the decoyman gives when he wishes them to enter the pipe. Sometimes it is unnecessary to whistle, the appearance of the piper, which, at a signal from his master, leaps over the low boards called dog-jumps, placed between the screens, being sufficient to attract them to the pipe.

What strikes the stranger as the most wonderful feature of decoying, is the curiosity displayed by the wild-fowl at the appearance of the decoyman's dog. Instead of taking

flight as soon as it commences to leap to and fro over the
" jumps," the fowl at once evince great interest in its movements ; and when the tame ducks, beside which they have
been feeding on the pool, begin swimming towards the mouth
of the pipe, they follow them. As soon as they are well
within the pipe, the decoyman, who until then has kept
himself carefully concealed, and perhaps has carried in his
hand a piece of smouldering peat so that the keen-scented
fowl may not become aware of his presence, shows himself
in front of the screens but behind the fowl, and by waving
his arm or handkerchief frightens them so that they rise from
the water and fly swiftly up the narrowing pipe. He follows
them and drives them into the bow-net, which he promptly
disconnects from the rest of the pipe, and the fowl are caught.
He then takes them out one by one and wrings their necks.
When wild duck, wigeon, and teal are plentiful, immense
quantities of them are taken in this way. The Rev. R.
Lubbock knew of three hundred mallard being taken in one
morning, also two hundred and twenty teal. The average
" take " of a decoy at the present time is said to be about a
thousand fowl in a season ; but this can scarcely apply to
Broadland, though fourteen hundred fowl were, I believe, taken
at Fritton in one week during the winter of 1899–1900. The
difficulty in preserving that absolute quietude essential to the
successful working of a decoy is one of the chief reasons why so
many of the old pipes have fallen into disuse ; and it is only at
Fritton, where the land surrounding the lake belongs to the owners
of the decoys, and fishing, shooting, and boating are prohibited
during the winter months, that this old-time method of wild-fowl
capture can still be resorted to with any likelihood of success.

From the time when the larches and birches first fleck
the woods with a green spray, until the golden and brown
leaves spread a rustling carpet on the woodland paths, Fritton
is the loveliest lagoon in Broadland ; but even when one has
rowed from shore to shore, seen the sunlit waters gleaming
between the boles of birch, oak, and beech, wandered through
groves where the paths seem a flickering fretwork of sunlight
and leaf shadows, inhaled the fragrance of the old-fashioned
flowers in the Old Hall garden, and listened to the drowsy

droning of the bees among the blossoms, one can have only a faint idea of the charm Fritton has for those who have known it long and known it well. The cruiser on Broadland waterways can seldom spare the time necessary to become acquainted with all its beauties; he can only imagine what the lake is like when its bordering woods are white and gleaming with hoar-frost, and every breath of breeze sets ice-crystals tinkling among the reeds. This is an aspect of Fritton with which only a favoured few are familiar; but a decoyman will tell you that there are times when, in the excitement of watching the wild-fowl paddling up the pipe of his decoy, he can feel neither the nip of the frost at his finger-tips nor the chill which is creeping into his bones. And if you ask him, he will say that it is in winter, and in frosty weather, that Fritton is seen at its best; for the sight of the wild-fowl swarming on the lake is far more pleasant to him than the singing of nightingales and reed birds and the shimmering of green leaves in the sunlight.

Of the Augustinian Priory of St. Olave, which stood near the ferry which crossed the river where St. Olave's Bridge now stands, there are only scanty remains, and these are of little interest; but if the voyager, after seeing Fritton, has an hour or two to spare before resuming his cruise, he may like to traverse the long willow-fringed dam which leads to Haddiscoe and visit Haddiscoe Church, which has the finest Norman round tower in Norfolk. There he can decipher the curious epitaph to an old stage-coachman, carved on a stone affixed to the outside of the churchyard wall. But unless he is interested in church architecture it will hardly be worth his while to cross the dusty marsh dam; he had better board his boat again and continue his voyage to Oulton Broad. At Somerleyton he will pass under another railway bridge, near which he may land and stroll up to the model village of Somerleyton, grouped around a pleasant green; and if he be there on a day when the gardens of Somerleyton Hall are open to the public, he cannot do better than see them and the fine Hall, which stands on the site of the old seat of the "Lords of the Island of Lothingland." When Fuller, in the seventeenth century, visited "Summerley Hall," he said that it was a place "well answering the name thereof: for here Sommer is to be seen in the depth of Winter, in the pleasant walks beset on both sides with firr trees, green all the year long." But the Hall to which Fuller refers, and which is said to have been built by a member of the Jerningham family, whose seat is now at Costessey, is demolished, and the present house, erected by Sir Morton Peto, has had no such exciting episodes in its history as had the old one, to which, we are told, on 14th March 1642, Colonel Cromwell's and Captain Fountayn's troops, and divers others, to the number of one hundred and forty, came, and, in addition to commandeering a large quantity of corn, carried away with them a quantity of arms and £160 in gold. For the Hall was then occupied by Sir John Wentworth, a Royalist, to whom the Lord General subsequently sent peremptory orders that he should "ungarrison" the place or it would be demolished with its fortifications. But when the Commonwealth ended, and King Charles came to the throne, his coronation was celebrated by the Somerleyton folk in a very festive style; for we read that barrels of beer, "duzzens" of bread, "tobacko," pipes, sugar, and "pruens" were purchased for the entertainment of the villagers, and a large quantity of faggots, broom, and firwood was provided for the building of a "bone fire."

Between Somerleyton and Oulton little is to be seen except marshes, and here and there an old windmill or an eel-catcher's house-boat. As these are objects with which the visitor to Broadland soon becomes familiar, he may be glad to know that there is an overland route to Oulton, which, if he is not sailing his yacht himself, he can take, sending his yacht on to the Broad in charge of the men who sail her. Leaving the road to Somerleyton station on the right as he returns from the village, he soon finds himself in a pleasant leafy lane running along the crest of the uplands where they slope downwards to the marshes. For some distance this lane, which is bordered by rose-garlanded hedgerows, except where it becomes a footpath across a small furzy warren, keeps to the uplands; but opposite the first cottage in the sparsely populated parish of Flixton there is a bylane or "driftway," as it is locally called, leading down to the marshes. At the

marsh end of this holly-bordered driftway there is, a little way
to the right, a rush marsh where sundews, bog pimpernels,
marsh helleborines, and the beautiful grass of Parnassus grow
freely, and even the dusky marsh cinquefoil, rare marsh pea,
and marsh fern may be found; but the Oulton path is to the
left, along the border of the marshes.   This path leads to
a footbridge over a narrow streamlet draining Flixton Decoy,
a small, strictly preserved lake hidden by its surrounding
woods.   Crossing the footbridge, the path, which still keeps to
the marshes, brings the traveller, by way of a short lane where
the scent of honeysuckle is often overpowered by the dis-
agreeable odour of white-starred ramsons, to a little hamlet
called Fisher Row.   This hamlet, which contains nothing of
special interest, is soon left behind, and the path, after passing
by a small marsh farmstead, should be abandoned at the point
where a driftway comes down to it near Oulton Church, which
is seen on high ground to the left.

Another footpath, branching off from the driftway just
opposite the churchyard gate, leads to a little colony of new
houses overlooking the Broad.   One of these houses stands on
the site of George Borrow's Oulton home, and the summer-
house in which Borrow wrote *Lavengro* and the *Bible in
Spain*, and sometimes entertained his Romany friends, is still
to be seen on the verge of a lawn, overshadowed by the firs
among which he loved to hear the wind make mournful music.
Apart from this old octagonal summer-house, which remains
in much the same state as Borrow left it, there is little of
interest in this particular neighbourhood; for the red-brick
villas and castellated houses which have sprung up on this side
of the Broad have, with some huge and ugly malt-houses
at its Carlton end, robbed Oulton of what little beauty it
once possessed.   Some fine old black poplars at the bend of
the road connecting this unsightly modern settlement with
Carlton Colville are, with the church and summer-house, all
that would remind Borrow, could he revisit Oulton, of the
scenes with which he was long familiar.   The old tithe-barn,
through whose tileless rafters the red light of sunset used to
glow so gorgeously that the barn looked like some charred
timber framework left by a receding conflagration, is gone;

and the spot which in Borrow's day was so isolate that it was said to be more approachable by water than by land, is only too easily accessible. The smoke of the Romany's camp fire is no longer seen like a blue haze against the dusky background of firs; and, as Dr. Jessopp says of other places which were once parts of Arcady, the face of the land wears a smirk rather than a smile.

Not only is the tithe-barn gone, but the old Wherry Inn no longer stands near Mutford Bridge, its site being now occupied by a large modern hotel. Oulton Broad is now a place for water frolics and regattas rather than communion with Nature. During the holiday season every train from Lowestoft discharges a flannel-clad crowd of pleasure-seekers on to the platforms of Oulton Broad and Carlton Colville stations; and it is only before the Lowestoft season begins and after it ends that the Broad enjoys peace and quiet. For three months in the year its boat-yards are thronged with yachting parties starting on or returning from Broadland cruising. Usually a little fleet of yachts, launches, and pleasure wherries is at anchor near Mutford Bridge. For Oulton is so near Lowestoft that many cruising parties do not trouble to take their yachts down the unattractive channel of Lake Lothing and moor them in the harbour yacht-basin; they visit Lowestoft by road or rail, and return to the Broad at night. The road from Oulton to Lowestoft is far prettier than the river way, and the railway journey is one of only five minutes.

But although Oulton lacks such beauty as has made Wroxham and Barton famous, it is a fine sheet of water for sailing; and when regattas are held on the Broad under favourable conditions, some good racing is seen. The water is deep everywhere except near the shore, and by way of Oulton Dyke, which is also wide and deep enough to admit of the passage of the largest craft which navigate the Broadland waterways, a day's cruise can be pleasantly extended up or down the Waveney. A popular trip with local folk who cannot devote much time to boating, is that to the little staithe near the curious church at Burgh St. Peter; but very few of the cruisers who land at the staithe and visit the church know that the latter stands on or near the site of a Roman camp. For almost all traces of the camp which could be seen a century ago, when the enclosure was said to bear " a striking resemblance to the form of those Roman towns whose outlines may still be traced in this country," have vanished ; and though an ivy-grown fragment of an old chapel, which formerly exempted the parish from the payment of tithes, still stands on a small mound which has been called the prætorium of the camp, a vivid imagination is necessary to reconstruct upon such evidence what may have been the Roman *Gariononum.* But the church tower, if ugly, is certainly unique, and the presence of Roman bricks in the church walls proves that the statements of antiquaries concerning the early importance of the place are not without foundation. Human remains, too, have been unearthed in large quantities near the river bank ; but whether, as is said, they were those of the slain in a battle fought near the staithe, is entirely a matter of surmise.

At Oulton, as in the neighbourhood of other large Broads, Broadsmen of the old type may be encountered,—men who still manage to exist on their scanty earnings as reed-cutters and eel-catchers. One of these men has a handy little sailing house-boat in which he spends the greater part of the winter, and in its cosy if somewhat cramped little cabin I have sat with him and chatted about the " good old days " when milk was a penny a pail, fresh butter ninepence a pound, and new country cheese threepence-halfpenny. Poor folk, he told me, could *live* then. His father had the " run " of the Acle new road across the marshes for his horses and cattle, which grazed on the grassy borders between the road and the dykes ; but " they maint du that now " ! Protecting and preserving had compelled him to abandon all his old methods of livelihood except eel-catching ; and if it had not been for the yachting folk, who found work for him in the summer, he did not know how he could have lived. I gently suggested that though the stopping of fish-netting may have entailed some hardship to such as he, trawling for fresh-water fish was calculated to spoil the rivers for the draw-netters as well as the anglers ; but he vehemently assured me that the trawlers caught nothing but

Frank Southgate

HAULING UP THE EEL-PODS

AN AUTUMN DAY

THE OCTOBER MOON

AN OCTOBER MORNING ON THE MARSHES

FROSTY SUNRISE ON ORMESBY BROAD

EEL-PICKING

A SUCCESSFUL SHOT AT WADERS – THE BIRDS' END OF THE GUN

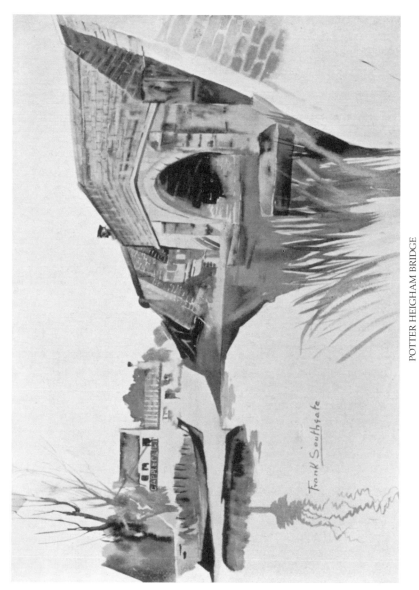

POTTER HEIGHAM BRIDGE

Frank Southgate

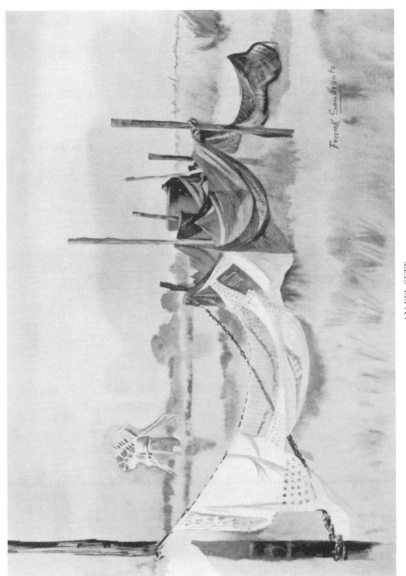

Frank Southgate

AN EEL-SETT

TOWING THE REED HARVEST

MARSHMEN WEED-LIFTING

MARSH HAY-CARTING BY THE YARE

"SCIENTIFIC" SPOTS FOWL

FLIGHT-SHOOTING – HARD HIT, MARKING HIM DOWN

ROOKS MOBBING A HERON

BREYDON – LOW WATER

eels, and when I ventured to doubt this, quoting the evidence of the witnesses who saw the fish landed at Yarmouth, he more than hinted that he had been in a better position than any one else to know what was caught. His house-boat, when I last saw it, was moored in the only quiet and unspoilt creek which the Oulton waters now possess, and I thought it characteristic of the old man who had so great a love of the river life, that he should have chosen the one spot which retained its primitive aspect and charm.

The Waveney between Oulton Dyke and Beccles is wide and deep, and with a fair wind a passage is soon made to the little town, whose massive church tower can be seen many miles across the marshes. Indeed, a speedy passage is generally considered desirable, except by those cruisers who are content with the beauty of waterside wild flowers and water-mirrored reeds and rushes; for this part of the Waveney presents few striking vistas, though it has some pretty " bits " here and there, where an alder carr has its jungle of towering willow-herbs, cat valerians, and marsh thistles, or a marshman's cottage stands close by the riverside, half hidden by willows and sallows. But even these marsh-bordered reaches are often remarkable for the wealth of colour they reveal. The green of the summer reeds, the lavender tint of the water-stained rush beds, and the ruddy hues of the sun-scorched leaves of dock and meadow-sweet—each, perhaps, with its counterpart in the unruffled water—give infinite variety to the low, level banks. On calm evenings, after the sun has set, the river is often like a sheet of glass; to look down into it is to see a sub-aqueous sky flecked with cloud-drift or gemmed with stars, and to feel a sensation of floating in aerial space. And when, after a hot summer day, the river banks are veiled with mist, one needs to look westward, where the upland's edge shows dark against the afterglow of sunset, to be assured that the extent of the still waters is not as vast as it is indefinable.

Beccles, apart from its fine Perpendicular church (which formerly belonged to the Abbey of St. Edmundsbury) and the view to be had from its churchyard, is chiefly of interest on account of the picturesque character of much of that part of the town which slopes down to the banks of the river just beyond

its road and railway bridges.   Here, the old malt-houses, boat-
yards, gardens, brightly painted wherries, some fine old trees,
and two or three houses of quaint styles of architecture,
make a series of riverside pictures worthy of an old Dutch
town and a painter of the Dutch school.   Not one in a
hundred Broadland cruisers sees Beccles from above the
bridges ; the majority of visitors, after strolling through the
town, carry away with them the impression that it is perhaps
the least attractive in the district.   Nor in the course of the
season do many people explore that part of the river which
lies between Beccles and Bungay, though it is, as the lock-
keeper at Geldeston maintained when he last opened the lock
for me, " uncommon pretty," and the river below Beccles not
" in it " when compared with it.   Several things unite to make
it unpopular with yachtsmen.   One of these is its shallowness ;
another, its mazy windings, which not only make sailing a
matter of difficulty, but are in places so tortuous as to convey
an impression that little or no headway is being made.

Then there are the locks at Geldeston, Ellingham, and
Wainford, two of which the cruiser must open for himself ;
while, early in the season, before the cutting is done, the water-
weeds almost choke up some of the reaches.   But in spite of
these drawbacks the trading wherries manage to get up to
Bungay all through the year, and those pleasure-seekers who
follow in the wake of the wherries are well rewarded for the
difficulties they encounter and overcome.   For they usually
have the twelve miles or so of waterway almost entirely to
themselves, they are all the time in the midst of a district
where the marshes are nowhere so wide as to make access to
the uplands difficult, and at the end of their journey they
reach as pleasant and picturesque an old country town as is
to be found in East Anglia.

I made this voyage not long ago in my little gun-punt,
the *Gipsy*, having for my companion the artist with whose
work this book will make the reader well acquainted.   We
had reached Beccles about six o'clock on a mid-June evening,
and were tempted by the fineness of the weather to continue
our cruise.   The breeze which had brought us quickly up from
Oulton died away just before sunset ; but the subtle charm of

the dark woods and misty meadows in the twilight, the revelation of beauty at every bend of the stream, the cries of redshank, snipe, and plover, and the songs of the reed birds, made our slow progress on the dusk-darkened waters very pleasant. So clear was the water, that even after the sun had gone down we could see the bright green weeds, and some of the little inlets were so covered with tiny white blossoms of water-crowfoot as to give them the appearance of being white with frost. The thick-stalked water-lilies were just showing their yellow heads above the stream ; thicker-stalked hemlock often brushed the sides of our boat—for the weeds were as yet uncut ; the air was filled with the aromatic odour of sweet sedge. A sense of complete isolation soon possessed us. After we had rowed a mile or so from Beccles, we did not pass even a rowing boat, and until ten o'clock, when we reached Geldeston Lock, we saw no sign of any kind of sailing craft—not even a wherry. But in a dyke near the lock a cheerful glow of light from a yacht's cabin indicated that other pleasure-seekers besides ourselves were taking an early-season cruise on the upper Waveney.

In the lock-house, which is also an alehouse, the landlord lock-keeper was entertaining half a dozen rustics, and after they were gone home we chatted with him for an hour or so about river and marsh life. We learnt that when he was a young man the Geldeston marshes, like those at Burgh Castle, were a favourite place for prize-fighting, the reason being, as in the case of Burgh, that the pugilists, if interrupted by the authorities of one county, could cross the river and resume hostilities in another, where the disturbing element was absent or had no power to act. Concerning King, Mace, and some noted Romany bruisers he discoursed in a way which would have moved George Borrow to many lamentations that the days of the pugilists are gone ; so vividly did he describe an encounter between a famous prize-fighter and a local celebrity known as " Blazer " High, that I, who could remember High only as a comparatively peaceable wheelwright in my native village, found myself regretting that I had not been born soon enough to witness just one of those stirring contests. But it was growing late, and we had not solved the difficulty of finding beds, so we were compelled to turn the conversation in another direction. There was no room for us at the lock-house, nor was it likely we could find accommodation in the village; and the last trains to Beccles and Bungay were gone. The prospect of having to walk to one of these towns did not please us, so, on learning that we had the alternative of sleeping in a big boat moored in a boat-house near the lock, we agreed to accept it. Laden with an old sail, a large rug, a couple of sacks, and an old horn lantern, we sallied forth from the inn into the dark night, and made our way to our draughty lodgings. By the faint lantern light the interior of the boat-house looked uninviting; so, after depositing our heterogeneous assortment of bedclothes in the boat, we extinguished the lantern and went for an hour's stroll across the Shipmeadow marshes. By feeling the firmness of the turf rather than by sight we kept to the footpath until the harsh " crek, crek " of a landrail tempted us to leave it, and we almost trod on the skulking bird before it rose from amid the long marsh grass. The path brought us to a lane into which, as we soon discovered, the waters of a ditch had been diverted, and after a brief experience of this oozy byway we returned to our quarters for the night.

The old boat-house was open towards the river, and, after two or three hours' sleep, we awoke to find the eastern sky radiant with a brazen dawn-light. A boisterous wind, increasing in force, was blowing, and some young poplars on the opposite bank of the river were bowing before it. The air was filled with the storm-song of tossing reeds, willows, and sallows ; along the riversides the sedge rustled loudly, white umbels of wild parsley waved wildly, and the brilliant blossoms of the water-flags were torn by the sharp-edged sedge blades. The unmown marsh grass rose and fell in green and grey waves, over which the bright yellow buttercups spread a tremulous golden haze. When a sedge warbler rose above the reeds it seemed as helpless as a wisp of thistledown, and was swept back into the reeds again. The sky was full of flying clouds, but every wind-gust blotted out their reflections in the water, which was constantly being dimmed like a breath-blown mirror.

For an hour or so we loitered about the lock-house, hoping

that the wind, which was dead against us, would moderate; and the lock - keeper, to entertain us, showed us a clever drawing given to him by an artist - angler, some stuffed birds, a couple of fine sea lamperns taken in the lock, and a perch weighing five pounds two ounces—the largest, he said, that had been taken in the river. But we were anxious to continue our cruise; so, after admiring the lock - keeper's treasures, we boarded our punt, passed through the lock, and began the toughest bit of rowing we had had for many a day. At times we found it impossible to make headway; the wind, if it did not force our boat into the bank, held it so fast in midstream that if it had not been a flat-bottomed punt we might have believed it aground. Yet we could not stop rowing, for once, when we paused a moment to watch a mole which had taken to the water and was swimming like a vole across the river, its little pink snout raised just above the surface, we drifted backward far faster than we had gone forward. The three miles of river between Geldeston and Ellingham seemed by far the longest miles of our cruise, and when we reached the fine old water-mill, which is the most picturesque feature of this part of the river, we had had, although it was only eight o'clock in the morning, enough rowing for that day. So we moored under the lee - side of a granary near the mill, and my companion, who was anxious to reach Bungay, set out for Ellingham station.

Two miles above Ellingham is Wainford Lock, adjoining which are huge maltings and a flour-mill. This is a very ancient place, for here was a ford on the Roman road from *Venta Icenorum* (Norwich) to the coast at *Sitomagus* (Dunwich), and here, in a later period, the Hundred Moot of Wangford or Wainford was held. The road ran to the east of the malt - houses, where Roman relics have been unearthed; and Dr. Raven, in his *History of Suffolk*, suggests that if the mill were pulled down valuable discoveries might be made; but only learned archæologists can find, in the narrow byroads which run from Ditchingham station to Mettingham, traces of the Stone Street of the Romans. However, a ramble from the lock to Mettingham, where there are some ruins of a castle built by Sir John de Norwich, one of Edward III.'s vice-admirals, is well worth taking; as is that to Ditchingham village and the Bath Hills which border the Waveney, where it makes a horseshoe bend round Bungay Common. But as these are places which can be visited as easily from Bungay, most voyagers on the Waveney prefer to complete their upward cruise before exploring the neighbourhood of that old Norman town. This they can soon do, for it is only about a mile from Wainford to Bungay Staithe.

Above Bungay Staithe the Waveney is unnavigable to sailing boats; but that part of the river which from the water-mill near the staithe makes a bend round the town and its large, breezy common, is worth exploring. The road over the mill-bridge leads to a footpath along the riverside and the Falcon Inn at Ditchingham, an old coaching inn far more famous a century ago than it is to-day. Here, boats suited to the shallows of the upper reaches can be hired, and the voyage upstream continued. For about a mile the river winds through marshes; but above a low wooden footbridge, beneath which, when the river is swollen by heavy rains, boats pass with difficulty, there is, on the Norfolk bank, the loveliest bit of scenery on the Waveney. A steep wooded bank or hanger, known as the Bath Hills, here slopes downwards to the very edge of the water, so that woodland wild flowers, such as anemones and bluebells, grow close beside the brilliant water-flags and dainty pink ragged robins, and the bright green leaves of that curious-looking plant, the setterwort, are seen within a few yards of patches of pink-spiked orchids. The water is so clear that the waving streamers and succulent stalks of the water-weeds are everywhere visible; and so sheltered is it that its surface is seldom ruffled, and reflects the overspreading horse-chestnuts, ashes, planes, and rowans like a mirror. For years this lovely reach was my favourite haunt in idle hours, and I was never tired of watching the shoals of fish darting by my boat, the brilliant-hued dragon-flies poising in films of vibrating wings, and listening to the wood doves crooning among the tree-tops. I remember that it was just by the old rifle butts behind which the wooded slope forms a natural bank that I first found the beautiful yellow archangel or weaselsnout in bloom, and near by *Daphne Laureola* and the acrid lettuce, three plants rare enough in Norfolk to make the finding of them here an interesting event in a botanist's life.

As a boy, I loved to scramble up the precipitous path behind the rifle butts—having first made sure that the local volunteers were not using the range, for the bullets often went wide of the target—for that steep path leads to a clematis-garlanded lane along the crest of the hills — a lane so embowered with trees that in summer it is a leafy crypt. But there are places where glimpses may be had of the wide common with its golden gorse, and beyond it the red roofs and church tower of Bungay town. It is a lane for idle hours and day-dreams, and I know that often, when I looked down on the river slowly winding through the cattle-dotted marsh-lands, I dreamt of the days when sea tides came flooding up the Waveney valley, bringing with them the Viking ships of the Norse raiders, whose raven banners were of such ill omen to the Saxon dwellers on the borders of the vale. For I had heard of the finding of ships' anchors and strange weapons in the peat of the marshlands, and had read of the Danes' ravages on our eastern shores. And all the romance of the red-roofed town, with its Norman castle and the mysterious underground passage which I firmly believed connected it with the castle at Mettingham, was brought near to me when I saw the town from this leafy height, and could detach myself from the familiar scenes I daily witnessed in its quiet streets. And when I read somewhere that the parish of Earsham, whose sky-pointing church spire I could see to the right of the town, had formerly paid a yearly sum towards the maintenance of the sea-walls at Lowestoft, which kept the sea from bursting in upon the marshes stretching away from the foot of the hills, the imagining of such an inrush of the sea afforded me mental diversion for hours together. The fact that centuries had elapsed since the ocean's pulse was felt beating so far inland, only gave the imagination wider scope for the spreading of its wings.

This leafy lane, which is in places so narrow that the path

9

is almost hidden by ferny parsley leaves and drooping brome grasses, skirts the borders of Mr. Rider Haggard's Ditchingham estate, and it is on a part of the slopes, known as the " Earl's Vineyard," that the scene is laid of a tragic episode in the early chapters of the novelist's romance, *Montezuma's Daughter*. Readers of that stirring story easily recognise here, too, other scenes described in it, and when they return to Bungay, and climb the steep street leading to the market-place, they find much in that quaint and quiet little town unchanged since the times with which the story deals. The round towers of the Bigods' castle, flanked by older earthworks, still frown down on the smiling pasture lands of the lush-grassed vale, and amid the crumbling but massive walls a shaft leads down to a grim, dark dungeon into which daylight has not penetrated for eight hundred years. Not far away stands a fine old church, originally that of the Benedictine nunnery which lost one of its abbesses through the ravage of the Black Death ; a little beyond it, the churchyards only separated by a street of almost sylvan aspect, an older church retains its Norman tower. In the market-place, nearly opposite the old Tuns Inn, a dome-roofed market-cross has handstocks still affixed to one of its pillars ; and in St. Mary's Street, facing the church, is a sixteenth-century house with richly carved corbels, the guest-house, some have said, of the nunnery whose precincts it once adjoined. But for the rest, the town is comparatively modern, for in 1688 it was almost entirely destroyed by an incendiary fire, which gave rise to the local saying, " As big a rogue as burnt Bungay." Yet it is not so very long since it was discovered that it possessed another relic of its past even more ancient than the earthworks amid which its Norman castle stands ; for when an old windmill beside the Flixton road was pulled down, its foundations were found to rest on a tumulus filled with human bones. I remember how the Bungay folk stood and wondered when it was seen that the skeletons lay in a circle, each with its feet towards a common centre, and how an interested townsman possessed himself of a fine set of ivory-white teeth !

The town is as charmingly situated as any in Broadland. No matter by what road you leave it, it is one more likely to lure you onward than make you think of retracing your steps. The best road is that leading to Mettingham, for, in addition to the delight of rambling through charming rural scenes, you have a definite object in view in following it. For it leads to the ruined castle I have once or twice referred to. This castle has no historical interest, but its lofty walls rising amid fine old trees make a striking picture, and its fine gate-tower is well preserved. From Mettingham a lane and field footpath lead to the verge of the uplands which border the Waveney valley, and the view from the uplands' edge is one of great charm and loveliness. To the right many miles of the vale lie revealed, with the river like a wavy silver thread in a cloth of green; to the left the picturesque promontory on which Bungay stands juts out into the lowlands; and through the midst of the vale the dark-sailed wherries glide along the serpentine reaches, like vessels which have lost their way. From the point where this prospect can be viewed it is not far to the road which leads back to the town and Bungay Staithe.

Not long ago, when the waters of the Waveney were checked in their downward flow by narrow-arched wooden bridges at Beccles and Bungay, floods were of frequent occurrence in the Waveney valley. Dwellers amidst and on the borders of the marshes often saw the swollen river overflow its banks, and for days together many miles of marshland were submerged. If these inundations occurred in winter, they were of little consequence except when they rose so high as to flood the lower rooms of the marsh-folk's houses; indeed, when frosty weather accompanied them, the submerged levels afforded excellent skating for the inhabitants of the towns and villages in the valley; but a summer flood was a more serious affair. Once in the month of July it rained heavily on several successive days, and the river rose rapidly. Still the marshes were not flooded until one night about a week after the rain began, and even on that night there was no water on the levels when the marsh-folk went to bed. But about midnight it swept across the valley, and from that hour until daybreak lights were burning in and around scores of cottages between Beccles and Bungay, where cottagers were hastily conveying upstairs the contents of the lower rooms, and removing pigs and poultry to places of safety. When day dawned the green marshlands had become a waste of waters, stretching in some directions almost as far as eye could see; and down the river was drifting a procession of haycocks which had floated off the meadows. The marsh dams at Ditchingham, Earsham, and Gillingham were impassable to foot passengers; to the houses bordering Ditchingham Dam the postman rowed in a boat. Farmers whose hay crops were ruined, and women whose household goods had suffered, looked depressed and disheartened; but to the children the flood was a novel and welcome experience. The marshes were transformed into an unexplored Pacific, an untraversed main, and as many of the lads as could get boats set out on voyages of discovery—voyages attended by dangers in the shape of submerged tree-stumps. For four days scores of marsh-folk were compelled to keep to the upper chambers of their houses; but at the end of that time they saw the cucumber frames in their gardens emerge, like welcome Ararats, from the flood. Since wider-arched bridges have been built over the river there has been no serious inundation.

CHAPTER IX

THE BURE AND ITS BROADS

A LARGE number of the yachting folk who visit Broadland confine their cruising to the Bure and its tributaries, some because lack of time prevents their exploring the Yare and Waveney; others because, as they often urge, the Bure and its tributaries bring them in touch with the best of the Broads and every kind of Broadland scenery. So long as the influent Ant and Thurne are included with the main stream, I am quite ready to admit that the Bure should be considered the chief river of Broadland and the best for loveliness and variety of charm; but, at the same time, I think that no one who knows the district intimately will deny that the more frequented and popular reaches of the Bure do not possess that unique and weirdly impressive beauty which is to be enjoyed at its best and subtlest on such wild wildernesses of reeds and water as Hickling Broad and Heigham Sounds. The most popular part of the Bure is that which lies between Acle and Wroxham, and embraces some of the best-known Broads; but I am not alone in thinking that while Wroxham, Ranworth, Salhouse, and South Walsham Broads are as pretty as it is possible for little lakes to be, and in late autumn and winter are undeniably lovely, they are lacking in that primeval, isolate beauty—I had almost written sublimity—characteristic of those Broads and river reaches which lie in the midst of wide level marshes and tracts of sedgy fen. Compared with Heigham Sounds at dawn or sunset, and Horsey Mere when the sun lights up the sandhill ridges of Horsey and Waxham, Wroxham and Ranworth seem to me simply pretty—as pretty as it is possible for wood-girt waters to be, no doubt, but not particularly impressive. But such comparisons are uncalled for. Degrees of beauty are hardly definable, and the appreciation of them is a matter of mood and temperament. On the Bure and its tributaries, and in the district which surrounds them, there is scenery to satisfy almost every one, and interest enough to occupy the mind of a visitor for a far longer time than most people can devote to it.

The lower waters of the Bure—that is to say, those reaches which lie between Acle Bridge and Breydon—are often described as uninteresting and featureless. Taking at random the opinions of three writers, I find one saying that "the landscape is singularly uninteresting, being composed of water, marshes, and sky, with very little to break the monotony"; another, that the country hereabouts is "lacking in picturesqueness"; and a third, that the banks are unlovely and the scenery beyond them very unattractive. But I have cruised on the lower Bure in company with an artist who maintained that almost every bend of the river presented a picture well worth painting. The ferries and ferrymen's houses, the windmills, and the marsh farmsteads and millmen's houses, with their long, low, thatched or red-tiled outbuildings, seen, as they generally are, with no other background than the sky, but with the gleaming river and perhaps an eel-fisher's house-boat moored in a creek in the foreground, form charming subjects for brush or pencil. Beyond the river walls, too, there are, during several months of the year, innumerable cattle-pieces worthy of the genius of a Paul Potter or a Sidney Cooper—hundreds of cattle often being visible between the walls and the far-off, mill-dotted sky-line. Runham Church also, with its shapely, slender-pinnacled tower rising from amid a grove of trees, makes a pleasant picture as seen from Herringby Staithe; and so does Stokesby as you approach it from Yarmouth, and see its fine windmill whirling its sails above the red roofs of the waterside cottages; while as for Yarmouth, as it appears for several miles beyond its bridges, Joseph Pennell has shown us what can be made of such a subject. Scenery possessing such features as these cannot justly be called tame, monotonous, and lacking in picturesqueness, especially when, as is the case with this part of the Bure, these features often group themselves into strikingly effective combinations. That there is abundant colour in these wide flat landscapes no one who sees the marshland studies which illustrate this book can doubt; the loveliest colour effects are to be seen on the marshes and along the river.

But unless the voyager can find pleasure in marshland scenery, there is little, I must admit, to tempt him to linger on the lower Bure. The churches at Runham and Stokesby are in no way remarkable, and all that is worth seeing in the villages can be seen from the river. At Acle, however, there is an interesting church about a mile from the old single-arched bridge which spans the river; and visitors with antiquarian inclinations can amuse themselves with trying to discover the site of Weybridge Priory, and so settle a matter of dispute among local antiquaries. For there was formerly a priory at Acle, an Augustinian house founded by one of the Bigods, Earls of Norfolk; and that it stood somewhere near Acle Bridge, which was formerly called Waybrig or Weybridge, is suggested by the name given to it in old documents. But not a trace of it remains, unless some slight depressions in the grounds adjoining the Angel Inn mark the position of its chief buildings, and the skeletons which have been unearthed there are those of the monks of Weybridge and the knights and dames who were buried in the Priory church.

All through the summer a good many yachts are moored above and below Acle Bridge, and on regatta day a lively scene is presented around the well-known Angel Inn. When I come to Wroxham I will try and describe one of these Broadland regattas; for the present I will only say that the water festival held at Acle towards the end of July is by no means the least popular, and when the river is thronged with all kinds of craft, and yachts afloat and flagstaffs ashore are a-flutter with bunting, the neighbourhood of the old brick bridge is one to be either sought or avoided—this, again, is a matter of temperament. Some cruisers prefer it when only a few wherries are moored at the staithe below the bridge, urging that the wherries are more in harmony with the weather-beaten bridge and inn than are the dainty yachts of the pleasuring folk. The average Broadland wherry gives plenty of colour to any scene of which it is a feature. I remember an evening when two of them were moored near the bridge. They were remarkable for their brilliant hues. The top of the mast and the sides of the hold of one were painted Pyrenese green; the square wooden chimney of the cabin was bright red, as were the rigging blocks and tabernacle; the cabin door was dark blue relieved by yellow bands; and the top of the tiller and its handle, the gaff and flag-frame, were white. The other wherry, which had only that morning left a Coltishall wherry-builder's yard, where it had been repainted, had red, white, and blue bands round the top of the mast, and beneath them was a two-feet band of burnished brass; flag, tabernacle, blocks, and cabin roof were vermilion, and the tiller and cabin door were royal blue and yellow. Both wherries were "light," and one showed something of a white, the other of a pale green keel. All these colours were reflected in the water, where they shimmered and melted one into another whenever a breath of wind or a passing boat sent ripples running towards the shore.

Above Acle Bridge the scenery of the Bure becomes more varied, but there is nothing to tempt any one to land until Thurne Mouth is passed and the ruined gateway of St. Benet's Abbey is seen close by the riverside, on some slightly elevated ground — once a kind of fen isle — among the Cowholm marshes. At first glance it may seem that there is little besides the gateway to call for attention; but a stroll along the riverside below the gateway, and a visit to the crumbling walls on the highest point of the old island, reveal much that is interesting. Close by the waterside the foundations— "groundsels" the marshmen call them—of several of the vanished monastery's buildings can be traced, while on the high ground are considerable remains of the walls of the cruciform abbey church in which the famous Sir John Fastolff of Caister Castle was buried. Distinctly traceable, too, are the foundations of the boundary wall, which extended from the riverside near the gateway a long way into the marshes, and returned to the river again some distance below the abbey church. This wall was buttressed, as can be seen from what remains of it; and it appears to have been bordered by rows of hawthorns and blackthorns, the stumps of which can still be seen. Apparently there were small towers at the angles of the wall, for there are some foundations which suggest this at the lower point where the wall reaches the riverside. Of the scanty ruins, however, the gateway is the most interesting portion. Its outer arch has a shield in each spandrel, a complete but empty niche on the right-hand side, and remains of another on the left. On the left side, too, are eighteen steps of a spiral staircase, over which are Restored pointed arches. A good many years ago a brick windmill was built within and upon the gateway; and within the tower, which is all that is left of this mill, is another arch with good mouldings, the inner foliated, having in the spandrels some fairly well-preserved carvings. There is also some vaulting with three bosses, and a piece of wall attached to the gateway: the latter probably formed part of the refectory. Until a few years ago the cattle which grazed on the neighbouring marshes could enter the gateway, but now it is surrounded by a railing which prevents their stumbling among and rubbing themselves against the crumbling masonry. But nothing has been done to protect the river bank, where the bones of the old monks of St. Benet's are often scoured from their unmarked graves.

According to the old chroniclers, the land on which the monastery stood was, in the eighth century, given by a local prince to a recluse named Suneman who, with other religious men, dwelt on it peaceably until the Danes ravaged East Anglia, demolished the hermitage, and killed its inmates. A century later a certain Wolfric followed the example of Suneman, and retired here; but when the Danes attained undisputed possession of the country, King Canute founded for the Benedictines the monastery of St. Benet-at-Holm. This monastery was a fortified house, and when the Conqueror sent a force against it, the monks, aided, no doubt, by the men of the neighbouring hamlets, were able to hold out for some time against the besiegers. But through the treachery of a captured monk named Ethelwald, the Normans eventually succeeded in entering the great gate and gaining possession of the monastery.   As a reward for his treachery, the monk had been promised the abbacy, and in fulfilment of this promise the Normans arrayed him in an abbot's robe, placed a mitre on his head, and went through the ceremony of installation. Then, disgusted with the man's conduct, they had him hanged above the gateway.[1]   Subsequent to this siege the history of the monastery is unexciting.   Many wealthy knights and nobles endowed it with lands and money, and when they died were buried in the fine abbey church ; distinguished guests were often entertained by the abbots, who amused them with falconry on the surrounding marshes.   Curiously enough, St. Benet's Abbey escaped the general suppression in 1537, its abbot at that time, William Rugge, being translated to the see of Norwich, to which the revenues of the abbey were also transferred.   He and his successors retained the title of Abbot of St. Benet-at-Holm, by right of which dignity the present Bishop of Norwich has a seat in the House of Lords. Previous to the Dissolution, the abbots had a residence or " grange " at Ludham, where parts of it are still embodied in the Hall Farm.   This grange afterwards became a country seat of the Bishops of Norwich.   The Hall Farm can be reached by a marsh wall or causeway which runs from the abbey gateway to the road which leads to the farm.

Almost opposite the gateway is a mile-and-a-half-long dyke leading to South Walsham Broad.   There are few more enjoyable things than a quiet row or a sail in a small yacht up this and other similar dykes in summer.   True, the tall reeds on either side hide the marshlands beyond them ; but this prevents one's attention being distracted from the wild flowers—the loosestrifes, willow-herbs, and hemp agrimonys —which deck the banks, and the birds which haunt these narrow water-courses.   It was while sailing up South Walsham Dyke that I saw a snipe standing on a post close to the water, and I shall never forget the perfect picture it made, nor the absolute disregard of human intrusiveness with which it looked about it from its elevated perch.   During that cruise I particularly noted how frequently snipes and redshanks were to be seen occupying similar positions, chosen probably

[1] It must be remembered that these stories are legendary.

because of the extended outlook they afforded. Swallow-tail butterflies are often plentiful on the marshes bordering South Walsham Dyke, and some of the little creeks, inlets, and cuttings made in the dyke banks by winter flight-shooters are full of treasures for the entomologist.

Although rather small, and by the luxuriance of its aquatic growths divided into two sheets of water, South Walsham is a very charming Broad, particularly that part of it entered by way of a narrow channel called the Weirs. It is a private Broad, but until recently it was generally supposed that the public had a right of way across it. For some time, however, there were occasional disputes between a riparian owner and the people of Ranworth, an adjoining village, as to whether this right of way extended to the inner and prettier portion of the Broad, and on Whit Monday of 1901 these disputes culminated in a rather lively scene. On that day, on hearing that some of the Ranworth people proposed making a public demonstration in support of the right they claimed, certain persons, presumably acting on behalf of the riparian owner, moored a large house-boat broadside across the narrowest part of the Weirs, blocking the channel leading to the Inner Broad. This in itself was a formidable obstacle for a fleet of small boats to encounter; and it was made the more so by having small hand fire-engines placed at its bow and stern, while from under the canvas of the house-boat a long glistening barrel was extended, resembling, according to an eye-witness of what took place, a Vickers-Maxim gun: in reality it was a long telescope from which the glass had been removed. During the afternoon several hundred people, among them the Vicar of Ranworth and the chairman of the Parish Council, assembled on the staithe, where they were approached by the riparian owner's agent and a Norwich solicitor. The former requested the crowd to leave the staithe; but the chairman of the Parish Council protested that the staithe was a public place, and until late in the day the villagers remained in possession of it. A good many uncomplimentary remarks were shouted to the persons on board the house-boat, but no attempt was made to force a passage through the Weirs. Subsequently the riparian owner established in a court of law his claim to the staithe; but when I visited South Walsham Broad a few weeks after the Whit-Monday proceedings, I found the Weirs open, and no attempt was made to stop me from sailing round the Inner Broad. Across the Outer Broad, which is entered by way of South Walsham Dyke, there is a right of way to South Walsham Staithe, from which the churches of St. Mary and St. Lawrence, both standing in the same churchyard, are distant about a mile. St. Lawrence's Church was partly destroyed by fire in 1827, and its tower is in ruins.

Quarter of a mile above St. Benet's Abbey is the mouth of the Ant, a river to be dealt with in the next chapter. Another mile or so, and the dyke is reached which leads to Ranworth Broad. To boats drawing no more than four feet of water this dyke is usually navigable; but cruisers in yachts of deeper draught generally continue their voyage to Horning Ferry, where they can land on the opposite bank to that on which the Ferry Inn stands, and stroll to Ranworth by the pleasant road which leads down to the ferry. Between St. Benet's Abbey and Horning Ferry there are two or three very pretty reaches; that which Horning Church overlooks from the left bank being perhaps the most charming up to that point. In this neighbourhood a few marshmen may occasionally be seen cutting peat by the riverside. The peat, locally called turf or hovers, is cut into square blocks, which are sold at a shilling a hundred. Rafts laden with these blocks often pass the Ferry Inn.

Ranworth is not the least delightful of the Broads lying between Acle and Wroxham; but the parish is more famous for having in its church one of the finest and best-preserved rood-screens in the county. Indeed, the committee of the Society of Antiquaries assert that as a whole there is "nothing of the sort remaining to equal it in England." "East Anglia," the committee's report states, "still contains a considerable number of painted screens, some of much merit, in its churches, but for delicacy and richness of detail that of Ranworth is unsurpassed. The beautiful diapers on the robes of the saints and apostles painted on the panels, and the elaborate flower-work which adds to and heightens the effect of the architectural features, make the whole composition suggestive of a great initial page of some splendidly illuminated manuscript." The paintings are said to recall the school of Meister Wilhelm of Cologne, and it is thought they may have been the work of German artificers who settled in Norwich during the fifteenth century. Especially to be noted are the figures of St. Lawrence and St. Michael, and the details of the vestments of many of the saints. The church has recently undergone a much-needed restoration; but, needless to say, the screen, which is as remarkable for the delicacy of its carved work as for the beauty of its paintings, has not been interfered with.

The Broad, like South Walsham, is private property; but there is a right of way across the eastern portion to the village. The western portion, which is divided from the other by reed beds, is a wild-fowl preserve and strictly private; formerly it was a noted place for decoying, very large quantities of duck, teal, and wigeon being captured during severe winters. The chief charms of the Broad in summer are its isolation, picturesque surroundings, lovely white water-lilies, and the glimpses one gets of yellow reed-stacks and old cottages and farmsteads on its shores; but it is seen at its best in autumn, when its reeds have attained their full height, and the leaves of its bordering trees have changed from green to crimson and gold.

While walking on a June day through Woodbastwick on my way to Ranworth, I came upon some marshmen reed-stacking close beside the road which leads down to Horning Ferry. It was rather late in the year for such work to be in progress, but I learnt that the reeds had been a long time drying, or they would have been stacked before. It was a characteristic Broadland scene, of which the chief features were the wide flat reed rafts being quanted up a dyke, the stacks with their light and dark layers of reeds, and the marshmen clad in clothes of a russet hue which harmonised well with the yellow reeds. On every side were flat, fenny lands, where purple-headed meadow thistles, dusky marsh cinquefoils, pale green marsh ferns, sweet gales, water-flags, and ragged robins grew amid young reeds, brown bents, and tawny and green rushes. I got into conversation with the reed-stackers, and learnt that in the neighbourhood of Woodbastwick the cutters reckon six sheaves to go to a fathom of reeds; while at Barton and elsewhere a fathom consists of five sheaves, the difference being due to the varying quality of the reeds. Ninety fathoms went to the making of a Woodbastwick reed-stack, so that each of the stacks which were being heaped up by the dykeside consisted of five hundred and forty sheaves.

The neighbourhood of Horning is one of the chief haunts of the Broadland flight-shooters, and some good bags have been made on the river between the ferry and St. Benet's Abbey. Some of the rare birds which have been shot in this district are in the Castle Museum at Norwich; but one of the finest cases of bitterns I know of is to be seen at the Ferry Inn, where is a splendid male bird shot by the landlord, and a female which fell to Mr. Christopher Davies' gun. A century ago the booming of the bittern was a familiar sound in Broadland; but in the Rev. R. Lubbock's time, the locally breeding bitterns had considerably decreased in numbers. The reed-beds of Hickling Broad, Heigham Sounds, and Catfield were the favourite haunts of the species; but in the middle of the last century it also bred at Ranworth, where one was shot in the act of feeding its young. Upton, near Acle, is believed to have been its last Norfolk nesting-place, for there two eggs were taken in 1868, and since then there is no trustworthy record of a nest having been found in the county. The marshmen used to call the bitterns "buttles"; and Dr. Emerson met an old man who had shot three in five minutes in Catfield Fen, where, the old man said, they used, like the herons, to alight on the trees. Almost every year I hear of bitterns being shot in Broadland, for these birds are early breeders, and the few which visit the district usually arrive before the close time begins. But even if they came a little later their fate would be the same. In the neighbourhood of Horning there is no escape for them, for in the shooting season the picturesque old Ferry Inn is frequented by almost as many gunners as there are anglers to be met there in summer.

There are some good colour effects among the old houses

of that part of the village of Horning which is passed about
half a mile above the ferry, where the river takes a sharp
bend to the left; but the impression they make upon the
voyager is forgotten as soon as he enters upon the first of
the delightful reaches which extend from this point up to and
beyond Wroxham Bridge. Above Horning the river banks
are in many places well wooded, and close beside the river
are several Broads. The presence of the first of these Broads
is betrayed, when Horning is passed, by the clamour of the
black-headed gulls, which have a colony on Hoveton Little
Broad. This Broad, which is about eighty acres in extent,
contains several small islets and some large beds of reeds,
upon and among which the gulls assemble in spring, make
their nests, and rear their young. But without special
permission it is impossible to witness the interesting sight
presented when the little gulls have been hatched off, for the
Broad is strictly preserved, and the little fluffy birds are
never disturbed while they swim about the edges of the open
pools and creep among the rushes and sedges. Even a finer
sight is presented by Hoveton Great Broad, which extends
from opposite the lower end of Wroxham Broad to a point
about a mile farther down-stream; for there a much larger
number of gulls breed yearly. But this Broad also is
preserved, and there are chains across the entrances to it from
the river. Yet even this colony is nothing like so large and
interesting as that at Scoulton Mere, near Watton in Norfolk.
There—where they are known as " Scoulton puits "—I have
seen the gulls rise from the water in such numbers as to
wholly blot out the trees behind them, and the clamour they
make is almost deafening. Beautiful birds are these wild-
crying puit-gulls, and their presence constitutes one of the
charms of Broadland. Whether seen circling above a Broad,
flying tern-like over a reed-bed, feeding on a Breydon flat,
or floating on the still water, they are delightful to behold ;
the gleam of their white wings against the blue of the
summer sky is a joy and an inspiration.

Not far from Hoveton Little Broad, on the south side of
the river, at a point where it turns sharply southward, is
Decoy or Woodbastwick Broad, which, like the Hoveton

Broads, is private water. It can scarcely be seen from the river—nor, as a matter of fact, can any of the Broads in this neighbourhood—on account of the riverside reeds, sallows, and alders. I have seen it suggested that it is a good plan for the visitor who is sailing in a large yacht to seat himself on the gaff of its mainsail, so that he may obtain a wider view of his surroundings; but not every one can enjoy the outlook, however picturesque it may be, from such an elevated and unsteady position. Nor is it necessary to climb so high to appreciate the loveliness of the river between Woodbastwick and Wroxham; while as for the beauties of Salhouse Broad, which yachts can enter by an opening on the left about a mile and a half above Hoveton Little Broad, they can be enjoyed at leisure. For Salhouse, though its fishing is preserved, is open to the public in so far that there is a right of way across it to the village. Connected with this Broad by a dyke is Salhouse Little Broad, a very pretty pool, where the fishing is also preserved. From a hill above the Little Broad the best view of the cluster of Broads in this neighbourhood can be enjoyed, not only the two Salhouse Broads, with their sylvan surroundings, but the Hoveton Broads and distant Wroxham, gleaming like a gem in a sylvan setting, contributing to the making of a scene of surpassing loveliness.

It is easy to understand how it is that so many pleasure-seekers are content, when they have once seen this part of the river, to confine their cruising to the Bure. There is charm and interest enough in a lovely little pool or "pulk" which lies about a quarter of a mile below Wroxham Broad to content the eyes and mind of a visitor all through a long summer day. The surface of the pool is almost covered with the flowers and leaves of white and yellow water-lilies, and close to the bordering rushes and sedges are pink patches of persicaria, so beautiful that even the chaste loveliness of the glorious nymphæas fails to distract attention from them. From among the dark green rushes coots and water-hens steal out at intervals, and swim to and fro until some involuntary movement betrays human presence and they disappear, the coots with a commotion which makes a drowsy warbler start singing as though in derision of the

water-fowls' fright. Then a reed bunting appears, and from
the top of a reed-stalk sings, with uplifted head, its plaintive
but rather unmusical song. Brilliant dragon - flies, " like
winged flowers or flying gems," some blue, others green, and
yet others with black - tipped wings, poise above the water,
wrapped in a film of wing-beats; perhaps a red admiral pays
a fleeting visit to the wild flowers which bloom around the
pool, and then, as the Ettrick Shepherd says, " floats awa'
in its wavering beauty . . . to some other nook of her
ephemeral paradise." Now and again a yacht or wherry
glides down the river, its white or dark sail showing for a few
moments through the foliage of the trees; but apart from
this there is nothing about the pool to suggest that all the
world is not contained within its sylvan and lacustrine fringe
of trees and reeds. Only a short distance away, beyond the
river, the marshlands are perhaps exposed to the full blaze
of a summer sun, just as when

> " A summer stillness held the land—
> The windmill drooped its idle sail—
> Trembling with heat, the crystal air
> Quivered and glistened, as it were
> A silver woven veil ; "

but over this shady pool a cool wind seems to breathe, and
on its banks a spring freshness and fragrance to linger.

Around Salhouse Broad alone there are a score of subjects
for an artist. The banks with their wild flowers and brown-
topped reed-maces, the rustic boat-houses, the inlets with
their coots and grebes, the reed and hay rafts, the staithe
with a wherry moored alongside, all tend to make the Broad
what it is—one of the most delightful and picturesque on the
Bure. And if the voyager lands and strolls through the
lanes and cornfields to the village church, he finds it hard
not to envy the dwellers in this lovely district. Inside the
church, which has a detached embattled tower, he finds, too,
something of interest, for it contains an old hour-glass stand,
a sanctus bell, and a crusader's tomb. After enjoying the
beauties of South Walsham, Ranworth, and Salhouse, such
a stroll is a pleasant break in a Broadland cruise, and the
voyager returns to the river better able to appreciate

10

Wroxham, which some have called the "Queen of the Broads."

So much has been written about Wroxham Broad that it is with diffidence I set down some of my impressions of it. As I have already suggested, it is not my favourite Broad; but I can quite understand how it is that thousands of visitors to Broadland cannot find words to express its beauties. Unless one lives near it and is often afloat on it, it is almost impossible to see it twice wearing the same aspect; in every season its moods are ever changing. One day it is as smooth as glass, mirroring every bird that flies over it and every flower that blooms along its reedy verge; the next its reeds are wildly tossing their feathery plumes, and the water is in such turmoil that a small boat is hardly safe upon it. And then, after a day of storm and drenching rain, comes an evening when the wind dies away into a gentle breeze that scarcely makes a whisper among the reeds, a glorious glow of amber radiance in the west lights up the Broad, and the night which follows is one of enchanting beauty. But before daybreak grey clouds overspread the sky, and in the dawnlight the surface of the Broad looks like a dull silver shield. Soon, however, the clouds begin to disperse, and some fine cloudscapes are reflected in the Broad as the rolling masses of white vapour are driven before the wind. By midday all the clouds are gone, and the water, where it is not agleam with sunlit ripples, is as blue as the sky. And of all the Broads Wroxham is, I think, the best on which to appreciate the changes the seasons bring—in spring, the fresh green of the woodlands on its western shore; in summer, the varied foliage of the trees and the luxurious aquatic growth of the swampy tracts which lie between the Broad and the river; in autumn, the glorious hues of the withering leaves; and in winter, the leafless reeds, golden as sun-ripened corn. Of its many aspects I hardly know which is the finest. If I have any preference, it is for that it shows on a calm November day when the sky is clear but a faint mist hangs over water and shore. Then the winter hues, which are often too hard and garish to be wholly pleasing, are softened and blended into something weird, mystic, and indescribably beautiful.

Wroxham Broad is about a hundred acres in extent; its length is about a mile and its breadth about three hundred yards. Although a decrease in its depth has become noticeable of late years, it is still deep enough to permit of the largest Broadland yachts sailing on it, and except near its shores there are none of those awkward shallows which make cruising on Hickling and Barton so difficult. On entering it from the river by the lower entrance—the only one now open—the voyager finds that on the west side the Broad is bordered by rising ground, for the most part well wooded but here and there revealing a green lawn in front of some half-hidden house; while on the east side a narrow tract of swampy ground, fringed with reeds and overgrown with sallow and alder scrub, separates the Broad from the river. According to a decision of the Superior Courts, the Broad is private property; but although a charge of half-a-crown a day is made for fishing—the money, I believe, going to the Norfolk and Norwich Hospital—and the riparian owners object to yachts being moored on the Broad except on regatta days, sailing and rowing are at all times freely permitted.

During the last week in July, when the cruising season is at its height, a slow procession of all kinds of Broadland craft makes its way up the Bure. At Acle and Horning regattas are held, in which not only regular racers but cruising yachts compete; then the whole fleet of wherries, pleasure-yachts, racers, and launches starts for Wroxham, where the season's most important regatta is usually held on the first and second of August. At nine o'clock in the morning of the opening day, the Broad presents a gay and lively aspect. By that time most of the cruising craft are moored and decked with bunting; but all day long small sailing boats keep arriving on the scene. Given fine weather, every one, from the chairman of the regatta committee to the juvenile occupants of the dilapidated marsh-boat which invariably gets in the way of the racers, is in good spirits. Yachtsmen don their whitest flannels and ladies wear their prettiest dresses; music is heard above the whispering of reeds and the fluttering of flags. In the neighbourhood of Wroxham Bridge a like gaiety prevails. Every train from Norwich, Yarmouth, and Cromer brings its load of yachting folk, whose yachts are ready to take them down to the Broad; blue-jerseyed crews stagger under the weight of well-filled hampers; trading wherries for a time become pleasure-craft, and are thronged with holiday-makers, each of whom is bent on enjoying himself to the utmost. In fact, every one realises that this is the great day of the Broadland season. Only the angler who, forgetting it was regatta day, has come to Wroxham for a quiet day's fishing on the Broad, and learns that there is not a rowing boat to be had " for love nor money," carries about with him a gloomy face.

At eleven o'clock the first race begins. Probably it is a race open to yachts of any rig or rating belonging to the local clubs. With a good sailing breeze, the yachts get away well together. The course is ten times round the Broad, and the winning of the race generally depends as much on skilful sailing as on the good qualities of the winner. One or two competitors usually drop out before the race is over : one gets her main sheet jammed ; another, after lagging hopelessly astern for an hour or more, vanishes through the entrance to the Broad. A certain yacht completes the ten rounds in about two hours ; but as her time allowance is fourteen minutes twenty-one seconds, ninety-nine of every hundred spectators do not know whether she is the winner until they read a report of the regatta in a newspaper next day. Then some of the cruising yachts have their turn. Great interest in this race is displayed by the cruisers in the competing craft, whose manifest glee when they are winning and depression when they are being badly beaten is often amusing. After a match for racing yachts, some of the wherries compete. This is a race which usually arouses some excitement ; but in the 1901 regatta only two wherries entered for the first day's race, some idea of which can be gathered from a report which appeared next day : " The starting gun fired at 4.15, and *Fawn* got away first. *Dauntless* was cruising about the top of the Broad, apparently in blissful ignorance that such a thing as a starting gun was required. She got off at last, but of course had no chance." The day's racing programme concludes with a dinghey race, for which there are usually a good many entries. Not infrequently, however, the start is made too late in the day, and the wind drops before the race is half over. When dusk comes down on the Broad a pretty scene is presented ; many of the yachts are illuminated, while rowing boats, carrying coloured lanterns, row in procession round the Broad. Across the still water comes the tinkling of banjoes and music of voices blended in merry choruses. Late into the night lights are burning in many of the yachts' cabins, and often the sounds of revelry cease only when the light of dawn is seen in the eastern sky. The second day's proceedings resemble the first day's. Races for racing and cruising yachts, wherries, dingheys, and open and half-decked boats, make up the programme, which is seldom completed until nightfall.

It is interesting to know that the very ancient ceremony of " beating the bounds " still survives at Wroxham. On a certain day in the year, the overseers, carrying willow wands decorated with milkwort, the rogation flower, and the heraldic colours of the parish, walk or " beat " round the parish bound- aries in order to see that no encroachments have been made and the old landmarks are still traceable. The " beaters " have the right to cross any lands, and pass through any garden or house through which the boundary lines run ; and they are accompanied by two lads, whose heads are knocked against several trees, posts, and other solid landmarks in order that they may remember them. When this ceremony was performed in 1901, the " beaters " succeeded in discovering an acre of land which for several years had been lost to the parish, and it was estimated that the expenses of the day's outing, which come out of the poor rate, were more than met by the rates recovered with this lost acre.

Just above Wroxham Bridge, opposite the King's Head Inn, is a small Broad, permission to visit which can be had at the inn ; but it is of little interest, and need not delay any one who is bent on exploring the navigable upper reaches of the Bure. From Yarmouth to Wroxham Bridge the Bure is, as East Anglian rivers go, a fairly wide stream ; but above the bridge it narrows considerably, though not so much as to make sailing very difficult. The scenery of these upper reaches is decidedly pretty, and between Wroxham and Coltishall the

banks are, from June to September, decked with the loveliest
of waterside wild flowers. After sailing some distance from
the bridge, a stranger may well be surprised that the church
he sees standing on a hill by the riverside is Wroxham
Church; but the mystery is explained when he is told that
a considerable portion of what is generally known as Wroxham
is situated in the parish of Hoveton St. John, and that the
parish of Wroxham really lies west of the bridge. The church,
embowered by trees, makes a very charming picture as seen
from the river, and is worth a close inspection on account
of its good Norman south doorway. It was while sailing
up the reach which the church dominates that I noticed, one
June day, the air filled with white down which the wind had
blown from the sallow catkins; everywhere little wisps of this
down were drifting before the breeze, and the water was
covered with them. Almost opposite the church is a small
sheet of water called Belaugh Broad, the last of the Bure
Broads, and one possessing no distinctive or remarkable
features.

Not far above Belaugh Broad is a channel, on the left,
called the Marl Pit Dyke, across the mouth of which a chain
is usually drawn so that yachts cannot enter it. This dyke
leads to a very pretty spot known as Little Switzerland,
which until a year or two ago was open to the public,
but which is now private. Next, on the opposite bank,
comes the village of Belaugh, with its church standing on
the summit of a steep bank sloping down to the riverside
gardens. In one of these gardens I was pleased to see a
notice-board set up which was in striking contrast to those
prohibitory ones which are such an unattractive feature of
the Bure's shores and Broads, for it stated that "Any one is
welcome to come in this garden." It seemed to me that
a great many of the riparian owners in Broadland might,
without experiencing any great annoyance, learn a lesson
from the owner of a pretty little garden in humble Belaugh.
The church, which a zealous Roundhead once said, referring
to its position, was "perked like one of the idolatrous high
places of Israel," contains a painted screen adorned with
figures of the twelve apostles; but the faces of the apostles

were obliterated by a "godly trooper," to whom, as to his brother Roundhead, they gave offence. The emblems held by the apostles are a shell and staff, a ship, two fishes, a chalice, a sword and casket, keys and a book, a lamb and book, a knife, a spear, a wallet of money, a fuller's bat, and a cross. The font is good fifteenth - century work, and there is an interesting brass (date 1471) to Sir John Curson, who is represented in full armour.

Coltishall, about two and a half miles above Belaugh, is in many respects a delightful place: undoubtedly it is the most picturesque waterside village in Broadland. Unlike Wroxham, it has not been spoilt by the erection of unsightly modern houses for the accommodation of visitors; for, in spite of its attractiveness, only a very few yachting parties extend their cruising above Wroxham Bridge. In its fine church, quaint old inns, houses with rounded gables, wherry-builders' yards, old malt-houses, charming gardens, well-wooded river reaches, cottage-bordered greens, fine old water-mill, and weather- and water-worn locks, it contains just the features calculated to enhance the charm of a village pleasantly situated by the riverside; and in its neighbourhood are enough places of interest to tempt a stranger to make it a centre from which to set out on summer rambles. The river flows close beside most of its picturesque buildings and delightful lawns and gardens, and pursues such a winding course that one might imagine it loves to linger in such a pleasant spot. One cannot help envying its inhabitants, even the humblest of whom has much to make him content, if not in love, with life. And even so long ago as the reign of Henry III. the Coltishall folk were eminently favoured, for that king "granted to all men, women, boys or girls born, or to be born, in this village of Couteshall, that they should be free from all villenage of body and blood, they and their families in all parts of England; and that they should not be forced to serve in any offices, for any one, unless they liked it; and that all frays or transgressions of bloodshed, bargains, and all quarrels and suits concerning the town of Couteshall should be determined every year before the king's officers at the letes there, and the natives of Couteshall should be free from toll by water and land in all fairs and markets throughout England, and from all stallage, poundage, and picage, being the king's tenants." The granting of this manumission to the thirteenth-century inhabitants of Coltishall was a great favour, for in those days most of the men, women, and children in English villages were villeins or slaves of the lords of the manors, who had the right to dispose of them to whomsoever they pleased.

That Coltishall was a place of some importance even in Saxon times, is indicated by the fact that a church was built here before the Conquest. The present church, an Early English building, has some curious figures on the battlements and west doorway. The large water-mill near the locks is not really in Coltishall but in Horstead. It is a fine old building, almost as picturesque as Constable's famous one at Flatford on the Stour; but, like all the Norfolk water-mills, it has a hidden undershot wheel, the force and fall of the Norfolk rivers not being sufficient to work an overshot wheel. A riverside footpath leads from the locks to Coltishall Bridge, from which Horstead Church, remarkable only for its ancient font, is distant about half a mile. In another direction, beyond the water-mill, a pleasant road leads to Heggatt Hall, a fine old Tudor house. Other roads lead to Tunstead, where the church has a curious raised platform behind the altar; and to Stratton Strawless, where, in the midst of woodlands, is one of the most interesting churches in this part of Norfolk. It contains some interesting memorials to members of the Marsham family, among them a fine black marble monument and a cross-legged mail-clad figure supposed to be that of Sir Ralph Marsham, who died in 1250.

Above Coltishall very few yachting parties care to go, for the eleven miles of river between Coltishall and Aylsham, though pretty, present no features not to be found on the upper waters of most small streams; and before Aylsham is reached three locks must be passed through and yachts' masts lowered for passage under no less than seven bridges. Should these obstacles fail to daunt the voyager, he finds at Oxnead some traces of the magnificent Hall which Sir Clement Paston built during the sixteenth century. This

Sir Clement, a distinguished naval commander in the reign of Henry VIII., and one who faithfully served Queens Mary and Elizabeth, is described as having been "a man of great stomach and courage," who "took a French galley, and in it the Admiral of France, called Baron St. Blancard, whom he brought into Englande, and kept him at Castor (Caister) by Yarmouth till he paid for his ransome seven thousand crowns over and beside the spoile of the said galleye; where among other things he had a cuppe and two snakes of goulde, which were the said Baron St. Blancard's; the which, during his life, he did upon high daies weare; and after left the same as a monument to his name." He is buried in Oxnead Church, where his marble tomb and alabaster effigy can be seen, also a long inscription in verse setting forth his remarkable qualities and brave deeds. He built Oxnead Hall in the reign of Queen Elizabeth. In 1676, when it was occupied by Robert Paston, Viscount Yarmouth, King Charles II. journeyed to it from Norwich and was lavishly entertained, an immense banqueting hall being built specially for the occasion.

Aylsham, which can be reached far more easily by road or rail than by river, stands in the midst of a district which has been called the "Garden of Norfolk." Formerly it was a place of considerable importance. Not only was the court of the Duchy of Lancaster held within it, but it was, in the reigns of the second and third Edwards, the chief centre of the linen manufacture. Its church, reputed to have been built by John of Gaunt, is of some interest; but from an antiquary's point of view cannot compare with those of Cawston and Salle, two fine Perpendicular buildings which can be visited from Cawston station. Both these churches have very fine and richly decorated roofs, curious tower galleries, and much heraldic carving. When he has seen these churches, especially noting at Salle a good brass, dated 1440, to Geoffrey Boleyn, the visitor can make a pleasant return journey to Aylsham by way of Blickling, where, on the site of the Boleyns' old home, is one of the finest Jacobean houses in England. The building of this fine old Hall was begun by Sir Henry Hobart, a Lord Chief Justice in the reign of James I.; it was finished by his son. The front of the house, as seen from the road, is very striking, its decorated entrance, surmounted by a clock-tower and flanked by square turrets, being led up to by a wide drive bordered by limes and clipped yews. It now belongs to the Marquess of Lothian, who on one day of the week (the precise day can be ascertained at Aylsham) admits the public to the chief rooms in the Hall and also to the park and gardens. Access can thus be had to a fine library of books selected by Mattaire, and containing many very old works and rare editions. This library is in a long gallery with a splendid Jacobean ceiling. Huge oak statues of Anne Boleyn and Queen Elizabeth, some good tapestry presented by the Empress Catherine of Russia to the second Earl of Buckinghamshire, and some portraits by Gainsborough, Reynolds, and Lely, can also be seen ; and in the gardens are some fountains and statues from the Pastons' old home at Oxnead.

So there is something to reward voyagers who ascend the Bure so far as it is navigable ; but as there is the return voyage to be considered, and all yachting parties do not care to confine their Broadland cruising to the Bure, it is, as I have suggested, often better to make the journey from Coltishall to Aylsham by rail. A day can then be devoted to visiting the places of interest just mentioned, and on the following morning the river can be descended as far as the mouth of one of the important tributary streams described in the two ensuing chapters. And after a few days spent on the pretty reaches of the Bure and among the many lovely nooks of the Bure Broads, cruisers will be the better prepared to appreciate the more unique and primitive charms of the Broads connected with the Ant and Thurne.

CHAPTER X

THE ANT AND ITS BROADS

THE Ant is a river which many yachting parties are unable to explore on account of its shallowness and the small arches of its bridges, so hundreds of pleasure-seekers who cruise in Broadland leave the district without seeing Barton Broad. As Barton is one of the loveliest Broads, this is to be regretted; but there is no help for it unless cruisers content themselves with the accommodation of a yacht drawing no more than three feet of water. Even then, if not careful, they are in danger of being " hung up," for Barton is very shallow except in the wherry channels, and the Ant, which is a very narrow stream, has, even below the Broad, some shallow reaches. When I cruise on this river, I much prefer to do so in my little flat-bottomed gun-punt the *Gipsy*, in which I can sail safely over the Barton shoals and explore many charming nooks inaccessible to even the smallest yachts. But the smallness of a Broadland gun-punt, and its lack of sleeping accommodation, prevent this type of boat being of use to the average cruiser.

It was in the *Gipsy* that I made a cruise on the Ant not long ago. Starting from Coltishall in the early morning, I loitered some hours among the Bure Broads, so that it was nearly dusk when St. Benet's Abbey came in sight, and I turned into the narrow river I had set out to explore. But on summer evenings the daylight seems loth to leave the open levels; for a long time after I had passed under Ludham Bridge there lingered an afterglow against which the windmills and distant rising ground were clearly defined. My progress was slow, for the many windings of the river seldom gave me, for more than a few minutes, the advantage of a light breeze that was dying away with the day. Above the bridge the only craft I encountered was a marsh boat, in which two lads were crossing from a riverside cottage to a neighbouring mill; the marshlands were deserted except by the grazing cattle; cottages and farmsteads were so few and far apart as each to suggest almost complete isolation; often the only sounds I heard were the rustling of the voles in the hovers and the harsh cries of the restless water-fowl. Gliding silently along, I watched the white mist rising from the water, the white moths fluttering amid the sedges, and the bats—the marsh-men's "flittermice"—flying waveringly along the banks and around the windmills. In a little creek I noticed a clump of reeds gemmed with glow-worms; not far from Irstead Church, which stands near the river bank a little way below the entrance to Barton Broad, I heard a nightjar churring among the trees.

In the deepening night-gloom little could be seen of the small flint and stone church; but it is worth visiting in the daytime, if only on account of its associations. For it was of this out-of-the-way parish on the verge of the marshes that William of Wykeham was rector, and a stained glass window to his memory has been put up in the church. In the days when he ministered to the spiritual needs of the Norfolk marshlanders, whose homes were then being devastated by the ravages of the Black Death, the tall, gaunt Hampshire priest was an almost unknown man; but when he died, after founding Winchester School and New College, Oxford, the world lost one of its best and greatest men. Fuller writes of him, "He was called *Long* from the height of his stature, though since it may apply to the perpetuity of his memory, which will last as long as the world endureth." He stayed but a few years in Norfolk, for there was more important work for him to do than could be done here; but Norfolk people are glad to believe that he learnt something of the needs of the nation while he dwelt in their county, and they do well to cherish his memory. For, as Dean Kitchen says, "very few are they to whom God has granted the happiness of being able to achieve so much in their time." A nineteenth-century rector of Irstead, the late Rev. John Gunn, was a noted geologist, who made the so-called Forest Bed his special study. The rectory formerly contained a fine collection of fossils taken from this remarkable deposit, which comes to the surface along the East Anglian coast. This collection is now in Norwich Castle Museum.

Irstead is the only village closely bordering on the Ant between the Bure and Barton Broad. The entrance to the Broad is a little way above that part of the river known as Irstead Shoals, where the bed of the stream is firm and pebbly. On the moonless night when the *Gipsy* glided on to the wide waters of the Broad, it was so dark that the channel posts were hardly visible, and sailing close to the fringing reed-beds I often heard the water-weeds which cover the shallows brushing against the sides of my boat. There were few stars to be seen, for clouds had drifted up from the west since sundown; a mist that was almost a fog hid the fenny shores. None of the landmarks—the trees, mills, and church towers—which in the daytime serve as guides to cruisers were visible; shoal water was only distinguishable by its dark patches of weeds and sparse growth of rush and sedge. But the little *Gipsy* sailed safely over the shallows, lifted her sharp bow over the matted water-weeds, and skirted the reed-beds like some large water-fowl seeking shelter for the night. Once she paused a moment, when some stout-stemmed rushes pressed close against her sides; but she dragged herself from their embrace and soon had a clear course again.

I had hoped to have run up Stalham Dyke and found lodgings for the night at a Stalham inn, but in the darkness I passed the mouth of the dyke without seeing it, and entered unknowingly the channel leading to Barton Staithe. A glimmering light tempted me to draw up at one of the landing-stages, and, stepping ashore, I found a group of marsh-men and wherrymen congregated on the settles outside a little "out-licensed" alehouse, which, however, was closed for the night. Knowing little about Barton—or Barton Turf, as the village is called, presumably on account of its having been largely concerned in the turf-cutting industry—I was uncertain as to whether I should find in the village a bed for the night; but my mind was soon set at rest. For, in response to my greeting and anxious inquiries, there stepped out of the darkness a genial wherryman, who offered to conduct me to his brother's house. Gladly accepting, I followed him up the road from the staithe to the village. Half an hour later I was sleeping soundly in as comfortable quarters as I have discovered in Broadland.

I awoke to find the sunlight flooding into my room and the fragrance of flowers stealing in at the window. Strolling down to the Broad, I could hardly believe that a few hours before I had lost my way on it. But a Barton villager whom I encountered assured me that I was by no means the first person who had done so, and that he himself, after an evening's eel-babbing, had been overtaken by a fog and compelled to spend a night on the Broad. For a fog magnifies a small clump of sedges until it looms as large as a reed-bed, and familiar landmarks seen through the mist assume strange and deceptive forms.

On that bright summer morning Barton Broad was seen at its best. A strong breeze had blown away the night-mists and was making the reeds and gladden bow before it, while wetting their green blades with splashes of spray. Two or three wherries were drawn up at the staithe, which with its old wooden sheds and reed, rush, and log stacks in the foreground, and a cottage or two among trees in the background, looked very picturesque. There was a group of marshmen outside the alehouse, where they often stay all day ; for a marshman by working three days in the week often earns as much money as a farm-hand who works seven, and he prefers to divide his week into equal portions for labouring and lounging. So, at any rate, said the wherryman who had come to my aid the night before, and the loungers did not contradict him. And they only grinned when he went to remark upon the fact that although when the marshmen went out babbing they invariably grumbled about the small number of eels they caught, there was always a large quantity missing when an eel-box was broken open in the night.

Freed from her moorings, the *Gipsy* was soon scudding across the flashing waters of the Broad, and for an hour or more I enjoyed a most exhilarating sail. There were two or three small yachts cruising up and down the channels, and it seemed to me I was rather envied by their occupants when they saw my little boat skimming safely over the shallows and along the edge of the reed-beds. A heron seemed indignant at my intrusion into one of his favourite haunts, for when I turned into a little inlet where the white water-crowfoot was in full bloom, the handsome bird rose suddenly within a few yards of me, greeting me with a loud, harsh cry. Then I headed again for the open water, where little wavelets slapped the *Gipsy's* sides and washed over her forward deck. But she shook the water from her like a water-bird after diving, and seemed to revel as much as I did in the freshness of the breeze. In Stalham Dyke, which I entered after this inspiriting sail, the water, in spite of the strong breeze, was scarcely ruffled, for the reeds were well " up," and in places grew so densely as to keep off the wind. So my progress became a more leisurely one, and I had ample time to admire the lovely white water-lilies for which the dyke is famous. There are people, whose knowledge of Broadland is confined to the more frequented Broads, who assert that the white water-lily is becoming rather rare in the district on account of its being so often gathered by visitors; but if they entered Stalham Dyke at any time during June or July, they would have no further fears as to the fate of this lovely flower. For among the large beds of reeds and rushes which now represent the " grown-up " Sutton Broad, there are acres and acres of water covered with white lilies, presenting a scene of floral loveliness not easily to be forgotten. Growing amid the smooth dark rushes, the lilies bloom in a green twilight, and the purity of their snowy petals is preserved far longer than is the case when they are exposed to the glare and heat of the sun. It is said that the white water-lily is seen nowhere in greater perfection than in the neighbourhood of Oxford; but I doubt whether even there it attains the size and beauty it does on Sutton Broad.

Much of the land bordering Stalham Dyke has only recently been reclaimed, and even now there are swampy tracts where it is hardly safe to set foot. On these quaking fens the sweet gale grows, and with it some lovely orchids and the graceful marsh fern. Formerly the royal fern was also to be found here in abundance; but I fear that it has met with the fate which some have dreaded for the white water-lily. As at Wicken Fen in Cambridgeshire, there survive in these swamps many of the old fen flowers which soon disappear from lands which are drained sufficiently to be used as grazing-grounds, and with them linger certain entomological rarities which favour such localities, and which, there is every reason to believe, will be lost to the country when the last of these fenny tracts is reclaimed. On hot summer days little clouds of midges hover over the reeds and sedges; gnats with antennæ twice the length of their frail wings alight on the decurrent reed-blades; and butterflies and dragon-flies are seen fluttering and poising everywhere. And the wild flowers which these insects and the moths fertilise flourish——the creamy meadow-sweet, the tall cat valerian, the hemp agrimony, the giant willow-herb, the purple and yellow loosestrifes, the meadow rue, and the strangely shaped orchids whose pink and purple spikes pierce the ruddy and golden bog mosses. But such swamps as these flowers grow in in rank luxuriance are rare, and in a few years, unless the sea again breaks in upon the low-lying levels of Broadland, there will be none of them left. Sutton Broad is now a Broad only in name, and several of the Broads marked on old maps of the district have wholly disappeared. Over the sites of some of them the mowing machines pass, cutting down hay crops where the reeds used to wave in the wind. As time goes on the reed and rush cutters will find their occupations gone, and they will have to seek other means of livelihood. This will be no easy matter, for the men of the rivers and marshes do not take kindly to changes. "A Norfolk Lament" in the *Eastern Counties Magazine* well expresses the views of one of them. In it an old marshman is made to say——

> "They're a sluggin' an' widenin' miles o' the deeks;
> I reckon the whool mash 'ull sewn ha'e to goo;
> An' us old mashmen 'ull fare like the freeaks
> I see last summer at Barnum's shoo.

.   .   .   .

Paarson say, ' Bill, yew dew narthin but growl ! '
  Well, bor ! I reckon theer's plenty o' rayson.
Whass become o' the flightin' fowl ?
  I never see fifty the whool o' last sayson.
Whass become o' the gre't deeak eeals ?
  Shillun a stoon we wuz glad to get for 'em.
Gone ! with the mallards an' snipes and teeals !
  If ye want any now yew ha' got to sweat for 'em."

Here we have a like complaint to that which the fenmen
made about the reclaimers two or three centuries ago. At
present, however, there are plenty of reeds and rushes around
Sutton ; early in the year the dry banks are almost covered
with stacks of them, and laden reed-rafts are continually being
towed or quanted up and down the dyke.

In the little town of Stalham there is not much to interest
the visitor, but it is a convenient place for Broadland cruisers
to take in stores. About a mile from the town, however, is
the fine church of Ingham, which contains some good tombs
with effigies. Formerly it possessed some very fine brasses,
but they were stolen nearly a century ago. This church is
of interest because it was at one time made collegiate in
connection with a college or priory of the order of Mathurines.
This order, which was founded in the twelfth century, possessed
only four houses in England, and the largest of these was
attached to Ingham Church, where some ruins of it can still be
seen. Its sacrist lived in the double parvise over the south
porch. The greater part of the church was rebuilt by Sir
Miles Stapleton, who also built the priory, and whose altar-
tomb is in the chancel. In an arch on the north side of the
chancel is the tomb and effigy of Sir Oliver de Ingham,
who under Edward III. was Constable of Bordeaux and
Seneschal of Gascoigne and Aquitaine. The knight's figure
is clad in mail, and at the back of the arch in which it rests
are faint traces of a mural painting. From Ingham Church
it is about half an hour's walk to Hickling Broad, which,
although not more than three miles from Stalham by road,
is a great distance by water.

When, the wind having died away, I rowed down Stalham
Dyke to Barton Turf, I found, just before entering the Broad,
an eel-sett spread across the dyke. The eel-catcher, who was

seated in the stern of a small house-boat drawn up on the bank, prepared to lower a part of his net so that the *Gipsy* could pass over it; but being in no hurry to get back to the staithe, I landed and chatted a while with the lonely fisherman. It was early in the season for sett-working, and very few eels were "running"; but so long as there was a chance of catching any the old man was quite content to spend the greater part of the night by the dykeside. But he was glad to have company; and finding that, like himself, I was a Norfolk man, he soon grew confidential. We talked about will-o'-the-wisps, or "lantern men," as he called them, and he said it was ten years since he last saw one; but he could remember the time when they were often seen dancing over the swampy lands which border the dyke. They were, he assured me, a kind of "morth" (moth), and he knew a man, who lived "up Wayford Bridge way," who had shot one, "but he never found it." In this he was less fortunate than a Barton Turf villager whom I subsequently met, for *he* had seen one in the daytime, and it was like a "devil's coach-horse" beetle! The end of its tail was its luminous part, which it turned up after the fashion of a scorpion! But I fancy that villager was confusing will-o'-the-wisps with glow-worms. The eel-catcher had seen his "morths" flying about over the marshes. Though not a very old man, he had known the time when Sutton Broad was open water, and he had often heard bitterns booming among its bordering reeds. And again I heard the familiar complaint that there "worn't no fowl to speak on nowadays, an' sune there wouldn't be eels enow in th' rivers to make it wuth while to use a sett." But, in spite of all the marshmen say, there are plenty of gunners on the marshes in winter, and I fancy there are quite as many eel-setts worked now as there have ever been.

I learnt that there were still some Hewitts among the Barton Turf marshmen. This interested me, for in Lubbock's time the Hewitts of Barton Turf—that is to say, the men among them — were all fishermen and gunners, gaining a livelihood by methods which Protection and Preservation Acts have to a large extent made illegal. It was, according to Lubbock, one of the Hewitts who discovered a new way of taking tench. He had noticed the sluggish nature of these fish, especially in sultry weather, and believed he could take them with his hands. He tried to do so, and succeeded. First he rowed his flat-bottomed marsh boat towards the weed-beds where the lusty fish lay close to the surface of the water. Generally there was a small shoal of them, and as he approached they darted away in all directions. Marking the spot—a bubble bursting on the surface of the water would indicate it—where one of them stopped, he slowly drew near it, then, baring his right arm to the shoulder, gently moved aside the weeds and peered among them until he saw the fish. Having found it, he carefully placed his hand under it, raised it gently but rapidly, and lifted it into the boat, where, says Lubbock, who loved to record such practices of the Broads-men, it " often remains motionless for full a minute, and then begins apparently to perceive the fraud practised upon it." The main thing to be avoided in this method of tench-taking is, he adds, the " molesting " of the fish's tail. An experienced " feeler " for tench would easily capture five or six dozen fish in a day; he himself had seen fifteen or sixteen good-sized fish taken in a short time. Hewitt's success induced other Broadsmen to follow his example, with the result that many of them soon got to prefer using their hands rather than a net in taking tench in shallow waters. Some of them do so to-day; but whether because they thus capture the largest fish, or because, as Lubbock asserts, the bow-nets are sometimes " examined " (!) before the owner takes them up, I cannot say.

Next morning I returned to the Bure, but on other occasions of my visiting Barton Turf I have spent more time there. The village is a very charming one, as a few outsiders have discovered, for they come and stay there every summer, and its church possesses a screen which some consider superior to that at Ranworth. On its panels are painted sixteen figures; but these, apparently, are not all by one hand, for some are much better done than .others. Among the saints repre-sented is St. Osyth, an East Anglian saint seldom seen on rood screens. She was, according to the monkish chroniclers, a daughter of King Frithwald and Wilburga, daughter of Penda, King of Mercia. She was educated by St. Modeven, who afterwards placed her in one of her nunneries. Exceptional Divine interest was soon manifested in her, for, being sent one day with a message to St. Modeven, and being drowned on the way, the spot where her body lay was revealed in a vision, and she was restored to life after being dead three days. Forced by her parents to marry Sighere, King of the East Saxons, she seized an opportunity of taking the veil; and her husband, finding her bent on living a reclusive life, built her a nunnery at Chirk, now St. Osyth, in Essex. This nunnery was plundered and destroyed by the Danes, who, failing to make St. Osyth abjure her faith, cut off her head. Immediately this was done the wondrous martyr took her severed head in her hands and walked to a neighbouring church, where, having knocked at the door, she fell down dead. She was afterwards looked upon as the patron saint of housekeepers, and on the Barton Turf screen is represented carrying keys. St. Apollonia, the dentists' saint, is also represented; and on a fine screen in the south aisle are depicted the royal saints Olaf, Edmund, Edward the Confessor, and Henry VI. In the vestry two interesting brasses with English inscriptions are preserved. At Beeston, a neighbouring village, the church has a good screen on which, as on that at Belaugh, the twelve apostles are portrayed. The western arm of Barton Broad extends to the bounds of the estate of Beeston Hall, for many generations the seat of the Prestons. Among the heirlooms of this family is an emerald ring given to Jacob Preston by Charles I. just before his execution.

Most writers of Broadland guides have hesitated to advise cruisers to ascend the upper waters of the Ant—that is to say, that part of the river which lies between Stalham Dyke and North Walsham—and although the country between Barton and North Walsham contains much that is interesting, and its scenery is, in places, exceedingly pretty, I can commend their hesitancy. For since the railway came to North Walsham and took much of the carrying trade out of the wherrymen's hands, only a few wherries have regularly used the river, and parts of it have become almost unnavigable. Even when its channel was quite clear, only small yachts could sail up it; and it has always been so narrow and winding that cruisers on it have generally found rowing or quanting the speediest methods of progression. There are, however, signs of improvement. Wayford Bridge has been rebuilt and its arch span widened.

Dilham with its lock and bridge, and Honing with its leafy long lane leading to the church, are among the pretty villages which the cruiser on the upper Ant can visit; but Worstead, about a mile from Briggate Lock, is more interesting than either of them. For Worstead was once an important town, the centre of a manufacture to which it gave its name, and its church is one of the finest in Norfolk. It was built during the most flourishing period of the town's history, and dates from the latter half of the fourteenth century. Its fine tower, 120 feet high, is in the Late Decorated style of architecture, and has some very interesting sound-holes with good tracery. The nave, which is Perpendicular, has a wide hammer-beam roof, and is divided from the chancel by a carved oak screen adorned with paintings of saints. The font is Perpendicular, and has an elegantly carved tabernacle cover surmounted by a floral finial. Across the tower arch extends a very fine and perfect gallery, erected at the beginning of the sixteenth century; the chancel screen is a century older. The screen at the west end is adorned with modern paintings, copied from pictures by Sir Joshua Reynolds. The south porch, which has a parvise, is well carved and groined, and the north doorway is interesting. Apart from the church, there is little in Worstead to suggest its former prosperity. It is now a village—a very pretty one, but, except for its church, in no way remarkable. Daniel Defoe, however, when he visited this neighbourhood in 1722, was much impressed by it. Between Cromer and Norwich, he wrote, "are several good market towns and innumerable villages, all diligently applying to the woollen manufacture, and the country is exceedingly fruitful and fertile, as well in corn as in pastures; particularly, which was very pleasant to see, the pheasants were in such great plenty as to be seen in the stubbles like cocks and hens—a testimony, though, by the way, that the county had more tradesmen than gentlemen in it; indeed, this part is so entirely given up to industry, that what with the seafaring men on the one side, and the manufactures on the other, we saw no idle hands here, but every man busy on the main affair of life, that is to say, getting money."

In North Walsham, too, there is a fine church, which, like that at Aylsham, bears the arms of John of Gaunt. It is a Perpendicular building; but its tower, which, with its spire, rose to a height of 147 feet, is now in ruins. The font has a good tabernacle cover with a pelican for its finial; and some screen panels, discovered in 1844, when the church was undergoing restoration, have been placed across the aisles and chancel. On the north side of the chancel is the tomb of Sir William Paston, who died in 1608. The effigy on this tomb, the work of a London mason, was set up during Sir William's lifetime; it represents him in full armour. He was the founder of the local Grammar School, at which Lord Nelson and Archbishop Tenison were scholars. Several of the Norfolk churches contain memorials to members of the famous Paston family, but the finest is in Paston Church, about four miles from North Walsham, where is a remarkably good monument, the work of Nathaniel Stone, to Catherine, wife of Sir Edmund Paston, who died in 1628. In the sculptor's diary the following entry has reference to this tomb: " In 1629 I made a tomb for my Lady Paston, and set it up at Paston, and was very extraordinarily entertained and pay'd for it £340." Another Sir William Paston, a judge in the reign of Henry IV., is also buried in this church. Other monuments by Stone are to Sir Edward and Sir Edmund Paston, and there is a brass bearing this inscription—

" Here Erasimus Paston and Marye his wyffe enclosed are in claye
 Which is the restinge place off fleache untill the latter daye
 Off sonnes thre & daughters nyne the Lord them parents made
 Ere cruell death did worke his cruell spite or fykell lyff did fade."

Of the Pastons' old home, from which many of the famous *Paston Letters* were written, the only trace is an old farm barn. The house stood not far from the coast, which in the fifteenth century seems to have been exposed to the attacks of pirates;

for we find Agnes Paston writing to her son that the pirates
" have thys weke takn iiij vesselys of Wyntyrton, and
Hapisborough, and Ecles.   Men be sore aferd for takyn of me
for ther ben x grete vesselys of the enemyis.   God give grace
that the see may be better kepte than it is now, or ellys it
shall ben a perylous dwellyng by the se cost."

A short distance from North Walsham, on the Norwich
road, stands an old stone cross erected to commemorate the
Litester insurrection of 1381.

But North Walsham and its neighbourhood can hardly be
called a part of Broadland.   When Barton Broad has been
crossed, no Broads of any size or importance retard the seaward
flow of the narrow, winding Ant.   True, there are a few
little pools—all that is left of what were once wide expanses
of water—but they in no respect differ from those which vary
the course of nearly every lowland stream.   Antingham Ponds,
in which the Ant has its source, are so shallow and " grown-
up " that they are not worth visiting, even if the channel which
leads to them were navigable.   At no time were they largely
visited by Broadland cruisers, and the time cannot be far
distant when even such a crazy craft as that in which Mr.
Christopher Davies adventured upon them will hardly find
open water enough to sink in.

CHAPTER XI

THE THURNE AND ITS BROADS

COMPARED with the Ant, the Thurne is a wide river, between Kendal Dyke and Thurne Mouth so deep that the largest Broadland craft can cruise on it. Flowing through one of the wildest and least populated districts in Norfolk, it is undoubtedly the best river for such voyagers as come into Broadland for a restful holiday, and they may well be content to devote the whole of their time to its pleasant waters, its fine Broads, and the wild, lonesome seaboard which lies a little way beyond the borders of Horsey Mere. If Broadland consisted only of this river, Hickling Broad, Horsey Mere, and Heigham Sounds, it would be a district unique within the borders of Britain; for while the beauty of the famous Bure Broads is of a kind not confined to Broadland, the charm and loveliness of Heigham Sounds, and its wide, wild marshes, are such as cannot be enjoyed elsewhere in England. In Heigham Sounds we have, as at Rockland, a Fenland mere in its primitive state, such as Whittlesea was ere the reclaimers came and transformed its reedy waters into pastures and cornfields. Almost unchanged in aspect from what it was a thousand years ago, secrets of the early world seem to be whispered still among the reeds; and there are times—as when dusk comes down on land and water —when it seems no hard matter to read them. Surrounded by scenes whose beauty man has done nothing or little to mar —where the handiwork is all Nature's—it is easy for the solitary cruiser to become a primitive child of Nature, a " summer-saturated heathen," and in so mingling his identity with hers, to drink in delight from the fountain-head of pleasure. After a few hours spent amid such scenes, he may become conscious of a return to primitive simplicity of thought and inclination, of an ability hitherto, even if possessed, unexercised, to distinguish the essential from the superfluous, and to rest content with the things which nearly every man can claim as his own. And unless he has lost one of the greatest gifts bestowed on man, it is possible for him, in a little while, to understand what Thoreau meant when he wrote that he had " never found the companion who was so companionable as solitude."

To a district where survives such untarnished loveliness and primevalness, there could hardly be a more fitting portal than the mediæval bridge which spans the river at Potter Heigham, and which, in part at least, dates from the twelfth century. Up to this point, and for a mile or so beyond it, the voyager's course lies between the widespreading marshes of the West Flegg and Happing Hundreds. On a declivity near the mouth of the river, on the east side, is the little village of Thurne, which gave its name to the stream. The church, which stands on the top of the hill, is a building in mixed styles, remarkable for containing one of the few existing bells made by William de Norwyco, a fourteenth century bell-founder. A good view of the ruins of St. Benet's Abbey can be obtained from the tower, in which there is a round hole that was formerly, tradition says, used as a " lookout," through which signals were made to and received from the inmates of the abbey. The nave has a good hammerbeam roof with carved bosses.

On a map of Norfolk by Tacden, issued in 1797, a Broad as large as that at Oulton is marked as being situated near the village: it was called Thurne Broad. All traces of it have disappeared, and Womack Broad, once a fairly extensive sheet of water on the opposite side of the river, seems likely at no very distant time to become equally indistinguishable.

Not very long ago, Womack Broad, which is connected with the river by a long dyke, was of fair size; now there is little more than an acre of it—a widening of the channel by which the wherries reach the village of Ludham at its north end. But it still has some pretty nooks and corners where marshmen's boats are moored or a cottage stands near its banks; and it is

worth visiting not on this account only, but because Ludham
Old Hall, once a residence of the Abbots of St. Benet's Abbey,
can easily be reached from Ludham Staithe. Very little of
the original building is left, for in 1611 it was almost destroyed
by fire; but a brick chapel, which Bishop Harsnet built when
the house came into the possession of the Bishops of Norwich,
is still standing, and is used as a barn. The village church is a
Perpendicular building, chiefly interesting on account of its
well-carved screen and font.

Between Womack Dyke and Potter Heigham are two or
three fine old windmills, good specimens of the picturesque
structures whose work, it is to be feared, will, at no very
distant date, be done by ugly brick or corrugated iron housed
steam-pumps. A spare half-hour may be well spent in
examining one of these old mills, especially if the millman
is present to explain the working of it. The interior is
often an eerie place, badly lighted, and care is needed in
climbing the steep, ladder-like flights of steps which connect
the floors; but the view from the top of the mill repays
one for the climb. The machinery consists of little besides
a long perpendicular shaft and some large cogwheels; but
the latter look very formidable, being usually without any
protective casing, and the racket made by some of the
mills as soon as they are set going is simply deafening.
Even on calm nights strange noises are heard in the dark
chambers — faint sighings, creakings, and groanings, rats
scampering over the floors, and birds fluttering among the
roof beams; so it is easy to understand why some of the
mills are believed to be haunted. Some, too, have tragic
histories; for lone millmen, compelled to stay all night in
them when a strong wind was blowing and the dykes were
filled with flood-water, have been caught and crushed in the
great cog-wheels. And tales are told of mills near Horsey
and Hickling having been used as storehouses by the smugglers
who ran cargoes on the East Norfolk coast.

Potter Heigham Bridge has been for a long time a favourite
subject with artists, but its surroundings have changed greatly
of late years. For Potter Heigham has become a popular
yachting centre, and along the banks of the river, both above

and below the bridge, there are now innumerable boat-sheds.
The old Waterman's Arms has been pulled down and a new inn
built, and it will not be surprising if before very long something is said about building a new bridge.   But to remove
the old structure would be a great pity, for Potter Heigham
Bridge, with its rounded central arch and flanking pointed
ones, is a fine example of mediæval bridge-building.   A few
years ago the village was almost as mediæval as the bridge.
Then it was that the curious gate-sign of the Falgate Inn
bore the lines—

> "This gate hang high
> But hinder none,
> Refresh and pay
> And travel on"—

an inscription which has since been repainted and, by being
made grammatical, made commonplace.   But this was at a
time when weight was attached to the sayings of old Mrs.
Lubbock of Irstead, a kind of "wise woman" or Mother
Shipton, who said, "Blessed are they that live near Potter
Heigham, and double blessed them that live in it."   She
was an uncanny old woman, this Mrs. Lubbock, for most
of her prognostications were of wars and rumours of wars.
She it was who stated that "the town of Yarmouth shall
become a nettle-bush"; that "England shall be won and
lost three times in one day, and that principally through an
embargo to be laid upon vessels."   "There is to come," she
added, "a man who shall have three thumbs on one hand,
who is to hold the King's horse in battle; he is to be born
in London, and be a miller by business.   The battle is to be
fought at Rackheath-stone Hill, on the Norwich road.   Ravens
shall carry the blood away, it will be so clotted.   The men are
to be killed, so that one man shall be left to seven women,
and the daughters shall come home and say to their mothers,
'Lawk, mother, I have seen a man!'"   Broadland cruisers
may find comfort in her forecast that "bridges shall be pulled
up, and small vessels sail to Irstead and Barton Broad"—
a prophecy which seems to point to the removal of that
awkward obstacle to navigation, Ludham Bridge.   But nowadays Potter Heigham moves with the times, and its "wise

women" are those enterprising village housewives who, as they significantly tell you, "take in" visitors.

A little way above the old stone bridge another bridge spans the river—an ugly iron one, over which runs the coast railway from Yarmouth to Cromer. Then, on the right, a short distance back from the river, the tower of the ruined church at Bastwick is seen. From this point onward to Kendal Dyke the scenery is, for the most part, a repetition of that of the lower waters of the Thurne; but the natural grouping of the waterside cottages and windmills is, in one or two places, even more picturesque than any to be seen below the bridge. In little inlets in the banks several house-boats are moored; but these do not all belong to the eel-catchers, some being moored here for the convenience of their pleasure - seeking owners. The eel-catchers, however, are much in evidence, and the setts between Potter Heigham and Heigham Sounds are considered to be by far the best situated in the Broadland rivers. For when the eels are "running," immense shoals of them leave Hickling Broad, Horsey Mere, and the Sounds, and on their way to the sea they must all pass through Kendal Dyke and down the Thurne.

Kendal Dyke in itself differs in no way from many other dykes and channels in Broadland; but there are many men, lovers of wild life and wild beauty, to whom it is, as it were, a water-path leading to a natural paradise. It is a waterway along which, if it were possible, every fresh voyager in Broadland should pass unconscious of what is before him; the impression made upon him by a glimpse of Heigham Sounds would then be uninfluenced by previous surmises and imaginings. For it is impossible for either the artist in colours or the artist in words to do anything like justice to this wild wilderness of reeds and water, and so convey a definite idea of it to one who has never seen it. To attempt to do so is trying to describe the indescribable; one can only give one's own impressions, and these, it seems to me, unsatisfactorily. For the average man has no opportunity of coming in contact with the absolutely primeval in Nature; and when he sees something which in a way suggests it, he is at a loss to find

words or other means to give expression to his feelings. He
has been born too late to have known what England was
like before it became, what an American writer has called it,
" a well-groomed country "; too late to have known it as a
land of wide forests, heaths, and fens. So, when he is suddenly
brought into the midst of a district which wears an aspect
borne by a great part of his native land centuries before he
became a dweller in it, and which strikes him at first as being
crude, untamed, and as it were unorthodox, it takes him some
time to get in harmony with his surroundings and adapt
himself to their moods.

In Heigham Sounds we have left to us a typical Fenland
mere of the pre-reclamation days. In all there are something
like 125 acres of water; but at first glance it is hard to
believe it, for some of the reed-beds have so increased in size
of late years that much of the open water which lies beyond
the largest pool, through which a channel runs, is hidden.
To estimate the size of such a sheet of water is difficult. On
almost every side the reeds, during the greater part of the
year, confine the cruiser's outlook, and there are no neighbouring heights to command a good view of the Sounds. Beyond
the reeds is a low, flat, fenny country, where rushes and sedges
are almost as plentiful as meadow grass. Here and there is
a solitary windmill, guardian and preserver of its surrounding
marshes. In one direction only is the outlook varied; there
a fir copse shows its blue-green foliage above the reeds and
against the sky. Everywhere else reeds and water, reedmace
and fen sedge; for of such are Heigham Sounds.

Little enough to rave about, some may say; and if they
come to the Sounds expecting to find a pretty Broad, like
Ranworth, Salhouse, or South Walsham, they will be disappointed, for there is nothing pretty about the Sounds.
But there is beauty, fascination, charm; and if one stays
long enough on this watery wilderness he will in time become
enthralled. For he will find that almost every day it has a
new aspect, a different mood, and that almost every hour
aspect or mood undergoes a subtle change. Colours such as
he never even dreamt were to be found on Nature's palette, will
be spread over the rippling water and will dye the quivering

air-films which veil the whispering reeds. Mirages, evanescent and beautiful, will bewilder him at noontide; mist-wraiths, vague and mystic, will haunt him at dusk and dawn. For him the wind among the reeds will make weird music, and at times whisper strange secrets of the early world in his ear. If he has any imagination, he will see visions and dream dreams. He will see not only coots, grebes, and herons, which are always around him, but the buzzards hovering over the fens and the ruffs dancing before the reeves among the sedge; and he will hear not only the "chucking" of the reed birds and the "chinging" of the titmice, but also the booming of the bittern and the creaking of the black tern. In the eel-catcher rowing his punt towards his sett he will see an old-time Broadsman spreading his hundred-yards-long draw-net and hauling it in so laden with roach and bream that he can hardly get it on board his boat again. Broadland as it was in the past, before Wild-Fowl Protection and Fisheries Preservation Acts altered the lives of the men of the rivers and marshes, will become as real to him as the Broadland of to-day.

For it was on and around Heigham Sounds that the characteristic wild life of Broadland was most abundant in those bygone days, and it is here that even now it can be studied under more favourable conditions than anywhere else in the district. The bitterns are gone, the black terns are gone, and so too are the avocets and spoonbills, the ruffs and reeves; but coots, water-hens, and grebes abound, and among the reeds can still be found that rare and handsome little fen bird, the bearded titmouse. This little bird, it is sometimes feared, will one day be numbered among England's lost breeding birds, for slowly yet surely its favourite haunts, the reed-girt marshland meres, are disappearing, and now that it has become very rare, the gunner, in spite of the legal protection afforded it, seldom spares it. Mr. J. H. Gurney, who has written a valuable and interesting monograph on this species, estimates that there were in 1898 not more than a hundred of these birds left in Broadland, and that of these the greater number frequented Heigham Sounds, where about half a dozen nests were reported to have been built in the spring of that year. In the spring and summer of 1901 they appeared to be fairly numerous among the reed-beds of the Sounds; every time I was there I heard their musical call-note and saw them taking short flights over the rustling reeds. Once or twice in the springtime, before the young reeds were "up," I caught a glimpse of one of them hanging first sideways and then almost head downwards on a last year's yellow reed-stalk; but for fear of disturbing them I did not try to find a nest. It was a sight worth seeing to watch the little acrobat going through his performance.

Mr. Gurney says that "in its nest and all that concerns the bearded tit the protective colour may be traced. The old cock's black moustachios . . . are like the dark corners in the reeds, and his tawny colouring harmonises with the brown tints of autumn. Nowhere is the harmony of Nature better seen than in the blending colours of the birds, insects, and flowers of Norfolk Broads, where everything seems made to suit its surroundings. Push your boat into the reeds and lie still, and then a more beautiful object than a cock bearded tit, clinging tail uppermost to a tall reed-stem, gently waving in the wind, it is difficult to imagine. Except in the vicinity of their nests, or when curiosity gets the better of them, they are decidedly shy, and inclined to hide low; but by their nests they are better to be seen, as they flit restlessly across one mown open space after another, and sometimes in their anxiety for their eggs betray their whereabouts. They become more unsuspecting when they have young, their care for whom causes them to defy danger and go straight to the very nest in the presence of spectators —yet they have instinct enough to creep to it rather than to fly. If there is the least wind, the reed pheasants, as they are called by the natives, are not very likely to show themselves, for, strange to say, what will wave the tops of the reeds will keep them at the bottom. I have been surprised when walking with an old marshman, an ex- perienced egger, to notice how often he heard their note when neither of us could see the bird, long experience in looking for them having sharpened his ear; but it is not loud at any time, though described by some persons as shrill, and by

Stevenson as ringing and silvery. Indeed, Lord Lilford, who was fond of the Norfolk Broads, says its note once heard can never be mistaken for that of any other European bird by a good ear, which no doubt he had. Several authors have alluded to the clear ringing of their call-notes, which an admirer (Crespon) compares to the sounds produced by the cords of a French mandolin."

I shall not soon forget a summer evening I spent on Heigham Sounds. A day of wild weather—of racing clouds, scanty sun-gleams, and sudden rain-squalls—was drawing to a close. The wind had died away, and hardly a ripple disturbed the water's reflections of the reeds and sedges. My boat was moored in a little inlet among the reeds, where my outlook was towards Whiteslea, beyond which some yachts' masts and two windmills stood out clearly against the sky. On the opposite side of the Sounds a pair of swans had fallen asleep, lulled, as it were, by the soft whispering of the reeds. All around, among the reeds, coots were calling harshly; from the marshlands came the crying of some unseen curlews; once a great crested grebe stole out of a reed-shoal and dived within a few yards of my boat. Cuckoos were calling in the old carr where the herons used to build, and were answered by others in a copse towards the Hickling end of the Sounds. As the hour of sunset approached, the coots crept from the cover of the reeds and swam out on to the open water, where they dived for food, undisturbed until the clanking of a rowlock sent them scurrying back to the reeds. Close to the reeds the bream were lurking, sending up little air-bubbles, which burst when they reached the surface of the water; at times a fish leapt half out of the water and sent a gleaming ring of ripples widening towards the shore. As the sun sank behind a long, low cloudbank, another sun seemed to rise towards it out of the depths of the Sounds; but both rising and setting suns soon vanished, leaving on sky and water an amber glow, darkened here and there by grey-green wisps of cloud. Across this band of amber light three herons, which appeared from the direction of Horsey Mere, went slowly winging westward, calling " frank, frank " as they went. Presently another heron came in sight, flying low over the reeds and water, and in the middle of the Sounds alighted on one of the channel posts, where it stayed a few moments, clearly outlined against the sky.

Whiteslea, though formerly a large sheet of water, is now little more than a fairly wide channel or reedy pool connecting Hickling Broad with Heigham Sounds. The entrance to it is at the western end of the Sounds, a little way to the left of the posts which mark the mouth of the Old Meadow Dyke leading to Horsey Mere. But Hickling, though its area has decreased of late years, is still the largest of the Broads. Not so very long ago, Hickling, Whiteslea, and Heigham Sounds together formed a Broad about 650 acres in extent; but the "growing up" of Whiteslea has resulted in Hickling with its 460 acres and Heigham Sounds with its 120 acres being considered distinct Broads. Hickling at first glance seems even larger than it really is, so low and flat are its shores; when mist hides its bordering reed-beds its waters appear limitless. The channel across it, from Whiteslea to Hickling Staithe, is marked by a long line of posts, which yachts must keep to starboard; but there is a branching channel leading westward to Catfield Staithe. Yachtsmen who are familiar with the Broad take care to keep close to the posts; for the width of the channel varies, and not even the wherrymen are always sure how far from the posts it is safe to venture. Except in the channel, the depth of water is hardly anywhere more than three feet; even small yachts, drawing not more than two feet, often find their progress checked by shoals and matted masses of water-weeds.

Lacking the wild beauty of the Sounds, Hickling Broad has little to recommend it to summer cruisers. But in the neighbourhood of the staithes there are some picturesque nooks and corners where wherries and old flat-bottomed reed-rafts and marsh boats are moored in dykes and inlets gay with brightly blooming wild flowers. The small sailing boats, too—which are the handiest boats for exploring this Broad—look very dainty little craft when they spread their white sails and race or tack across the wide waters. Sometimes you may see what

look like small haystacks—one, perhaps, with a sail hoisted
above it—floating down the channel; these are reed-rafts laden
with hay, which the marshmen are quanting or sailing from
the banks of the Old Meadow Dyke to Hickling Staithe. But
these characteristic craft are more often afloat in winter, when
the reed-cutters are at work on Hickling, Whiteslea, and the
Sounds; then the reed-rafts are continually passing, laden or
empty, up and down the Broad. But when sharp weather
sets in, and the Broad is frozen, as it sometimes is, for weeks
together, the rafts disappear, and even the heavy wherries
cannot break their way through the ice. Instead, one or two
ice-yachts are seen, and maybe a marshman's gun-punt
mounted on wooden runners. These glide with amazing speed
over the smooth ice, where there is ample room for them, and
skaters, as a rule, are few. At such times other bird-voices
than the familiar ones of coot and grebe are heard among the
reeds—the voices of wild-fowl driven southward from the
frozen North. But the "Hickling Skater," the ghost of the
young soldier who used to meet his sweetheart on the Swim
Coots marsh on the Heigham side of the Broad, no longer
startles the belated skater by dashing past him on the ice; for
that strange wraith has not been seen for many years.

About three quarters of a mile from Hickling Staithe is
the village of Hickling, where there is little of interest except
the church. Of the Augustinian Priory founded by Theobald de
Valoins in 1185, some scanty remains can be seen attached to
a farmstead about half a mile north of the church, but the
walls have almost disappeared. One of the old windows has
been built into the porch of the priory farmhouse. Formerly
Hickling was a place of some importance; it was a market
town, and in the reign of Henry III. was granted an annual
three days' fair. Catfield, where is the nearest railway station,
is a village about two miles from Hickling Staithe. Its church,
a Restored Decorated building, contains some good work; but
more interest attaches to the rectory, which was for some
time the home of the poet Cowper. Stalham is about four
miles from the Staithe, and can be reached by way of Ingham,
where are the fine church and the priory ruins referred to
in the chapter on the river Ant. An isolated pool called

Calthorpe Broad is situated about a mile north of Hickling Priory; but it is scarcely worth while for a stranger to go out of his way to obtain the special permission necessary before he can see it. Indeed, the visitor whose time is limited does well if he contents himself with a sail across Hickling Broad and then returns to Heigham Sounds. For if he has come straight away from Potter Heigham he will not yet have sailed up the Old Meadow Dyke and seen Horsey Mere.

The Old Meadow Dyke is one of those navigable channels which in several cases connect Broads with the rivers or with other Broads. It is about a mile and a half long, very narrow, and branches off in a north-easterly direction from the Sounds, near the point where another channel leads from the latter into Whiteslea. In many respects it closely resembles the waterway between the Bure and South Walsham Broad, but it is rather deeper than that dyke, and its course not quite so tortuous. Its water is usually very clear, so that its subaqueous weeds,—narrow and broad leaved pond-weeds, matted thyme-weed, and dark bunches of hornwort,—which grow luxuriantly, can easily be seen and identified. On both sides of the dyke are wide stretches of marsh, rather more fenny than those bordering the main rivers. On these marshes, and by the waterside, some rare sedges are to be found; also some fine tall water-grasses, among them the tall fescue (*Festuca elatior*, Sm.), the aquatic meadow grass, and the purple reed grass. During July, when the meadow rue, willow-herb, and flowering rush are in full bloom, the dyke banks are very beautiful, and the fragrance of the meadow-sweet on sultry days is almost overpowering. In places the waterside flowers attain such a height as to conceal the haymakers at work on the marshes; they have to be cut down with scythes before the reed-rafts can be loaded with hay. Where such a clearing is made, cruisers on the dyke get a wide view, and see the stalwart marshmen swinging their scythes among the long grass, exposed to the scorching blaze of the summer sun. For on marsh nor dyke is there shelter from the sun-glare, except where the reeds rise high around some narrow inlet, or a reed-thatched cattle shed stands in the midst of the grass and flowers.

As the voyager approaches the Horsey end of the dyke, he becomes aware of the presence of a rare feature in Broadland scenery. Before him, in the distance, he sees a long, ragged ridge of maram-hills, the sandy sides of which, when lit up by the sun, stand out in striking contrast to the green of the marshlands in the foreground and the blue of the sky beyond. When he reaches the Mere, he finds these sand-hills clearly outlined on the horizon, but little else, except perhaps the salt savour of a sea wind, to indicate that he is within a mile and a half of the sea. The Mere, though smaller than Hickling and Barton, is wider than Wroxham, whose beauty, compared with that of this lovely lagoon, seems somewhat commonplace. Like Heigham Sounds, it continually reveals fresh loveliness and weaves new spells of enchantment. It is an almost circular Broad, fringed with reeds, beyond which, in one direction, is a narrow belt of woodland. Innumerable coots nest among the reeds, and their cries are often the only sounds which break the silence of the placid waters ; for yachtsmen, daunted by the difficulties of the Old Meadow Dyke, seldom visit the Mere, and the only rowing boats seen on it are those belonging to its owners.

With the exception of a private fishing-house on a little wooded promontory almost opposite the mouth of the Old Meadow Dyke, hardly a human habitation is visible from the Mere ; and as a rule the cruiser who visits it finds no one afloat on its waters. This was the case when, in the twilight of a summer evening, I sailed on to Horsey. The little *Gipsy*, gliding before a dying breeze, crept slowly through the water, which, although the sun had set and the sunset's glories faded, still had the sheen of a silver shield. A pale mist almost hid the bordering reeds and magnified the coots on the open water so that they looked like the large gulls seen at night on the Breydon flats. Above the mist, in the direction of Hickling, a tall windmill loomed like a phantom guardian of the Mere. The coots were silent ; not a whisper was heard among the reeds, which the failing breeze scarcely stirred ; not a sound came from the hidden village behind the trees, not a murmur from the sea. The Mere slumbered like a lake in Dreamland, over which the night was drawing a dewy coverlet, white and smooth except where a little islet of sedge and sallow ruffled its filmy folds and the *Gipsy's* white sail, slackly waving from the mast, swept aside the ethereal gauze. There was something suspensive in the stillness and silence: earth, sky, and water seemed to be breathlessly watching and waiting. Such absolute quietude was almost weird. One could fancy the world so waiting, hushed and awed, for the final cataclysm.

But it was only the calm before the storm. Next morning, when, with little more than the peak of my punt's sail showing above her decks, I ventured out on to the Mere, a wild wind was whipping the surface of the water into white-crested wavelets, and robbing some of the alders and sallows of their as yet green leaves. The sun was shining brightly, except now and again when, for a few moments, a flying cloud darkened it and cast a shadow on the distant sandhills. Not a coot was to be seen where the evening before there were a hundred; but over the flashing water some seagulls were wheeling, their white wings gleaming in the sunlight. On the marshes the tall grasses tossed and gleamed amid a foam of meadow-sweet, the sheen of their slanting stems suggesting the spears and lances of a hidden army of fays. From every side came the varied notes of the wind's song—from the grasslands a sibilant " sishing," from the reed-beds a shriller symphony, from the sallows a whistling of lashing wands, and from beyond the sandhills and the deep-breathing woodlands the incessant roaring of the surf on the shore.

Landing near the entrance to the Old Meadow Dyke, I strolled along a marsh wall which led to the nearest windmill. At times, when wind-gusts swept down upon me, I could hardly make headway; at every stile and marsh gate I was glad to rest a while and regain breath. Nowhere along the footpath was there shelter from the furious blasts; and at length I abandoned the path and trespassed on a swampy marsh which lay a few feet below the wall. There, as there was no chance of further cruising until the storm moderated, I wandered amid waving tufts of white cotton-grass, and sought for sundews on the brilliant-hued patches of bog-moss. I could not find them; but there were beautiful little pink-belled bog pimpernels trailing over the moss, adder's tongues sending up their slender spikes, thistles nodding their purple heads, and moneyworts creeping amid the grasses and sedges. Fragile eyebrights hid amid the long grass, where, too, the tiny starwort lurked; but the straggling purple-blue marsh pea was conspicuous in several places, and there were signs that the lovely grass of Parnassus would soon be in bloom. Among the fragrant spiræas a swallow-tail butterfly fluttered, and innumerable five-spotted burnets were abroad in spite of the wind; but most of the insect life of the swampy marsh lurked among the sedges, grasses, and bog moss. There, in a dense jungle of stems, blades, leaves, and blossoms, thousands of minute beetles and ephemeral midges were living their little lives, never venturing out of the green twilight of their marish underworld. They had their enemies, animal and vegetable, but the wild wind left them as undisturbed as it did the inhabitants of the depths of the sea.

Returning to the wall, I met a marshman on his way to the mill. Talking of the weather reminded him of the November gale of 1897, when the sea broke through the sandhills and overflowed the Horsey marshes. " If yow'd ha' sin th' sea come in," he said, "yow'd ha' thowt we wor all a-goin' to be drownded. It come in acrost th' Warren for nigh three hours—till th' tide went out; an' if it hadn't ha' bin for th' deeks bein' pretty nigh empty at th' time, I don't know what would ha' happened. An' mind yow," he went on, " sich a thing never owght to ha' happened. There's th' Commish'ners; it's their bisness to luke arter th' merrimills, an' if they'd a-done it as they should ha' done, th' sea 'ud never ha' got tru. Kapin' th' sea out ain't a one-man-an'-a-boy job, as some o' th' Commish'ners fare to think 'tis. Why, there was one Commish'ner he say tu me, ' What's wantin' is plenty o' faggots.' Says I to him, ' Sir, there wor faggots enow all riddy to be used long afore th' storm come, but no one was towd to use 'em.' ' Ah,' he say, ' that was werry wrong; it owght ter taach us a lesson.' Says I, ' Some folks take a daal o' taachin',' an' he larfed; but, thinks I, it ain't no larfin matter. But *he* didn't own no land out this way; *his* property wor all out Norwich way. Another man what come to hev a luke round when th' mills wor a-clearin' th' deeks fared a sight more consarned about th' fish bein' killed by th' salts than he did about anything else. 'Shockin',' he say, 'shockin'!' 'That 'tis, sir,' says I; 'some o' us mash folk stand a gude chance o' bein' drownded if suffin ain't done.' 'Ah,' he say, 'that 'ud be werry sad, but I wor a-thinkin' about th' fish'!"

After leaving the marshman, I rowed back across the Mere, having a hard struggle to reach the entrance to the narrow reedy dyke leading to the staithe and the big turbine pump-mill. I then rambled down to the village, formerly, before the road to Somerton was made, one of the least accessible by land on the East Norfolk coast. The church, which is only a few minutes' walk from the Mere, is a very ancient building in the Gothic style, containing one of the oldest screens in Broadland. Apart from its screen and a few old poppy-heads, it is of little interest.

Shortly after midday the gale moderated, but there was a strong breeze blowing when I again crossed the Mere and entered Waxham Dyke. This dyke, sometimes called the New Cut, is a very narrow channel leading from the north side of the Mere northward to Waxham and Palling. Until lately it was in a very neglected state, owing to the wherries having temporarily ceased trading with Palling; but a revival of the carrying trade has led to its being bottom-fyed, and it is now possible for shallow draughted yachts to follow in the wake of the wherries. When I last sailed up the dyke, however, the bottom-fying had not been completed, and just beyond a rough driftway leading to the hamlet of Waxham a dam was placed across the dyke, barring further progress towards Palling. So, leaving the *Gipsy* in the hands of a millman whose mill and cottage stand on the bank near the bottom of the driftway, I set out for a stroll towards the coast.

At Waxham the sandhills rise to an impressive height, constituting a barrier through which it seems impossible for the sea to break. Standing on their summit, one sees stretching towards Horsey on the one hand and Palling on the other, a long serrated ridge of sand hillocks, rising in places to a height of fifty or sixty feet. But high as is this ridge, its breadth,

compared with that of the denes or dunes between Yarmouth
and Caister, is inconsiderable, and so insubstantial are its
sandy slopes, that every exceptionally high tide scours away
tons of sand.   Inland lie wide levels of marshland, shimmering
in sun haze or checkered with light and shade.   They have
been won from the sea—won by a process largely natural—
but the sea seems bent on winning them back again.   For the
character of the coast has changed since the days when the
lowlands were reclaimed.   Then, the wearing away of cliff promontories to the northward resulted in the forming of natural
sand barriers lower down the coast; now, the promontories
are gone, and the wave-scour is felt to the southward, where,
whenever a strong wind from the westward swells the sea tides,
the sandhills are weakened.   Old landmarks are disappearing;
Eccles church tower, which a few years ago stood amid the
sandhills about two miles from the Town Gap at Happisburgh,
is gone, just as the village went which once clustered about its
walls.   Thousands of acres of land, too, are gone into the sea,
which, unsated, continues its incessant siege.   Sea Breach
Commissioners make feeble attempts to withstand this siege,
but the enemy is far too strong for them.   Their successes in
the past were chiefly due to the assistance of natural forces;
their failures in the future—for everything seems to point to
failure—will be through lack of that assistance.   Lyell, in his
Principles of Geology, suggests that the protection afforded by
the sandhills can be only temporary.   "Hills of blown sand,"
he writes, "between Eccles and Winterton have barred up and
excluded the tide for many hundred years from the mouths of
several small estuaries, but there are records of nine breaches,
from 20 to 120 yards wide, having been made through these,
by which immense damage was done to the low grounds in
the interior.   A few miles south of Happisburgh, also, are hills
of blown sand, which extend to Yarmouth.   These dunes
afford a *temporary protection* to the coast."   And again, after
dealing with the reclamation of the marshlands, he remarks,
"Yet it must not be imagined the acquisition of new land fit
for cultivation in Norfolk and Suffolk indicates any permanent
growth of the eastern limits of our island to compensate for
its reiterated losses.   No delta can form on such a shore."

Waxham is now only a small hamlet without a boat on its beach ; formerly it was a considerable village, with large tracts of cultivated land extending eastward beyond where are now the sandhills.   These lands belonged to the Hall, an old home of the Wodehouse family, a member of which, Sir William Wodehouse, who lived here in the reign of James I., is said to have been the builder of the first wild-fowl decoy constructed in Norfolk.   Near the ruined church, a short distance from the sandhills, from which it can best be seen, stands the Old Hall.   It is now a farmhouse, much altered and modernised, but it is surrounded by its original turreted wall, in the midst of which is a square, pinnacled gateway.   Traces of fine old doorways and windows, of good carved work, and of a paved pond, are still to be seen ; and the Wodehouses' old barn, said to be the biggest in Norfolk, quite dwarfs the dilapidated church which stands beside it.   An ancient inhabitant of a neighbouring cottage climbed through a gap in the sandhills while I looked down towards the Hall.   " Ah," he said, " that's a place as has seen some changes.   They say as how there used to be miles an' miles o' land betwixt that owd Hall an' th' sea."   Local tradition may exaggerate the acreage of the land the sea has encroached upon since the Hall was built, but no one can doubt that the old house has seen some changes.

A straight road on the landward side of the sandhills leads from Waxham to Palling, a little fishing village, which, if the visitor has patience and plenty of time to spare, can also be reached by the New Cut.   The road journey, however, is one of a very few minutes, and as a pleasant stroll back to Waxham can be taken along the seashore, it is perhaps preferable. Palling, with its quaint old cottages, drawn-up yawls and beach boats, and roads and footpaths leading down to the beach, is a typical Norfolk coast village.   Its beachmen are considered to be very expert boatmen, and the frequency with which they have rendered aid to vessels driven on to the dreaded Hasboro' Sands has gained them an enviable reputation.   Among the men to be encountered at the village inns and on the beach are some who, when their characteristic reticence has been conquered, can tell stirring tales of wreck and rescue.

A well-known writer of powerful but pessimistic romance
has suggested that the time is close at hand when the
orthodox beauty of smiling champaign country and the
obvious loveliness of many famous landscapes will cease to
appeal to thinking humanity, who will find the severe
simplicity of heathland scenery and the "chastened sublimity
of a moor" in greater harmony with their moods. When
that time arrives, he adds, places like Iceland may "become
what the vineyards and myrtle gardens of South Europe"
are to us now, and Heidelberg and Baden will be "passed
unheeded" as we hasten "from the Alps to the sand-dunes
of Scheveningen." When the time which this writer considers
imminent arrives, the attractiveness of such a line of sandhills
as lies between Waxham and Palling should be fully appreciated.
At first glance these sandhills seem barren and dreary; and
one might well imagine that the seasons' changes have no
effect on them, that they are impervious to the influence of
spring showers, summer sun, and winter frosts and storms.
But the field botanist knows that on these apparently barren
ridges the rose-tinted sea convolvulus blooms, and close
beside it the prickly sea holly, the pink-flowered restharrow,
and the yellow-horned poppy. And even the rambler who
is not a botanist finds a certain fascination in the long line
of broken ridges—a fascination like that of a bleak moor or
barren mountain-top. The irregular outlines, like those of
a mountain range in miniature, seen against the dawn-light
or sunset's golden glory — or, perhaps, looming through a
mist of rain or wind-blown spray—are singularly impressive.
In the twilight, when the hillocks' sloping sides are in the
shadow, but the sparsely grassed crests are clearly defined
against an afterglow of daylight, the sandhills assume a
primeval and even awesome aspect, yet one which attracts
and appeals more than simple loveliness.

After cruising on Hickling Broad, Heigham Sounds, and
Horsey Mere, the voyager may perhaps be disappointed when
he sees Martham or Somerton Broad, the only other Broad connected with the Thurne. This was formerly a fairly large
Broad, but its open water is now inconsiderable. To see it the
yachtsman must ascend the Thurne about two miles above

ABOVE ST. OLAVES

Frank Southgate

BECCLES

GELDESTON LOCK

MILL COUNTRY ABOVE STOKESBY

ACLE BRIDGE

REED-STACKING

BELOW WROXHAM BRIDGE

DRAINAGE MILL NEAR BARTON. AUTUMN

COLTISHALL LOCK

RISING MISTS, COLTISHALL

DRAINAGE MILL ON THE ANT

ENTRANCE TO BARTON BROAD

Frank Southgate

BELOW POTTER HEIGHAM

POTTER HEIGHAM BRIDGE

SUNSET, HEIGHAM SOUNDS

Frank Southgate

Kendal Dyke. Should his yacht draw much water, however, he will do well to moor it in the neighbourhood of Martham Ferry, which he passes a little way above the dyke; for the narrow channel by which the Broad is reached is often so weed-choked that only rowing boats can pass through it. The Broad is surrounded by dense reed jungles, in which the black-headed gulls have lately established a colony. Westward are marshlands stretching away to Heigham Sounds and the Old Meadow Dyke; northward and eastward, too, are marshes; but southward the land rises gradually towards Martham, whose church tower is the most conspicuous feature of the landscape.

Not far from the south-east corner of the Broad is the village of West Somerton. In this village the celebrated Norfolk giant, Robert Hales, was born. He belonged to a family of giants, each member of which was over six feet in height. He himself stood 7 feet 6 inches in his stockings, and weighed 452 lbs. In 1848 he was engaged to go to America in company with Tom Thumb at a salary of £800 a year. His family is still represented in the village by some stalwart farmers and farm-hands. But the chief attraction West Somerton has for cruisers is the fine series of mural paintings discovered in the parish church during its restoration in 1867. The largest of these paintings, depicting the Day of Judgment, is thus described by Mr. T. H. Bryant in his valuable work on the Norfolk churches: "Our Lord is represented seated, with the globe beneath His feet, upon a rainbow; . . . but of the figure of Christ nothing but the feet remain, one of which has the mark of the nail. The central upper portion of the painting had been destroyed at some time, when part of the nave was rebuilt. On either side of our Lord is a seraphim presenting to Him a kneeling figure. The one on His right hand, perhaps the Virgin, bares her bosom and holds her right hand to her breast, as if pleading her maternity; lower down are two angels, habited in albs and wearing the usual type of angelic crowns, summoning the dead to judgment, the right-hand angel being (the) more distinct, his trumpet having a cross-engrailed banner upon it. Below are eleven more or less nude figures, rising in various attitudes and with varied expressions of countenance. Amongst them are a king and queen, mitred and tonsured ecclesiastics, and two knights, whose sharp-pointed bascinets suggest *circa* 1350 as the date of the picture. S. Christopher occupies a space on the south side of the nave ; he is represented holding in his right hand a staff, and bearing the Infant Saviour upon his left arm. Opposite, upon the north wall, and enclosed within a border of decorated work, is a small painting of the Resurrection ; this has faded somewhat, but the figure of the Lord is represented habited in a green vesture, stepping out of the sepulchre, holding in His left hand the cross-banner of the Resurrection and His right in the attitude of benediction. One of the soldiers' bills is lying upon the ground fairly distinct. There are also representations of the Entry into Jerusalem and the Flagellation. Indications exist of the walls having once been covered with paintings." The church also contains a Perpendicular pulpit and a bell cast by Thomas Belyeter at the Lynn Foundry in the fourteenth century.

Two other churches, Winterton and Martham, are well worthy of the attention of the visitor who devotes some time to exploring the surroundings of Martham Broad. Winterton is a coast village about a mile east of West Somerton ; with its church, a fine building in mixed styles, the yachtsman who has cruised on the Thurne Broads will for some time have had a distant acquaintance, for its tower, about 125 feet high, is a striking feature of the wide view obtained from any slight rise in the neighbourhood of Hickling, Heigham, and Horsey. On closer acquaintance, however, the south porch proves to be more interesting than the tower, though unfortunately its fine carvings are much mutilated. Daniel Defoe, who visited Winterton in 1722, remarks upon the dangerous character of the coast between Winterton Ness and Yarmouth, where, he says, the cottage-garden railings, the pig-stys, barns, stables, and sheds were all built of ships' timbers, " the wreck of ships and ruin of mariners' and merchants' fortunes." And he goes on to tell how, in the year 1692, during a terrible storm, two hundred ships and a thousand lives were lost off the coast in one night. A lofty lighthouse, from the lantern of which a good view of the neighbouring Broads can be had, warns the seaman off this treacherous shore.

Martham can be visited from the Broad, but is more easily reached by the road from the ferry above Kendal Dyke. It is a large and pleasantly situated village, famous for containing the finest church in the Flegg Hundreds. This church is a splendid Perpendicular building, built at the beginning of the fifteenth century. The windows, some of which contain old stained glass, are particularly interesting; the font is good Perpendicular; and the south door is decorated with some fine mediæval carvings. The chancel was rebuilt and the nave restored in 1855 at a cost of £8000; this was done as a memorial to the Rev. Jonathan Dawson of Rollesby Hall. There was at one time a chapel in the south aisle dedicated to St. Blithe or Blida, the wife of Benedict and mother of the farm-hand Saint Walstan, who was born at Bawburgh, near Norwich. St. Blithe was probably buried in a Saxon church which stood on the site of the present one, and when the latter was built her tomb was embodied in it. In 1522, Richard Fuller, a Norwich tanner, gave ten shillings towards the repairing " of the church at Martham, where St. Blithe lyeth." The church register contains some curious entries. In 1619, " John Smyth, servant to Nicholas Cootes, brocke his legge at the footbaull, one the 6 day of ffebruary being Sunday, and was buried the eleventh day of the same month." The " footbaull " at which this unfortunate man was injured was probably a camping match played on a Sunday. Another entry states that a certain woman had two children at a birth " which, through the mistake of two or three good old women, were baptized Edward and Robert, when the aforesaid Edward was a daughter and Robert a son."

CHAPTER XII

ORMESBY, FILBY, AND ROLLESBY BROADS

IN the days when those Norse Viking raiders whom the early English historians indiscriminatingly call Danes established a considerable settlement in that East Anglian district now contained in the Norfolk Hundreds of East and West Flegg, there lay, between what are now the Hundreds, a large arm, extending northward and eastward of the estuarine valley of the Bure. Into that wide arm or bay the Norsemen brought their ships, leaving them safely moored on it or drawn up on its shores, while they founded a little colony in the neighbourhood by taking possession of the homes and holdings of the Saxon dwellers on that isolate island tract which lay to the north of the entrance to the great East Anglian estuary. They had little difficulty in subduing the land. The Romans, who had built strong fortresses to guard the mouth of the estuary, were gone; the Saxons of this part of East Anglia, probably few in number and knowing little of warfare, were unable to resist invasion. To a seafaring folk like the Norsemen the district offered many attractions. In every direction bays or inlets ran up into the land, not unlike—though very much smaller than—those which fretted the rugged coasts of their native land. On the banks of these inlets they could easily establish themselves, exist on the fish which abounded in the estuary and the wild-fowl which flocked to its swampy shores, and disregard the threats of any Saxons who may have been able to retain possession of the higher lands in the heart of East Anglia. They were practically secure against attack; when they manned their warships and set out on raiding expeditions into the interior of the countries of the North Folk and South Folk of East

Anglia, it was scarcely necessary for them to leave any of their fighting men to guard the homesteads they had built or seized. That they held the island district of the Fleggs some considerable time, seems probable, for they have left their mark upon it—the names they gave their settlements are borne by the Flegg hamlets to-day. In the names Rollesby, Mautby, Thrigby, and others, are embodied those of Norse sea-kings; and Ormesby is in all probability derived from the Norse "orm," a serpent, a name the Vikings often gave their ships.

When the mouth of the great estuary narrowed and the swampy lands of the Broadland valleys became comparatively firm and dry, the "orms' bei" or ships' bay was separated from the main channel of the Bure valley waters except in so far as it was connected with it by the dykes which drained the new lands formed between Stokesby and Flegg Burgh. As in the case of Fritton, the bay became a land-locked lake, which gradually decreased in size until its area was less than a thousand acres. It then stretched from the borders of Thrigby to those of Hemsby, spreading out arms in several directions, and in places narrowing and shoaling so that horsemen could ride through it. In course of time, bridges, led up to by raised causeways, were built over these narrow shallows, and the lake was so divided into what are practically three distinct Broads. But although the northernmost of these Broads is called Ormesby, the southernmost Filby, and the middle sheet of water Rollesby, even the natives of the district, not excepting the owners of the Broads and the lands adjoining them, can give no definite information as to their precise limits. Indeed, some writers affirm that there are in reality seven Broads adjoining one another, namely, Old Burgh, Filby and Burgh, Filby, Water Lily, Rollesby and Ormesby, Waterworks, and Hemsby Broads. But if every inlet or arm were to be called a Broad, and every sheet of water were to receive a different name from each of its adjoining parishes, the list of Norfolk Broads would be a formidable one.

For years it has been the dream of certain Broadland cruisers that "one day some one" will make the Muck Fleet navigable and so make it possible for yachts to sail from the Bure to Filby Broad. But year after year passes, and nothing is done; nor is it likely that the riparian owners will ever consent to a scheme which, if it were carried out, would result in Ormesby becoming as popular with yachting folk as Oulton and Wroxham are to-day. In all probability visitors to Ormesby, Rollesby, and Filby will always have to content themselves with journeying to these Broads in the prosaic manner of road and rail travellers, and when they go afloat on them it will be in the somewhat antiquated rowing boats on hire at the inns.

The scenery of these Broads is pleasantly varied. The shores are well wooded; there are quiet creeks not unlike those of Barton, islets fringed with fen sedge, willow herbs, and purple-topped marsh thistles, swampy tracts redolent of water-mints and bright with purple and yellow loosestrife, underwoods garlanded with honeysuckle and white bells of the great convolvulus, gardens where handsome peacock butter-flies flutter among Canterbury bells and hollyhocks, and bays beautiful with white water-lilies. The reed and rush beds are many acres in extent; their varied greens in summer and amber and tawny hues in winter are among the most striking effects visible from the open water. Coots and grebes are abundant on Filby and Rollesby; the woods are full of crooning pigeons, and during the summer months the reeds are musical with warblers. In winter, large numbers of wild-fowl visit the Broads, especially Filby; but the shooting is preserved.

To explore the Broads in one of the boats on hire for the purpose is somewhat difficult, for the bridge-spanned channels which connect them are very shallow, often having less than six inches of water in them; and the boats are too heavy to be easily dragged under the arches. Attended by such diffi-culties, a day's pleasuring becomes tedious and wearying. Less laborious and far pleasanter it is to content one's self with seeing one of the Broads. The visitor who does so misses little, for the three chief Broads possess no marked distinctive features; having seen one he may rest assured that he loses nothing by leaving the district without seeing the others.

Unless he is an angler, he is unlikely to become enthusiastic over either Rollesby, Ormesby, or Filby. For the Trinity Broads—as they are sometimes called—lack that wild beauty which is the great charm of Barton, Heigham Sounds, and Horsey, and their prettiness, when all has been said about it, is of too commonplace a kind to help to extend the fame of Broadland.

Perhaps the most enjoyable way of spending a day in this district is to devote an hour or two to the Broads and the rest of the day to exploring the neighbouring hamlets. If the visitor does this, his time will be pleasantly and profitably occupied. Most of the villages bordering the Broads are picturesque and primitive. The churches of some of them are of considerable interest; and at Caister, about midway between Yarmouth and Ormesby, there is a ruined castle, which, in spite of the ravages of time and the vandalism of Yarmouth trippers, remains a fitting monument to one of Norfolk's famous men. From Ormesby Broad it is not far to the church of Ormesby St. Michael, or Little Ormesby — a building in mixed styles, standing beside the road leading to the station. This church is perhaps the least interesting in the district; but the parish can boast that, among several families which, about the year 1630, left it for the New Hampshire and Massachusetts settlements, were the ancestors of the famous American statesman, Daniel Webster. The church of Ormesby St. Margaret, or Great Ormesby, is more worthy of attention; for, in addition to having some curious bosses in its roof, it contains a brass to Alice, the second wife of Sir Robert Clere and aunt to Queen Anne Boleyn. For a long time this brass was kept in the parish chest; but it is now, I believe, refixed in the matrix of its original stone, lately discovered in the chancel. There are frequent references to the Clere family in the *Paston Letters*, for the Cleres held several manors in this neighbourhood at the time when the Pastons held Caister Castle. Sir Robert Clere's tomb, which is without an inscription, is near the north window of the church; and some traces of the family's coat of arms can be seen on the font. The south doorway is good Norman work,

13

The manor on which the Hall stands anciently belonged
to the Ormesby family, a member of which, Gunnora de
Ormesby, was the mother of Alice Perrers, the mistress of
Edward III. Great Ormesby village is prettily grouped
around a tree - shaded green. It was formerly a place of
some importance, — a market town whose inhabitants were
exempt from serving on juries, from contributing to the
maintenance of knights of the shire, and from " theolony,
stallage, cumrage, pontage, pennage, picage, murage, and
passage." But in spite of all these privileges it is now a
comparatively unimportant village. Where there were at one
time five churches there is now only one.

A by-road branching off southward from the Ormesby road
where it skirts the village green leads to Mautby, a parish
bordering on the Bure. Here again we come in touch with
the Pastons ; for Margaret Paston, whose letters are the
most delightful in the famous collection, was a daughter
of John de Mauteby, who held the manor in the middle of
the fifteenth century. Undeniably, it is Margaret Paston who
gives life to the *Letters*, which, although invaluable to students
who would acquaint themselves with the conditions of life in
England during the reigns of the kings of the houses of York
and Lancaster, would be somewhat dry reading if it were
not for her love for her lord and careful guardianship of his
interests. Her fond love for her children, too, is often
manifested, though there are times when we might think her
mercenary if we failed to understand the customs of the age
in which she lived. For instance, she writes to her " right
worshipful husband " as follows : " I was at Norwich this week
to purvey such things as needeth me this winter ; and I was at
my mother's, and while I was there, there came in one Wrothe,
a kinsman of Elizabeth Clere, and he saw your daughter, and
praised her to my mother, and said that she was a goodly
young woman ; and my mother prayed him for to get for her
a good marriage if he knew any ; and he said he knew
one . . . the which is Sir John Cley's son, that is Chamberlain
with my Lady of York, and he is of age eighteen years old. If
ye think it be for to be spoke of, my mother thinketh that it
should be got for less money now in this world than it should

be hereafter, either that one or some other good marriage."
From this epistle it might be imagined that Dame Margaret
considered mutual love an unessential adjunct of matrimonial
contracts ; but elsewhere she reveals a kindly interest in a
love-sick maiden.   Writing to her son, Sir John Paston, who
was probably with King Edward IV. at Pomfret at the time,
she says, " I would you should speak with Wekis [Wykes, an
usher of the King's Chamber], and know his disposition to Jane
Walsham.   She hath said, since he departed hence, but [unless]
she might have him, she would never marry, her heart is so sore
set on him ; she told me that he said to her that there was no
woman in the world he loved so well.   I would not he should
jape her, for she meaneth good faith."   But, like a careful match-
maker, she is anxious that her young friend's matrimonial
prospects should not be entirely marred by this usher who loved
and rode away, for she adds, " If he will not have her, let me
know in haste, and I shall purvey for her in other wise."
Then the careful mother shows herself, for she goes on to
say, " As for your harness and gear that you left here, it is
in Daubeney's keeping ; it was never removed since your
departing, because that he had not the keys.   I trow it shall
get injured unless it be taken heed to betimes. . . . I sent
your grey horse to Ruston to the farrier, and he saith he shall
never be nought to ride, neither right good to plough nor to
cart ; he saith he was splayed, and his shoulder rent from
the body.   I wot not what to do with him."   This letter
was conveyed to her son by the rector of Filby, as appears
from a postscript : " I would you should make much of the
parson of Filby, the bearer hereof, and make him good cheer
if you may."   Delightful Dame Margaret !   Her gentle wraith
seems to haunt the meads of Mautby and the ruins of her
Caister home.   She was buried in Mautby Church, in
accordance with the instructions of her will, in which she
desires to be interred " in the aisle of that church at Mawteby,
in which aisle rest the bodies of divers of mine ancestors,"
and that under a " scutcheon of arms " should be inscribed
the words, " God is my trust."   Her tomb has vanished
with the south aisle in which it stood ; but at the south end
of the nave is a marble tomb and cross-legged effigy of

Sir Walter de Mauteby, one of her ancestors, who died in 1248.

Within the bounds of the parish is a boat ferry on the Bure. It is called Mautby Swim, being one of the spots where cattle used to swim across the river to and from the marshes. Adjoining Mautby is Filby, a village on the main road from Yarmouth to Norwich. Its church, which has a fine Perpendicular tower, with figures of the four Doctors of the Church for pinnacles, overlooks Filby Broad, and is only a few minutes' walk from Filby Bridge. A belfry door with seven locks, some painted screen panels, and a fine west window, are its most interesting features.

Nearly a hundred acres of Rollesby Broad are situated in the united parishes of Burgh St. Margaret and St. Mary, now known as Flegg Burgh. St. Mary's Church is in ruins, and of little interest; but St. Margaret's contains some good Norman work. The lordship of Burgh St. Margaret was granted by King John to Hubert de Burgh, Earl of Kent—that same Hubert whom, in Shakespeare's play, the king, when he would have him murder the youthful Prince Arthur, addresses thus :—

> "O my gentle Hubert,
> We owe thee much ; within this wall of flesh
> There is a soul counts thee her creditor,
> And with advantage means to pay thy love :
> And, my good friend, thy voluntary oath
> Lives in this bosom, dearly cherished.
> Give me thy hand. I had a thing to say,—
> But I will fit it with some better time.
> By Heaven, Hubert, I am almost asham'd
> To say what good respect I have of thee."

Adjoining Flegg Burgh is Clippesby, where the church contains two good brasses, one of which Cotman calls "one of the best and most pleasing" in the county. It is on the tomb of John and Juliana Clippesby, and is dated 1594.

But the historical interest of the neighbourhood of the Trinity Broads chiefly attaches to the ruins of Caister Castle. This castle, one of the oldest brick houses in England, was built by Sir John Fastolff, the cost of its building, it is (very incredibly) said, being defrayed by the ransom money received

for a French noble whom Fastolff captured at Verneuil or
Agincourt. Its builder was a Norfolk knight, a famous soldier,
and a much-maligned man. He was a prominent leader in
the wars of the reign of Henry V., and for his gallant conduct
at Harfleur, Agincourt, and Verneuil had honours heaped upon
him; but he was called a coward because at Pataye the troops
under his command, panic-stricken by what they had heard
of the supernatural powers ascribed to the Maid of Orleans,
fled in disorder before the Frenchmen. "From this battell,"
says Holinshed, "departed without anie stroke striken, sir
John Fastolfe, the same year for his valiantnesse elected into
the order of the garter. But for doubt of misdealing at this
brunt the duke of Bedford tooke from him the image of St.
George and his garter; though afterward, by means of friends
and apparent causes of good excuse, the same were to him
againe deliveryd against the mind of the lord Talbot."
Shakespeare, in *King Henry VI.*, makes a messenger from
the battlefield of Pataye say that, through the bravery of
Talbot, the battle would have been won by the English

> "If sir John Fastolfe had not play'd the coward:
> He being in the vaward, (plac'd behind,
> With purpose to relieve and follow them,)
> Cowardly fled, not having struck one stroke."

And again, by Talbot, Fastolff is charged with being a
"dastard"; while the king calls him "stain to thy countrymen." Holinshed based his charges on Monstrelet's account
of the battle, and Shakespeare credited Holinshed's statements; but in the *Chronique d'Angleterre*, written by Waurin,
who was present at Pataye, it is confidently asserted that
the battle was lost through Talbot's foolhardiness, and that
Fastolff fought until it was plain to every one the English
were defeated.

The Fastolffs held lands at Caister early in the fourteenth
century; but we hear nothing of their having a residence here
before the reign of Henry VI., when Sir John built Caister
Castle.[1] He was then an old man; but he seems to have

---

[1] Undoubtedly they *had* a house here before the castle was built, for Sir John was
born here.

lived in great state in his new home until 1459, when he died, and was buried in a chapel he had founded in connection with St. Benet's Abbey. At his death the castle came into the possession of John Paston; but Thomas Mowbray, the powerful Duke of Norfolk, asserted that "Sir John had given him Caister, and that he would have it plainly"; and in 1469 he laid siege to the castle. Its defenders numbered only twenty-eight, but they seem to have made a gallant defence. In the end, however, "from sore lack of victual and gunpowder," they were compelled to surrender. Lengthy legal proceedings ensued. Margaret Paston, in a letter to her husband, writes, "My Lord of Norwich said to me that he would not abide the sorrow and trouble that you have 'abyden,' to win all Sir John Fastolff's goods." But the duke retained possession until his death, when the king confirmed John Paston's right to the estate, and until 1599 the castle was the chief seat of the Paston family. In that year they removed to the fine Hall Clement Paston had built at Oxnead. Sixty years later the castle was sold to William Crowe, a son of the builder of a fine old house at Yarmouth, now the Star Hotel. Crowe, who was a wealthy merchant, is said to have used it as a country residence. After his death it was allowed to fall into decay.

In its original state it was a large quadrangular building, containing, besides the state apartments, twenty-six large rooms. It was surrounded by two moats, the inner containing the greater part of the buildings of which there are ruins remaining, the outer a college which, though founded by Fastolff, was not erected until the Pastons' time. The chief entrance—a square, ornamented gateway—was on the west side. The principal remaining portions are the north and west walls, and a circular tower, about ninety feet high, at the north-west corner of the quadrangle. These ruins are surrounded by the inner moat. Of the outer moat there are no traces; but some walls and a small round tower embodied in a house adjoining the ruins undoubtedly formed part of the castle, and, with the college buildings, were contained within the outer moat. Visitors' scrawlings on the walls have done much to disfigure the ruins; but in spite of this Caister Castle is one of the most interesting ruins in Norfolk. Seen as it is against a background of fine trees growing beyond the moat, its tower and walls are strikingly picturesque.

Caister formerly had two parish churches, but of one of these only a portion of the tower remains. The other, a building in mixed styles of architecture, stands just outside the village, beside the road leading from Yarmouth to the Castle. It is of little interest except for the fact that its churchyard contains the tomb of Sarah Martin, the philanthropic seamstress to whose memory a window is erected in Yarmouth parish church. Of the Roman station which, with Burgh Castle, guarded the entrance to the East Anglian estuary, nothing remains, but its site is pointed out on a hill north-west of the church, where a Roman kiln and pavement and several skeletons have been unearthed. That the camp simply consisted of earthworks seems probable, from the fact that no remains of masonry have been discovered.

CHAPTER XIII

WILD LIFE ON BREYDON

By Arthur Patterson

HISTORY, more or less traditional, has handed down to us the probable fact that, so recently as the time of the Roman occupation of Great Britain, the site on which Great Yarmouth now stands was entirely submerged, and that on a great arm of the sea, lying between the high lands of Caister and Burgh and known as *Gariensis Ostium*, Roman war-galleys sailed right up to Norwich. But an accumulation of alternate layers of moor and silt gradually pushed back the waters from the great alluvial flat, until all that remains of the estuary now exists in the Broads connected with the rivers Yare, Bure, and Waveney. With one exception, all these Broads have become freshwater lagoons, and it is a rare occurrence for freshets during neap tides to make it even brackish, though occasionally roach, pike, and carp are drawn down by the ebb and caught weakly struggling on the surface of Breydon, the largest sheet of Broadland water, which, being estuarine, naturally becomes charged with the salt tides. The surrounding area, now carefully ditched and drained and more or less dry, constitutes a vast level of rich marshlands, on which thousands of cattle are fattened during the summer months, and good crops of hay are produced. What this great tract was like before the raising of the "walls" to shut in Breydon and the rivers—especially when a high tide converted it into an immense lake, dotted with islets and swarming with wild-fowl—one can only conjecture.

The processes of reclamation must have been slow and

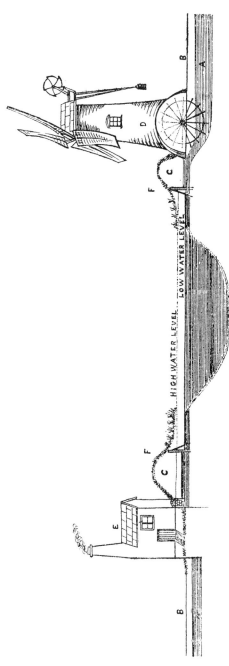

DIAGRAM SHOWING THE SYSTEM OF MARSH DRAINAGE.

A. Depth of Marsh Dyke. *D.* Water-Wheel.

B. Marsh Level. *E.* Steam Pump-Mill.

C. Section of River-Wall. *F.* Sluice-Gate.

frequently hindered by inundations. An extensive series of "walls"—long, zigzagging, triangular-shaped mounds, following the trend of the rivers and Breydon—were thrown up above the level of high water, and faced on the inner or water side with a sloping frontage of large flints. The dykes or ditches, formed where the soil was dug up for making the walls, constitute drains for the marshes. They are fed by innumerable cross-cut dykes, and their surplus water is discharged into the tidal waters beyond the walls. The accompanying diagram illustrates the way in which protection and reclamation have been carried out together.

The picturesque tower pump-mills still in use in many parts of the district date back to the early part of the eighteenth century: formerly there were many of them around Breydon. Their *modus operandi* is simple. A large water-wheel is set in motion by the mill-sails, and the water thrown into a dammed-up receptacle separated from the river or the short ditch which intersects the rond between the wall and the river; a sluice gate, fixed in a brick archway in the wall, is opened at the fall of the tide to let out the accumulated water. Steam, however, has largely superseded this slow and uncertain method, and drainage goes on independently of the caprices of the winds. The marshes have naturally settled and solidified, to the great detriment of the many species of birds which used to leave Breydon and feed on the molluscan and crustacean life of the marshes whilst the mud-flats were covered by the tide, and flock back again when the water fell.

The Breydon walls have to be carefully tended, mended when occasion demands, and kept to a necessary height. Certain "sets" of the tide have to be watched, and especial protection afforded at times by relaying and renewing the flints, and, if need be, by adding a rough stuccoing of concrete. The walls are sufficiently wide at the apex to form a footpath, and during the greater part of the year a ramble along them is an interesting experience. Beside them the Sea Southernwood (*Artemisia maritima*) grows luxuriantly, whilst the Scurvy Grass (*Cochlearia officinalis*), the Sea Aster (*Aster tripolium*), and the Sea Milkwort (*Glaux maritima*) are found in abundance, large tufts of the first mentioned often springing up among the jagged flints lapped by the tide. Very rarely, when severe gales have created unusually high tides, breaches have been made in the wall, and miles of marshland flooded. Such an inundation occurred at the upper end of Breydon in December 1894, when there were two flood tides without an ebb! Myriads of worms perished; and on the abatement of the flood, early in January, enormous flocks of Lapwings and Gulls assembled on the marshes.

From the walls jutting out into Breydon are a number of ronds, or irregular and broken patches of original swamp, covered with coarse saline grasses, Scurvy Grass, and the Jointed Glasswort (*Salicornia herbacea*). These ronds are being slowly but surely broken away by the constant lapping and beating of the waters; crumbling, they help to make the great stretches of mud-flat still wider and higher, and tend towards the gradual "growing-up" of Breydon. There is little doubt that these ronds and the marshes beyond the walls were formerly united, though to-day the former are slightly higher than the drained area.

Taking a look down Breydon from the upper end, at Berney Arms, when the tide is in, one sees a noble lake bisected by two parallel rows of posts or "stakes," red on the one hand and white on the other. Between these posts is the navigable channel; beyond them the water shallows abruptly over the mud-flats. The view is extensive and often interesting, with sometimes quite a fleet of laden wherries, with huge, gracefully swelling, high-peaked sails, coming up on a fair wind, or tacking and quanting against a less favourable breeze. Here and there on summer days are snow-white yacht-sails, whilst the punts of the eel-catchers are seen at intervals gliding about the deeper runs among the flats. At other times the blustering nor'-westers fling down sombre shadows from cloud-land, and the darkened surface of the water is churned into white-crested waves; it is then wild and bleak by day, and the curtain of night falls upon a dreary and depressing scene.

Breydon's aspects, indeed, are many and various. There are to be seen the most wonderful sunrises and the grandest sunsets. The outlook changes every hour. On fine days, even at low water, when the flats are bare, amazing colourings —vivid greens, gold, and brown—are seen at dawn and sunset; and with the seasons the dense matted masses of Wigeon Grass (*Potamogeton pectinatus*) on the flats change from pale green to brown. But the sunsets are the most magnificent spectacles—when the sun, seeming to draw nearer and nearer to you, sinks out of sight just beyond the farthest mud-flat, flinging long bars of radiance into the sky and a wide lane of liquid fire along the water. And then the moon comes up, and her silver light reveals the Gulls quarrelling over their lessening resting-places on the flats. You hear their wild screaming, the wail of the Curlew, the shrill pipe of the Sandpiper, the harsh croak of the Heron; and at times you are startled by the boom of a wild-fowler's punt-gun. Even in winter, when the sky is overcast, and snowstorms rage, and ice spreads from the channel to the walls, Breydon has its fascination, for then the wild-fowl alight in the opening wakes, or settle bewildered on the water, and the Hooded Crow is seen, vulture-like, searching for dead or dying birds which the gunners have been unable to retrieve.

But Breydon is not as it was in the earlier half of the last century. Then, some of the flats which now are barely covered at high water, were easily sailed over by deep-keeled wherries; while others, that are now dry on the ebb, were almost always under water. And there are drains and runs and channels which have opened in late years and deepened several feet in a remarkably short period: twenty or thirty years ago they did not exist.

In the days referred to, a semi-amphibious fraternity, provided with boats, nets, and guns, earned a livelihood on Breydon all the year round. There was always a sufficient depth of water for them to work their nets or get within reach of wild-fowl. To-day Ducks often sit in safety, for the gunner, with all his manœuvring, fails to get within shooting distance of them. Grey Mullet used to tumble and splash among the Wigeon Grass hour after hour, wisely timing their return to deeper water when the tide went down. Various Ducks and allied species of fowl came in their season to feed; but now the drying and hardening of the flats have killed off much

of the food for which they came. The flats, however, are still
alive in places with ragworms and *Nereidæ*, and for these the
long-billed waders search and probe. Mollusca are commonly
met with, but in decreasing numbers. The Common Winkle
abounds, and often with it is found its relative, *Littorina
neritoides*. Small Cockles are sparingly found a few inches
below the surface, also quantities of the Clam (*Mya arenia*)
and the smaller *Scrobicularia piperita*. At low tide, tiny jets
of water ejected by these molluscs may be seen squirting from
the holes everywhere dotting the mud : the Curlew knows well
their meaning, and profits by them. The Mussel, now condemned by the local authorities as unfit for food, is abundant,
and if it were not for the sewage, might be cultivated on the
Bouchet system with profit to many. The tiny *Hydrobia ulvæ*
dots every Potamogeton blade in dozens, and, with small
Winkles, provides a welcome food for many wild-fowl. In one
or two corners or small bays in the walls, locally known as
"shell corners," are considerable deposits of shells of these
species, accumulated by eddying currents—a process precisely
analogous to that which formed the Crag, which has so long
puzzled geologists.

In the glare of the sunlight, the muds in places, viewed
aslant, are seen to be all "on the work"! Close inspection
reveals myriads of *Corophium longicornis*, the long-horned
crustaceans so industriously gathered by Dunlins and the
smaller waders. Let the water but rise sufficiently, the keen
eye of the naturalist will discover that almost transparent
Opossum Shrimp, *Mysis chamæleon*, scurrying around every
pool, pile, or weed-clothed flint stone. For these and the
Common Shrimp, Flounders and smaller fishes, such as Gobies
and Blennies, eagerly hunt ; and left among the stranded
flotsam and under the seaweeds *Gammarus marinus* gives the
Turnstone or "Tangle-picker" profitable employment. The
Sandhopper (*Talitrus locusta*) is also plentiful. The Common
Shore Crab (*Carcinus mœnas*) literally swarms among the weeds
and under the edges of the ronds, affording a rich and never-
failing supply of food for various fishes and birds. While at
liberty this scavenger of the waters does good service in
clearing away submerged carrion ; failing which, he scrambles

after Shrimps and any little fishes he may overtake. The
Large White Prawn (*Palæmon squilla*) also occurs.

The fish life of Breydon has decreased considerably in
recent years. The Salmon has but casually ascended this
basin for a century or two, although one was discovered on a
flooded marsh near Norwich a few years ago, and Sir Thomas
Browne (1662) refers to fifteen being taken at Trowse Mill.
The Salmon-trout may rarely be seen throwing itself out of
the water in summer, probably disliking the flavour of the
sewage-tainted flood. Until about the seventies more ambitious
Breydoners boasted the ownership of a Mullet net, a long seine
with pocketing meshes on either side. In the earlier half of
the last century large catches of Mullet were made, occasionally of several pounds' value. The sport was exciting, and
at times disappointing, when one bold fish, awaking to the
situation, would leap the nets, followed by others. An outside
net a few feet beyond the first would often effectually baffle
them. It was for love of the Mullet that Cormorants used to
frequent Breydon. The older gunners speak of a Cormorant
perched on every stake as quite an ordinary matter. But
since the destruction of the Fritton colony some years ago
these birds have been *rara aves* on Breydon. The rare sub-
variety of the Mullet, *Mugil septentrionalis*, has once been
taken, and a record Mullet weighed nine pounds in weight.
No one now goes fishing for this species specially.

Flounders, locally "Butts" (*Pleuronectes flesus*), are still
common on Breydon, although by no means so plentiful as
formerly. Three decades ago the practice of staking nets
across the flats at high water, and gathering in the spoil at low
water, was not an uncommon or unremunerative business.
In August the "grass-fed" fish were in excellent condition.
In January, when the larger examples came up, "darting"
was much practised. A Butt dart consists of a rake-like
appliance with barbed teeth placed vertically; it is securely
attached to a slim pole perhaps twenty feet long. "Darting"
is simply jobbing with this implement, and transfixing with
the tines any unlucky fish that may come in its way. In
frosts, these fish are very sluggish. Young Flounders, next to
the Eels, are the quest of the Herons which frequent Breydon

during the greater part of the year. Butt-darting and Butt-picking are now only sporting exercises. The latter is carried on in summer, when the Flounders have drawn off the flats into the narrowing runs. The pole is light and comparatively short, and the tines are made of straightened cod-hooks.

The fish chiefly sought for on Breydon is the Common Eel, which in summer is captured in great numbers. During the time it is on the "run" considerable quantities are taken on the "bab"—a bunch of worms threaded on shoemakers' hemp or worsted, and weighted with a leaden sinker. The Eel-babber usually fishes by night, though occasionally by day, on the flood by preference, and drifts down-stream on the ebb to dispose of his catch. He fishes from an old punt or, preferably, from a low-built, "double-ended" open boat—a much better adapted craft to drop the Eels into from the bab than the small-welled punt. Babbing consists of bobbing the bait up and down. When the Eels bite it is difficult for them to disentangle their small teeth from the hemp, and before they can do so the fisherman deposits them in the boat. Formerly there were more Eel-babbers than now, and in summer they made a good living. In winter those that remain drop the babbing-pole and take up the Eel-spear, and work the muds in which the Eels burrow on cold days. Much alone and exposed to all weathers, the men are hardy, taciturn, and unambitious. Occasionally, however, they may be persuaded to spin yarns; and their experiences, usually savouring of the marvellous in natural history, are often worth listening to. For instance, two or three of them were smelting up Breydon on one occasion, and an object, at first thought to be a floating bush, was curiously approached. It proved to be a Sturgeon resting on the water. Cautiously a noose was prepared and slipped over the tail of the fish, which, on feeling restraint put upon its movements, dashed off and succeeded in freeing itself. Becoming again quiet, once again it was stalked, and a surer noose affixed to it. Again it dashed away, towing the boat about a hundred yards; but the men eventually stunned it by smashing its head with an iron bar. It weighed eleven and a half stones, and some difficulty was experienced in getting it into the boat. On another occasion an Eel-catcher named Jack Gibbs struck a Conger-eel with his pick and secured it, the fish weighing no less than thirteen and a half pounds. These are fair examples of the unusual experiences of Breydoners.

Some half a dozen men are in the habit of laying a few Eel-pots in the Breydon channel and in the river, and catch occasionally some good Eels. The pots are long, funnel-shaped structures of wickerwork; the bait consists of a few pints of Shrimps, themselves taken in a small trawl-net on Breydon. Only one or two men to-day practise this latter method of fishing, the catches having fallen off so much as to be un-remunerative. Years ago fine Soles and several other species of fish were taken in this way. Up to a comparatively recent date great shoals of Codlings came up on the flood, and large hauls were made by netting. At such times local anglers by the score, commandeering all available boats, made famous catches of these bold-biting fishes. In October the species was regularly looked for. Singularly enough, young Pollack turned up for a year or two; in May 1887, indeed, they were very numerous, since when they have been exceedingly rare.

The capture of one other fish, the Smelt (*Osmerus eperlanus*) keeps a few men employed in the season. This fish, which ascends to the fresh waters of the upper rivers to spawn, occurs abundantly in Breydon. Smelt nets are finely meshed and of various lengths, from eighty yards upwards. The net is a miniature seine, and locally termed a draw-net. The fish are surrounded, one man remaining on a flat while the other rows the boat and drops the net in a half-circle. Both ends of the net are then gradually brought together, and its contents are shot out on the mud. Sometimes several score Smelts of various sizes are taken; occasionally the catch is varied with a few Flounders, an Eel or two, many viviparous Blennies (locally " Eel-pouts "), and a number of small Herrings. Now and again a quantity of Atherines (*Atherina presbyter*), locally called " Smolts," are netted; also Crabs galore, and at chance times a stranger in the shape of a Five-bearded Rockling (*Motella mustela*), a Fifteen - spined Stickleback

(*Gasterosteus spinachia*), or a Sand Launce (*Ammodytes lanceo-latus*). Small shoals of Whiting occur occasionally.[1]

But it is for its bird life that Breydon is chiefly famous, for there is not another spot of its size in the British Isles where a larger variety of birds has been seen or so many rare species taken; indeed, on its muds have occurred several species which until then were not known to occur in Britain. Each period of the year sees a continuous arrival of different species, whilst atmospheric conditions limit the numbers or account for large influxes.

In spring—in May especially—many birds " in the red," or other striking attire of their nuptial state, call here for a rest and feed on their northward journey; with a fair wind their numbers may be large. Bar - tailed Godwits, Knots, Curlew-sandpipers in russet plumage, are met with in lesser numbers than of yore; but so sure is the time of their coming, especially in the case of the Godwits, that a very ancient saying—" Twelfth of May—Godwit Day "—is a familiar one with the local gunners. Certainly some are seen before and others after that date, but on that day the " rush " is still looked for. But the days are gone when the " lumps "—the highest parts of the flats left bare by the rising tide—were hidden by closely packed flocks of these birds, with which the Grey Plover in its livery of black and grey, the Turnstone, the Ringed Plover, and the Dunlin associated. Still these species regularly appear. The Godwit and Knot will feed almost under your boat's prow; the Dunlin, streaked with greys and browns above and with a horseshoe patch of black on its breast, runs nimbly ahead of you, feeding as it goes, but ready to flit to some distant flat the moment the more suspicious Ringed Plover takes alarm and noisily wings away; along by the flint walls the Common Sandpipers flit in twos or threes, while the wary Whimbrel (locally " Half-curlew " or " May-bird ") utters its clamorous pipe, and the Greenshank joins in with its clear, bell-like *pleu pleu*. Not less noisy are the Redshanks that come to nest on the neighbouring marshes. But he is a fortunate man who chances to detect the Kentish Plover (*Ægialitis cantiana*), the Pectoral Sandpiper (*Tringa*

[1] For a list of fishes known to occur in Breydon, see Appendix.

maculata), or the Little Stint (*T. minuta*) among the commoner species; and equally to be envied is he who gets within easy sight of a couple or more of Avocets or a small party of Spoonbills fishing in the shallows. Yet it is more than probable that in the springtime the Spoonbills will be found here. Then, too, we look for the passing of the Black Terns and Lesser Terns, among which may occasionally be noted the rarer Caspian Tern (*Sterna caspia*), or the even rarer White-winged Black Tern (*Hydrochelidon nigra*).

Then, too, there are the various Ducks — Wigeon in particular—in their fine spring plumage. The Wigeon, with which consort the Shoveller, the Pintail, and the Tufted Duck, comes in large flocks, and spends days together feeding on the tender stalks of Potamogeton. Gulls, Black-headed and Black-backed, are also plentiful, and, as the tide serves, may be seen flying or running, picking up their food; while the Turnstone, tossing over the tangled bunches of weed to get at the crustaceans beneath, the Curlew and Whimbrel, probing in the mud for worms, the Shoveller spooning for small molluscs, the smaller birds snapping up *Gammaridæ*, and the handsome Herons, standing thigh-deep in the water, seeking for Eels and flat fish, provide abundant interest for the naturalist.

Fortunately the close season for a time prevents the birds being disturbed by the loud boom of the punt-gun and the sharper crack of the fowling-piece. Yachtsmen, while their yachts are passing up or down Breydon, sometimes shoot at birds flying by or resting on the flats—a reprehensible practice, which, it is hoped, will ere long become a thing of the past. All through the spring and summer the watcher skims around in his little punt, or from the cabin of his quaint ark-like house-boat scans the flats with a view to detecting delinquents and preventing illegal gunning. The local gunners, to their credit be it said, respect the close season.

In August the birds begin to return on their southern migration. Species such as I have already mentioned are then seen, the young birds of the year invariably arriving before their lagging progenitors. For a month they are unmolested, and during this time many Terns, Sandpipers, Plovers, and the like pass safely southward; but in September the walking gunner perambulates the walls, and the punt-gunner glides about the drains and runs, whilst a few—a very few—Breydoners lay aside bab and Eel-spear in order to devote their attention to the Ducks and shore-birds. Success depends largely on wind and weather. Long spells of westerly and southerly winds prevent the arrival of many birds, which undoubtedly migrate along the eastern side of the German Ocean; but south-easterly winds bring in the Plovers and "stir up" other birds. As winter approaches, the Wild Ducks of various species drop in, and then it is the wild-fowlers display that hunting instinct and cunning which is often inherited. Slowly and stealthily, sculling with one oar astern, the wily gunner gradually gets within range of the feeding fowl. Sometimes the latter will bunch up and suspiciously eye the floating object coming towards them. Occasionally they take flight; but often they unwarily allow a near approach. Then the fowler, poising his huge gun, takes his "sights" and knocks his foot on the floor of the punt. The startled birds take to wing in a compact flock, and are hardly above the surface of the water ere the gun pours forth its deadly pound of shot, cutting a lane through the midst of the flock. The victims drop dead or wounded on the tide. Those within reach the gunner speedily gathers, rowing after the badly wounded, and with his shoulder gun killing those that are wildly fluttering beyond his reach.

In snowy and frosty weather wild-fowl are often abundant, hundreds of birds which have been sheltering on the Broads then making for the open waters off the foreshores or for Breydon. At such times Swans, Geese, Pochards, Wigeon, Scaup, Teal, and many others are looked for. Among the species which have been met with here are the Whooper, Bewick's Swan, and White-fronted, Pink-footed, and Bernacle Geese. "Hard-weather" fowl, too, become numerous, among them the Scaup, Tufted Duck, and Golden Eye; and, unable to stay longer on the frozen Broads, hundreds of Coots wander up and down the shallows, feeding on the decaying "Wigeon Grass."

Among the rare birds which have been shot on Breydon are the White-tailed Eagle, Osprey, Purple Heron, Black Stork,

Siberian Pectoral Sandpiper (*Tringa acuminata*), Gull-billed Tern (*Sterna anglica*), Mediterranean Herring-gull (*Larus cachinnans*), Mediterranean Black-headed Gull (*L. melanocephalus*), Sabine's Gull (*Xema sabinii*), and the Iceland Gull (*Larus leucopterus*). The late Mr. E. T. Booth obtained many of the choicest birds in his collection (at Brighton) on Breydon.

To review briefly the *Mammalia* whose claims to being Breydonian may be allowed: an occasional Seal (*Phoca vitulina*), and, in one instance, a Grey Seal (*Halichœrus gryphus*) may be mentioned; Common Bats (*Vesperugo pipistrellus*) and the Noctule (*V. noctula*) flit about on summer evenings; the Weasel sparsely inhabits the banks, where it finds abundant prey in the shape of Brown Rats. On several occasions Porpoises have been observed wallowing in the shallows.

A few words may be added about the men who, in decreasing numbers, frequent Breydon. Next to the eel-babbers, the wherrymen are the most conspicuous. Formerly they had much of the fisherman and sportsman in their composition; but the keenness of the competition between the wherries and the railways now necessitates their being simply wherrymen. The race of Breydon wild-fowlers is almost extinct: the late John Thomas may be said to have been the last of the professional gunners. His father and grandfather were fowlers before him. Many of his adventures and experiences were exciting and entertaining. That his profession is not unattended with danger, the fact that he, at different times, sustained a broken collar-bone, had fingers blown off, and received other injuries, will testify. On one occasion he possessed a worn-out punt-gun so weak in the lock that it often missed "cracking the patch" twice running, and sometimes had to be exploded by means of a blow from a piece of iron kept handy for the purpose! He made some big shots, once securing over a hundred Dunlins after one discharge of his punt-gun. Avocets, Spoonbills, Swans, and Temminck's Stints also fell to his gun; for in the old days he shot all the year round. His big bag of Dunlins, however, was not so profitable as a bag made by his grandfather, the following account of which appears in Paget's *Sketch of the Natural History of Great Yarmouth* (1834): "A remarkable case (of bird-slaughter) occurred to an old man named Thomas, who one morning, on awakening in his boat on the flats, saw not far from him a number of wild-fowl sitting in a crowd close together on the ice. From his boat being nearly covered with snow, he had escaped their observation while they were collecting in the night. He immediately fired (his gun carrying about a pound of shot), and with those killed outright and the wounded, which he and his dog caught before they could make their escape, he secured no less than thirty couple of wild-fowl, consisting principally of Wigeon and Teal."

PART II

CHAPTER XIV

BIRD LIFE[1]

By the Rev. M. C. H. Bird, M.A., M.B.O.U.

I N writing on the above subject, it may be best to commence
with some of those birds which are especially characteristic
of the district, and as such the Bearded Tit (*Panurus
biarmicus*) stands pre-eminent. A few years ago it was, I
believe, included in a list of "Lost British Birds"; but
although at one time it seemed to hover on the verge of
extinction, it has now reasserted itself, and, in spite of much
and constant persecution on many Broads, attained such a firm
foothold, that, with the aid of legal and local protection, I see
no reason why it should not continue to be with us as long as
the Broads themselves.

It is nevertheless a curious fact that, although within the
past decade this species has certainly increased in numbers,
there has been no regularity in that increase year by year;
the increase in one year has not necessarily been followed by
a still greater increase in the next season. Taking the two
years last past, for instance, there were not so many nests
around the larger Broads in 1901 as there were in the
previous spring, and yet there were no apparent anomalies of
weather or of persecution to account for the noticeable drop in
numbers. 1900 was a bonus year with *Panurus biarmicus*,
but what became of the surplus? It is the same with all birds.
One good Partridge season, for instance, does not argue that a

---

[1] A list of the birds of Broadland appears at the end of this book.

better will succeed it; the doubtful friends of the Rooks go so far as to say that a colony of these birds will decrease unless some of the young be slaughtered.

Reed Pheasants, as Bearded Tits are called by the Broadsmen, have everything now in their favour except the greed of collectors. They are very secretive in their habits, and double-brooded—if, indeed, they do not sometimes attempt to rear more than two clutches in a year. In fact, I know that this was the case with one pair of these birds in 1900, and a nest of eggs on 18th July 1901 is also suggestive. During the month of August and up to Christmas small roving parties may be met with at some distance from their breeding haunts; tit-like, they are ever on the move, but it is very doubtful whether any actually migrate,[1] and this residency makes the Reed Pheasant to be at the present time *the* most interesting bird we have, since all the other rarer birds that ever breed, or attempt to breed, here now are migrants (such as the Ruff and Spotted Tail, Harriers and Garganey), and therefore less liable to extinction so far as our locality is concerned.

An up-to-date monograph on this gem of the Broads appeared in the *Zoologist* for 1900, from the able pen of Mr. J. H. Gurney. Their metallic call-note *ping! ping!* often betrays their whereabouts; but when disturbed they have a habit of dropping down amongst the rank vegetation, and creeping mouse-like from one reed to another, and so escaping observation. Conspicuous in the hand, at liberty they are protectively coloured, especially when winter has changed the tints of the reeds and the wind has blown away the leaf; then their rufous or tawny plumage harmonises perfectly with the dead and dying vegetation. Even their slightly curved tail blends in shade and conforms in shape with the bending reed stem, heavy with the added weight of the three or four drachms of this bright speck of bird life. In fact, to those who know their note at any rate,—and once heard it can never be forgotten or confounded with that of any other bird,—they are more often heard than seen. But, like all other birds, when once seen, they will, to the practical observer, soon betray their

---

[1] One was observed at Languard Lighthouse in February 1887, and H. Gätke mentions several occurrences in Heligoland.

nesting site, although the actual nest (built almost on the ground, and composed of reed leaves lined with reed bloom), large and somewhat clumsy though it be, will take some looking for.

From babyhood these birds are beautiful to prying eyes, although the beauty is concealed until hunger opens the nestling's mouth, when upon the roof may be seen four rows of onyx spots set in deep pink carnelian. The adult birds are hardy enough; but in severe winters, when the reed-beds are frozen, loafing gunners take advantage of the ice and stalk the Reed Pheasants. In 1890 and 1895 several thus suffered.

A recent contribution to ornithological literature, the second edition of Harting's *Handbook of British Birds*, gives a novel method of imitating the ringing call-note of the Bearded Tit, namely, by balancing a penny on the middle finger of each hand and striking the edges together.

The Great Crested Grebe, once nearly as scarce hereabouts as the Bearded Tit, has increased even more abundantly. Shy and wary as a lone Curlew, it will admit of no near approach, diving noiselessly upon the slightest alarm, and not coming to the surface again until almost out of sight of the naked eye. Unless one is "in the know," whoever would take that lump of rotten weed to be a Loon's nest? And yet, perhaps, within two seconds of your finding it, the old bird was incubating, and at the moment of your arrival she not only glided off into and under the water, without raising a ripple on its surface, but also, with a right and left movement of her beak, covered up her eggs before leaving them. I have watched these actions, and at close quarters they are so rapid that the eye can scarcely follow them. The jerk, too, with which the Grebe regains her position on the nest is peculiar; her clawless feet are placed too far behind for her to climb on to it, nor does she ever attempt to fly to and then alight upon it. A fresh-laid Grebe's egg is a very different object to one that has rested for weeks on and in a miniature hotbed of decaying vegetation. The newly hatched young birds, as in many other species, differ much in appearance from their parents, their neck and head being zebra-striped, and the pates adorned with a pinky shield. The old bird's loud and deep *honk! honk!* bears no comparison with the soft, musical babbling of the young.

Schooling soon commences, and the first lessons in diving are taken on the parent's back. I have a couple of neck feathers of an old male, taken from the mouth of a youngster less than a week old: they gave way after affording the little one beak-hold for a more than two-hundred-yards' dive!

Grand and handsome birds, indeed, the adult males are in breeding plumage, with their frills and ear-tippets well up and their iris fully coloured. When pursued they seldom rise; but if they do, their flight is both peculiar and graceful—straight as an arrow and seldom much above water level. They trust chiefly to their rapid swimming and diving powers; just before the latter means of progression are taken advantage of, the body is mysteriously submerged ere the neck is bent, the head inclined, and the final plunge taken. When danger threatens, a Grebe will never swim into the bush, but always dives when within some thirty yards of the reed; and when once the reed-bush is reached not even an otter could catch him.

In summer, any time after 4 p.m., a lookout may be kept for a sight of the Short-eared Owl, a few pairs still remaining to nest on, and fatten on the voles which abound in, the rough marshes around the Broads. A grand sight it is to watch the powerful, buoyant, long-sustained, and noiseless flight of *Otus brachyotus*—a different thing altogether to the forced and lazy flapping of the foreign representatives of this species that, breeding farther north, come here to winter with us, and to be now and then flushed whilst we are out after Snipe in the marshes, Rabbits on the sandhills, or even Partridges in the swede-fields. Woodcock Owls we call them then, because they and *Scolopax rusticola* often arrive here simultaneously. And there are many more such Owls here in winter than in summer; but in the former season they do not show themselves, whereas the breeding birds, having perhaps a family to provide for, brave the sunlight in seeking for food. I had a very enjoyable evening some few years ago hunting for an Owl's nest. A friend had fixed the whereabouts, and we concealed ourselves in the nearest sallow bush. For hours we watched the male bird alternately flying and resting—going away beyond the range of our glasses, then coming back within a few yards of us; flying high and strong for half an hour or more, until my eyes were tired of following him; now hunting for prey, now toying up in the air and joyfully clapping his wings over his back like a pouter pigeon. Every now and then he dipped down amongst some marsh stuff, and several times we sallied forth from our ambush, thinking we had learnt his secret, but only to return disappointed. We knew a nest was near, but we little suspected how near; we believed that incubation had commenced, but did not anticipate that it was over. The failing light compelled us to relinquish our watching. Leading the homeward way, I had not gone a score yards when the female Owl rose at my feet, betraying six young ones, all in the ascending scale of development. The eldest, fully fledged, drew himself up, and, with head thrown back and glaring amber eyes, snapped his beak menacingly; the " pitman,"[1] with sightless eyes and body bare of feathers, stretched out his neck and compressed his body to the ground, trusting to perfect stillness for concealment. Meanwhile the cock bird dashed up and down close to our heads, and the hen, throwing herself down on the ground, rolled and flapped about Partridge-like, trying to distract our attention from her young.

It was a delightful picture of parental solicitude, and how could any nature-lover further disturb such a family? The prime mistake we unwittingly made was, of course, selecting a site for our supposed concealment too near to the position of the nest, which was within two hundred yards of a public water-course. Local marshmen say that the first hatched nestlings frequently devour their youngest brothers and sisters, but this I cannot vouch for.

Another bird characteristic of the district, and more abundant than is generally supposed, is the Grasshopper Warbler (*Locustella nævia*). The ability to catch the sound made by a Bat's membranous wing has been suggested as a test of good hearing. I have accompanied more than one visitor to Broadland who was unable to hear, at a little distance, the peculiar reel of the " Scissor-grinder." Were it not for its

---

[1] *Petit* man or cad—the smallest of the clutch.

distinctive note, the bird would probably escape notice altogether, its crepuscular habits and small size rendering it, in
the rank marsh stuff, most difficult to locate; the reeling, too,
is, like the voice of the Landrail, somewhat ventriloquial, and
unless the songster himself be seen, his exact whereabouts—at
many yards' distance, at any rate—is difficult to determinate.

A rough marsh, with a few sallow bushes and brambles
growing here and there, is its favourite haunt; but the nest
is seldom found except by the most experienced "eggers,"
though several are annually cut out by the marsh mowers.
A year or two ago I saw one that had been so discovered: it
contained five eggs, and was placed on the ground amidst
grass and candle rushes (*Juncus effusus*) only, so that when
this covert was cut the nest was left quite open. The man
to whom the swathes belonged, thinking that there was no
likelihood of such a naturally shy bird returning, under such
circumstances, to finish the process of incubation, with his
shut-knife[1] cut out the perfect nest and the grass sod containing it. Noticing that one egg was broken, he picked it
out and threw it on one side, putting the nest down out of
harm's way whilst continuing his mowing. In a few moments
the male bird came and carried away the broken eggshell in
his beak. Taking this act as an evidence of continued
parental solicitude, Nudd, the marshman, replaced the nest, and
a few days afterwards I was invited to witness the unusual
sight of a Grasshopper Warbler sitting on her newly-hatched
young on a marsh as level and bare as the palm of one's hand.
The fledglings subsequently flew in safety.

I have notes of several Sedge Warblers' nests being
successfully moved; but this bird is of a much more confid-
ing nature than the Grasshopper Warbler. Parental instinct is
very highly developed in the wildest animals, and by taking
advantage of this instinct, with the help of our reasoning
powers, we are enabled now and then to discover and peep
into the secret cradle of a rare bird, situated though it be in
the midst of a thousand acres of marshes, every square yard
of which is to the untrained eye almost exactly alike, and to
hunt all over which, without watching the birds and appreciat-

[1] Shut or shutting knife = pocket knife, as opposed to a table or case knife.

ing their moods and movements, would be an utter waste of time and trouble.

The ubiquitous Coot may certainly be said to be characteristic of the avi-fauna of the Broads. It has increased tenfold within the last decade, and though in summer a pair or two are to be found on every Broad, Hickling is *par excellence* their winter rendezvous, as well as their favourite breeding haunt. Careful protection during the springtime, and perhaps the decrease of the egg-devouring Harriers, has tended to this desirable result. Giant Pike, too, are not quite so numerous as of yore. These voracious freshwater sharks, being able to accommodate many downy mites in their capacious maws, doubtlessly used to levy toll on the young of all water fowl.

In spite of their commonness, how few people have any idea of the peculiar beauty of a baby Coot, not all dingy black, as the old birds mostly are, but with head and neck adorned with bristles of yellow and scarlet, the filaments tipped with white! They are hatched in a large and conspicuous nest composed almost entirely of, and always lined with, the leaves of the previous year's reeds. The eggs are never covered when the old bird leaves them, nor need they be, for they are protectively coloured, being of a ground colour assimilating to the leaves on which they rest, and, like them, peppered with small black dots and markings—the work, in the reed foliage, of a parasitic fungus.

Let me here confess that my oft companion on many a harmless ramble, Alfred Nudd of Hickling, most observant of marshmen, called my attention to this mimicry years before I ever saw it chronicled in print. For a full and perfect description of a local Coot shoot, I must again refer my readers to the work of our county ornithologist, Mr. J. H. Gurney having contributed such a paper to the *Transactions of the Norfolk and Norwich Naturalists' Society*.

The eggs of the Coot differ very much in size, as indeed do those of all other birds. Measurements alone are of little value for purposes of identification; but the larger the egg of the species the more noticeable is the variation, and the greater the series examined the more such variations are found. But with the Coot there seems every season to be two types of egg, one large and the other small, the latter scarcely exceeding those of the Moor-hen in bulk. In fact, I have seen examples quite as diminutive, and for two years in succession I have come across a clutch of Moor-hen's as large as the typical Coot's. Two sizes of Coots, too, appear in the winter game-bags, one weighing a third more than the other. We may conclude, therefore, that the smaller are not a distinct race—as in the case with the home-bred and foreign Mallard that occur here in winter — and that the local marshmen are right in describing those eggs laid by the smaller Coots as "pullet" eggs, *i.e.* those of birds under two years old. Although Coots are generally seen on water, and procure most of their food therefrom, they also eat grass, and tread on land. Moor-hens are, of course, abundant round the Broads, but not being so sociable are neither so numerous nor so much in evidence as the Coots. Their unlobated feet betoken their adaptability to less watery localities; by night they stray far inland, and at such times their loud and distant *thuck! thuck!* has puzzled many an observer of bird notes. They frequently roost in trees by day, and I have found their nests elevated ten feet above land or water; but I have never seen their eggs covered when the parent leaves them either before or during incubation, not even on such much-frequented rivers as the "Backs" or "Freshman's" at Cambridge, much less so in our reed bushes, marshes, coverts, or wayside ponds.

Water Rails (*Rallus aquaticus*) still lay their delicately tinted eggs in "slads" away from the open Broads; the nest, though large, is well concealed, but not difficult to discover when one knows the likely spots or listens in the evening for the "sharming" of the birds.

The Montagu Harrier, still annually occurring as a spring migrant attempting to nest, may as yet be included as lending character to our extensive marshes. There can be no doubt that this beautiful bird would be at any rate as plentiful as the Kestrel, were it not for the fact that it is also a hawk, and, moreover, a rare hawk, and therefore looked upon not only as deleterious to game and gamekeepers, but also valuable to shooters and collectors.

I must not tell all I know about either the depredations made by or upon this bird, or I shall perhaps damage both its chances and its character. I will therefore merely attempt to describe some few hours passed not many years ago in its company. At one time I had three Montagus and a pair of Marsh Harriers in view, with a Short-eared Owl or two also within ken, Rails "sharming" and Snipe drumming and bleating around, Redshanks incessantly uttering their monotonous, plaintive, but musical whistle in the distance, whilst more of the larger Gulls than I ever remember before noticing together at that season of the year were washing and slaking their thirst in the mere near by. The advent of a passing Heron lent diversion, and several Yellow Wagtails and now and then a Swallow-tail Butterfly added colour to the scene. Ere our quest was over a little party of Lesser Redpolls visited the young birch trees on the marsh wall adjacent to our hiding-place, and an unexpected Kingfisher— one of a pair, as I subsequently ascertained, that were breeding not far away—alighted on the "ligger" which spanned the nearest dyke. Added to which, Swallows, Martins, and, towards evening, several Swifts hurried to and fro over our heads, whilst countless Sedge and Reed Warblers "noised" incessantly on every side of us, and Wood Pigeons cooed with contentment within earshot. Nor must I omit the Cuckoos, especially numerous that year, which, two at a time, were now and then perched motionless for minutes together upon the same stunted thorn bush about a hundred yards away, apparently taking no notice of one another while resting; but if one started off the other followed, and they chevied one another, chuckling and clucking meanwhile, but whether in love or anger who shall say? Meanwhile the sky was cloudless, the sun intensely powerful, flies immensely irritating in the shade, and the gnats at "shutting-in-time" even more so.

Nudd undertook to watch the three Montagus, whilst I was intent upon the two Marsh Harriers. I watched until my eyes were weary of watching and my arms tired of holding up the glasses. When the birds crossed one another, we became sometimes a bit mixed in the species. Sometimes we lost sight of one bird for many minutes together. The male, say, would suddenly disappear behind the tall reed to the right, and then suddenly reveal himself far away on the left; or one would alight on the bare marsh wall, on which mud had recently been thrown and was now baked and cracked by the sun; here another bird would bring it food. Next, one of the Marsh Harriers would be "mobbed" and suffer persecution at the hands of two of the Montagus; but the Marsh never attacked the Montagu, from which we argued, and rightly, as subsequent events proved, that the larger birds had not yet nested, and that the smaller had already laid.

For hours, however, we could make nothing out for certain; but shortly before sunset a female Montagu was suddenly lost to sight, and one of the males was viewed away to the distant sandhills. Just as we were beginning to think it were no use staying longer, a speck appeared in the azure, the male returned, and hovered over where we had last lost sight of his mate. "Uick! uick! gluee! gluee!" he cried, as he apparently dropped some prey; and the female, rising a few yards, caught it in the air. Nudd threw up his cap for joy. Waiting a few moments to let the hen bird settle herself, "Now you may go," says Sam Harmer (*alias* Captain Hanks); and away we went, all excitement, to the spot—carefully marked before starting; and so true was the long line taken, that without deviating a yard Nudd came within a few feet of putting his feet on the sitting bird, which, until we were too near, trusted to stillness for escaping observation. There were four eggs in the nest, the first I had ever seen *in situ;* but I regret to say that neither they nor subsequent clutches laid in the same district within the past five years were allowed a chance of hatching off, although report has it that one young bird at least was successfully reared a year or two ago in a neighbouring parish.

Rival eggers try to shoot the male of any bird whose embryo offspring they desire to secure; for should the female have commenced, she generally will go on laying, or at any rate sitting, without her husband to attend upon her, his attentions frequently betraying the whereabouts of her sanctuary.

Local observers state that Harriers tread in the air, and should one of a pair of birds be killed early in the season, the other will go away and soon bring back another partner. I have also heard it said that male Harriers appear first and select a nesting site, if not actually commencing to build, before bringing the female to inspect and approve and complete their preparations. Nudd aforesaid and poor old Sam Harmer—now, alas! ending his days in the workhouse —can bear witness that the aforegoing is no overdrawn picture, but the simple truth as to what passed before our eyes whilst we were sitting in one spot, or at any rate not moving more than a dozen yards from it, in half as many hours; although it may have fallen to the lot of few to see, as I have seen, the nests of both Marsh and Montagu Harriers in one day, and to find those of the Montagu and the Short-eared Owl on the same marsh. The Marsh Harrier's nest, commenced but never finished, was placed about a foot off the ground in the midst of a large and dense bed of that rare rush, *Cladium jamaicense.*

Still characteristic of the Broads, for some few—several in spring and one or two in autumn—still annually visit us, the Ruff and Reeve must now, I fear, be included in the list of lost breeding species. Both in 1900 and 1901 a lone Reeve stayed very late and raised the hopes of some of us that what had been would, to a certain extent, be again; but since 1889 no Reeve's nest has, to my knowledge, been found.[1] It is not necessary that a pair should be seen to ensure nidification, for the Ruff is polygamous, and troubles himself not with parental cares. Within the last decade I took a local friend over to Hickling on the chance of seeing some of these curious birds, and we were successful beyond our highest anticipations. It was a bright May morning, the wind was right, and as we neared Swimcoots wall our worthy quanter, glasses in hand, spied a party of Ruffs and Reeves come and alight inside the marsh. Promptly lying down at the bottom of the boat, we let her drift towards land, and ere she grounded, some ten yards from the shore, first a Reeve, then a Ruff, and then

---

[1] In Harting's *Handbook of British Birds*, 2nd ed., p. 184, a nest is reported in 1897, near Hoveton Broad.

15

another Ruff, came over the narrow foot and grassy slope, until we had counted eight different and distinctive plumages of the almost adult males. For nearly half an hour we watched them, until, for some unaccountable reason, they took wing, and fled rapidly away to the right of us, over to the hovers in the Warbush.[1]

Whilst we held them in view on Swimcoots we saw no serious fighting. Now and then two males would play the game-cock; but more often than not they would set at and challenge one another without even attempting to spar, and when a feint was made it ended there, and if an actual blow was struck it never told, and the striker was the first to move away and commence feeding again. In fact, they were difficult to watch, for they were incessantly on the move. Some of the Ruffs, none very white or yellow in the frill, were in very nearly full feather; but we saw no attention paid to the three Reeves accompanying them.

Terns—Common, Lesser, and Black—occur regularly on spring and autumn migration: the last-named used to breed here, but have now quite ceased to do so. The last egg at Hickling was laid upon a lump of weed drawn up by the sun when the water was low; and the last pair that probably intended to nest at Rollesby were shot. The rare White-winged Black Tern has been procured at Hickling several times, and also at Barton.

Amongst the Ducks, the Shoveller has increased; but the Garganey, or Summer Teal, retains a very doubtful hold as a breeding species. Within the past ten years the Spotted Rail reared a brood in the parish of Brunstead. Very late in August, a cousin, a steady old retriever, and I, tried ineffectually our best to catch some of a clutch, unable or unwilling to rise, although one — as thin as the proverbial rail—passed between my legs as I stood knee-deep in water, mud, and marsh stuff. There was no case of mistaken identity, for I had already shot one of the parent birds before thinking, much less knowing, that there were any young about; the note and behaviour of the other old bird left no doubt in my mind as to the species of herself or the little

[1] So called because men used to hide here from the pressgangers.

ones accompanying her. Never but once have I seen either of the smaller Crakes or Rails, and then not near enough to distinguish it. We were after Duck and Snipe, when my old bitch flushed it some ten yards ahead of me, and in its low, short, backward flight it covered first her and then my right-hand companion, and as he was on the outside and coming round upon the beat, I had not a chance to shoot ere it alighted between us; and although there was too much water for it to get its feet to the ground, the thick vegetation gave it ample foothold, and in spite of careful and prolonged hunting, and much snuffing and tail-wagging on the part of our canine accomplice, we never flushed that tiny mite again.

The Norfolk Plover has ceased to breed in the hollows amongst the sandhills within the last twenty years: I can remember the time when they might be seen night after night taking the same line of flight at Winterton. Here, too, on the upland fields, the Dotterel used regularly to appear at turnip-sowing time: one or two are now and again still taken on Yarmouth Denes, and I have a couple which, in different years, killed themselves by colliding with telegraph or telephone wires. This bird is one of the exceptions tending to prove the ornithological rule, that where the female only incubates, there she is protectively and less highly coloured than her mate; here the male alone sits, and therefore has to be contented with less conspicuous attire.

There are so many birds that a visitor is almost sure to come across whilst cruising on the Broads, that it is difficult to summarise. In spring and early summer the Redshank will not allow itself to pass unnoticed, nor is the phonetic Peewit much less shy in forcing itself under observation; and the unbird-like wing sound of the Summer Lamb [1] is sure to betray the downward flight of the Common Snipe.

The great gaunt Heron, too, suddenly disturbed from swallowing an edible frog, perhaps, on the banks of Deep Dyke, will slowly sail across the ronds, uttering his loud *frank! frank!* as if his size alone were not sufficient to attract attention to his huge wings, long rudder-like legs,

[1] So called from its peculiar wing sound at breeding-time.

flowing crest, and old-world *tout ensemble*. In autumn time, I have counted as many as forty of these "arrangements in grey" resting or fishing for eels in Swimcoots big slad. But such an assembly is as nothing to the great bunches of Wigeon which come to us in May *en route* for their more northern breeding grounds, or to the hundreds of Pochards which precede the winter's hard frosts. I have seen Somerton Broad, both north and south portions of it, one day so thickly covered with Red-heads that it would have been impossible to put down a punt without touching one, and the next day the water was "laid," and the "Pokers" had perforce departed. But even such a gathering is outnumbered frequently by the clouds of chattering Starlings which in autumn assemble to roost amongst the reeds, and in their eagerness for supremacy, and to gain the highest perch, do much damage to the thatching stuff, breaking down acres of the reed by their weight and flutterings. Sometimes, too, the water is literally alive with Gulls. Never shall I forget sleeping in an open boat in the midst of a local breeding colony of Scoulton Cobs! A pretty picture they make in daylight, and a pretty noise, too, at daybreak!

Here, as nowhere else in England,—away from the coast, at any rate,—may annually be seen, sometimes in good-sized herds, the stately Whooper and more Goose-like Bewick Swan, driven hither, probably, by gathering ice in more northern regions: each species upon such emergency frequents the more expansive Broads. On the approach of winter, — as early as mid-October, sometimes, — attracted by their Mute relatives, perhaps, Swans of equal size with them, but with full wings, straight necks, and beaks carried at right angles thereto, may be observed. These are the Great Wild Swans, come in here for rest and fresh water; and wild indeed they are, at any rate so long as the Broad keeps open. The carriage of the head and neck betokens their distinction from *Cygnus olor*, and this at a distance at which the different disposition of black and yellow on the beak cannot be noticed. Their smaller size and more lumpy appearance on the water sufficiently identify the Bewicks. The latter birds keep much closer together on the water than the Whoopers, and appear to be more sociable. Both species frequently have head and neck feathers tinged with rufous red, probably from feeding in waters saturated with iron sulphate, or "that old sulphur," as the marshmen call it.

An old male Whooper I have weighed up to twenty-two and a half pounds; an adult Bewick scaled ten pounds less— both in excellent condition. The double-walled keel to the breast-bone of each I have now in front of me. Between the two walls the windpipe passes and returns ere it enters the lungs,—a provision of nature for warming the air for breathing whilst the birds are feeding in water below freezing-point, perhaps; for when "ground" or "mare's ice" is forming on the Broads, the whole volume of water is of a temperature below $32°$, and only kept from consolidating by the action of the wind. Thus is the rare phenomenon of a Broad freezing up to leeward accounted for. I have had the nose of my quant a knob of ice, and brought up ice-covered weeds at every shove, whilst the surface of the water was unfrozen. On the other hand, the suddenness with which the ice on Hickling breaks up may be judged from the fact that I once helped to push a punt across the Broad in the morning, laid in a wake on the other side all day, and came home in open water after flighting - time. The power of the huge sheets of ice, crashing against and running over one another, can be gauged by the fact that their striking against the steam-driven posts which stake-out the channel is sufficient, in a few hours, to lay the posts at an acute angle with the water. But such is not a day on which to admire the Whoopers; a bright, crisp day, with blue sky and still waters, is the time to see and admire the majestic wing-sweep and dazzling white plumage, hear the distinctive *honk! congk!* and observe the final wedge-like formation of some forty long-necked strangers, — a formation which, after being once or twice put up, they assume to ease their aerial passage seaward, until departing daylight or early dawn may (should the weather threaten) tempt them to return inland.

Under certain conditions, the immediate vicinity of the Broads seems — not counting game — a veritable Avernus; but when once skaters and ice-boats have cleared away, and the prolonged frost has broken up for good, how great and sudden is the change in bird life!—right on, then, until next mid-November at the earliest, every acre of marsh, reed-ground, and quiet open water is alive with ever-varying feathered forms. Not that we can now boast of so numerous an avi-fauna as the pages of even so recent an historian as Lubbock tells of; but since he wrote, some new species have been added to our local list, whilst others, that had dwindled down towards extinction, within the last twenty years have increased in numbers. In former days, when Ornithology had not been made quite such an exact science, the immigration of many waifs and strays and storm-driven strangers was allowed to pass unrecorded, if not unnoticed; but within later times Shore Larks and Little Auks, Sand Grouse and Blue-throated Warblers, have put in more frequent appearances, whilst the Turtle Dove and Tree Sparrow, Great Crested Grebe and Woodcock, more than hold their own as breeding species. The Stock-Dove is certainly decreasing on the sandhills, and the Common Plover on the marshes. A good many Redshank and Snipe still nest with us; but never again, perhaps, will it be possible for one gun in Broadland to kill thirty-three couple of the latter in a day, and one hundred and sixty-six couple in a season, as my father did at Somerton in 1868. Some estimate of the present-day wealth of bird life in Norfolk may be arrived at by comparing the British list with that of the county. The latest schedule of British birds published with authority is found in the new (1901) edition of Harting's Handbook, in which four hundred and twenty-eight species are enumerated, sixty-five of which are marked as doubtful. Up to January 1899 (and I know of no later additions), Messrs. Gurney and Southwell, in the *Transactions of the Norfolk and Norwich Naturalists' Society*, credit our county with three hundred and eight representatives, and make mention of eight other uncertain ones. The length and position of our coastline, facing the east and shouldering round to the north, with saltings adjoining, our many fresh-water Broads, marshes, and reed-beds, together with the far-famed Breydon mud-flats, and extensive game coverts in close proximity to the shore,—all these taken together form an attractive network of decoys for any species of bird that may chance to come within sight of them.

So sharp an outlook is now kept for varieties, that probably not a single avian stranger stays more than a day to rest here without its presence being detected, even if its skin is not secured. Some of the scarce and tiny Warblers may, indeed, escape observation during the summer months; but it is practically impossible for any larger bird to defy detection, so many trained and eager eyes are always and everywhere on the lookout for something to annex, or to report upon. No other county, probably, has, for the last thirty years at least, been more thoroughly and systematically worked, both for birds and eggs.

Upon the local ornithology of the past I need not dwell. Suffice to say that up to 1542 the Crane is supposed to have bred here, and until 1671 the Spoonbill. The Cormorant ceased nesting in the county about 1825, and the Avocet at about the same time. The last Black-tailed Godwit's egg was taken at Reedham in 1857. Probably the Black Tern and Bittern will never again rear their young in Broadland; the Reeve seems disinclined to stay; and the Harriers are certainly doomed, in spite of Protection Acts and prohibited areas. The Garganey Teal seems to be mysteriously vanishing as a breeder; the Spotted Rail retains a doubtful foothold; nor does either the Short or Long Eared Owl tend to increase. The recent rise in price of litter has caused more marsh stuff to be cut between haysel and harvest; this is detrimental to nidification in general, although favourable to snipe-feeding and snipe-shooting, and affording more playground to the Ruffs.

A few years ago I heard a marshman give as one reason for the Ruffs' and Reeves' absence nowadays, that they had nowhere to alight upon,—one of their most favoured haunts not having been mown for six or seven years. Now London 'bus and cab horses have absorbed that ancient herbage, and yet the Ruffs and Reeves do not linger long, although a nest was reported at Hoveton in 1897.

Lost as breeding birds are the Spoonbills and Godwits, with some dozen other species which formerly bred here; but the *animaux implumes* that now annually visit the Broads are of greater value to the greater number, and with less species we have more numerous benefits. The ague has departed as well as the Avocet, and bullocks now batten where the Bittern once boomed; but in spite of egging and shooting, steam drainage and other inventions, we still possess a richer avifauna than any other county in England. Eleven species, at least, in the British list were first noted in this favoured district.

CHAPTER XV

ENTOMOLOGY

By Claude Morley, F.E.S., etc.

NORFOLK possesses in its Broads a physiological feature found nowhere else throughout the British Isles to so large an extent. Nowhere do marsh plants, marsh trees, and marsh animals of all kinds flourish so perfectly; and consequently marsh insects are here in greater profusion than elsewhere. You do not see them, because it is not intended that you should; if you could the birds could, and then the insects would be destroyed, and the plants, which they benefit us so greatly by keeping within bounds, would flourish to such an abnormal extent as to choke up the waterways and their adjacent marshes, just as the dense scudd blocks the White Nile. This is one of the surprising things about our marsh insects; another is the way they protect themselves from their feathered enemies. Some that live on the Great Water Dock are green, and pass their existence on the leaves; others that are red inhabit only the flowers of the Purple Loosestrife; yellow ones live in Honeysuckle, and black ones in the mud of the river margins. Some water beetles mimic fallen acorns; and others, as though for a joke, exactly resemble the droppings of the birds themselves. Those that live on the reeds are long and narrow, those on broad leaves are round and flat like seeds. You can see a ship on the horizon, a skying partridge, or even the drift of your neighbour's business, but you will not find insects in their natural environment till you have had considerable practice at the art.

One of the disadvantages of this fascinating study is its very magnitude; in fact, the number of different kinds of insects (which term does not include spiders, wood lice, nor crustaceans nowadays) is computed to be very nearly if not quite fifteen thousand in Britain alone. This world of insects is divided into nations as distinct *inter se* as are those of the world of man. They differ from one another as completely in habits and tastes, and far, very far, more in structure and colour, than *Homo sapiens*. Therefore it will be most convenient to search our Broads for each of those great nationalities or *Orders* in turn, remarking only that justice is meted out by no means impartially, because a very great deal more is known of some orders than of others. Personally, I should guess that of British entomologists quite seventy-five in a hundred study only the moths; so, of course, moths are better known than are the insects of any other order; though of late years the beetles have come in for a larger share of attention.

We are, then, going to the Broads to collect Moths; but let us first bear in mind there is one grand and glorious butterfly, which takes our breath away when it appears for the first time to us sweeping over the alder carrs in marshland, or opening and closing its wings while basking in the sunshine on a flower by the riverside, exhibiting the long projections of its hind wings, which have earned for it the name of Swallow-Tail. But you should not catch it; so many have been caught and killed by greedy collectors and curious folk, that it is becoming very rare, and is now found nowhere in Britain but in these Broads and in the fens of Cambridgeshire, where, I fear, it is less common than it was a few years ago. Of course, collectors are only a secondary cause of its threatened extinction; the primary one is the draining of the wet places in which alone the Hog's Fennel, the food-plant of its caterpillar, will deign to grow. There is another butterfly, now but a phantom reminiscent of original bog, unbounded river, the Bittern and Savi's Warbler, which at the beginning of the last century used to gladden one's heart with a sight of its large copper-coloured wings; but it gradually died out, and is now known only in old-time collectors' cabinets, a veritable treasure. The periodic butterflies, the Queen of Spain and the Camberwell Beauty, occasionally appear singly at various villages, and are quite as common here as elsewhere in England; but one can never rely on a personal encounter.

Yarmouth is the gate of Broadland, and before proceeding farther you should try to discover a Bedstraw or Oleander Hawk hovering about its portals, since they have both been found here, as well as the very rare *Cloantha perspicillaris*. When the Broads themselves are at length reached, work the numberless alders for the Dotted Footman, said to occur nowhere else in Britain, but which may here be had in return for the requisite searching in July and August. The last record of the Gipsy Moth living "wild" is from Cawston, and in the old days Curtis and others used to take it quite commonly at Horning. The well-named Marveil-du-jour Moth has been recorded from Aldeby, and the delicate Essex Emerald from Horning, though it is, I believe, not found in such numbers as is the case in its southern home.

The coast sands are so much a feature of Broadland,—in some places, as at Horsey, almost touching the marshes,—that I may be forgiven for calling attention to one or two of the local species which are found upon them. Of these, one of the, most noteworthy is the Lyme Wainscot, which is abroad in July, though the caterpillar is better obtained in May by shaking the Lyme Grass on the dunes over a newspaper. The Fen Leopard, whose caterpillar only feeds within the Cambridge reed-stems, has been introduced (no secret is made of the fact, since it was becoming scarce in its old haunts) at Ranworth, and there appears, having escaped its great enemy, the Reed Bunting, to be gaining a satisfactory footing in congenial surroundings; and in the same way the Scarce Chocolate-Tip has been "laid down" in Barton Turf. Nevertheless, there is no need to introduce alien species, unless, as in the above instances, it is for their own preservation; the vast array of indigenous ones will amply repay even the most advanced student, and to the tyro furnishes worlds unconquered. The favourite method of collecting imagines is to rig up a large white sheet between two poles and place a strong light before it; to this decoy, luminous for miles across the marshes, moths will flock on a damp, warm, breathless night from all quarters. In this manner have been taken such rarities as the Buff

Footman, the Black Collar, the Bordered and Scarce-Bordered Straws, as well as their cousin the Scarce-Marbled Clover. While searching for the Lyme Wainscot you might easily pass over the Scarce Pearl, which has been found resting on the grass-stems of the sandhills at Yarmouth, where you may also attract to your sheet-lantern the exclusive *Anerastia farrella*, and are sure to find *Nyetegrates achatinella* among the maram grass early in July. Taken as a whole, you should secure the Sand Dart, the Portland Moth, the Shore Wainscot, and *Eupœcilia pallidana* on these sand dunes at the proper time of year. Another splendid ground is the cluster of Broads on the Bure about Ranworth; here the Powdered Pearl, *Peronea perplexana* and *lorguiniana*, among other rarities, have been found; and mention must also be made of *Crambus padellus*, which is nearly confined to this spot, as is *C. fascelinellus* to Yarmouth. Last and greatest of the moths I shall here indicate—for the majority is too numerous for mention—is Fenn's Nonagria, for this fine species is our own monopoly, occurring nowhere in the world outside the cluster of Broads about Horning, where, however, it is by no means rare, though not discovered till 1864. The caterpillars may be found on their food-plant by searching with a lantern after dark, and the moths themselves fly at dusk early in August amongst the gently rustling reed-maces. I saw many of the larvæ there in June, 1901.

The coleopterist in Broadland must have a water-net, for nowhere in the length and breadth of this country can it be used with greater effect than in our rivers, Broads, and brooks. No other county can touch us in the number of water-beetles, predacious and phytophagous,[1] for there have been recorded one hundred and seventy-three out of a total of two hundred and twenty kinds in these islands, some of which are almost unique and others exclusively Scotch. Of the predacious ones, *Hydroporus halensis* — English names are nearly unknown among beetles—is a "good thing," and one that will appear in an occasional pool, such as existed formerly at Brundall station, in plenty, and then not be seen again for years; it has also been recorded for Horning and Stalham. *H.*

[1] Plant-feeding.

scalesianus, first found in Norfolk, *H. neglectus* at Horning and Stratton Strawless, *H. ferrugineus* and *oblongus*, *Agabus striolatus*, of which we have a monopoly, *Ilybius guttiger*, and *Rhantus grapii*, all occur at Horning, and should not be mistaken for the common things they so much resemble.

Let us next metaphorically sit down in a mud flat to see what is running about seeking what it may devour, since perchance *Pogonus luridipennis*, first found here in 1806, but not taken now for many years; some of the rarer *Bembidii*, such as *fumigatum* and *saxatile*, the long-lost *Pterostichus aterrimus*, which used to bask on the wet mud by the Broads and fly in bright sunshine, to mention only a few rarities in the way of ground beetles, might fall to our lot. Among the roots of the reeds might lurk the rare *Ætophorus*, and we are sure to get *Odacantha*, whose brilliant red and green coat is conspicuous among the reed-refuse, especially in May. Many of the rove or cocktail beetles will be seen scurrying about, more especially those of the genera *Stenus*, *Trogophlœus*, and *Homalota*; of these there are so many good things obtainable that space cries Hold! But I must just whisper *Stenus proditor* and *opticus* by sweeping at Horning, often after dark; *Homalota atomaria*, *perixigua*, and *hodierna* in vegetable refuse, also at Horning, and add that good *Heteroceri* should also be found in this way.

A great deal remains to be discovered about our rove-beetles, which have not yet received adequate attention. To instance a single genus, with, for the most part, swampy proclivities, *Bledius* is but ill represented by nine kinds; *Arenarius* and *Cassicollis* have been taken but a few miles south, in Suffolk, and a little farther, *Spectabilis* and *Bicornis* at Harwich. For the short-winged *Clavicorns* we are on classic ground, since at Norwich in 1825 was published Denny's Monograph on these atoms. *Blythinus burelli* was first found here in 1824 and named by Denny after its captor, and the same may be said of *Sparshalli* in 1823. Mr. Sparshall's collection of beetles is preserved in the Castle Museum. It is a most curious circumstance that such common things as the Great Stag-Beetle and *Helops striatus*, which abound throughout Suffolk, should be so rare as to be almost unknown in Norfolk;

yet such would appear to be the case.   Marsh frequenters like
Telephorus figuratus, thoracicus, and *lateralis, Silis ruficollis,
Malthodes dispar,* and *Anthocomus terminatus,* all occur with
more or less frequency.   Of the fine longhorns, *Agapanthia
lineatocollis,* which is common in the Cambridgeshire Fens,
has not been found for years; but I expect *Oberea oculata*
is to be discovered on the sallow bushes in August if they
are searched systematically.   Those essentially aquatic-plant
beetles, the lovely metallic *Donaciæ,* you will find when, as
Elliott says—

"The reed-maces gently are rustling,"

as well as all the other kinds known in Britain, excepting only
D. obscura.   In like manner all the *Galerucæ* are common on
the osiers and water-lilies, with *Phyllobrotica* on the skull-cap.[1]
Ceuthorhynchus querceti has only recently been added to our
native fauna by Mr. Champion from several examples taken in
Horning Fen, and in all probability it is there attached to the
wild radish.   An idea of what you are looking for is in this
case very necessary, since it is a small beetle with a strong
superficial likeness to several common kinds.

Every one who is fond of beetles—and it is only necessary
to notice their adaptability and wonderful economy to love
instead of hating them, in which so many ignorant and superstitious people persist—ought to be interested in the bugs.   Oh
yes! a nasty word, I grant you; but nasty only from association: in America all insects are designated "bugs"; and do the
peasants of East Anglia dislike lady-birds because they call
them "golden bugs"?   On the contrary, bugs—by which term
is meant here only that nation of insects which has a proboscis
and semi-membraneous wings—are of the utmost value to us,
for they insert their proboscis into the plant-stems to suck up the
juices, thus keeping down rank and superfluous growth.   Bugs
are at sight divided into two groups: those that hop and those
that don't.   The first section of Norfolk includes many rare
kinds, and the coleopterist could nowhere begin to study them
to greater advantage.   Such rarities as *Plociomerus fracticollis,*
which is quite common here, the large *Reduvius peronatus,*
often attracted at night by artificial light, and many fen

[1] *Scutellaria galericulata.*

species of *Salda*, may be had with a little exertion. The little *Hebrus pusillus* and, I expect, *ruficeps* will be found in wet moss; the curious *Ranatra*, *Aphelocheirus*, and rare *Gerris rufoscutellata* may also fall to your water-net. Mr. James Edwards has worked very thoroughly the hopping bugs of Norfolk, and the result has so well repaid his labours that *Typhlocyba debilis*, of which only about four specimens are known, and *Deltocephalus costalis*, a fen species nearly confined to Ranworth Broad, have been recorded from the county, which boasts in all a list not likely to be equalled from any other locality.

Of the nation of the Locusts, Crickets, and Cockroaches, so abundant abroad, there are but forty kinds here, and of these very few are recorded from our swamps, simply because they have never been looked for. But they deserve attention, if only on account of their omnivorousness and peculiar method of chirping. Every species has its own especial chirp, and if you have a good ear it is not difficult to tell what kind is talking in an adjacent osier-bed; but, like detecting a green beetle on a green leaf, perfection requires practice and patience. The sound is not emitted from the mouth at all, but is produced by the rough hind hopping-legs, which are rubbed briskly against the wings, like the pins of a musical box on their teeth, an invention thus long forestalled in Nature. Cockroaches are, no doubt, only too common—I call them Cockroaches, but some people say Black Beetles; an invidious term, because they are not black and are not beetles! They will eat anything from blacking to ships' biscuits, and there are several wild kinds that never live in houses, but are found in woods and among heather. One rather good Grasshopper, only found in very wet places and sure to turn up in Broadland, is *Xiphidium dorsale*, a very handsome green and chocolate insect, common south of the Waveney.

One would expect caterpillars that live invariably at the bottom of shallow fresh, stagnant, or running water to be abundant in our moist places, but such seems to be the case to no exceptional extent in either Norfolk or Cambridgeshire. The great, grand Dragon-flies—or " Horse-stings," as they are locally known, though quite harmless—seen hawking in darts along the margin of the river and the reeds of the pools, were once ugly creepy things resembling nothing so much as crayfish, that lived in the mud, subsisting on aquatic insects, which they stalked in an underhand kind of way, with a great arm usually tucked away under the head but capable of being shot forward at will to seize their prey when the latter thought itself out of reach.   The only kind really worthy of note is *Æschna rufescens*, said by Paget, in his *Natural History of Yarmouth* (1834), to have been taken in the Halvergate marshes.   It is still expected to occur in that vicinity, though I do not think it has been found since his time.   The very name " Water-flies " suggests such a locality as one for their discovery ; but in point of fact I fancy no kinds of extraordinary interest have been noticed.   These in their earlier stages are the caddis-worms, so curious on account of the queer cases they construct to protect themselves from the attacks of voracious Dragon-flies and Water-beetles.   You may see a bit of stick or a bundle of tiny pebbles actually walking with no visible means of propulsion about the bottom of a shallow ; but on looking closely a little black object is observed protruding from the front end.   This is the head and forefeet of a worm—really a caterpillar—which is capable of retreating into its shelter at the least swirl of danger.   Very curious cases have been constructed of coloured beads and even metals by allowing caddis - worms in captivity no more natural building materials.

And now let us for a moment briefly glance at the greatest and most potent of all insect nations, the *Hymenoptera*, under which heading are included groups differing as widely as do the Kaffir, the Briton, and the Hindoo, but united, as under a common flag, by their possession of four small transparent wings, linked together by a series of tiny hooks and a hard, chitinous [1] body.   It is here that we find the marvellous sagacity, almost intelligence, of the ants, bees, and wasps, whose inventions in the way of architecture and militarism, we are beginning to realise, have long preceded many of our own : the foresight of the Sawflies, which secrete their future progeny in a little slit cut between the cuticles of leaves ; of the Ichneumons, most

[1] Mail-like.

marvellous creatures, perhaps, of all creation, whose long ovipositor is plunged into some unwary caterpillar, there leaving the fatal egg, which produces a white fleshy maggot and eventually destroys its unwilling host, from whose empty skin the plump parasite rises, just as the original Egyptian ichneumon was supposed to unaccountably arise from the despoiled crocodile's egg. But this vampire does not always emerge; sometimes a small green hymenopteron comes forth, and you know that the Ichneumon, while preying on the moth, has itself been devoured from within by this verdant evil, which is consequently called a hyper-parasite—an interesting process illustrative of Swift's "big fleas and little fleas," and which would go well to the rhythm of the "House that Jack built." No county has had its Ichneumons better worked than have those of Norfolk by Mr. John B. Bridgman, who also found many of the rarer Wild Bees here, including *Sphecodes ferruginatus*, *Nomada obtusifrons*, and *Macropis labiata*, and also of the Saw-flies. His grand collections are in the Norwich Museum, and are worthy of an especial visit, being a monument to what even a busy man can do almost single-handed upon a neglected group of insects.

I have heard a man who studies the Beetles of the world (a prodigious task!) say that there are only three sorts of flies, namely, house-flies, dragon-flies, and "other flies." This was, of course, in simulated contempt, for no one knew better than he that the last term comprised some three thousand different kinds in England alone, and that dragon-flies, scientifically speaking, are not flies at all in the proper sense. Of house-flies there can be said to be only some dozen kinds, for most of those found indoors are nothing but chance visitors. But many of the "other flies" are very interesting on account of their varied habits and habitats. They are found everywhere, from the mines they bore in the leaves of the tallest trees, to the roots of the tiniest plants; from scavengers ridding the earth of carrion and offal, reducing it to the best possible manure, to the Bot-flies laying their eggs on the skin of cattle, whence they are licked by the beasts into their stomachs, where the resultant maggots thrive and grow fat to maturity; from, in fine, flies which literally live on elephants, to others which

16

prey upon and destroy insects no bigger than themselves. In the Broads we find a great many marsh flies, whose caterpillars pass their life in or upon the surface of water, such as many of the *Stratiomyidæ ;* or in the spongy club-mosses, but more especially in the water-plants and reed-beds, all of which swarm with Gnats, Mosquitoes, Craneflies, and Hoverers. The last-named are very useful entities in the balance of Nature ; they have active, carnivorous caterpillars, frequenting plants infested with Green-blight or *Aphides*, which they seize in their powerful jaws and devour with gusto in great numbers. There is, I think, a fortune awaiting the man who will keep a menagerie of these destroyers, to be let out on hire to florists and others whose rare cuttings and bulbs are attacked by plant-lice. Two very common hoverers throughout the Broads are *Tropidia milesiformis* and *Pyrophæna ocymi ;* I have also taken the rare *P. rosarum* at Wroxham.

I have pointed out in this chapter but few of the beauties of Broadland's insects. Plenty of others will be found awaiting observation there ; but they must be looked for. It is pleasant to be on your wherry and watch the winged wonders of air and water ; but if you are content to do this you will find when you get home that " the devil bubbled below the keel, ' It's human, but is it Art ? ' " No ; watch the incessant war of the insect world, both direct and subtle, that is waging around you, but *also* discover its cause and effect ; find that with it activity is stimulated, the most useful in Nature only is preserved, that the fittest only survive, the noxious perish, and that without it worlds—the worlds of insects, of plants, and consequently of animals and man—would stagnate, putrefy, and finally rot. We do not yet comprehend what we indirectly owe to our tiny fluttering friends, but glimmerings begin to pierce our blindness.

CHAPTER XVI

POND LIFE

By H. E. Hurrell

IN pursuance of the study of this important branch of Natural History, the student has one of the most delightful tasks before him that can possibly be imagined—that is, if he be an enthusiast; and no one, unless he be "over head and ears in love" with the subject, will be able to derive from it the unqualified delight and constant enjoyment that is the certain lot of all earnest students, or be able to solve the many little zoological problems that crop up now and again in the course of his perambulations from pool to pool. Research in pond life offers triple advantages: it takes the seeker after knowledge into a world totally different to that in which he has otherwise lived; it gives him a wider view of the great plan of creation, and takes him away (for a time at least) from the cares, the bustle, and the business anxieties of a workaday life. No study could be at once more entertaining, more informative, or more useful, than the elucidation of the mysteries relating to the life-histories of the habitants of our inland waters. There is no lack of opportunity given to the most busy man, provided he be an earnest student; in and around the mighty city he can find plenty of living organisms coming under the general term of pond life —for wherever the river rushes and swirls or a garden pond exists, he will be sure to find, on intelligent search, objects that will employ his leisure to an almost unlimited extent, and provide him with pleasure and information that is only obtainable from a "speaking" acquaintance with the merry movements of the fairy forms with which he will continually come in contact. Or if he have an hour or two to spare, he has but to take a short trip to the country district immediately surrounding the town in which he resides, to be at once in the midst of unlimited " game."

He requires no beater to drive the animals he is in search of from their cover, or dog to retrieve them, but hies him to the first farmyard pond, wayside pool or ditch, where he is provided with " sport " that not only gives him present interest, but certain and abundant material for home examination and study. The pond-life cult has this advantage over almost all other Natural History pursuits—it brings before the notice of the acute observer an immense variety of objects that, while not belonging to his particular department, afford him a fund of information that is not obtainable in any other way. In seeking for specimens, he must necessarily become acquainted with the beautiful water-plants—too often miscalled *weeds*— that confront him on every hand; and not only this, for the autumn and winter months provide a variety of species as well as the more prolific months of spring and summer, and the various natural aspects of the countryside, its ever-changing panorama of plant and flower, the bursting of the trees into leaf, the grandeur and wealth of their summer foliage, and the beautiful shading-off of their leaves into the kaleidoscopic hues of autumn, together with the harvest and fruiting periods,—all these tend not only to whittle down the anxieties of life and make it more worth living, but afford permanent and useful study that no book could furnish, no lecturer, however eloquent, convey.

The waters of the Broads district are rich in the matter of their micro fauna, and can compare well with any part of the country; in one or two instances it furnishes species marked down in the text-books as rare. This is certainly the case with the beautiful Cordylophora, which is to be found in the vicinity of Hickling Broad and Heigham Sounds in immense quantities during the summer months and late into the autumn. Allied to the Hydra, it is a much more interesting and attractive creature, and when seen fully extended is an exceedingly graceful tenant of a small aquarium.

Passing by numerous larvæ of insects and beetles whose life-history comes within the province of the entomologist and the coleopterist, the attention of the pond-hunter (for so he is ignominiously termed) is attracted by two very well-known forms, viz. the Entomostracan, *Daphnia pulex* (Water-flea), and the true Crustacean, Cyclops. There are several species of the former, which abound in immense numbers in open ponds and ditches, and during the summer the water is so full of them that it is frequently coloured a deep red, caused by the presence of many millions of these tiny animals disporting themselves therein. The Water-flea is interesting from all points of view: its movements are very peculiar, its progression being effected by a series of sudden jerks brought about by the use of branched antennæ, while the brilliant compound eye with which it is furnished and the shell in which the creature is enclosed make it a very good and entertaining object under the microscope. There is a very fine species of the Daphnia to be found in Ormesby Broad, and which on account of its size has been named *D. elephanta*. This water-flea possesses an enormous eye, brilliantly coloured and highly interesting from many points. Unlike the majority of Daphniæ, this species substitutes for the spasmodic jerks so characteristic of the family, a bold stroke with the arms, which sends it along at a swift pace through the water, giving its movements the appearance of flight.

The Cyclops family has three special representatives, which include *Cyclops quadricornis*, *Diaptomus Castor*, and Cantho-camptus. This pretty little fellow gained his name from the formidable single eye occupying the central portion of its head, and as seen with its double egg-bag attached to its body is extremely interesting. *Diaptomus Castor* is a lovely fellow, and is possessed of a pair of very long antennæ, with which he strikes out boldly and all but flies through the water. The remaining species, Canthocamptus, is known not only by its smaller size but by its zigzag movement.

Another lively little animal is the Cypris, which lives and scuttles along in its bivalve shell with the greatest of ease, and the collector is sure to catch in his tube-net at the right season (spring to autumn) plenty of water-mites, some a brilliant red, others a beautiful green, and all of them more or less spotted with black. In the brackish waters near Great Yarmouth the fresh-water shrimp is sure to be met with. Other forms are the water-louse, notable for the fan-like plates attached to the under part of its body for respiratory purposes. This is a ravenous creature to keep in an aquarium, and his movements must be closely watched if it is intended to keep any *Polyzoa* alive in the same tank or aquarium. The diving spider has always been a favourite "catch" with naturalists, and these may be found at all seasons and can be obtained in the winter-time by breaking the ice on a pond and watching for the appearance of an individual of the species. These, in brief, are but a few of the larger so-called micro forms to be found in Broadland waters. There is, however, another world of life and movement at the other end of the scale, viz. the Infusorial Animalcules: they abound wherever vegetable matter exists, and nowhere so much as in the weedy ditches around Hickling and in the vicinity of most of the other Broads. Saville, Kent, and others have dealt fully with these; but there is plenty of room for further research on the part of those having time and opportunity. Mention should, however, be made of the beautiful tree-like form of the Vorticelli family, viz. *Zoöthamnium arbuscula* and kindred Vorticellidans which are to be found in plenty on the rootlets of sedges growing by the margins of all our rivers where the salt tides do not reach them, and in all the Broads without exception.

THE ROTIFERA

Of all the wonderful inhabitants of the waters in the Broadland district, probably none can compare for interest with the Rotifers, or "Wheel-bearing Animalcules," as they were originally called, on account of the almost perfect semblance of a wheel-like motion going on at the head or crown of the animal. Prior to 1840 or 1850, very little was known about this full-specied order, owing probably to the defective optical and mechanical appliances then in vogue. This is clearly demonstrated from the fact that an early observer noted the circumstance that he was not able to give a correct drawing of the animal under observation, because it would rush across the field of view. All present-day microscopists know that with a Rousselet Compressor, or similar appliance, the smallest animal may be kept perfectly still and made amenable to the will of the operator. To this may be ascribed the great popularity now enjoyed by the study of the Rotifera.

Some of the early observers made somewhat shrewd guesses into the anatomy of these tiny animals, which vary from $\frac{1}{10}$th to $\frac{1}{500}$th of an inch in size, and some queer diagrams appear in their books and writings; but a few, although not enjoying the benefit of the modern highly finished instruments and corrected lenses, came wonderfully near to a perfect description of many of the families and a large number of species, showing what enthusiastic students they must have been. As a matter of fact, the discovery of the various species (now numbering about 250) may be said to have gone hand in hand with the perfecting of microscopic lenses and appliances up till about twenty-five or thirty years since. The earliest English observer of whom there is any record is John Harris, F.R.S., rector of Winchelsea, who detected the common rotifer which he describes in the *Philosophic Transactions* of 1696. Leeuwenhoek was the first to find and describe *Limnias ceratophylli* (one of the Melicerta family) in 1705, Eichorn, Baker, Müller, Joblot, and others being the discoverers of some twenty species prior to 1838. After this date a large number of microscopists seem to have given attention to the subject, with the result that every year substantial additions were made to the list.

Norfolk is well represented in the late Mr. Thomas Brightwell of Norwich, who published in 1848 his *Sketch of a Fauna Infusoria for East Norfolk*, a monograph dealing principally with rotifers found almost exclusively in the Broadland district. The sketch is, for the period at which it was written, exceedingly well done, and is beautifully illustrated by the author's wife; but, like many of his contemporaries, Brightwell placed Rotifers amongst the Infusoria. Out of about ninety species enumerated and described, 25 per cent. were rotifers. Thanks to the labours of the late Mr. P. H. Gosse, F.R.S., and

Dr. C. T. Hudson, the whole class Rotifera has been focussed into a grand work compiled jointly by them, and entitled *The Rotifera or Wheel Animalcules*, published in 1886. There were scores of treatises, essays, and reviews in existence prior to this by the same writers and a number of other scientific observers, but this may be considered the most complete and reliable of all up to the date of its publication. The finding of a large number of new species both in British and foreign habitats necessitated the publication of a supplement, which appeared three years later. Like many other subjects, there can be no finality about it, as from time to time new species are being added by students all over the country. To such men as Mr. C. F. Rousselet of London, John Hood of Dundee, and a few others, is to be credited the immense amount of interest now taken in the subject, the former gentleman having elaborated a plan of mounting all the species fully extended and with lifelike perfection.

A recent single-handed exploration of the Broads district has led to the enumeration of a large number of species, but from the natural aspect of the district there must be a large number yet to be placed on the list. Rotiferan life appears to be largely dependent on the chemical property of the water in which it exists. There are many species that are to be found in the brackish and saline waters of the ditches surrounding Yarmouth that are not to be seen in the fresh water more inland and beyond the reach of the salt tides. The rotifers found in lacustrine waters such as Ormesby Broad, Fritton Lake, and Wroxham, are, as a rule, much finer specimens than those found in smaller pieces of waters, doubtless owing to the quality of the food to be obtained, and other conditions under which they live. *Brachionus pala* is to be secured in almost every part of East Norfolk, but nowhere is there such a grand example of the species to be found as in Ormesby Broad, where it not only attains a larger size than elsewhere, but is beautifully transparent and altogether a magnificent species.

As the form and structure of the Rotifera may be " caviare to the general," the following definitions given in Hudson and Gosse's great work will be helpful :—

"The Rotifera are small aquatic animals varying from $\frac{1}{8}$th to $\frac{1}{500}$th of an inch in length, and derive their name from a wheel-like appearance produced by fine circlets of hairs (*cilia*) seated on the front of their heads. A few species are marine, but the great majority known to us belong to fresh water, and are to be found in ditches, ponds, reservoirs, lakes, and slowly running streams. . . .

"(1) They swim by means of hairs on the front of their heads; (2) they possess a simple stomach and intestine and peculiar jaws; (3) they have muscles which are sometimes striated, and which often pass freely through the cavity of the body; (4) they have a well-developed vascular system; (5) their nervous system consists of one ganglion with nerve threads radiating to their organ of sense; (6) they are diœcious, have ova of two kinds, and do not pass through any distinct metamorphosis."

Rotifers are most lively and industrious creatures, for, whether viewed at morning, noon, or evening, they are always at work. As a matter of fact, some of them are so formed that they have no opportunity of resting, and are condemned to perpetual motion during the term of their natural life. For the purposes of classification the Rotatoria have been divided in four main orders, as follows :—

I. Rhizota (the rooted), which always remain rooted or fixed to weed or algæ when adult, like the Floscule, Melicerta, and Stephanoceros.

II. Bdelloida (the leech-like), that swim with the ciliary wreath and creep like a leech, as the Philodinadæ, in which family are found *Rotifer vulgaris* and *neptunis*.

III. Ploima (the sea-worthy), that only swim with their ciliary wreath, such as *Brachionus pala, Hydatina senta,* and a large number of other species.

IV. Scirtopoda (the skippers), that swim with their ciliary wreath and skip with Arthropodous limbs, such as *Pedalion mirum.*

The list which appears in the Appendix is not intended as a complete record of the species to be found in the Broads district, but so far as it goes it is authentic, specimens of every one of the species having been found by the writer, who has confined his researches to the ditches, ponds, and pools in East Norfolk, and the chain of Broads running from Ormesby *viâ* Hickling to Wroxham, with an occasional visit to Fritton Lake, Oulton Broad, and the now much neglected Surlingham Broad. That the list may be largely extended is frankly acknowledged; but the work of making a systematic visit to all the places named at different seasons of the year could not be accomplished by one individual, though to get a correct idea of the number of species to be furnished from the district visits at frequent intervals to all the places referred to would be necessary. While it is to be regretted that so few microscopists and naturalists have developed a penchant for the study of rotiferan life, the subject is of such engrossing interest that it is to be hoped it will be taken up by naturalists living in Norfolk, so that Broadland's micro fauna may be properly and fully described. So far as the rotifers are concerned, the list in this book could, under these circumstances, easily be doubled and possibly trebled.

In the neighbourhood of Great Yarmouth some of the most prolific ditches have recently been sacrificed to the exigencies of bricks and mortar, and where but a year or two since the rotifer-hunter could make sure of taking in his tube-net a score or so of species, there is not a drop of water left, the ditches having been filled in and built over. This will necessarily occur in the vicinity of all large towns; but it will be a long time before any serious difficulty will be placed in the way of the micro naturalist, who, if he be but in earnest, will test every semblance of a pool or collection of still water, from the water-butt in his back yard to the magnificent sheets of water which are the pride of East Norfolk.

Now a word as to securing these most beautiful of Nature's wonderful creatures.

The apparatus required is simple and cheap in the extreme when the importance of the study is taken into consideration. The absolute requisites are a tube-net and rod, a rake, a few wide-mouthed bottles, and a small flat-sided tank for examining water by the pond-side. An aplanatic lens of an amplification of about eight diameters is also indispensable for use outdoors, and also for mounting and other

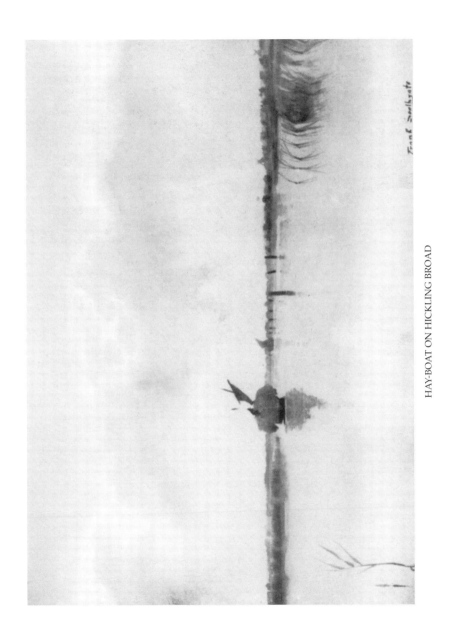

Frank Southgate

HAY-BOAT ON HICKLING BROAD

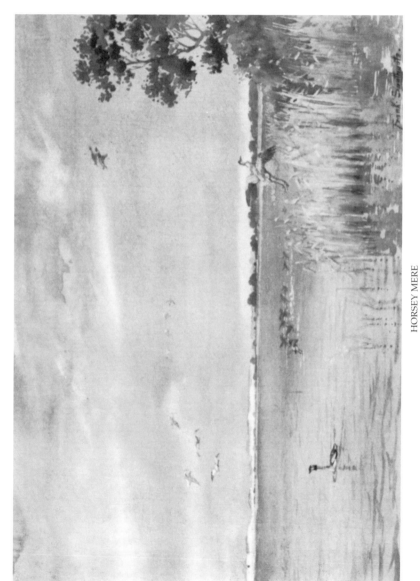

Frank Southgate

HORSEY MERE

WAXHAM OLD HALL, FROM THE SAND-HILLS

ORMESBY BROAD. AUTUMN

THROWING THE CAST-NET

PUNT-GUNNERS' HOUSEBOATS ON BREYDON – WATCHING FOR FOWL

BREYDON ROND

SMELT-FISHING, BREYDON

PUNT-GUNNING ON BREYDON

"MARK COCK"

MONTAGU HARRIER

MARSH HARRIER AND WOUNDED TEAL.

REDSHANK

HORNING FERRY

PLEASURE BOAT INN, HICKLING BROAD

HORSTED MILL

purposes at home. This last may be had from Messrs. Watson's, High Holborn, or a triple folding lens may be obtained from almost any optician. On the principle that nothing is better than the best, the aplanatic lens is recommended as far and away the best and in the end the cheapest, as it saves time, trouble, and temper in the examination of species.

The purpose of the tube-net is to strain or *sift* the water so as to get the maximum of life with the minimum of water. The form of net in use by most collectors is about six inches in diameter at the mouth, tapering down to fit the mouth of a tube of about two fluid ounces capacity, special tubes with a flange for more perfect security being obtainable at Mr. C. Baker's establishment, 244 High Holborn. The net may be made of linen of good quality, or, what is better, of silk similar to that used in flour mills for sifting the finest flour. The *modus operandi* is to draw the net with considerable force through the water, and then give it a rotary motion with a wrist action so as to facilitate the straining of the water through the net material. In this way all life, large and small, gets imprisoned in the tube below. The tube need not be emptied at each dip; ten, twenty, or an indefinite number of dips may be made before emptying its contents into a bottle or jar; but care must be taken lest the organisms already caught escape when the net is plunged into the water.

The rake is principally used for pulling up weeds on which the rooted forms are to be found. A sharp hook similar to that used in blackberrying is also useful, but not nearly so good as the rake—one of five or six teeth set fairly close together serving the purpose admirably.

THE POLYZOA

Of all the larger forms of so-called micro pond life the Polyzoa are amongst the most exquisitely beautiful: they may be appropriately termed fresh-water feathered beauties, on account of the similarity of their delicately formed crests to the down of birds. As seen by the unassisted eye in their natural habitat, or in a micro tank at home, they look like minute living feathers attached to a fleshy mass, and certainly provide the most beautiful of all the micro fauna.

The undoubted king of the Polyzoa, crowned as he is with his double crest, is *Lophopus crystallinus*, a veritable treasure to the microscopist on " show " evenings, and a never-failing source of enjoyment to the student, who can never tire of looking at the charming crest as it is gradually protruded and unfolded. The Lophopus is one of the six Polyzoons to be found in English waters, and is generally to be taken in clusters of from four to six or even more individuals on dead or dying vegetation in slowly running streams or shady ditches. The principal feature of all the class is the beautiful plume or crest, which in Lophopus assumes the shape of a double horseshoe, each tentacle being delicately ciliated so as to assist the animal in securing its food, the tentacles themselves aiding by closing on their prey and making its escape absolutely impossible. A very interesting and pretty sight is that of Lophopus engaged in an attempt either to swallow or get rid of a Volvox which has involuntarily strayed within the range of the double crest. The beautiful globe is much too large for the polyzoon to " bolt," and the currents set up by the cilia on both appear to prevent its escape. The contest is evidently unpremeditated, and both Lophopus and Volvox seem to appreciate deliverance from their dilemma. Lophopus is not to be easily secured, though when found is generally to be taken in large quantities. *Anacharis alsinastrum* (thyme-weed) is its principal selection in Broad-land waters, and upon the tips of the leaves of this well-known water-plant the familiar orange-coloured sac in which the polyzoon lives is to be found.

The searcher for the polyzoa can do no better than find the shadiest nook in some dyke leading from a Broad or river, and examine the rootlets of willow trees and haul up portions of the roots of such sedges and water-plants as may be growing there, the iris for preference, as on this plant the writer has found not only Lophopus but other forms in great profusion during July and August. The principal exception in respect to the shadiness of the polyzoon's retreat is in the case of *Cristatella mucedo*, which is a light-loving animal, generally best procured in sunny situations. The crest of this species is not quite so fine as that of Lophopus, but the creature itself is much more numerous. It is unique in that each polyzoon, although independent so far as its special functions are concerned, is attached to a sort of gasteropodic foot, which creeps slowly over the water-plants, aiding the animals in their search for food. So social, however, are Cristatellans, that in spots where the conditions are specially favourable they are to be met with in vast numbers. On Hickling Broad and all along Kendal Dyke leading from the Thurne to Heigham Sounds they are generally to be obtained in plenty, whilst on the reeds and sedges in the vicinity of Surlingham and Brundall they are sure to be found just below low - water mark. Sometimes the long-leaved water-plants are covered with Cristatella as with a beautiful down or filmy mould : there can be no mistaking it when once seen, and its glories as a microscopic object are *par excellent*. Like all the members of its class, it is reproduced by statoblasts, a sort of bud formed within the animal and liberated when death and decay takes place. The statoblast of Cristatella is the largest and most interesting of them all, and bears well-formed hooks, which cling tenaciously to water-plants, and in the early spring split open and liberate the young polyzoon, which speedily multiplies by a kind of gemmation into a colony. It may be added that Lophopus also has locomotive power, but of such sluggishness as only to be noticeable on comparing its relative position day by day, as it would probably take a week to travel two or three inches.

Fredericella sultana is a beautiful polype, and lives in a well-formed tube which encircles or encrusts the roots of the larger water-plants or surrounds the stem of anacharis and other weeds. Its crest of tentacles is more circular in shape than those of the polyzoons previously referred to and much smaller, the animal when fully extended looking like a silver star if viewed by dark-field illumination. It loves the soft waters of the river-fed Broads and open water spaces, on the margins of which it can scarcely be missed if systematically searched for. And here again it may be well to state that the very best implement to use is an ordinary rake, with which to pull up the submerged roots of plants, which should be examined in the palm of the hand *under water*, when the polyzoa may with a very little practice be seen and should be detached (with the rootlets) and placed in a bottle or jar with plenty of water from their habitat.

Plumatella repens is another delightful crest - bearing polyzoon, having its tentacles displayed in somewhat of a horseshoe form. As its specific name implies, it creeps or spreads itself along the object on which it grows. In the Broads district it is fairly abundant, and should be sought for on reeds and rushes at about a foot below the surface of the water. In the summer and autumn of 1901 it was very general in all parts of Fritton Lake and in Heigham Sounds. Paludicella is a polyzoon very much like Fredericella; but its tube is flatter, and instead of the polypes emerging from the end of the tube they protrude from a tiny opening near the end of it. This is a very beautiful animal, and should not be missed. It produces buds entirely distinct from the other polyzoa.

Alcyonella is also included in the fresh-water polyzoa, and grows in sponge-like masses in similar places to its confrères. As a matter of fact, the student of pond life need have no lack of material upon which to base his researches, for summer and winter alike provide abundance. The prime necessity for every worker is enthusiasm, and with this he is bound to succeed.

CHAPTER XVII

BOTANY

By the Rev. G. H. Harris, B.A.

THE district commonly known as the "Norfolk Broads
District" is drained by three rivers—the Waveney,
Yare, and Bure—flowing into the sea at Yarmouth
as one river, the Yare. The famous Broads are simply
expansions of these three rivers, occurring here and there
in their course. They are slow rivers, so they cut no deep
channels, but readily extend themselves into any depression
the country they flow through may afford. As the country
is, for the most part, uniformly flat and marshy, it follows
that a "Broad" may be found at any point from the source
of these rivers to their outlet into the sea. Accordingly,
Broads fall into two classes, as they are near to or remote
from the sea: first, those which are brackish because they
are affected by tides or salt springs; secondly, those beyond
the influence of the ocean, which are of course ordinary sheets
of fresh water.

There was a time when there were more Broads and
when the present Broads were larger; but various causes
have co-operated to restrict these waters more and more
to the river channels. For instance, Hickling was, not long
ago, larger by the whole extent of Chapman's Broad, and
Blackfleet Broad still figures on the Ordnance Map. But
these are now nothing more than stretches of marshland
intersected by dykes. And, similarly, all the Broads are
surrounded by what was originally water or bog, but is
now marshland in all stages of dryness, ranging from the
ordinary cornfield to the wild, sour, intractable salt-marsh.

These considerations affect the distribution of the Flora. We get, on the one hand, a flora peculiar to the salt-marsh near the coast; and, on the other hand, an inland flora, which falls into two classes, (1) that of the unreclaimed marsh, of which the Hickling district is typical, (2) that of the reclaimed country farther inland, much of which is drained by the Yare, and whose flora presents features in common with the ordinary flora of arable districts. Needless to say, in such a division as this there must be a good deal of overlapping; but, in a rough way, there is such a division, and it will be convenient to observe it.

There is yet another sort of country bordering on the Broad District, but in its physiographical features quite distinct from it, namely, the sandhills and denes of the coast. The propinquity of the coast at Horsey to the Broads, and the central position of Yarmouth, make it so certain that the sandhills of the former and the denes of the latter will be visited by a good many cruisers in Broadland, that it becomes necessary to describe their Flora as a part of that appertaining to the Broads District. To begin, then, with these.

The vegetation of the sandhills proper consists largely of Maram Grass, with here and there large patches of the uncommon and shyly flowering Lyme Grass. A careful search will reveal spikes of a very rare grass, closely allied to the Maram, and common on the sandhills of the opposite coast, namely, *Ammophila baltica ;* and if the searcher on the sandhills to the north of Yarmouth is lucky, he may light on that rare Rue, *Thalictrum dunense.* In the loose sand, the Purple Sea Rocket, the Sea Purslane (*Arenaria peploides*), the Sea Holly, the Saltwort, and the Prickly Restharrow may be seen everywhere. Near Winterton the Sea Buckthorn (*Hippophæ rhamnoides*) flourishes, despite the rapid inroads of the sea, which annually invades its homes, and sometimes carries it away in masses. It bears in plenty its edible orange berries, which the natives used to cook, and still call by the curious and underivable name of "Wye-bibbles."

The "Denes" of Yarmouth are flat, sandy plains to the

south and north of the town. Those to the south are quite remarkable botanically. The greater part of the short fine grass is a variety of the ordinary *Poa annua*, namely, *Poa bulbosa*. This grass has provided, not against a rainy day, but against a good many dry days to be spent in a dry place, by developing bulbs at its roots. The grass itself dies down early; the bulbs fall away, and may be found for the rest of the year blowing about with the sand. In the spring they vegetate and make the new grass of the following summer. In addition to this species, another rare grass, *Weingaertneria canescens*, which grows in purplish tufts, and possesses a marvellously beautiful awn, worth examining, is plentiful on both Denes. Again, if we connect both Denes, no less than twelve species of Clover can be found. This list includes such rarities as *Trifolium subterraneum*, *T. scabrum*, *T. glomeratum*, and *T. suffocatum*. These rarer forms are mostly South Denes plants. Botanically, this small triangular strip of Denes, bounded on the north by the town, by the sea on the east, and by the high land of Gorleston on its third side, and isolated therefore from any kindred soil, must be nearly unique. In length only a mile, in breadth a quarter of a mile, and yet three rare grasses and four rare clovers, to say nothing of a fine crop of Henbane, make it a happier hunting-ground for the botanist than all the rest of the sandhills and denes, from Lowestoft to Happisburgh, put together.[1]

Let us now pass to our division into tidal and fresh-water districts.

Surrounding the waters of Breydon at Yarmouth, and Lake Lothing at Lowestoft, and along the coast from Winterton to Happisburgh, is a certain amount of land that may be described as salt-marsh. During the last century, house-building and greater attention to river walls considerably limited this area, and there is little now but the immediate vicinity of the above-mentioned estuarine Broads, with patches of marsh here and there, that deserve

---

[1] *Trifolium suffocatum*, *T. subterraneum*, *T. glomeratum*, and *T. scabrum* also occur on the Denes at Lowestoft, where, as at Yarmouth, the grass largely consists of *Poa bulbosa.*—ED.

17

the name. The flora of the salt-marsh has, in consequence, lost some striking representatives.

Here it may be interesting to pause in order to note quite briefly flowers conspicuous in the Broad District by their absence, both (1) those that one would expect to find there, and (2) those that used to be found, but are found no longer, or with difficulty. In the former category are the Blue Meadow Crane's-Bill (*Geranium pratense*), that fine flower so decorative to the Thames banks; the Marsh Violet (*Viola palustris*), with its large circular leaves; the Comfreys; and, on the heaths, as last but not least, may be mentioned the pet flower of the poet, the sweet-smelling Thyme. In the latter class are the Yellow Horned Poppy, which has disappeared from the beach of late years; the Sea Heath (*Frankenia lævis*), which in 1834 was reported to be getting rare and has now quite gone; whilst none of the Sea Lavenders (*Statice*) have been seen for one hundred and twenty years, although growing freely both to the north and south of our district. More recently the queer little Thorough - Wax (*Bupleurum tenuissimum*) and a very rare Orache (*Atriplex pedunculata*) have yielded to the stress of change, and they blow no longer on the shores of Breydon. There is also the Marsh Flea Wort (*Senecio palustris*), which has had one foot in the grave for years, but still lingers, a notable survivor amid the gradual decay of a noble and illustrious Flora.

It will be noticed that all these flowers, with the exception of the last named, are flowers of the beach and salt-marsh. A dearth of flowers will perhaps never happen, so long as the Broads remain, whatever draining may do. But a dearth of the characteristic Broad Flora is threatened. In face of this it may not be amiss to utter a protest against adding to the unavoidable conditions of extinction a condition that is avoidable, namely, the diminution of rare plants by specimen-collecting for Herbaria. The practice of those collectors who, not at all in the interests of science, but simply for the gratification of their personal ends, do not scruple to increase their collections even if the extinction of a plant is to be the result of their undisciplined and unfruitful zeal, is greatly to be deprecated. More than one plant has, to the writer's knowledge, been decimated in this way; and even if actual extinction has not been the result, it has reduced to a minimum the chance of the plant maintaining itself against present odds.

There is, however, a fair number of typical marsh flowers still to be found. There is the grey, drooping, Maritime Wormwood (*Artemisia maritima*), with which may be found the Scurvy Grass (*Cochlearia officinalis*),—no grass, however, as any botanist knows, but a plant closely allied to the Cabbage. The Wild Celery, too, and the Wild Fennel, and the small but pretty Sea Milkwort, can easily be found. In the autumn the Michaelmas Daisy turns many a muddy bank into a garden of flowers. The Sea Thrift is not so common as one would expect, but grows sparingly on the shores of Lake Lothing, together with the Golden Dock (*Rumex maritimus*). The muddy shores of Breydon and Lake Lothing have, in addition, thick beds of the Marsh Samphire (*Salicornia herbacea*), which many think is the plant Shakespeare alludes to in *King Lear*. It is, however, quite different, and never grows in situations of which it could be said—

> "How fearful
> And dizzy 'tis to cast one's eyes so low!
> The crows and choughs, that wing the midway air,
> Show scarce so gross as beetles."

And with the Marsh Samphire are other beds — of the red-tinged Sea Blite.

Farther into the marsh the handsome Marsh Mallow grows. In the dykes which everywhere intersect the flats, the stately Flowering Rush (*Butomus umbellatus*) lifts its handsome head of rose-coloured blossoms, and intermixed with it may be found some of the species of that poisonous white umbellifer, the Water Dropwort (*Œnanthe pimpinelloides* in the salt-marsh, and farther inland *silaifolia*, *crocata*, and *Phellandrium* may be mentioned). This plant has enormous stems and roots. The latter are embedded in the semi-liquid black mud of the dyke bottom, and if lifted out will generally repay any one hunting for larvæ for his trouble. A singularly graceful water-weed is the Horned Pond Weed (*Zannichellia palustris*). It is a feature of the dykes and pools in the neighbourhood of Burgh Castle.

The fresh-water Broads have, of course, many flowers in common. And here it may be said that so far as the Broads have a Flora peculiar to themselves, it is scientific in its interest rather than scenic. It is, perhaps, fortunate that so few of the remaining rarities are calculated to impress the picnicker. Many beautiful flowers do adorn the banks of all the Broads, but they may be found everywhere in England where there is water—although in the Broads they seem to grow with an exceptional luxuriance. Of such is that exceedingly lovely flower of the Gentian family, the Buck-Bean, the flowering season of which is, by the bye, over with the end of June, so it is missed by the ordinary summer visitor ; and together with this, flowering about the same time, is the Marsh Cinquefoil, with its curiously conventional-looking blossom. The two Water Parsnips (*Sium*) also grow in profusion, and the Greater Spear Wort is everywhere prominent, with its large yellow flowers. Two of the Bladder Worts are fairly common, and the third (*intermedia*) can be found. The Sundews are scattered all through the district, loving most the beds of Sphagnum. In the south the round-leaved is the commonest, but in the north *Anglica* is as common. That very distinctive St. John's Wort, *Hypericum elodes*, favours a similar habitat. One of the most difficult flowers to find in the Broad District, a flower which is a prize wherever it is found, both for its beauty and its rarity, is *Gentiana pneumonanthe*. This, too, grows in damp, heathy places. The Water Soldier (*Stratiotes aloides*) is extraordinarily plentiful in places, but never seems to seed, although in the far past it did so, as is shown by the fossil seed-vessels which have been found locally. The Arrow-head is also very common, and two Bur-reeds, *Sparganium ramosum* and *simplex*. Of the Great Spiræa, the Hairy Willow-herb, the Red and Yellow Loosestrifes, no more need be said than that these fine wild flowers, characteristic of aquatic scenery all England over, grow in these open and sunny marshes in unusual abundance.

The deep-water Broads, such as Wroxham and Fritton

(with which we may class generally the country drained by the Waveney and Yare), lie in a comparatively cultivated district, and are not, botanically, so interesting as the shallower Broads, particularly those connected with the Ant and Thurne, two tributaries of the Bure, lying to the north of that river. Still, Filby Broad can boast of a fine growth of the Water Hemlock (*Cicuta virosa*). The classical locality for the very rare Wintergreen (*Pyrola rotundifolia*) is in the neighbourhood of the Yare, and the Fragrant Bog Myrtle (*Myrica Gale*) is hereabouts common. In addition, the Great Meadow Rue (*Thalictrum flavum*) may be found at Horning and at Burgh Castle, and the Sweet Reed (*Acorus Calamus*) at Beccles.

It is the great stretch of marshland and wet common beginning below the high land of Martham, and stretching away to Palling on the east, Barton on the west, and Crostwight on the north, including the extensive Broad system of Hickling and the watersheds of the Ant and Thurne, that is the storehouse of botanical treasures. To the non-botanical public much of it is ugly and ungraceful, but the botanist revels in its new and interesting forms.

In June the banks are rich in Carex. The little brown spikes of this Protean genus are alike as egg to egg to the passer-by, but on examination they will be found of many species, each striking out a distinct and original line for itself, in which the disposition of male and female flowers in the spike plays an important part. To the botanist the distinctions are well marked, and members of the family are not half so difficult to discriminate between as a cursory acquaintance would seem to declare. Many of the species are rare, and among the best prizes available in the district. And there are one or two that are really ornamental, such as the two larger species, *paludosa* and *riparia*, whose dark elegant spikes, contrasting strongly with the bright greens of the young grass, are among the first of the signs of approaching summer.

These are common anywhere; but *Pseudo-Cyperus*, which has gracefully drooping yellow-green spikes, very distinctive, is not generally common, but is frequent on the Broads. It flowers later than most of the *Carices*, and its spikes may be seen when the summer is far advanced. Roughly speaking, there are between thirty and forty species of Carex, some very common and some difficult to find. Among those generally uncommon are *divisa, teretiuscula, paradoxa, limosa, distans, filiformis, divulsa,* and *extensa.*

Another family of plants which plays a large part in the plant life of the Broads is *Scirpus. Scirpus lacustris* is the tall reed that lines so many of the river banks. This, it is worth remarking, is the true Bulrush, which name is generally given to the handsome and well-known Reed Mace, which also (both species) grows in abundance. *Scirpus maritimus* is one of the prizes of the Hickling district. *Juncus* (which is the Rush proper, as *Scirpus* is the Reed and *Carex* the Sedge) grows everywhere in most of its many varieties (here ten can be found).

Akin to these, rare elsewhere, but in the Hickling district growing by the marshful, is the Prickly Twig Rush (*Cladium jamaicense*), tall, gaunt, and harsh, a true daughter of this wild country. The pretty black-headed *Schœnus nigricans* is another rare rush-like plant to be found in plenty on Barton Broad, and elsewhere, in close association with the Meadow Plume Thistle (*Cnicus pratensis*) and the Grass of Parnassus, which last, the latest of the Broad Flora to flower, is to be seen at its best about the beginning of September. In the far north of the district, the Berry-bearing Alder (*Rhamnus frangula*) is plentiful. Its cherry-like fruit is conspicuous in the late summer months.

In the shallow Broads, the true water-weeds, those whose habitat is neither the marsh nor the bank, but the water itself, are very interesting, perhaps more interesting than any other part of the Broads Flora. The depth of the Broads in this district averages only about four to six feet, and so they offer a desirable home, of which the water-loving plants are not slow to avail themselves. In many places, particularly in Somerton and Hickling Broads, a tangled forest of plants grows, a very Eden for fish, whose forms are easily distinguishable as they thread a sinuous way through the watery jungle. For the water is at most times pretty clear, and when calm as well, every leaf and ribbon of these delicate water-plants can be seen waving gently to the motion of whatever imperceptible current there may be. A great part of this aquatic tangle is formed by the lime-encrusted, offensive-smelling family of the *Characeæ*. When fished up, these plants are pleasant neither to the eye, to the nose, nor to the touch. They have an aggressive *noli-me-tangere* look, and are horrid with bristles. But seen through the softening medium of the waters, and in company with such elegant plants as *Potamogeton pusillus*, the Water Milfoils, and the Hornwort, the impression left is that of a miniature forest where fir and larch grow mixed in a striking though harmonious contrast.

In summer, in the shallows of Hickling Broad large yellowish white spots appear on the bottom. The Rev. M. C. H. Bird tells me these are in their origin masses of floating weed. They are made up, no doubt, principally of *Chara*. These masses are drawn up by the sun in dry summers, when the Broad is low, and often form a nesting-place for water-birds. On such a mass of weed the last Black Tern that nested in this district laid its egg. Finally, the lumps sink to the bottom and there decay. Being composed largely of the lime-encrusted *Chara*, the vegetable part of the lump disappears and leaves an insoluble deposit of lime, to be seen as the conspicuous light-coloured spot which is quite a feature of the Broads.

Among these water-weeds is one of the latest additions to the British Flora, *Naias marina*, discovered by Mr. A. Bennett in the eighties. There are also such rarities as *Nitella flexilis* and *opaca*, and *Lychnothamnus stelliger*, to be dredged up from the bottom. In the leaf-axils of the last named is a beautiful white star-shaped formation, by means of which the plant reproduces itself, and not, apparently, by the usual means of propagation.

The Pondweeds (*Potamogeton*) are many in number and various in form. About fifteen species can be found, from the broad, flat leaf of *natans*, beloved of tench, that floats on the surface of many still dykes, to the wavy, ornamental leaf of *crispus*, the grass-like leaf of *gramineus*, and the curious leaf of a form of *lucens*, with its midrib prolonged like a claw.

There are two classes of plants in which most visitors, botanists or non-botanists, take a lively interest, and which therefore may well be reserved till now for special notice. They are the Ferns and the Orchids. Our geographical division will still apply, as the country of the Ant and Thurne is rich in the Orchids of the district, while Ferns, as will be shown, are everywhere scarce. With respect to the latter, the luxuriance of *Osmunda regalis* does much to compensate for the paucity of species. This magnificent fern, although depleted in many spots by the fern-gatherer, still grows in great beds six feet high in the Catfield country. Its popular name of " Flowering Fern " is, as is the way with popular names, more descriptive than correct. " The hunly fern as flars ! " as I heard a Cockney crying in Yarmouth market, with that assurance of omniscience which is a Cockney's most valuable asset ; just as I heard another, generous out of his abundance, correct an erring brother with " A brike ain't a fern, I tell yer." Well, a brake is, of course, as much a fern as *Osmunda* is not a flower. But *Osmunda* devotes a special frond to the work of reproduction, and there collects its spore-holding vessels ; hence the popular name. Outside *Osmunda* and the common sorts, the Broads District has not much to show. There is no rock and little rain, two essentials to the thriving of the Fern tribe. However, the Marsh Buckler (*Lastræa thelypteris*) is common, and the Adder's Tongue is plentiful in certain places—especially Hickling. In the heathy districts to the north the Hard Fern (*Lomaria spicant*) is very abundant.

With respect to the Orchids there is a fair choice, though not of the more magnificent, albeit the particularly beautiful Marsh Helleborine is very abundant in the Ant district. In the spongy bogs where *Sphagnum* is still found are *Malaxis paludosa* and *Liparis Læselii*. On the dryer heaths are *Listera ovata*, *Gymnadenia conopsea*, and *Spiranthes autumnalis*. In the Norwich district there are spots where the chalk outcrops and where the chalk-loving Orchids may be found, but these hardly come within the scope of this paper.

Orchids tend to decrease. There are those natural causes I have mentioned above, all working against the well-being of the Orchid tribe. They are legitimate. But the people, trowel-armed, who, ankle - deep in mire, dig furiously at everything unhappy enough to bear the name of Orchid, these are not legitimate, and ought to be extirpated before the Orchid.

CHAPTER XVIII

A SKETCH OF THE GEOLOGICAL HISTORY OF THE BROADLAND

BY F. W. HARMER, F.G.S.,

Membre Associé Etranger de la Société Belge de Géologie; Membre de la Société Géologique de France, etc.

THE Zoology and the Botany of the East Anglian Lakeland are each of them full of interest, but when these have been studied, it may still be useful to inquire why the natural features of this region, to which the special character of its fauna and flora are largely due, differ so widely from those of other parts of Great Britain. For this purpose we must learn something of the strata by which it is underlain, and of the physical changes which, in past ages, it has undergone. The subject is a large one, however, and can only be dealt with here in the most general way. One can only attempt rapidly to show, as by the shifting scenes of a panorama, the conditions of the district at some of the more important stages of its geological history.[1]

The principal strata which occur at or near the surface, or are known from borings, are given in the following schedule, their stratigraphical relation to each other being shown in the section (Fig. 1).

---

[1] Those who desire to study the geology of the district more seriously are referred to an admirable résumé of the subject recently published by Mr. H. B. Woodward, F.R.S., in the *Victoria History of Norfolk*.

	Recent . .	{ Blown sand, marine beaches, peat, estuarine and fresh-water deposits.
Tertiary or Kainozoic	Pleistocene .	{ Valley gravels, etc. Plateau gravels. Chalky Boulder Clay. Middle Glacial Sand. Norwich Brick-earth. Contorted Drift of coast section. Cromer Till. Pebbly gravels and sand (Westleton Beds). *Leda myalis* Sands and Arctic fresh-water Bed.
	Pliocene . .	{ Forest-Bed series; estuarine and fresh-water. Weybourne Crag (zone of *Tellina balthica*); marine. Chillesford Clay; estuarine. Norwich Crag; marine.
	Miocene . . *Oligocene* .	} *Not represented in East Anglia.*
	Eocene . .	{ London Clay. Reading Beds.
Secondary or Mesozoic	Cretaceous .	Upper Chalk.

The deposition of the Chalk, the oldest of the rocks of this region, carries us back to a period incalculably remote although geologically very recent, when East Anglia, with other parts of the continent of Europe, was covered by the ocean; it belongs to the latest part of the Mesozoic or Secondary epoch, an age of great reptiles, or " sea-serpents "—to speak more correctly, of sea-lizards (enaliosaurs)—and of flying dragons (pterodactyles). The skeleton of an animal of the former group, *Leiodon anceps*, was discovered some years since in a quarry at Norwich. The invertebrate fauna of the Mesozoic period was characterised by the great abundance and variety of its cephalopodous mollusca, among which the Ammonites may be specially mentioned.

The Chalk of the Broadland, belonging to the upper part of the Cretaceous formation, resembles, both in appearance and chemical composition, the calcareous ooze now forming at the bottom of the Atlantic. It may have accumulated under somewhat similar conditions in a sea of considerable depth, and at some distance from land. Apart from the siliceous flint nodules everywhere present in it, generally in horizontal layers, it consists almost entirely of carbonate of lime, originating not from the degraded material of older rocks brought down by rivers, but from the accumulated remains of minute organisms which lived in the Cretaceous sea. Among the more common invertebrate fossils of the Upper Chalk may be named *Belemnitella mucronata*, *Terebratula carnea*, *Rhynchonella plicatilis*, and *Ananchytes ovatus*.

The deposition of the calcareous ooze of the Atlantic at the present day seems to be exceedingly slow. At the first attempt to establish telegraphic communication between Europe and America, the cable broke in mid-ocean; when the broken end was recovered, after an interval of some months, it was found that while the portion which had rested on the sea bottom was coated with chalky mud, no appreciable film had formed on the part which had lain uppermost. The deposition of the Chalk, which at Norwich exceeds 1200 feet in thickness, may have been somewhat more rapid, but if not, it probably represents a period to be measured in millions of years.

A reference to the diagram (Fig. 1) will show that the surface of the Chalk forms a platform upon which the later deposits rest. Dipping to the east, the Chalk disappears beneath the level of the river Yare a few miles below Norwich, but it may be studied in quarries at Thorpe, Whitlingham, and elsewhere near that city, at Coltishall in the Bure valley, and in the cliff section to the north-west of Cromer.

Our first panoramic glimpse of the geological history of the Broadland area is that of a deep rolling sea, an arm of the Atlantic, with no land in sight.

The scene changes. East Anglia has emerged, and forms part of the European continent, the ocean having retired far to the west. Such a state of things continued for a period of unknown duration, sufficiently protracted, however, to allow for the disappearance, not only of the reptilian fauna of the Mesozoic epoch, but of its more characteristic mollusca also. The Ammonites, just referred to, had in Secondary times a world-wide range; but there is no evidence of their survival to

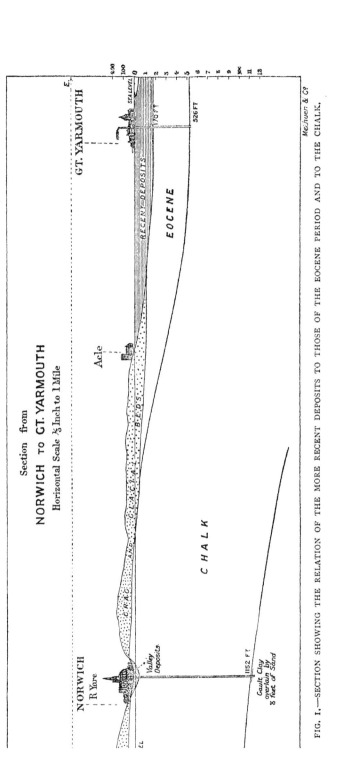

Section from

NORWICH TO GT. YARMOUTH

Horizontal Scale ⅓ Inch to 1 Mile

NORWICH
R Yare

GT. YARMOUTH

Acle

Valley
Deposits.

CRAG AND GLACIAL BEDS.

RECENT DEPOSITS

EOCENE

CHALK

1152 FT

Gault Clay
overlain by
8 feet of Sand

526 FT

170 FT

SEA LEVEL

Methuen & Cº

FIG. I.—SECTION SHOWING THE RELATION OF THE MORE RECENT DEPOSITS TO THOSE OF THE EOCENE PERIOD AND TO THE CHALK.

the Tertiary period. Unfortunately, the geological record is silent as to the condition of East Anglia, or as to its fauna and flora, during the long interval separating the Secondary and Tertiary epochs.

The Tertiary period has at length dawned, and the eastern part of Norfolk and Suffolk is once more covered by the sea, though to a less depth than during the deposition of the Chalk.

No deposits of Older Tertiary (Eocene) age come to the surface in the Broadland, but strata, 51 feet in thickness, supposed to represent the Reading series, and 305 feet of London Clay, were met with in a well boring at Yarmouth, the surface of the Chalk upon which they were found to rest having been reached at a depth of 526 feet below sea-level (Fig. 1).

The land then lay to the west, probably at no great distance, while a large river brought into the East Anglian area sediment, first more or less sandy, and afterwards of fine mud. Farther south, beds of rolled pebbles were formed of flints derived from the destruction of the chalk cliffs, then forming the sea margin.

The climate of Britain was then much warmer than it is now; turtles and crocodiles, palms and bananas, flourished in these latitudes, while the mollusca which swarmed in the rivers, estuaries, and seas were allied to those now found in tropical or subtropical regions.

Placental mammals, of a more generalised character, however, than those of the present, make their first recorded appearance, in great variety and abundance, in the Eocene deposits. All that are known from Secondary strata are aplacental, a lower as well as an older type of animal life, now confined to Australia and South America, which is represented by the marsupials and monotremes of those countries. We have comparatively little information as to the mammalia of Great Britain at this time; but the fossil remains of *Palæotherium, Anoplotherium, Xiphodon*, and other well-known forms, are found in France, in rocks of a somewhat later (Oligocene) date. Such animals may not improbably have then existed in the Broadland area.

The distribution of land and water during the Eocene

period differed widely from that of our own time. From the south and east of England the sea extended in one direction over the north of France, and in another into Belgium. The Atlantic was connected with the Pacific by an ocean which stretched across the Mediterranean region, over the south of Europe and the north of Africa, into Asia Minor, Arabia, Persia, to the Himalayas, and thence to Sumatra, Borneo, and the Philippines.[1]

Once more the Broad district became land, the sea retiring from it, though not far, and such conditions persisted during the Oligocene, Miocene, and older Pliocene epochs.

With the advent of the newer Pliocene, represented in East Anglia by the Crag formation, famed for the beauty and variety of its fossils, and by the so-called Forest-Bed, modern geological history commences. At that time the map of north-western Europe had acquired generally its present form ; animals and plants of existing genera, and often of existing species, inhabited the British Isles, while the molluscan fauna of the German Ocean closely resembled that of European seas at the present day.

The upper horizons of the deposits referred to, known as the Red and Norwich Crags, consist of sand, often containing in great profusion the drifted shells of dead mollusca. Although to a great extent hidden by the glacial strata overlying them, they cover a considerable part of the counties of Norfolk and Suffolk as with a sheet, more or less continuous for fifty miles from south to north, representing the littoral accumulation during Pliocene times of the German Ocean, which then extended somewhat farther to the west than it does at present. The richness of the invertebrate fauna of the Pliocene sea of East Anglia may be shown by the fact that the writer has collected from one small exposure of the Essex Crag, not larger than a good-sized dining-room, more than five hundred different species or well-marked varieties of mollusca, polyzoa, etc.

---

[1] The geographical conditions of the Cretaceous and Eocene periods are more fully discussed by Mr. A. J. Jukes-Browne, F.G.S., in the *Student's Handbook of Stratigraphical Geology* (Stanford).

In consequence of a combined movement of elevation in the southern part of this region, and of subsidence towards the north, the whole Crag basin moving as on a pivot, its southern margin was gradually shifted, the sea retiring towards the north. The upper Crag beds, originating upon or near the shore as beaches or shoals in shallow water, indicate successive stages of this movement. Hence it is that the older of these deposits are to be found in the south of the Crag area, the newer in the north. Moreover, during this epoch the climate of the northern hemisphere was gradually changing, becoming colder as the Glacial Period approached. The earlier horizons of the Crag contain a molluscan fauna more or less allied to that of the Mediterranean at present. As time went on, the southern shells died out, their place being taken by northern and Arctic species which invaded the German Ocean from the north. The fauna of these strata assumes, therefore, a more boreal facies as we trace them from Essex northward. The Crag beds of the Broadland belong to the Norwich, Chillesford, and Weybourne zones, the most recent of the series. The first-named may be observed in a quarry near Thorpe Asylum, and sometimes, when not obscured by talus, in the historic pit close to the river Yare, at Bramerton, a few miles from Norwich. The Weybourne Crag, characterised by the earliest appearance and great abundance of a shell still living in the North Sea, *Tellina balthica*, may be seen at Weybourne and other points on the Cromer coast.

The fossils of the older horizons of the Crag are more varied and interesting than those of the Broadland area, for the same reason that the conchology of the Mediterranean at the present day is of a richer character than that of British seas, and their mollusca or polyzoa may be more conveniently studied from centres like Aldeburgh, or Orford, on the Suffolk coast, than in Norfolk. Important collections of Crag fossils are to be found, however, in the Castle Museum at Norwich.

At present, dead shells are but rarely met with on the eastern shores of Norfolk and Suffolk. One may sometimes walk for a mile at Yarmouth or Lowestoft without finding more than a chance specimen, but they are cast upon the

18

Dutch coast, or driven into the estuaries of that country, in enormous quantities, being collected there for the manufacture of lime; 100,000 tons of shells are annually dredged for this purpose, for example, from one spot near the Hook of Holland.

The abundance of dead shells on the Dutch coasts, and their comparative absence from the beaches of East Anglia that face the east, seem to be equally due to the fact that the cyclonic disturbances which approach this country from the Atlantic pass for the most part, especially during winter, when storms are most frequent, with their centres to the north of the region in question. Hence gales there occurring are generally westerly (from south-west to north-west), and dead shells are driven towards the shores of Holland rather than towards those of Norfolk and Suffolk.

It seems necessary, therefore, to suppose that the prevalent direction of the strongest gales may have been from the east during the later part of the Crag period. The study of the meteorology of the Pliocene epoch suggests that such may have been the case, the cyclone tracks then lying farther to the south, owing to a difference in the relative distribution of the areas of high and low barometric pressure.[1]

Throughout the Pliocene period the North Sea received, as it now does, the drainage of the Rhine and its affluents. Deep borings show that Holland is underlain by deposits of sand or clay of great thickness, the Rhine mud of a former epoch. The Netherlands thus represent the old delta of that river, of which the latest Crag beds of East Anglia may have formed the western edge.

At one stage of the Pliocene history, that represented by the Chillesford Clay, when the land stood somewhat higher and the German Ocean lay farther to the north than during the deposition of the Norwich Crag, an estuary existed in the Broadland, which was possibly one of the channels by which the great southern river reached the sea. The Chillesford Clay is shown in a brickyard near Wroxham station, from

[1] As to this, see a paper by the present writer, "On the Influence of the Winds upon Climate during the Pleistocene Epoch," *Quarterly Journal of the Geological Society*, vol. lvii. p. 407. 1901.

whence it may be traced along a sinuous line into East Suffolk. It is generally characterised by the abundant presence of minute flakes of mica, derived, it is suggested, from the Devonian schists of the Ardennes, or from micaceous rocks farther south.

During the deposition of the so-called Forest-Bed of the Cromer coast, at a period somewhat later than that of the Chillesford Clay, the Rhine once more flowed over East Anglia, but at this stage its course lay farther to the east. The estuarine part of the Forest-Bed series, a deposit now of gravel and again of clay, is exposed from time to time at the base of the cliffs at various parts of the coast, as between Cromer and Hasboro' in Norfolk, or at Corton and Kessingland in Suffolk. It contains the stools of trees, generally of spruce or Scotch fir, with many mammalian fossils, especially of two large elephants, *Elephas antiquus* and *E. meridionalis*, and of different species of deer. Remains of bear, hyena, machairodus (a large extinct carnivore allied to the tiger), hippopotamus, rhinoceros, and other animals have also been found in it, some of them allied to forms now living to the south of Great Britain. A few specimens of distinctly northern species, such as the musk ox, *Ovibos moschatus*, and the glutton, have been met with, but generally the mammalia are of a southern character.

The Forest-Bed and its fauna were at one time supposed to represent the site and the animal life of a former East Anglian woodland. The tree stumps, however, are not found in place, but have been drifted; the fossil remains of the larger mammalia never occur as perfect skeletons, but as isolated and often fragmentary bones or teeth. It seems possible, therefore, that some of the southern species may represent the fauna of regions to the south rather than that of Norfolk and Suffolk. Animals browsing in herds on the low grounds bordering the great southern river may have been from time to time overtaken and swept away by sudden and violent floods, their remains being in this way carried down to their present resting-place. There are interesting collections of Forest-Bed fossils in the Natural History Museum at South Kensington, and in the Castle Museum at Norwich.

Associated with these estuarine deposits are some of a fresh-water character, implying slight changes in the position of the Rhine, and probably in the level of the land. The area which was at one time occupied by the estuary and its mud flats became, as the course of the Rhine was shifted to the east, a region of marsh and bog, and of shallow lakes.

Our bird's-eye view of Norfolk at this period is one of low, sandy plains, probably covered by woods of Scotch fir or of spruce, with groves of beech, oak, or elm in places, and a tangled undergrowth of hawthorn, bramble, and hazel. On the west, rolling chalk downs ; on the east, Broads and swamps filled with aquatic plants such as now live in the district, and fringed with thickets of alder, willow, and birch. Farther to the east lay the great estuary, often swollen and turbid, and then sweeping down, with other flotsam and jetsam, the stools of trees torn from its undermined banks, and from time to time the carcasses of elephant or deer. Beyond the river, a vast plain, now covered by the sea, but at that time dark with pine forests, stretched eastward to the distant horizon, and thence to Holland.

The plant and animal life of East Anglia at this period was varied and abundant.[1] The Broads and streams, which then as now swarmed with fish,—pike, bream, perch, and roach,—were margined with the water-lily and the water-plantain, and with masses of dock, sedge, and reed. The marshes were gay with meadow-rue and cotton-grass, and with buttercups and the golden flowers of the *Caltha*, while here and there arose a great clump of the royal *Osmunda*. Flocks of geese and wild duck, undisturbed by sportsman or tourist, made their home in these inland waters ; while in the evening, the owl, on noiseless wing, scoured the country in search of its prey. Squirrels flitted through the trees, and frogs croaked in the damp meadows, dotted then, as they are to-day, by the rounded hillocks of the mole. From their holes in the river banks, or their lairs in the reed-beds, otters issued for their nightly fishing, while beavers were busy in the con-

[1] Our knowledge of the flora of the Forest-Bed deposits is largely due to the researches of Mr. Clement Reid, F.R.S.

struction of their dams. Smaller animals, such as mice, shrews, and water-voles, abounded, and the poisonous adder lurked in the woods.[1]

Such was then the aspect of the Broadland, presenting more or less the features which were in after times to make it famous; but once more the scene changes. The climate of the northern hemisphere has now become of Arctic severity, and the Great Ice Age is holding East Anglia in its wintry grasp. Enormous glaciers are issuing from the Scandinavian fiords; the northern part of the German Ocean is blocked with ice, a great lake possibly existing towards the south, into which the summer drainage of the Rhine was poured. The disturbing influence of the North Sea ice is evidenced by the contortions which may be observed in the Cliff section near Cromer. At one stage of the Glacial Period the masses of snow and ice which accumulated on the hilly and mountainous regions of England and Scotland sent out great ice streams towards the lower ground. In the opinion of my friend and coadjutor, the late Searles V. Wood, jun., one of these, the " Great Eastern Glacier," descended from Lincolnshire, travelling southwards between the Chalk Wolds and the Oolitic escarpment (the Lincoln Heights). Spreading itself out like a fan as it reached East Anglia, it extended as far as Yarmouth in one direction, the Thames valley in another, and into the midland counties in a third. A thick sheet of clay, possibly the *moraine profonde* of this ice stream, covers a great part of the eastern counties of England. This deposit, called by Wood the "Chalky Boulder Clay," consists of material derived from the degradation of the various Cretaceous and Jurassic rocks over which the ice moved. It is absent from the northeastern part of Norfolk, the region lying between Norwich and Cromer. The ice to which the Chalky Boulder Clay was

[1] Those who desire further information as to the Crag and Forest-Bed, are referred to Mr. Reid's " Pliocene Deposits of Britain " (*Memoirs of the Geological Survey*), which contains the opinions of that gentleman at the time of its appearance in 1890. The views of the present writer are more fully stated in three papers published in the *Quarterly Journal of the Geological Society*, vols. lii. p. 748, liv. p. 308, and lvi. p. 705. 1896, 1898, and 1900. A summary of these appeared in the *Proceedings of the Geologists' Association*, London, vol. xvii. p. 416. 1902.

due could not, therefore, have come from the direction of the North Sea, as has been sometimes supposed. (Fig. 2.)

Interesting exposures of the glacial deposits of the Broadland may be seen in the cliff sections of the Cromer and Lowestoft coasts.

As the Glacial Period waned, and the ice melted over the higher parts of Norfolk, it seems to have shrunk into the valleys, eroding and deepening them ; patches of boulder clay being found in many places at the valley bottoms. A glacier appears, for example, to have moved down the valley of the Yare, eastward from Norwich. At a quarry in the parish of Whitlingham, on the south bank of the river, the chalk has been greatly disturbed, the lines of flint in it, originally horizontal, having been forced up into an anticlinal (Fig. 3). At Thorpe, immediately opposite, on the north bank, the glacial beds present similar evidence of disturbance ; while on the low ground, within the valley, boulder clay rests on the glaciated surface of the chalk.

Another transformation. The Glacial Epoch is rapidly passing away. Floods of great violence, due partly to the melting of the ice and partly to meteorological disturbances of greater intensity than those of our own times, ravaged the eastern counties, at one time heaping up in places coarse flint gravel, as may be seen in some large excavations near the Infantry Barracks at Norwich ; at another, carving out of the morainic detritus left by the ice the diversified and picturesque scenery of Norfolk and Suffolk. The constant alternation of hill and dale, the size and number of the valleys by which the district is intersected, out of all proportion to its area, or to the streams which flow, or ever could have flowed, in them, and the masses of flint gravel just referred to, could not have originated under conditions similar to those which now prevail, however prolonged.

No conclusive evidence that man existed in the Broadland before the Glacial Epoch has yet been obtained, though it is believed by some geologists that such may have been the case. There is no doubt, however, that an immigration of uncivilised folk into East Anglia took place shortly after

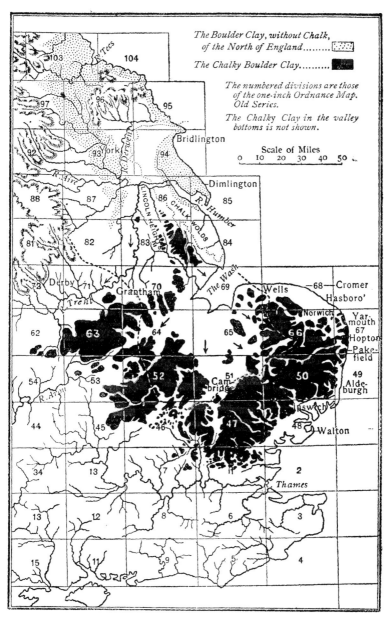

FIG. 2.—MAP SHOWING THE EXTENT AND DISTRIBUTION OF THE CHALKY
BOULDER CLAY, THE MORAINIC DETRITUS, ACCORDING TO SEARLES V. WOOD,
JUN., OF THE GREAT EASTERN GLACIER. THE SUPPOSED DIRECTION OF THE
ICE-FLOW IS INDICATED BY ARROWS.

279

its close. Savage tribes, ignorant of the use of metals, possibly driven northward by the pressure of stronger races, followed the retreating ice into these then inhospitable regions; for the same reason, a similar race of men, the Eskimo, have now wandered to the far north. Here and there evidence of the former existence of these Palæolithic men occurs in the Post-Glacial deposits of the district. One symmetrically formed unpolished flint hatchet was found by the writer many years ago in the gravels of the Yare valley at Cringleford, three miles south of Norwich. At Hoxne, in the Waveney valley, near which place there must have been at this period a settlement of such people, many flint implements have been found, and they have also been met with in river gravels near Thetford and Brandon. At a later period the Palæolithic men were displaced and possibly driven northward by the arrival in England of the Neolithic races, who used polished weapons and were in other respects more civilised than their predecessors. The further discussion of this branch of the subject belongs, however, to the archæologist.

Borings which have been made in the low ground bordering the Yare and the Wensum show not only that the original valleys are much wider than the narrow channels in which those rivers now run, but that they have been excavated to a depth considerably below sea-level. They are generally filled with peat, underlain by gravel, which latter reaches in places a height of twenty-five feet or more above that of the highest floods of the present day. An exposure of these gravels may be seen on the right hand as the train leaves Thorpe station (Norwich).

As the excavating power of water depends more or less upon the gradient, it follows that the formation or deepening of the valleys, so far as this was due to the action of running water, could only have taken place when the land stood relatively to the sea at a higher level than it does now. The height to which the valley gravels extend shows equally that the floods to which they were due were of greater volume than any which now occur. England may have been at this time joined to the Continent, and the torrents which then swept through Norfolk and Suffolk may have mingled in their after course with those of the Rhine.

The valley gravels thus represent a period of greater elevation. A later stage, however, in the evolution of the Broadland was accompanied by subsidence, during which the North Sea re-invaded its former basin, gradually creeping up the Norfolk valleys, converting the lower part of them into estuaries. Estuarine conditions continue to this day in the southern part of East Anglia, as in those of the Orwell and the Stour. It may be interesting to inquire why the development of the latter has been arrested at this stage, while the valleys of the Broadland are choked with sediment or peat.

The constant encroachment of the sea upon those parts of the coast that are exposed to the tidal scour is a fact only too well known to the unfortunate owners of the land, the waste being often greater where the cliffs are high. So long as the latter are buttressed by talus, or by the accumulation of beach, they are safe; but when these are eaten away by the waves, and the cliff acquires a face more or less vertical, it falls by its own weight, its disintegration being hastened by the action of land-springs. The fallen material protects it for a time, but eventually history repeats itself, and a further strip of land falls a prey to the hungry sea.[1]

A considerable portion of the material derived from this waste of the land remains upon or near the shore, accumulating principally at comparatively sheltered spots. From another portion, however, have been formed those long, narrow sandbanks which fringe certain parts of the coast, lying parallel to it, at no great distance from the shore.

As is well known, the beaches of the eastern coasts of Norfolk and Suffolk have a tendency to travel from north to south, the currents running in that direction—those of the flowing tide—being the stronger. Efforts are frequently made to arrest this coastal movement, and so to cause accumulation at certain points by the construction of groynes; but the protection of one spot is gained at the expense of other localities. Lowestoft affords a striking instance of this. The

---

[1] The District Council of north-east Norfolk is at present perpetrating the almost incredible folly of removing shingle from the beach at Bacton for mending the roads.

two long piers which enclose the harbour at that place form a gigantic groyne. Large quantities of sand are constantly accumulating therefore to the north of the north pier, a sandy plain extending from the pier head to the foot of the cliffs (the sea margin of a former period), upon which the old town of Lowestoft stands. On the contrary, little or no sediment can reach the shore to the south of the south pier, and the local authorities, so far as they are there endeavouring to protect the cliffs by groynes, seem to be engaged in an unequal and hopeless struggle.

The amount of material available for the formation of beach is strictly limited, depending on the waste going on towards the north. Where the cliffs are composed of sand, the beaches lying to the south are more or less sandy; where of gravel, they are stony. An example of the latter state of things is presented by the great shingle bank (derived from the pebble beds of a former extension of Dunwich cliff, now destroyed) which extends southward from Aldeburgh in Suffolk. The river Alde approaches the sea at right angles, immediately to the south of the latter town, until within about one hundred yards of it. It then turns abruptly to the south and runs parallel to the shore, and near it, finally reaching the sea at Hollesley, nine miles to the south-west. It is the gradual travel of the beach southward, and the accumulation of the shingle bank between the river and the sea, that has altered the course of the Alde. Similarly, the destruction of the cliffs of North Norfolk in former times has given rise to the great sand-bank upon which Yarmouth has been built. Until this bank had finally established itself across the mouth of the Yare estuary, the tidal currents kept possession of its V-shaped valleys, heaping themselves up inland at high water, where the valleys become narrower, to a level higher than that of the sea outside. Were it not for the existence of this sand-bank, and the fact that the influx of the flowing tide is now confined to the narrow channel of the river between Gorleston and Yarmouth, similar conditions would obtain at present.

The estuarine condition of the Broadland valleys may have continued until a comparatively recent period, as suggested by Samuel Woodward in a map of Roman Norfolk published

in 1833.[1]   Such a view is supported by the positions chosen by
the Romans for their camps at Burgh, Caister, and elsewhere.
There is an old map in Yarmouth (the Hutch map) which
shows a similar state of things as existing in Norman times.
In the district known as the Flegg Hundred, a triangular area
in East Norfolk, bounded by the river Bure and the Hundred
stream (Fig. 4), most of the names of the villages end in *by*, a
proof of their Danish origin, while the majority of those on
the opposite bank of the Bure have Saxon terminations.[2]   It
would seem, therefore, that in those troublous times the Flegg
Hundred may have formed a region marked off by some
natural boundary, which served to protect its inhabitants from
sudden attack.   Moreover, the *Saxon Chronicle* states that in
A.D. 1004, Sweyn, with thirty ships, plundered and burned
Norwich, marching afterwards from thence to Thetford.   The
inference has been drawn that the failure of a Saxon attack
on the ships, in the absence of many of their defenders, may
have been due to the estuarine condition of the Wensum valley
at Norwich at that period.

There is no evidence to show when the Yarmouth sand-
bank began to accumulate.   Originating first as a submarine
shoal, it grew until, at some time previous to the Norman
Conquest, it had become an island frequented by fishermen.
We learn from the report of a survey made by Edward the
Confessor, about A.D. 1050, published in Domesday Book,
that Yarmouth had then seventy burgesses.   The sand-bank
may at that time have obstructed, though it did not wholly
prevent, the daily flow of the tidal water into the estuary.
That this was so is further shown by the existence of *salinæ*,
pans for evaporating salt water, which are recorded as having
then existed at Halvergate and Cantley, in the Yare valley,
and in that of the Bure at Runham, South Walsham, and
other places some miles inland.

The protracted struggle between the growth of the
Yarmouth sand-bank and the scour of the tidal currents marks

---

[1] *Archæologia*, vol. xxiii. p. 358.   1833.

[2] Thurne, Repps, and Bastwick are also Danish, and possibly Runham and
Martham, the latter being, in Mr. Walter Rye's opinion, corruptions of Runholm and
Martholm.

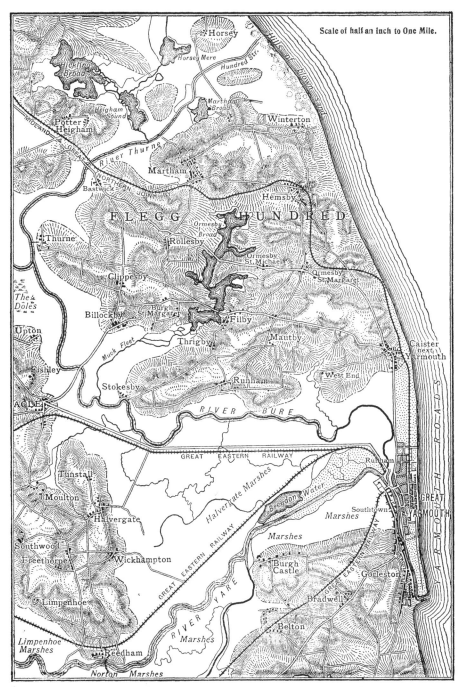

FIG. 4.—SHOWING THE SITE OF A PORTION OF THE ANCIENT ESTUARIES OF THE VALLEYS OF
THE YARE AND THE BURE, AND THE WAY BY WHICH THE SEA HAS BEEN EXCLUDED FROM
THEM BY THE GRADUAL ACCUMULATION OF THE YARMOUTH SAND-BANKS.

another stage in the history of the Broadland. Gradually but irresistibly creeping southward, the sand drove the mouth of the Yare before it. At one time the river reached as far as Corton, a few miles north of Lowestoft, but in the sixteenth century an artificial opening to the sea was made for it at Gorleston; its farther progress towards the south is now barred by the piers at the latter place. Accumulation is taking place to the north of these piers, as at Lowestoft, and the cliffs to the south of them are wasting. All trace of the former channel of the Yare, for example, to the south of Gorleston, has been destroyed by the encroachment of the sea (Fig. 4).

The conditions of the valleys of the Stour and Orwell, of the Alde, and of those of the Bure and the Yare, thus represent successive stages in the process by which the Broads have acquired their present features. The first-named are still open to the sea, because a smaller amount of material derived from the waste of the coast immediately to the north of them is there available. Similar causes are at work, however. A sandy spit extends southward from Felixstowe toward the mouth of the estuary of the Stour, and many submerged sand-banks exist in the offing. The access of the tidal currents to these valleys is, however, for the present unobstructed.

For a long time the river Bure kept for itself an opening to the sea to the north of Yarmouth, but this was finally silted up in the fourteenth century. With the exclusion of the sea from the estuary of the Yare by the blocking of its northern mouth, and of any similar opening which may have existed between Horsey and Winterton, the final stage in the evolution of the Broads commenced. Towards the sea, sediment, consisting partly of mud brought down by the rivers, which are turbid when in flood, and partly of tidal silt, was deposited in sheltered places as banks or shoals. Such deposition is still going on, as for example in Breydon Water, over the mud flats of which, as Mr. A. Patterson informs me, a small boat can hardly pass now where thirty-five years ago a wherry could sail.

Farther inland, beyond the point to which the tidal waters could penetrate, aquatic vegetation flourished in the water-logged soil and along the banks or the shallower parts of the streams.

The first effect of the exclusion of the swiftly flowing tidal currents from the valleys of the Broadland was to transform all the land below a certain level into a sheet, or possibly into several sheets, of inland water, which gradually became smaller, and were finally reduced to a series of lakelets, by the deposition of mud and the accumulation of decaying vegetation. At a later stage, and by a similar process, impassable swamps became meadows, and cattle now graze in the former haunts of the crane and the bittern.[1]

From the valleys of the Waveney and the Yare freshwater lakes have nearly disappeared. The Broads of Rockland and Surlingham in the latter are gradually becoming smaller. Marshes, protected from inundation, during the summer at least, by river banks, extend from Norwich and Bungay to Yarmouth and Lowestoft. Along the Bure, however, Broads still exist, occupying possibly the deeper parts of the old valley, holes which have not yet been filled up. The agencies by the operation of which they came into existence are still at work, and will eventually bring them to an end, the more quickly perhaps because the rivers, the current of which tends to keep their own channels open, do not run through the Broads, but past them.[2]

A portion of the Broadland, that traversed by the Hundred stream (Fig. 4), once open to the sea, is now protected from its incursion by hills of blown sand and by the sandy beach accumulating at their base. The sand dunes at this spot, however, are being gradually moved inland by the agency of the winds, the sea following. When Sir Charles Lyell visited Norfolk in 1839, he found the ruined church tower of Eccles (a small village on the coast to the south-

---

[1] Breydon is the shrunken representation of the large sheet of water which must at one time have covered the low ground shown in the map (Fig. 4), extending from Yarmouth to beyond Reedham in one direction and to the north of Acle in another.

[2] A comparison of the recent maps of the Ordnance Survey with those issued half a century ago will show that the Broads, taken as a whole, have been considerably reduced in extent during recent years.

east of Hasboro') half-buried in the sand-hills.[1] Twelve years afterwards, the latter having shifted, it stood clear of them to seaward, and it has since been entirely destroyed by the waves. Compared with the enormous dunes of some parts of the Dutch coast, which are two miles in width, for example, in the island of Texel, our own sand - hills afford a less secure protection to this part of the Broadland than could be desired. Much of the land is there below the level of high water, and were a breach in the cliffs once made, the sea would take possession of the lower reaches of the Bure valley, and again convert the old Danish settlement of the Flegg Hundred into an island. It is probable that the safety of the district depends as much on the stability of the beach at this point, as on that of the sand-cliffs; but step by step the sea is gaining on the land, and it is to be feared that nothing can permanently prevent its continued encroachment. A visit to this locality may be made by the tourist by way of the Hundred stream, which is navigable in a small boat to within a short distance of the coast.

The present conditions of the Broadland, with their unique and seductive beauty, represent one only out of the many fleeting episodes of its long history. Past ages have brought it never-ceasing change, change of regeneration, however, as well as of decay. What may be in store for it in the more distant future we cannot tell, but to-day natural forces are working towards the obliteration of its distinctive features, while the remorseless sea is threatening its very existence. Fortunately "the mills of God grind slowly," and the East Anglian people, as well as the visitors they yearly welcome, may still hope to enjoy, for some generations to come, their much-valued heritage.

[1] *Principles of Geology*, 10th ed., vol. i. p. 513. Mr. Walter Rye informs me that a patent for the erection of this church on a new site was granted in 1338, the one previously existing at Eccles having been destroyed by the sea.

CHAPTER XIX

ARCHÆOLOGY

By William A. Dutt

SEEING that the greater part of Broadland consists of marshlands that, geologically speaking, are of very recent formation, it is not surprising that the district possesses slight traces of the earliest inhabitants of Eastern England. In the valley gravels of the upper Waveney, and elsewhere in East Norfolk and East Suffolk, flint implements of the crudest form, assignable to the Palæolithic period, have been discovered, whilst Neolithic and bronze relics have also been found; but such primitive structures as cromlechs and dolmens are entirely absent. The lack of stone suitable for the construction of such monuments sufficiently accounts for this; but it is just possible that a stone circle which existed in a field called Stone Close at Gorleston, near Yarmouth, and which was unfortunately destroyed in 1768, may have dated from prehistoric times. It is not unlikely, however, that this circle, which consisted of massive stones ten feet high, was the work of the Norsemen, who established themselves in the Flegg Hundreds about two centuries before the Conquest; for we know that similar circles were raised in Scandinavia to commemorate famous Vikings and mark the places of their burial. That traces of lake-dwellings have been discovered in only one corner of the district—at Filby—seems at first more surprising than the absence of cromlechs and dolmens, for the shallow Broads are as well adapted to the purpose of the builders of such dwellings as the meres at Wretham near Thetford, where drainage revealed some interesting remains of lake-dwellings; but their absence is accounted for by the fact that the Broadland valleys were in an estuarine state so recently as the time of the Roman Occupation. On Mousehold Heath, near Norwich, and on Marsham Heath, near Aylsham, there are some pits or hollows similar to the remarkable " Shrieking Pits " which existed until a few years ago at Aylmerton, and those of the so - called " prehistoric village " of Stanlake in Oxfordshire. These excavations, supposed to be primitive dwellings which were originally roofed with sods of earth or some kind of thatch, may have been occupied by people of that Aryan race known as the Iceni, or by earlier Iberian inhabitants of the district.[1]

Of the Roman Occupation of East Anglia, Broadland possesses a grand relic in Burgh Castle, situated on high ground overlooking the junction of the Yare and Waveney. In an earlier chapter I have written at some length about this notable stronghold ; but I may add here that its walls, which are 14 feet high and 9 feet thick, form three sides of an irregular parallelogram 640 feet by 370, containing an area of over five acres. On its east side are four round towers of solid masonry, on the top of each of which are small holes or depressions, conjectured to have served for the reception of watch-turrets. Large portions of the walls on the north and south sides have fallen ; but the east wall, which, like the others, is built of flints, rubble, and red tiles embedded in mortar, is well preserved. It is noteworthy that the towers are not built into the wall, but are bonded into it near the summit. When one of them fell some years ago, it was found to have been built on a foundation of oak planking and a kind of concrete. The principal entrance appears to have been in the middle of the east wall. Whether there was originally a west wall has long been a matter of dispute. Harrod, who made extensive excavations in 1850 and 1855, found, by digging a series of trenches, layers of broken mortar, flints, and tiles ; and he maintained that he had succeeded in tracing a west wall for about 200 feet. He thought it not improbable that the greater part of the flints of which the

---

[1] On Broome Heath, near Bungay, a mound or tumulus was opened and a human skeleton unearthed ; but the entire absence of any work of art prevented the discoverer hazarding any opinion as to the age of the interment.

wall consisted were carted away and utilised when Burgh Church was built, and that the action of the water, which formerly came quite up to the foot of the slope above which the camp stands, together with the cultivation of the soil within the camp, had resulted in the collapse and obliteration of the wall's foundations. Other archæologists have contended that the remains discovered by Harrod were those of a quay against which the Roman galleys were moored, and that the sea or estuary constituted a sufficient defence for one side of the camp. On the occasion of the members of the Norfolk and Norwich Archæological Society visiting Burgh Castle, Mr. F. Danby-Palmer, in discussing the purposes for which the camp was used, expressed an opinion that it may have been a naval rather than a military station, and that the headquarters of the Stablesian Horse must be sought for at Bergh Apton or Wheatacre Burgh on the mainland, instead of on the " Island of Lothing." Dr. Raven, the Suffolk historian, however, thought it no more remarkable that cavalry should have been stationed at Burgh Castle than at Richborough and Reculvers, and stated that a great number of horses' teeth had been found in and around the camp.

Burgh Castle is the only relic of the Roman Occupation likely to attract the attention of the visitor in Broadland. The camp at Caistor St. Edmund is well preserved, but is not accessible by any Broadland waterway. Concerning the existence of traces of Roman roads, antiquaries have grown somewhat sceptical, and cruisers in Broadland will scarcely choose to devote their time to this difficult problem. Roman relics have been unearthed at Caister, Burgh-next-Aylsham, Bungay, Lowestoft, and elsewhere in the district. Many of these are preserved in the Castle Museum at Norwich.[1]

---

[1] At Geldeston a beautiful Roman glass vase and some earthen vessels were discovered ; at Barsham, a gold Roman ring. Several urns of this period were found at Buckenham during the making of the Norwich and Yarmouth railway. Coins have been found at Reedham, Thurton, Fritton, Gorleston, Bungay, Ditchingham, Caister, Burgh - next - Aylsham, and elsewhere. " The late Mr. Leighton, in the course of some excavations, discovered on the low cliff at Reedham the ground-plan or foundations of a circular tower, which he believed to have been a Roman Pharos . . . a lighthouse on the hill at Reedham would

Concerning the antiquity of such huge earthworks as that on which Norwich Castle stands, and those at Bungay, there has been much dispute, some antiquaries going so far as to credit them with equal antiquity to the round tumuli of the Stone Age. Harrod, after careful examination and excavation, came to the conclusion that they are of earlier date than the Roman Occupation, thus giving some support to certain writers who argued that these artificial hills were constructed for the performance of the religious rites of the Iceni. That some sort of British earthworks were occasionally utilised by the Romans there is strong evidence at Castle Acre in Norfolk and elsewhere; but it is now generally agreed that such mounds as that on which Norwich Castle stands were constructed during the Anglo-Saxon period, when they were surmounted by wooden buildings. Some remarks on this subject, contributed by the Rev. C. R. Manning to the *Original Papers of the Norfolk and Norwich Archæological Society*, are well worthy of consideration. In writing of the Castle Hill at Denton (an earthwork situated a little way beyond the recognised bounds of Broadland), he urges the necessity for remembering that the castles on or amid earthworks constructed by the chief lords of our English (Saxon or Angle) ancestors were *domestic* buildings, "intended for permanent habitation as well as defence"; whereas the British earthworks were *tribal*, and constructed for the defence of large bodies of men, and the Roman works were *military*, "and adapted for the encampment of soldiers under well-defined rules of warfare." "As the chief lords and leaders (of the English) had dwelt in their northern homes, so they continued to live and build here, regardless of the previous occupants or their methods. They cast up a truncated cone of earth, formed out of the contents of the circumscribing ditch . . . upon it they constructed a wooden building, defended with stout palisades, and approached by a bridge thrown over the ditch. . . . Connected with the mound were base-courts for shelter of servants and the offices, and usually a larger enclosure at a little distance for the

have been visible from the Roman station of Garianonum, and from a large extent of the estuaries of the Yare and Waveney." — Mr. Greville Chester in *Norfolk Archæology*.

herding of cattle.   In several cases earthworks of earlier date
were made use of, and sometimes natural hills were brought
into requisition, and scarped so as to save labour ; in others,
and more frequently, the works were new and artificial from
the first."   Whether the huge mound at Norwich is entirely
artificial is uncertain.   There is some reason for believing that
it originally formed the end of a ridge of upland some half a mile
long ; but, according to Gough's *Camden's Britannia*, in 1784,
when a well was being sunk in the basement of the castle
keep, the workmen at a great depth came upon a trackway
which had crossed the site on which the mound stands.
Tradition asserts that Uffa, the first king of the East Angles,
who reigned about 575, threw up the mound, probably on the
site of an Icenic encampment ; for Caer Gwent—the *Venta
Icenorum* of the Romans—undoubtedly comprised a stronghold
on the before-mentioned upland ridge.   The earthworks at
Bungay, though still considerable, are greatly reduced in
height.   They were for a long time believed to have been
constructed for the defence of the Bigods' castle, but antiquaries now assign them to the same period as those at
Norwich and Denton.

The Anglo-Saxons, who were a peace-loving people, gave
their attention, so long as the Norse raiders would allow them,
to cultivating their lands ; and as they constructed no encamp-
ments, and built few more durable buildings than wooden
houses,[1] it is not surprising that we now possess slight traces
of them apart from the names of certain villages and the
mounds on which their kings and lords erected their castles.
In other parts of Norfolk are remains of huge embankments
or "dykes" which may have been heaped up by them ; but
though these dykes may have served as a protection against
the encroachments of neighbouring peoples, their chief purpose
was, in all probability, that of boundary marks.   Norwich was
one of the seats of the kings of East Anglia during this
period, and Uffa, who united Norfolk, Suffolk, and Cambridgeshire in one kingdom, may have built a wooden castle on or

---

[1] Visitors to Bungay should, however, not fail to visit South Elmham St. George
(five miles south-west of Bungay, and one and a half miles east of Homersfield
station), where are the ruins of a Saxon church known as the " Old Minster."

near the site of the existing Norman keep. Anna, another
king, held his court where is now the Norfolk capital, and
bestowed his castle, with the lands pertaining to it, on his
daughter Etheldreda when she married Tonbert, a chieftain of
the Gyrvii. Monasteries were established, at Cnobersburg
(Burgh Castle) by Sigebert about 640, and at Cowholm near
Ludham by a company of hermits, presided over by one
Suneman, about the year 800 ; but of these religious establishments not a fragment remains. Nor is it easy to determine
whether Saxon work is detectable in any of the churches
of Broadland, though some of them are of great antiquity.
Bradeston Church, near Brundall, retains in its chancel some
work which may be pre-Norman, and some small windows at
Coltishall are believed to be Saxon. The building of the round
towers which are so plentiful in Norfolk, and not uncommon in
Suffolk, was formerly attributed to the Saxons, and even now
there are students of the different styles of ecclesiastical
architecture who believe they are able to distinguish Saxon
work in some of these structures ; but though such work
may exist in the foundations, most of the round towers seem
to be of a later date. From Domesday we learn that a considerable number of *salinæ* or salt pans existed in Broadland
at the time of the Norman Conquest, mention being made of
their presence at various places in the Flegg Hundreds and
even at South Walsham on the Bure. In all there were
something like a hundred of them, and they were undoubtedly
flat pans into which the salt water was admitted at high tide
and retained so that salt might be obtained by evaporation.
At Herringby on the Bure there were six *salinæ ;* and a few
years ago, when a drain was being cut in the Herringby
marshes, a square enclosure, believed to be one of these pans,
was discovered close by a buried thicket of ash and alder trees.
Although the Danes or Norsemen frequently ravaged the
Norfolk coast during the reigns of the Anglo-Saxon kings,
and an encampment at Warham near Wells is thought to have
been constructed by them, the only indications of their settlement in Broadland are the names of some of the villages,
particularly in the Flegg Hundreds. Canute is said to have
founded St. Benet's Abbey in 1034, on the site of Suneman's

hermitage, which the Danes had destroyed. Tradition says that at the time of the Norman Conquest this monastery was so strongly fortified that it "resembled a castle more than a cloister." There is nothing among the scanty ruins remaining on the Cowholm marshes that can be assigned to a pre-Norman period.[1]

A description and history of the Norman castle at Norwich and the splendid Norman work in Norwich Cathedral can hardly be looked for in a brief chapter devoted to the Archæology of Broadland; but a little may be added to what appears elsewhere in this book concerning Bungay Castle, which, like the keep of Norwich Castle, was probably built by Roger Bigod, Earl of Norfolk. Subsequently the manor of Bungay, with nearly two hundred other manors in Norfolk and Suffolk, was inherited by Roger's second son Hugh, his eldest son William having been drowned when the *White Ship* foundered in 1120. Hugh Bigod was a very turbulent lord. He rebelled against King Stephen in 1137. Two years later he declared himself a supporter of Matilda, and in punishment for his disloyalty the king took from him Bungay Castle. A year or two later he regained possession of the castle, which he held until the accession of Henry II., who had it destroyed. It was not, however, totally demolished, and in 1163 Earl Bigod set about restoring it, only to have it again destroyed in 1174, when, after a final act of rebellion, the faithless baron was relieved of his estates. The latter were restored by Richard I. to a second Roger Bigod; and in 1294 Edward I. granted to another Roger, fifth Earl of Norfolk, leave to fortify the castle, of which some massive fragments can still be seen in the midst of the picturesque old town on the Waveney. On the death of this earl the castle passed into the hands of the Uffords,

---

[1] " My list of Saxon antiquities from the Waveney and Yare valleys is but meagre. A golden bulla . . . was turned up at Palgrave; this object, however, is regarded by some antiquaries as a relic of Roman workmanship. Pagan-Saxon urns have been found near the Minster, St. George's, South Elmham, and at Stow Park, near Bungay. On the Suffolk banks of the Waveney two parishes preserve the name of St. Felix the Burgundian, the apostle of the Eastern counties. . . . I am not aware that any antiquities have been discovered, either near the Waveney or Yare, which can be safely assigned to the Danish invaders. A sword in my own possession, dredged up in the river at Norwich, strongly resembles one figured in Professor Worsaæ's interesting work."—Mr. Greville Chester in *Norfolk Archæology*.

Earls of Suffolk, and subsequently to the Howards, Dukes of Norfolk. The principal remains are two low circular towers and considerable portions of the walls of an octangular ground-plan which enclosed a keep about 54 feet square, three sides of which are still standing, their walls being from 6 to 11 feet thick, and from 15 to 17 feet high. In the midst of the mound on which the castle stands a square shaft of considerable depth descends to a small "pitch-dark" hole, which some have thought to be a dungeon, but which is more likely to have been the bottom of a well from which the holders of the castle obtained water in times of siege.[1]

East Anglia possessed a very great number of monastic houses,—abbeys, priories, nunneries, colleges, and hospitals,— Norfolk alone containing considerably more than a hundred. Of these, St. Benet's Abbey and the religious house which Sigebert established at Burgh Castle were the earliest foundations in Broadland. Of the Benedictine Priory at Aldeby, founded in the reign of Henry I.; Hickling Priory, a house for Austin Friars, founded in 1185; Ingham Priory, one of the few English establishments of the Mathurines or Trinitarians, founded in 1380; and the Augustinian Priory of St. Olave at Herringfleet, founded in 1239,—the remains are very fragmentary and of little interest: while of a priory or cell at Horstead on the Bure, a hospital at Great Hautbois, Lessingham Priory, West Somerton Hospital, Herringby College, Weybridge Priory at Acle, and the Benedictine nunnery at Bungay, there are now no traces. In my chapters on the Yare and Bure I have given some description and an outline of the history of Langley and St. Benet's Abbeys. The greater part of St. Olave's Priory was demolished many years ago; but a considerable portion of the crypt, which is now used as a house, is intact, the groining being very well preserved. This priory was founded by Roger Fitz-Osbert near the old ferry across the Waveney, its site being one of the "holms" or islets of rising ground among the fens. It was dedicated to the Virgin and St. Olave the King and Martyr.

[1] For a description of Caister Castle, see pp. 196–199.

Bromholm Priory, in the parish of Bacton, which cruisers on the Ant to North Walsham can easily visit from Paston station, was founded in 1113 by William de Glanvile for Cluniac monks as a cell to the important priory founded by the first Earl Warrenne at Castle Acre. Of the original building nothing remains. The gatehouse, by which access is gained to the ruins, seems to have been enlarged about the middle of the sixteenth century, when John of Tytleshall was prior, for while its lower part is Transition-Norman, and the piers on each side are Transition-Norman and Early English, above the capital the stonework is Perpendicular. On the right of this was the porter's lodge. Of the priory itself Harrod asserts that the oldest portion is a fragment now standing apart from the rest of the ruins, and which formed the north transept of the church: it probably dates from the latter part of the twelfth century. The most interesting remains are this old portion, and those of the dormitory and the chapter-house. The last-named are the most picturesque, and undoubtedly date from the time when the priory became famous on account of its acquisition of the "Holy Rood"; for these remains and those of the dormitory are Early English. The dormitory appears to have been large, and lighted by a row of small windows on the east side. The church was cruciform, the nave extending west of the cross aisle about 115 feet, while the cross aisle was about 90 feet from north to south. As proving the fact that the priory was considerably enlarged early in the thirteenth century, Harrod draws attention to a fragment remaining against the east wall of the north transept; "not only is it later in style than the wall it abuts upon, but it does not range with the walls of the transept." This enlargement was probably contemporary with the building of the chapter-house and dormitory. At the west end of the church are some traces of brick vaults, and the presence of a fireplace in a vaulted room beneath the dormitory suggests that this room was the calefactory. Unfortunately these ruins have for many years been utilised as outbuildings in connection with the farm on which they stand, and neglect is responsible for several portions which were interesting at the time of Harrod's survey being now almost indistinguishable in consequence of the growth of ivy and accumulation of rubbish.

How Bromholm became possessed of its famous relic is related by Matthew Paris, from whose account it appears that after Baldwin, Emperor of Constantinople, was defeated and made prisoner at Adrianople, his English chaplain "left the city of Constantinople privately," carrying with him many valuable relics, including a wooden cross which was declared to be a portion of the Cross on which our Saviour was crucified. This cross he showed to some of the monks of St. Alban's; but they were incredulous of its authenticity, and the chaplain, after offering it to several monasteries, disposed of it to the "very poor" chapel of Bromholm. From this time (1223) "divine miracles began to be wrought in that monastery, to the praise and glory of the life-giving Cross; for there the dead were restored to life, the blind recovered their sight, and the lame their power of walking; the skin of lepers was made clean, and those possessed of devils were released from them; and any sick person who approached the aforesaid Cross with faith, went away safe and sound. This said Cross is frequently worshipped, not only by the English people, but also by those from distant countries, and those who have heard of the divine miracles connected with it." This account Capgrave to some extent "confirms" by the assertion that this wonderful relic was the means of thirty-nine persons being raised from the dead. Among the pilgrims to Bromholm was Henry III., who spent some time here with his court; and Harrod thinks it not improbable that Edward I., who stayed with John, Earl Warrenne, at Gimingham, also paid a visit to the shrine.

By a papal Bull obtained in the year 1298, Bromholm freed itself of the control of the Prior of Castle Acre. Among its patrons were the Pastons. Sir John Paston, who died in 1466, was buried in the Priory Church, when there were great festivities, of which Mr. Dawson Turner gives some account in his history of Caister Castle. "For three continuous days one man was engaged in no other occupation than that of flaying beasts, and provision was made of 13 barrels of ale, one barrel of beer of the greatest assyze, and a runlet of red wine of 15 gallons. . . . A barber was occupied five days in smartening up the monks for the ceremony ; and 'the reke of the torches at the dirge' was so great that the glazier had to remove two panes to permit the fumes to escape." At the Dissolution the site of the priory was granted to Sir Thomas Wodehouse, who held the neighbouring manor of Waxham. Of the Wodehouses' fine old hall there are some remains just within the sandhill bastions which protect the coast from the sea.

Concerning the Broadland churches so much could be said that one might well hesitate to attempt any account of them here. The finest Norman architecture in the district is, of course, in Norwich Cathedral ; but some of the village churches contain good work of this period. The round towers at Herringfleet and Haddiscoe are perhaps the finest in East Anglia. Notable features of the tower at Herringfleet are its circular-headed windows enclosing double triangular arches ; these, though often described as Saxon, are undoubtedly Norman. This church also contains an interesting example of the Norman star moulding. In the tower at Haddiscoe, too, there are triangular-headed, two-light windows, and the north door has some rich carving. Good Norman doorways are also to be found in the churches at Chedgrave, Aldeby, Clippesby, Great Ormesby, and West Somerton ; but none of these are so fine as the grand one at Wroxham. Fritton Church possesses an interesting Norman apsidal chancel. Gillingham Church, near Beccles, is also of this period, and has a remarkable ground-plan.

Early English work is not uncommon in Broadland ; but nowhere in the district is it so good as in the ancient church at Burgh-next-Aylsham, the chancel of which Sir Gilbert Scott described as " one of peculiar beauty and interest, and at the same time one of which it is peculiarly difficult to conjecture the original form and extent. The south side," he adds, " consists, on its upper and principal level, of a continuous range of beautiful and similar lancet lights, arched within, and absolutely simple without. Its lower stage consists of a continuous arcade standing upon a stone seat. Both stages are of admirable design and beautiful detail. On the opposite or north side of the chancel the design, though at perfect unity with the south side, is from its circumstances somewhat different. Here a continuous range of windows could not exist, inasmuch as there was a side chapel running alongside of the chancel. This chapel was entered from the chancel by a beautiful arch, breaking through the lower range of arcading about the middle of the present chancel wall. Westward of the arch there remain no ancient windows,—one at least two centuries later than the date of the building has been inserted,— but eastward of the arch the arcading of the windows appears again as on the opposite side ; but the two remaining arches being alongside of the chapel are blank. Eastward of these and of the chapel, the chancel still continued, though now destroyed. . . . The architecture of the chancel and of the arch into the former side chapel is of the *finest* character, and of a date not very abundant in the remains of its productions. It is neither Transitional nor Developed Early English, but of an intermediate stage between the two. It unites the square abacus, the type of the one style, with the round abacus, the type of the other. It is probably of the same date with the work of St. Hugh at Lincoln, dating about 1200. The roof is probably of the same date as the nave."

Of Decorated work the district has some good examples. At Aylsham the main arcade, of which the piers are alternately circular and octagonal, is of this style, and there are good portions at Brunstead, Crostwight, Happisburgh, Belaugh, Knapton, Stokesby, and Paston. In Ingham Church we have an interesting specimen of Late Decorated work with a very fine tower.

More interest attaches to Broadland's Perpendicular churches, especially to those at Worstead, Salle, Cawston, Martham, Lowestoft, Bungay, Beccles, North Walsham, and Winterton, to say nothing of St. Peter Mancroft and St. Andrew's Hall at Norwich. The towers of the churches at Bungay, Beccles, and Winterton are grand and lofty ; while at Beccles and Salle the main arcades, and at Cawston the magnificent open roof, invariably excite admiration. The Cawston roof, which is one of the best of its date in England, has double hammer-beams, the lower arches of which are borne by wooden shafts rising between the clerestory lights. Curiously carved cherubs with outspread wings adorn the cornice, and full-length angels are supported by the projecting beams. At Salle and Loddon, too, there are good roofs; but neither are so fine as that at Knapton (a village about three miles from North Walsham), which is ornamented with rich carved work and more than a hundred figures. Tradition has it that this roof, destined for some continental church, was found on board a Spanish vessel wrecked on the neighbouring coast; but an entry in the register records its erection by one John Smithe in the year 1503. At Martham there is some excellent flint-work, a good south door, and some interesting windows filled with Flemish glass. The lofty tower and richly decorated south porch at Winterton also belong to this period; and at Worstead, formerly the seat of an important industry to which the place gave its name, is a noble building, which no one who visits Broadland should fail to see. It represents the period of transition from Decorated to Perpendicular, and has a beautiful tower with some sound-holes which alone are a sufficient reward for a long journey by road or rail.

Broadland churches are famous for their painted and carved rood screens. The best known is at Ranworth; but the screens at Barton Turf, Worstead, and Fritton are fine, and those at Belaugh, Filby, East Ruston, Ludham, Horsey, and Aylsham claim attention. Some of the old tombs and monuments are very interesting: that of Sir Oliver de Ingham (died 1343) in Ingham Church is perhaps the most notable.[1] The tomb of Sir Roger and Dame Margaret de Bois, also at Ingham, is of interest, though much mutilated. At Mautby are some ancient memorials of the Mawteby

[1] A good description of this tomb appears in the *Original Papers of the Norfolk and Norwich Archæological Society* (vol. viii. pp. 216-218). It is a high tomb placed beneath an arched recess in the north wall of the chancel. On it is the effigy of Sir Oliver, "which represents him reposing in an unusual or forced position, reclining somewhat on his right side, with his arms folded over his body and his legs crossed. He appears wearing a conical basinet, to which a camail of mail is attached. The body armour apparently consists of a hawberk of mail with short sleeves, which protect the shoulders and half the upper part of the arms," which are further protected by brassarts, elbow plates, vambraces, and the hands by gauntlets.

family, including the earliest existing in Broadland probably, that of Sir Walter de Mawteby, who died in 1248; though at Stratton Strawless there is a cross-legged effigy of one of the Marshams of almost equal antiquity. Oxnead, North Walsham, and Paston churches contain some fine monuments to members of the Paston family. Mural paintings, some of unusual merit, have been discovered in several of the Broadland churches since the early part of the nineteenth century. At Trunch there is a magnificent baptistery or self-supporting font-cover of rare form and Late Perpendicular date.

Apart from Blickling Hall, Waxham Old Hall, and Heydon Hall, the last-named of which is not far from Blickling, the domestic architecture likely to come under the notice of a visitor to Broadland is not particularly interesting.

Blickling Hall stands on an historically famous manor. Before the Norman Conquest it was held by King Harold, the site of whose "palace" is pointed out about a mile from the Hall! The Conqueror gave it to Herfast, his chaplain, who was the first Norman bishop of East Anglia, and it was afterwards held by Bishop Herbert de Lozinga, the builder of Norwich Cathedral. Subsequently it came into the possession of the Dagworths, one of whom, Sir Nicholas Dagworth, built a manor house which remained until the early part of the seventeenth century, when Sir Henry Hobart, a Lord Chief Justice of the reign of James I., erected the existing Hall. From the Dagworths the manor passed to the Erpinghams,—one of whom was the builder of the fine cathedral gateway at Norwich,—and afterwards to Sir John Fastolff, the builder of Caister Castle. Fastolff sold it to Sir Geoffrey Boleyn, ex-Lord Mayor of London and great-grandfather of Queen Anne Boleyn.

"Over the hawberk is worn an emblazoned cyclas. . . . The legs are encased in chausses of mail, with jambs of plate or leather in front; the feet are protected by laminated sollerets and rest against the figure of a lion. Above the head is represented the tilting helm with mantling, but the crest, an owl, is gone; the helm is supported by two mutilated statuettes of angels clad in albs and copes, with a morse connecting each of the latter in front. On the left side of the effigy are the remains of the sword. . . . The effigy is represented as lying on a bed of flint boulders. . . . This appears to have been a whim of the artist." In only one other church in Norfolk, that of Reepham, is an effigy represented lying on a bed of stones.

Norfolk people, crediting the statements of Spelman, Blomefield, and other historians, claim that Anne Boleyn was born at Blickling; but like claims are made on behalf of Hever Castle in Kent and Rochfort Hall in Essex. That she spent some years of her childhood at Blickling is certain; and there is a tradition, mentioned by Agnes Strickland in her *Lives of the Queens of England*, that after she was beheaded her body was secretly conveyed from the Tower and buried in the church at Salle, the manor of which was held by the Boleyns before they purchased Blickling. Blickling Hall contains a fine library of twelve thousand books, ten thousand of which were selected by Mattaire. Among its treasures are some valuable Aldine publications, two copies of Coverdale's Bible, the Sedan New Testament, and a French MS. Bible of the thirteenth century. In the hall are two large wooden statues, one of Queen Elizabeth, the other of Anne Boleyn. Some draperies, gowns, and nightcaps worn by Anne Boleyn are among the heirlooms. Some of the rooms have finely ornamented chimney-pieces, one of which was formerly in the Norwich house of Sir Thomas Browne, the author of *Religio Medici*, while another originally formed a window arch in Caister Castle. The front of the Hall, which bears the date 1626, has a richly decorated entrance, above which are the arms of its builder, Sir Henry Hobart. In the gardens are some statues which originally adorned the terrace of Sir Clement Paston's Hall at Oxnead, and in the Park is a curious pyramidal mausoleum in which are buried an Earl of Buckinghamshire and his two wives.

Heydon Hall, which was a seat of Lord Lytton, the novelist, is a fine Tudor house still in the possession of the Bulwer family. At Crostwight the Walpoles had a large manor house, of which some interesting portions remain.

CHAPTER XX

YACHT-RACING

By A. Townley Clarkson,

Honorary Secretary of the Norfolk and Suffolk Yacht and Sailing Clubs' Association

PLEASURE-BOAT sailing and racing were reckoned among the sports of what is now known as the Broads district at an early period; but it is difficult to determine exactly when days were first set apart for properly organised racing. We know, however, that water frolics were held in the middle of the eighteenth century, and that pleasure boats owned by various gentlemen residing in the district competed in the races; but the terms "regatta" and "yacht" do not seem to have been commonly used until about 1850. The water frolics were held at Thorpe near Norwich and Burgh at the top of Breydon Water; at any rate, these appear to have been the most important places in the earlier years of the nineteenth century. Similar frolics were held elsewhere, but they were not annual events like the two mentioned. Thorpe Water Frolic was quite a social function, and about 1830–40 several thousands of people yearly flocked to the meadow just below the present railway bridge, which, on some occasions at all events, was kept as an enclosure, a charge of half-a-crown being made for admission. Burgh Water Frolic was also regarded as an important event, and was attended by the Mayor of Great Yarmouth in state. It seems to have had its origin in the annual visit paid to St. Olave's Bridge and Hardley Cross by the Yarmouth bailiffs, some account of whose proceedings, and their attendant joviality, is given in

another chapter.[1]   For many years the occasion of this frolic
was looked upon as a gala day by the inhabitants of Yarmouth;
but the passing of the Municipal Corporations Act of 1835
prevented the application of the borough funds to the maintenance of the pageant,—the official expenses of which had increased from a modest thirty shillings allowed to the bailiffs
in the sixteenth century, to about £100 a year,—and the
Mayor ceased to attend in his official capacity.   The frolic,
however, continued to be a great carnival for many years
afterwards, but it gradually became less popular, and was
finally discontinued some twenty years ago.

The yachts which took part in the races of the first half
of the last century were lateen-rigged as to the foremast, which
was stepped almost up in the yacht's eyes; while on the
mainmast, which was placed exactly amidships, was carried
a large boom and gaff mainsail.   In the later boats a mizzen
was substituted for a main mast.   One famous yacht of this
type is still in evidence on Barton Broad.   She was built of
oak in 1834, for Mr. Plowman of Normanstone, Lowestoft,
and was called the *Paragon*.   Sir Jacob Preston bought her
in 1837, and changed her name to the *Maria*.   She is 23
feet long, with 8 feet beam and 3 feet draught of water.

In calculating the measurement for time allowance in
racing, the only factor was length, taken from the foreside of
the stem to the afterside of the stern-post.   The boats were
built with very short counters, and it was not until about
1850[2] that the builders recognised the advantage of running
them farther, which they ultimately did to the extent of a
third or even more of the length between perpendiculars, when

---

[1] See pp. 18–20.

[2] The following advertisement appeared in the *Lynn Advertiser*, dated 10th
August 1850:—

"NORWICH REGATTA, *Monday*, 19*th August* 1850.

"A Silver Tankard of not less value than Fifteen Guineas will be given for Cutter
Rigged Pleasure Boats not exceeding 28 feet on the ram.   Time to be allowed for
length, quarter minute per foot.

"A Cup of not less value than Eight Guineas for Boats rigged with Foresail and
Mizzen not exceeding 16 feet on the ram.   Time to be allowed for length, quarter
minute per foot.

"A Prize will be given for an Amateur Sculling Match.   A Handsome set of Shirt
Studs, value Six Guineas.

it was found necessary to penalise them; this was done by adding half the length of the counter to the length from stem to stern-post. This measurement remained in force until after the founding of the Norfolk and Suffolk Yacht Club, when the Thames Rule of computing tonnage was adopted, half the length of the counter, however, still being taken in for length.

About 1847, cutters—that is to say, yachts carrying a boom and gaff mainsail and one large jib, but no stay foresail—made their appearance. The *Wallace*, 19 feet, owned by Mr. Randell Burroughes of Thorpe; the *Tantivy*, 19 feet, owned by Messrs J. B. and H. Morgan of Norwich; and the *Venus*, 19 feet, owned by Mr. Francis of Beccles, were the first racing yachts of this class. At this time the 16th Lancers were quartered at Norwich, and several officers of that regiment took an active interest in sailing, Captain Coster becoming owner of the *Kestrel*, and Captains Heaviside and Shelley and Mr. Lockhart Scott owners of other yachts. Mr. Alec Bence of Thorington also had a boat, and a club was formed called the Amateur Cutter Yacht Club. This was the beginning of united action; but the life of the club was brief, owing to the funds being exhausted by a grand *déjeûner* at Wroxham.

In 1859, Colonel George Wilson of Beccles and Mr. Green of Wroxham started the idea of forming a club, and a meeting was held at Norwich, at which Mr. Henry Morgan acted as Secretary *pro tem.* The result was the formation of the Norfolk and Suffolk Yacht Club, Colonel Wilson being elected Commodore and Mr. C. W. Millard Secretary at a meeting held on 16th April 1859 at Mr. Millard's office in Norwich. The Committee consisted of Messrs. W. H. Scott, Fred Green, and A. J. N. Chamberlin, representing the river Bure; Messrs. H. P. Green, W. Jecks, and J. B. Morgan for the Yare; and

"A Prize for Four-oared Boats, to be rowed by Non-commissioned Officers and Privates of the 11th Hussars. The First Boat to receive £4, the Second do. £2.

"A Prize for Watermen's Four Oars not exceeding 24 feet in length. First Prize £4, Second do. £2.

"A Prize for Watermen's Sculling. First Prize £3, Second do. £1.

"A Prize for Watermen's Punts. First Prize £3, Second do. £1.

"All boats intending to sail must be entered at Cattermole's Gardens, Thorpe, or by letter to the Secretary. No entry will be received after 10 o'clock a.m. of the day of the race."

Messrs. E. Swatman, W. S. Everitt, and Henry Farr for the Waveney. To these were added the Commodore, the Vice-Commodore (Mr. E. S. Trafford), the Rear-Commodore (Mr. F. Brown), the Treasurer (Mr. H. Morgan), and the Secretary. At a subsequent meeting, Messrs. Samuel Nightingale, T. M. Read, and W. M. Bond were added to represent Great Yarmouth.

The first season's programme was for races to take place at Cantley on 16th June, at Wroxham on 14th July, and at Oulton on 11th August. Two races were sailed on each of these days, the first for cutters, the second for lateen-rigged yachts (foresail and mizzen). The prize in each race was £15 at the two first-named places; but at Oulton and in subsequent races the amount was divided into two prizes, the first £10 and the second £5. The cutters which started in the first race at Cantley were—

Tantivy	.	.	.	.	Morgan	.	.	.	6 tons.
Oberon	.	.	.	.	Morton	.	.	.	5 ,,
Union	.	.	.	.	Chamberlin	.	.	.	3 ,,
Kestrel	.	.	.	.	Butcher	.	.	.	12 ,,
Belvidere	.	.	.	.	Read	.	.	.	9 ,,
Clara	.	.	.	.	Smith	.	.	.	3 ,,

For the lateen yachts race the starters were *Osprey*, Swatman; *Maud*, Asker; *Atalanta*, Wilson; and *Amateur*, Brown. Unfortunately the records do not mention their tonnage.

The lateen-rigged yachts were gradually superseded by cutters, and by 1863 only two appear in the list of entries at Oulton on 6th August, namely, the *Vampire*, owned by Mr. W. S. Everitt, and the *Enchantress*, owned by Mr. H. P. Green. The entries on that occasion were as follows:—

For the first race—

Belvidere (cutter)	.	10 tons	.	W. H. Clabburn.
Wanderer ,,	.	14 ,,	.	R. J. H. Harvey.
Myth ,,	.	9 ,,	.	{ R. J. H. Harvey. { J. L. Barber in charge.
Red Rover .,	.	14 ,,	.	S. Nightingale.
Alabama ,,	.	14 ,,	.	E. S. Trafford.

In the second race—

Vampire (lateen)	.	9 tons	. W. S. Everitt.
Belvidere (cutter)	.	10 ,,	. W. H. Clabburn.
Bittern ,,	.	7 ,,	. Morgan and Hansell.
Myth ,,	.	9 ,,	. R. J. H. Harvey.
Enchantress (lateen) .		8 ,,	. H. P. Green.
Blanche (cutter)	.	7 ,,	. R. Morris.
Woman in White (cutter)		6 ,,	. J. L. Barber.

It is interesting to note the dimensions of two of the lateeners, both of which were famous craft in their day—the *Enchantress* and the *Miranda* (Mr. Blake Humphrey). They were 19 feet between perpendiculars, with 6 feet length of counter, about 10 feet beam, and 4 feet draught of water; and the foreyard for their largest racing suit is said to have been some 70 feet long.

With the alteration of rig came a change in the form of the hulls of the yachts. The enormous foresail right up forward in the lateener had necessitated very full bows. These became finer in the cutters, giving an easier entrance; while the lengthened counters gave a vastly improved delivery from the water aft, resulting in a boat admirably adapted to their own particular waters, namely, a shallow-bodied vessel of light displacement, which, with a beam great in proportion to its length and a deep keel, was rendered capable of standing up to its enormous spread of canvas.

In the 'seventies and 'eighties it was no uncommon thing to find a dozen yachts, on board of which their owners could live, and in fact did live in comfort, entered for a race.[1]   Now,

---

[1] The *Firefly*, a well-known 10 tonner built for Messrs. J. and H. Morgan in 1874, was typical of that class in the 'seventies. With a low freeboard, hardly any sheer, long and flat in the floor, the body of the boat not drawing more than 2 feet, her hold of the water being obtained by a deep keel, almost if not quite straight, which made the total draught of water about 4 feet 6 inches. Length over all 32 feet, some 10 feet of which was counter partly submerged, and beam 10 feet. The length of the bowsprit out-board being about the same as the length from stem to stern-post, namely, 22 feet, gives an idea of the enormous jib carried; but unfortunately the dimensions of the yacht's other spars are not obtainable.

The following particulars of the cutter *Arrow*, built for Mr. B. V. Winch by Kemp Bros. in 1877, may be taken as fairly typical. Length over all, 38 feet 6 inches; length on deck, stem to stern-post, 29 feet 6 inches; length on water line, 34 feet; beam, 10 feet; draught of water, 6 feet; bowsprit out-board, 26 feet

unfortunately, the evolution of yacht - building has brought
about a type useless except as racing machines, and the larger
class of racing boat has disappeared.

In 1874 a race from Yarmouth to Reedham and back
brought out the following starters :—

Red Rover	.	.	15 tons	.	S. Nightingale.
Firefly	.	.	10 ,,	.	J. B. and H. Morgan.
Lethe	.	.	10 ,,	.	G. Gaudy.
Alarm	.	.	10 ,,	.	B. V. Winch.
Kismet	.	.	11 ,,	.	F. Taylor.
Glance	.	.	11 ,,	.	P. E. Hansell.
Helen	.	.	24 ,,	.	R. W. Burleigh.
Gem	.	.	6 ,,	.	J. and F. Mack.
Vinaex	.	.	9 ,,	.	Sir S. B. Crossley.
Belvidere	.	.	9 ,,	.	J. Barnby and H. Teasdel.
Gleam	.	.	6 ,,	.	C. A. Preston.
Vivid	.	.	6 ,,	.	G. F. Crane.
Spray	.	.	7 ,,	.	F. G. Foster.
Little Mary	.	.	8 ,,	.	B. P. Phillips.

And so the records go on ; but after 1880 there was a falling-
off in the number of the larger yachts racing, until now, as
has been the case for some years past, except in handicap
races, which have brought out large entries, the racing on the
inland waters of the district is confined to boats of the 30
feet rating class and under.   But so far as racing of one
sort or another is concerned, there were never more races
sailed in one year than have been contested during the last
few seasons.

In the autumn of 1902 the clubs of the district considered
the reason for the few boats on the waters built for class
racing.   This has resulted in the Royal Norfolk and Suffolk
Yacht Club and the Yare and Waverley Sailing Clubs deciding
to revert to the length and sail area measurement in force in

2 inches ; boom, 31 feet 6 inches ; area of mainsail, 822 square feet ; area of jib, 520
square feet ; total amount of ballast, 7 tons.

The *Trixie*, built by W. Brighton in 1883, was a most successful boat in the
smaller class, and made a fine record under the ownership of Mr. E. Tilyard.   Her
length over all was 27 feet 6 inches ; length on deck, stem to stern-post, 20 feet
6 inches ; length on water line, 24 feet ; beam, 6 feet 6 inches ; draught, 3 feet 9
inches ; bowsprit out-board, 22 feet ; boom, 25 feet ; ballast, 4 tons.

The *Wanderer*, built for Mr. J. Lee Barber by W. Brighton in 1886, was a very
fast boat, and gained many prizes.   Her draught of water was less than the *Arrow*,
and her displacement was somewhat lighter, her beam being under 9 feet.

the earlier days of the last decade, a rule which has been adhered to by the Upper Thames Sailing Club with marked success, and which may be hoped to produce equally good results on these waters.

In 1876 the Yare Sailing Club was formed for the encouragement of racing among the smaller class of decked and open boats, and it has flourished ever since. Holding regattas at Cantley and Oulton, and also on the Bure, it has admirably answered the purpose for which it was formed, and has done much to encourage sport.

The Great Yarmouth Yacht Club was formed in 1883, with a view to encouraging racing on Breydon Water.

The youngest club is the Waveney Sailing Club, having its headquarters at Oulton Broad. It was formed in 1895, and fully justifies its claim to be one of the most sporting clubs of its kind. With an annual subscription of only five shillings and a membership for 1901 of 340, it has held eight regattas with 32 races, the entries for which were 181, besides managing several races which were not down on the formal programme.

One matter of note on which the sailing men on these waters may well pride themselves, is the absence of " protests." Though perhaps partly due to the fact that nowhere are committees more ready to take cognisance of any foul sailing should it come under their notice, even without formal protest, this happy condition of things is chiefly owing to the thoroughly sportsman-like feeling which prevails among all those taking part in the races.

At a conference held at Norwich in October 1894, presided over by the Commodore of the Norfolk and Suffolk Yacht Club (Colonel H. E. Preston), and attended by delegates from the Norfolk and Suffolk and Great Yarmouth Yacht Clubs and the Yare Sailing Club, it was resolved to form an association to be called the Norfolk and Suffolk Yacht and Sailing Clubs Association, the object of which should be the adjustment of programmes so as to avoid clashing of dates, the consideration of systems of measurement, the issuing of certificates of rating, and the arrangement of any other matters affecting racing so as to ensure uniformity of action among the clubs of the district. Mr. A. Townley Clarkson was elected Secretary and Official Measurer. It was decided that any resolutions passed should be in the form of recommendations to the clubs affected. The earliest recommendations passed comprised the substitution of the rules and regulations of the Yacht Racing Association (with slight alterations to meet the requirements of racing on inland waters) for those hitherto in force, and the constitution of the Association as a court of appeal to which questions and disputes might be referred. These suggestions were adopted by the clubs, and the Association has since proved its usefulness by promoting the objects for which it was formed.

In 1898 the senior club of the district, then under the commodoreship of Mr. T. M. Read, one of its early members, celebrated its accession to Royal rank by a dinner at the Royal Hotel, Lowestoft, when, on the motion of the Earl of Stradbroke, seconded by Mr. H. S. Foster, M.P., a vote of thanks was tendered to H.R.H. the Prince of Wales, the Patron of the Club, for his assistance in obtaining the Warrant. After his accession the King evinced his interest in local yachting by expressing his pleasure to continue to be Patron of the Club.

It may be mentioned that the Royal Norfolk and Suffolk is the only club in the district which caters for sea-going craft, for which it provides some fifteen races in the course of the season. The other clubs rightly consider that with their more limited means they fully take their share in the promotion of sport, while confining themselves to the inland waters.[1]

---

[1] The total number of regattas advertised by the Norfolk and Suffolk Yacht and Sailing Clubs Association to take place on the rivers and Broads during the season of 1901 was twenty-nine. In addition to these, the Royal Norfolk and Suffolk Yacht Club held races at sea on six days during the season.

CHAPTER XXI

FISHING [1]

BY A. J. RUDD

THE Broadland of Norfolk and Suffolk, being for the most part flat, is watered by rivers unusually slow of current. In these rivers coarse fish abound in far greater numbers than in any other part of England, and the bottom fishing of the district is among the best in the world. We are not favoured with periodic visits from the lordly salmon now, though in years gone by the Yare was a salmon river, as may be seen from old records, in certain manors of the district, which contain accounts of purchases of these fish from the owners of the mills which span the rivers. Nor are trout to be found in any quantity in any but the uppermost parts of the streams. In the upper Wensum they have been preserved for some years, and have thrived to a degree unsurpassed except in a very few of the more highly preserved waters of the southern counties. In the upper waters of the Bure they are also found, but are not nearly so large nor so plentiful as in the Wensum. These trout waters are strictly preserved by the lords of the manors and the riparian owners.

The waters available to the angler-tourist are the Yare below Norwich, the Bure below Wroxham, and that part of the Waveney which lies between Geldeston and Breydon Water. On the Yare bream and roach are caught in great quantities during the summer months, the best part of the river being from Surlingham to Cantley. On the Bure, bream, roach, and perch are taken, with sometimes a few rudd and an occasional tench. On the Waveney, bream are chiefly taken

---

[1] For a list of the Fishes of Broadland, see Appendix.

on the lower reaches, and roach on the upper, towards Beccles. In the latter part of the summer a number of pike are caught on all these waters on baits trailed behind rowing boats, or even yachts, when the wind is very light; but pike-fishing is more a winter sport in this district than in most parts of England.

The principal fish, then, for the visitor are bream and roach, and for these the same tackle serves for all the waters. Before describing the tackle necessary for the rivers and Broads, it may, however, be as well to look at the fishes for a short time, commencing with the pike, which is the great game of the district. Here it thrives to a remarkable degree, the slow-running rivers and the large lagoon-like Broads suiting its habits admirably, while the myriads of small roach found in every piece of water afford it an inexhaustible supply of food. This fact no doubt accounts for its being so difficult to catch at certain times of the year. The best pike-fishing is obtained in the winter months, from November to the beginning of March; and the best places are, of course, the preserved Broads. Here pike grow to an immense size, twenty pounds not being considered by local anglers a fish worth preserving. Some of this size are taken every season, and fish of twenty-five or even thirty pounds are not uncommon. The heaviest fish I have seen was a magnificent specimen of thirty-six pounds.

Next to the pike, the perch is the best fish we have in our waters, both for the sport he gives when hooked, and his excellent table qualities. He is the handsomest of fresh-water fishes, with his beautiful iridescent bronze coat barred with dark green, and his brilliantly vermilion-coloured fins. The perch is distributed over all the waters, but not in very large quantities.

Bream, as I have said, are found almost everywhere. These fish attain a very large size, five pounds being a not uncommon weight, and six pounds by no means a record. When of this size, the bream is a brown, flat-sided, lazy creature, and has been aptly compared with a pair of bellows.

The roach is a far more sporting fish, and is also to be found in all the waters. Of more athletic build than the

A BURE BANK

SALHOUSE GREAT BROAD

FIG 3. SHOWING THE DISTURBANCE OF THE CHALK AND OF THE
CRAG BEDS OVERLAYING IT, BY THE YARE GLACIER, IN A QUARRY
AT WHITLINGHAM, NEAR NORWICH

CHAPTER HOUSE, LANGLEY ABBEY

THE LATEENER "MARIA," BUILT IN 1834

REGATTA ON HICKLING

HALF-RATER ON WROXHAM

BREAM-FISHING NEAR ST. BENET'S ABBEY

HICKLING BROAD

DUCK-SHOOTING FROM REED SCREENS OVER DECOYS

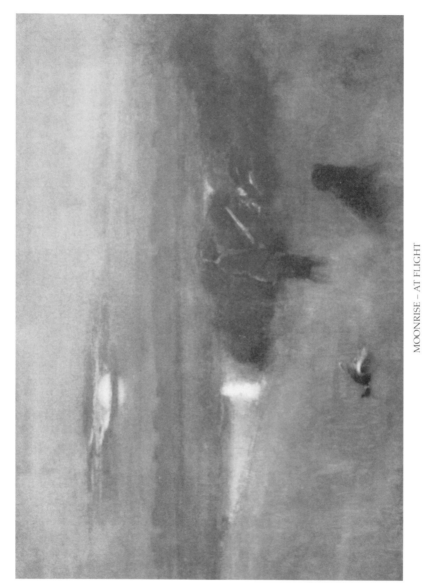

MOONRISE – AT FLIGHT

DUCK-SHOOTING OVER DECOYS IN A WAKE

ALL IN A DAY'S WORK

GREEN'S COTTAGE BELOW ACLE BRIDGE

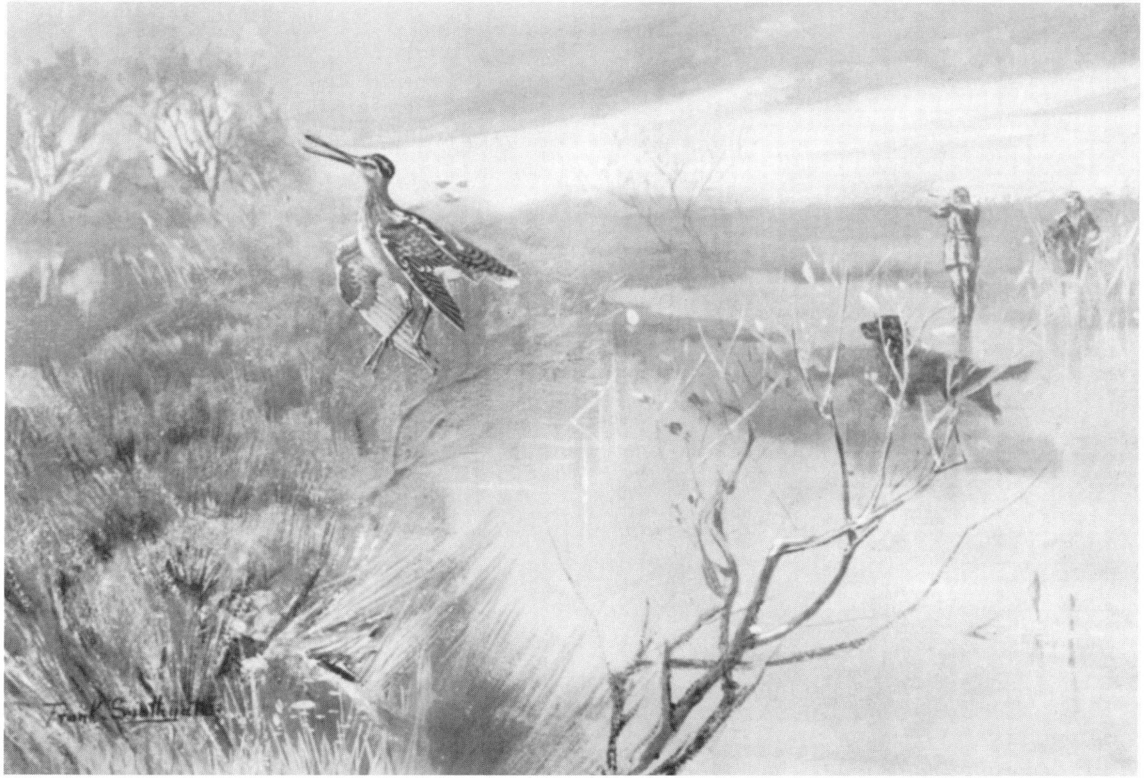

SNIPE-SHOOTING

LAYING AT WIDGEON

bream, he takes the angler's bait with less deliberation, and gives proportionately more play when hooked. The only fish the angler is likely to mistake for a roach is the rudd. The latter are found on many of the Broads and some of the Bure reaches in fair numbers, and are good fighting fish. The difference between the two fish is that the dorsal fin is directly over the ventral in the roach, whereas in the rudd it is placed some distance behind it. The rudd, too, is rather more golden in colour than its cousin, and the fins are of a brighter red.

Tench are more numerous in our rivers than most anglers imagine; on some of the Broads where the rod fails to catch half a dozen in a season, they are taken in great numbers in bow-nets. During very hot weather a few are taken in the Bure at Wroxham and Horning, and in the Yare at Buckenham.

Every angler who has fished in Norfolk waters knows the ruffe, or pope, as he is called in the north. A miniature perch, he bites as freely at anglers' baits, and sometimes one gets such a lot of them in the swim that they are an intolerable nuisance, for they are not big enough to give any sport, and are of no use for eating.

Bream and roach are the principal fish caught by the angler in Broadland, and, indeed, it is scarcely worth while trying to make a basket of any other kinds, except very occasionally when the perch are on the feed; and, again, one might have a day at the rudd on such waters as Barton.

The rod for fishing in these waters should be light enough to strike a roach, and strong enough to play a heavy bream. One about twelve feet long, or even a little longer, and with a perfect action, not too much down in the butt, is a useful weapon. It should be fitted with fixed rings, and a suitable reel carrying about thirty yards of fine silk line, which may be the ordinary plaited silk or the same water-proofed, as the angler prefers. The reel should be fitted with some kind of guard or guide for the line, preferably the " Rudd-Barton " combined brake and line guide, which serves the double purpose of keeping the line in its proper position and forming an efficient brake either for casting from the reel or putting pressure on the fish. Some floats, casts, hooks, and a landing-net complete the outfit.

Of baits for coarse fish the best are worms, either lob or brandling, for the bream, and paste or gentles for the roach. Ground-bait is sold ready made in a powder form by most tackle-makers, and has only to be mixed with water and kneaded into firm balls. Boiled wheat and boiled rice are also used, and are splendid ground-baits for roach and bream : the choicest corns of either can be used as hook-baits, occasionally being more seductive than any other lure.

In Broadland the river banks are for the most part reedy, and being, moreover, private property, there is very little bank-fishing. Boats are plentiful and cheap at most fishing stations, and from a boat one can fish far out into the stream with a short rod. This is most essential, as the rivers are deepest in the middle, and it is there that the fish congregate. There, too, the water, being constantly on the move either up or down, and often disturbed by passing yachts and barges, is more free from weeds than nearer the edges.

During the summer months the best places to fish are on the middle reaches of the rivers. On the Yare, during July and August, good sport is to be had from Brundall to Cantley, and occasionally down as far as Reedham. The Bure is always good from Horning to Acle Bridge, and the Waveney from Beccles to Oulton Dyke. Above and below these points the amount of sport to be obtained fluctuates with the condition of the waters. High up-stream, these rivers are, of course, subject to rise and fall according to the amount of rain, and they are clear or thick as the rain has been little or much ; low down they are affected by the rise and fall of the tide at Yarmouth Bar. During certain winds the water in the rivers is very much higher and salter than during the prevalence of winds from other directions ; sometimes the salt water comes up for miles, and consequently the fish are driven up the rivers. Bream do not object to a slight brackishness as do roach, and they are often found very low down the rivers, especially if the tides have been low and the salt water has been kept down by a heavy rainfall. At certain times of the year, generally in September and February, a large quantity of bream come up the Yare as far as Norwich, and are caught in great numbers within the city boundary. The reason for this periodical migration is difficult to understand, unless it be that the fish like the thick water; and, of course, the water is always more discoloured in these months that at any other time of the year, except during very hot weather, when a curious phenomenon occurs. The water, as the weather becomes warmer, is gradually discoloured to a degree eminently suited to the roach fisherman, by the constant disturbance of the thick beds of mud at the bottom of the rivers and Broads, occasioned by the expansion and liberation of the gases generated by the decomposition of the mud. When a heavy storm occurs, say at Norwich, the rain discolours the water as far down as Bramerton, below which all the colouring matter is deposited or filtered out by the weeds. From Bramerton downwards the effect of the storm is to clear the water by lowering its temperature and causing a cessation of the rising of the gases from the bottom. As I have endeavoured to explain, these different conditions of the water all affect sport more or less; but by the exercise of a little judgment the visiting angler can generally rely on getting all the fishing he cares for on the middle reaches of the rivers, where these conditions are not so pronounced as higher up or lower down stream.

In selecting the swim for a day's fishing, the angler should find a place sheltered from the wind, at the side of a long reach or in the hollow of a bend in the river—never off a point. It does not matter which side of the river he fishes, except in one part of the Bure—from Horning to St. Benet's Abbey—where the Ranworth side is the best, owing to the water being deeper there. When fishing on "a Broad," if shelter cannot be obtained from the banks or reed-beds, the boat should be moored across the wind so as to keep it off the water in front of the angler. Not that the wind is any disadvantage, except for the difficulty of seeing a bite when the float is constantly moving up and down on the ripples. On the other hand, a slight ruffling of the surface is of advantage if the water is clear, as it prevents the angler being easily seen by the fish. If no lee can be obtained, legering should be resorted to in place of float-fishing.

In fishing for roach with float tackle, the exact depth of the water should be ascertained by means of the plummet, and the float so set that the hook travels along just clear of the bottom. Any alteration in the depth of the water, owing to the rising or falling of the tide, should be met with a corresponding alteration in the depth of line from float to hook. In fishing for bream this is not so essential. So long as the bait is on the bottom, it matters not whether the hook drag by one inch or six. When changing hooks—a bream for a roach hook, or a roach for a bream hook—this alteration should be made to suit the habits of the fish. A roach must not be given an inch of slack or his bite will be missed, whereas a bream, if given line enough, will almost hook himself.

In fishing the Yare below Buckenham, the Bure below Thurne Mouth, and the Waveney below Burgh St. Peter, or anywhere where the current is strong, the leger is generally used in preference to float tackle, as the latter is so soon swept down by the rapid flow of the water that the swims are very short. Most anglers know what a "leger" is; but for the benefit of those who do not, I may say that it consists of a yard or more of gut, on which a pierced bullet is threaded: a hook is fixed above and below the bullet, which lies on the bottom. The line being kept taut from this to the rod-top, the bite of the fish is detected by the "feel" instead of by sight. The bait, being always quite on the bottom, seems to be generally more effective than with float tackle, larger fish being taken with the leger as a rule. In legering for bream, lob worms are the most frequently used bait; but large pieces of bread paste kill roach and bream equally well. It is a good plan in legering to squeeze a lump of ground-bait round the bullet and cast it out in that way; it is then kept closer to the hooks than when thrown out in handfuls into the stream. The leger should be cast down-stream, not across, as many anglers cast it, as this prevents the hooks being washed back on to the line by the current. The weight of the lead should be just sufficient to hold the bottom and no more, as it is a great advantage to be able to let it go farther down-stream, a yard or two at a time, by slightly lifting the point of the rod. By this means the hooks are kept over the ground-bait, which, as it breaks up, is carried down by the current.

On the main rivers, and on such deep Broads as Wroxham, it is not necessary to fish very far away from the boat; in fact, the working line below the rod-point need be no longer than the rod itself; but for fishing on shallow waters like Barton and Hickling Broads, and Heigham Sounds, a long line must be cast. At these places the water is so shallow and clear that it is impossible to get very close to the fish with the boat, and to be successful the angler must be able to throw out at least twenty yards of line. A fairly heavy float is necessary: some experienced fishermen use a pike pilot-float with a small barrel lead to keep it down and give sufficient weight to enable a long cast to be made. Bream and rudd are the fish principally caught on these waters. The latter are excellent fighting fish, yielding good sport to any one who can cast a fly or a bunch of gentles on a fly rod. There is no better sport than rudd-fishing on a warm summer evening. The Broad, with its fringe of green rushes and reeds, is at its best in the soft sunlight; not a sound breaks the stillness save the cries of the water-fowl or the splash of the fish; except where the fish are rolling about at the top of the water, the surface is as smooth as a mirror. The boat is rowed quietly to within casting distance of the reeds, and, tackle being in readiness, a cast is made towards the shore. The flies alight on the water without a splash, and are then slowly drawn towards the angler. And now a great wave breaks the placid surface, and the tightening line and bending rod tell of a good fish hooked. Have a care or he will take your delicate cast round the nearest bolder [1] and smash you to a certainty! Steadily putting pressure on the fast-tiring fish, you draw him away from his safety and your danger, till a dip of the net lands him, kicking and gasping, in the bottom of the boat. So you go on; cast after cast you rise the fish but do not always hook them, and now and again you lose cast, flies, and fish as some monster defeats you. Almost any thick-bodied flies will do for rudd; but there are occasions when half a dozen gentles on a fairly large hook, cast in the same way as the fly, is a better

[1] See Glossary.

lure. Great care has to be exercised in throwing the gentles, for they are tender creatures, and anything like a jerk will flick them off the hook.

Although the Broadland waters abound with pike, these fish are not often caught by the summer visitor. In July and August, it is true, some quantity of small fish is taken, but nothing in comparison with what are caught later in the season. Occasionally pike feed well in the early part of the autumn on the Yare, and great numbers are caught on spoon and other baits, either trailing behind rowing boats or cast out and drawn in again in the usual spinning style. As many as twenty fish in a day have fallen to a single rod, the fish ranging from three to ten pounds in weight, and, in the strong water of this river, giving excellent sport for their size. During the late autumn, as a rule, sport with the pike is not very good; but with the advent of cold wintry weather the fish become ravenous, and from the end of November to the middle of March good bags may be relied on, upon any of the Broads. Of waters that are open to the tourist, either by reason of their being tidal and free, or on payment of a small fee where private, Rockland on the Yare and Oulton on the Waveney may be mentioned as free, and Hickling Broad and Heigham Sounds on the Thurne, Barton Broad on the Ant, and Woodbastwick, Salhouse, and Wroxham Broads on the Bure can be fished on payment of from two to five shillings a boat a day. These waters may be considered to rank, for the amount of sport they give, in the order in which I have placed them. Rockland yields an immense number of fish in the early season, after which it is liggered to a regrettable extent. Oulton is very good, but it is much fished; the other Broads are all good at times. Some amount of local knowledge is necessary for success on such large waters as Hickling and Barton, but the angler who patiently and skilfully fishes along by the reedbeds fringing the margin of the Broads or the banks of weed in the middle will be sure of sport.

Of the various means of catching pike the most common in this district is with live bait on snap tackle; next to this, spinning with a dead fish on a flight of hooks. Spinning is no doubt the more artistic method, and is also the most killing.

With a spinner the angler covers more water than by any other means, and the bait is presented in a more attractive manner. Very often when the angler has tried all over a bay with live bait without so much as a touch from a fish, the first cast with a spinning bait hooks a good fish. As an instance of this, on one occasion in the winter of 1900, two anglers had been fishing all day from the same boat without a run, when late in the afternoon one of them thought he would try spinning. He did so, and at the very first cast took a fish of twenty-six pounds within a few yards of his companion's float, and followed up this with two other fish of twenty-two pounds and twenty pounds. This is not a solitary instance, but the results here were better than in any other case I know of.

In spinning on a Broad, it is a good plan, if the wind is light, to allow the boat to drift with the wind down one shore, and as the water is thus covered to cast out first up to the reeds and then out into the open till the end of the Broad is reached. The angler should then cross the Broad and pursue the same tactics along the other bank. Of course, if the wind is strong such manœuvring is impracticable; the plan then is to moor the boat opposite each bay in succession, moving on as each has been thoroughly fished. Sometimes it is as well to put out a live bait into the bay while a spinner is cast out on the other side of the boat; but this is not recommended if the fish are at all on the feed, and should only be adopted as a last resource when things have been very slow and one feels the necessity for retrieving the fortunes of the day somehow.

When fishing with live bait alone, the usual way is to fish in the different bays as recommended for spinning on a windy day; and it is generally found that the angler who can cast his bait nearest to the reeds without getting " hung up," has the best sport, because the fish, as a rule, lie quite in the reeds and only come out to feed. In some places, where the reed-beds are very wide, it is a good plan to drive the fish from their lairs before beginning to cast for them. This may be done by taking an oar or a mooring pole and splashing about with it in the water near the bank, or, if the reeds are not too dense, the boat may be forced round the back of the

21

bed.   In some places the reed-beds are quite hollow beneath, and if the fish are not driven out the sport is very limited.

On many of the Broads the water is very much deeper at one end or side than at the other: this is particularly notice-able on such Broads as lie alongside the rivers, and points to the fact that at one time they formed parts of the rivers. This should be noted by the pike-fisher, as, according to the season of the year, the pike lie in deep or shallow water, deep at the beginning and shallow at the end of the season, pre-paratory to their ascending the dykes and drains to spawn.

CHAPTER XXII

WILD-FOWLING

By Nicholas Everitt

IN the early days when Broadland was one vast fen-land, the district must have been a veritable paradise for the wild-fowler. Drainage, as we know it, was practically unknown, and the Yare, Waveney, and Bure valleys were vast swamps, overflown by the flood tides, and everywhere intersected by reed-beds and open sheets of water such as may be seen in the south of Sweden, the morasses of Spain, or on the lower banks of the Danube. When the river walls were built and the Dutch water-mills introduced, bird life on the marshlands became more confined, whilst year by year, as the drainage improved, it decreased perceptibly. Even the last twenty years have made a vast difference, and the bittern and ruff are almost objects of curiosity.

Twenty years ago good wild-fowling was to be had on the Broads. Flight shooting then was easy, now it is difficult to locate, and more or less jealously watched by keepers, who have the interests of their pheasants at heart and do not believe in free shooting. Thirty years ago, before boat-letting became an industry, the yachtsman could shoot over many hundreds of miles of waterway. Probably he would be as unmolested to-day as he was then, if it were not for the fact that liberties have been frequently taken by unthinking visitors, and damage inflicted alike to man, beast, and bird; cattle even having been found on the marshes adjoining the river seriously wounded and sometimes dead. It now seems to be the aim of all land proprietors in the district to put a stop to free shooting, and gunners on the Broads are restricted to the smallest possible limit, unless they hire private shootings.[1]

The best shooting in Broadland is found upon Ranworth Great Broad, Hoveton, Hickling, Barnby, Buckenham, Wood-bastwick Broads, and Horsey Mere; but most of these are let with the shooting on the adjoining estates, and the purse must be deep to enable any one to rent a tract if only for a single season.

It is the custom on private waters to erect small reed-screens or shelters, which are made by raising platforms, three or four feet square, about a foot and a half above high-water mark, and surrounding them by four reed-screens four and a half to five feet high. The shooter can conceal himself behind them with ease, and they are approached from the mainland by narrow banks or boarded plank-ways. In connection therewith, decoys, alive or artificial, are often used with considerable success.

On the day of the shoot, before the party starts (for some prearranged place), a stated time is set and given to each shooter, and whatever happens no gun is allowed to be fired before the time agreed upon. This is done in order to give each gun a chance of getting to his stand before the fowl are alarmed. One of the party (generally the host) proceeds to quant through and between the many reed-beds which intersect or border the shores of the Broad, and as soon as the time limit has expired any one may take advantage of the best shot offered.

At first gun-fire the fowl on the water rise and circle in all directions; possibly there may be only a very small quantity, possibly there may be from five hundred to a couple of thousand, and during the ensuing ten minutes every barrel

---

[1] A sub-section of a by-law made by virtue and in exercise of the Great Yarmouth Port and Haven Act, 1900, prohibits the use of any firearm or air-gun by any person "while using, or while in, upon, or about the rivers Yare, Bure, or Waveney, or the banks or shore thereof, or any land of the Port and Haven Commissions, provided always that this sub-section shall not affect the rights of the riparian owners of the land on either side of the river." In the preamble to the by-laws it is stated that this and other by-laws apply also to navigable tributaries except Oulton Dyke and Oulton Broad and their banks. Mr. Everitt expresses it as his opinion that this by-law is bad at law, and if contested would be upset.—ED.

may become uncomfortably warm. After this fusilade the birds leave the water for quieter and more secluded quarters; but within half an hour a great number will return, and if the shooter is still concealed and remains quite quiet, they will dip to the surface of the water and offer further opportunities. Large quantities of fowl, however, are not killed in this way, forty to fifty being a good bag, although on one occasion the writer was fortunate enough to be one of a party which gathered seventy-three duck and mallard and one coot before lunch in a shoot of this description.

On Hickling Broad (which consists of several hundred acres of open water, reed-beds, and swamps) there has been held from time immemorial an annual coot-shoot, which is a very interesting function to attend. Until recent years the fixture was open to anybody who chose to participate in it, but since the Hickling Broad case was fought in London the shooting has been let, and this local event, so far as the general sporting public is concerned, has become a thing of the past. The lessee of the sporting rights, however, continues to hold annual coot-shoots, which are carried out upon lines very similar to those of former years. The guns divide into two parties—one manning the boats, the other keeping to the shore. During the summer coots breed almost unmolested on all the private Broads, and in the winter congregate in vast numbers on the largest sheets of open water they can find, remaining there until driven away by the frost. The coot rarely takes to wing unless driven to do so by force of circumstances. The party on shore proceed to some bay previously agreed upon, which they surround, concealing themselves behind reed-stacks, gate-posts, screens, or the friendly shelter of the river-wall, whilst the boats spread out in line and row after the birds, which swim before them faster than a boat can be rowed or pushed. They are thus driven, like a flock of sheep, in the direction required. When the boats press the birds into the bay, they swim to the reeds, then endeavour to fly back to the open water by circling overhead. So soon as the birds are completely surrounded, all the guns show themselves, and a battue, which must be participated in to be fully realised, takes place. At these shoots some hundreds of coots are bagged, and the sport — though dangerous — is considered good.

Sixty years ago there were many men in Norfolk and Suffolk who obtained a livelihood in winter from punt-gunning, wild-fowling, and eel-spearing; but the two first named, as occupations, have practically become extinct.

The punt-gun is not allowed on Hickling Broad, Horsey Mere, or Heigham Sounds; these happy hunting-grounds are all claimed as private property. To use a punt-gun on Oulton or any other free Broad would be dangerous now, for so many gunners conceal themselves in the reed-beds that death or serious injury would sooner or later result. Indeed, the game would hardly be worth the candle, except possibly during the first fortnight in November, when migratory fowl are much in evidence.

On Breydon Water some twenty or thirty professional gunners were always to be found; but they have dwindled down to as many as can be counted on one hand, and now that yet another railway bridge is built over the easternmost end of the flats, the muds, saltings, and creeks are less likely to be patronised than heretofore. What few fowl settle there are pretty certain to select the Burgh end, bounded on the north by what are known as the Dickey Works, in preference to the neighbourhood of the Old Ship Run; but of course during a hard frost sport will always be obtained on Breydon, and good sport to boot.

Perhaps the most favourite branch of wild-fowling indulged in in Broadland is flight-shooting, which must again be sub-divided into two branches: (1) the evening flight, and (2) the morning flight.

Most shooters patronise the evening flight. Wild-fowl, as is commonly known, spend the day in the seclusion of some unfrequented or undisturbed haunt, and at sundown take wing to their feeding grounds. During the months of August and September, when the fields abound in corn, they flight, in the twilight, to the uplands, and excellent sport may be enjoyed by the fortunate individual who can obtain leave from some farming friend to shoot the fields so favoured. The best localities in Broadland are in the neighbourhood of

Ranworth, Hoveton, Horning, and Potter Heigham, and twenty to thirty duck and mallard is no record bag to obtain from an evening's fowling. One small field the writer knows of is surrounded by four Broads and forms an island in their midst. In August, when this field has been cultivated with barley, peas, or suchlike products, it is a veritable flight-shooter's paradise; but the owner knows its value, and the shooting rights are never likely to be let.

As the season advances and the corn is gathered from the fields, wild-fowl flight from the Broads to the rivers, spring-drains, and secluded ponds, where they know they will find the food they love. These points of advantage must be watched for and noted by the fowler, who if he is not fortunate enough to be able to hire or obtain the necessary permit to visit them, must do the next best thing he can by placing himself in the line of flight.

During August and September, the yachtsman who is moored for the night in the neighbourhood of Horning Ferry may be astonished at the number of boats going down-stream towards St. Benet's Abbey shortly after sundown. If he inquires, he will be told that the Horse Shoe Reach (about a quarter of a mile below the ferry) intersects one of the most favoured lines of flight for fowl coming and going between Ranworth Great Broad, Woodbastwick, and other wild-fowl sanctuaries. As the gloaming increases, the booming of guns, echoing and re-echoing over the marshes, tells of the sport that is being obtained.

Evening flight does not last more than half an hour; the shooting is difficult, and the birds still harder to obtain after they have been shot.

Morning flighting is more for those who have private waters frequented by wild-fowl, than for the promiscuous gunner who picks up just what he can obtain.

On the assumption that the wild-fowl which frequent a certain water leave it at dusk for the purpose of obtaining food, or to visit other haunts to which their inclination or instinct lead them, the morning flighter betakes himself, an hour before daybreak, to the water so frequented, and conceals himself in reed-screens or huts made for the purpose. When the wild-fowl return to enjoy the seclusion of sanctuary during daylight, they receive a welcome quite unexpected and much too warm for their approbation. But this sport does not afford the same charm as evening flighting, because of the irregularity of the return of the birds and the fact that the shots they offer are by no means so sporting as those obtained in the gloom of eventide.

During the spring of the year the common green plover, peewit, or lapwing scatter themselves over the commons, brecks, and moorlands of Norfolk for nesting purposes. As the autumn advances they collect in enormous flocks, frequenting both upland and marsh, and just before a frost excellent plover-shooting may be obtained at evening flight. About an hour before sundown, thousands upon thousands of these birds, which have been feeding during the daytime upon the upland fields, may be seen flying overhead in vast flocks; but when the sun has set they break up into twos and threes and flutter about in all directions over the marsh levels, like leaves driven before a storm, uttering their weird cries and offering to the shooter as many shots as he cares to take, alike sporting and most difficult. Again, large flocks of golden plover rest a while in Norfolk on their way southwards. Early in the evening these birds may easily be distinguished from others, as they, like geese, invariably fly in the V formation; but later in the evening they fly so near to the ground they are very difficult to see.

Snipe and redshank breed fairly freely on the wet swamps around Hickling, Ranworth, Horsey, Hoveton, Oulton, Surlingham, and other Broads. Before the Wild Birds' Protection Act of 1880 came into force, the landowners of these districts were wont to organise parties for the purpose of shooting young redshank in June, before they made off to the saltings; but now they can only be shot at places like Wells, Blakeney, and Breydon Water, during Maybird time, which is early in the month of August.

Snipe, however, remain on the marshes where they are bred until shot, or until compelled to migrate southwards owing to frost, and some fair bags may be obtained in the neighbourhood of Hickling, Horsey, Barton, Upton, Ranworth, and Beccles; but year by year, as the marshlands are more drained, the weight of these bags diminish.

Another branch of wild-fowling which is more or less peculiar to Broadland consists of shooting on decoy-flighting ponds; this, however, is a more or less artificial sport. The owner of a suitable shoot where wild-fowl can be encouraged, digs, or otherwise forms, a series of small ponds at different parts of a beat. In these ponds he raises a considerable number of half-bred fowl, or hatches off a quantity of wild ducks' eggs. The young birds are hand-fed, and allowed to do as they please until November. During the early part of that month the migratory fowl arrive, and are soon attracted by the hand-reared birds, with a result that the migrants take up their quarters with them, or at all events become nightly visitors to their ponds. As soon as the foreign birds have established a strong "lead in," the flight-shooter commences operations, visiting one pond once a week all through the season. Screens or blinds are made and placed round each pond, so the whole of the water can be commanded by the guns. The incoming fowl are generally allowed to alight upon the water before they are disturbed; then a noise is made to alarm them, the birds fly up and are shot at, but not as often killed, as, owing to the uncertain light, they are very difficult indeed to hit. A rather extraordinary thing about this decoy-pond flight-shooting is that the hand-reared birds never seem to get shot. They mostly spend the day-time on the pond, leaving it early in the evening for the adjoining marsh ditches, where they pass the night. If this sport is properly worked, magnificent flighting can be obtained at very small expense.

The stalking horse is almost forgotten in Norfolk, and is used only in the remote fenlands. The marshman or fowler who uses it rarely divulges the secrets of his art, unless it is made to his pecuniary advantage so to do, or there is some other powerful reason urged upon him which he is unable to resist.

Shooting over wakes or broken places in the surface of an ice-bound Broad, with the assistance of decoys (as practised on the coast of Scotland, Ireland, and elsewhere), is comparatively unknown. Shore-shooting is also not worthy of the name in Broadland. It is true that a few schoolboy gunners still visit the banks of Breydon Water, but their bags are light in comparison with the number of miles they tramp. The shooting in the roadsteads off the coast—which can hardly be included under the heading of "Wild-fowling in Broadland"—is dependent upon the weather rather than the number of birds in the neighbourhood.

Speaking generally, it is not correct to say that wild-fowling in Broadland is practically a thing of the past; it is better to describe it as being more or less confined to private individuals. The rights of the public are being gradually curtailed to the narrowest possible limits, and so jealous is the game preserver, the Broad-owner, and the riparian proprietor, that the time when such rights will no longer exist seems to be drawing very near.

CHAPTER XXIII

FOLK-LORE—SOME LOCAL LEGENDS AND SAYINGS

By James Hooper and William A. Dutt

THOUGH East Anglia cannot boast any such wealth of legendary lore as the west of England, a very fair crop of legends, traditions, and characteristic local sayings may be gathered from various sources.

One of the most impressive phantoms, and one of the best known in Norfolk, is Old Shuck,[1] a demon dog, as big as a fair-sized calf, that pads along noiselessly under the shadow of hedgerows, tracking the steps of lonely wayfarers, and terrifying them with the wicked glare of his yellow eyes. To meet him means death within the year to the unhappy beholder. As Shuck sometimes leaves his head at home, though his eyes are always seen as big as saucers, he is, as Mr. Rye says, " an animal more avoided than respected." One of his chief haunts is Neatishead Lane, near Barton Broad; but he also favours Coltishall Bridge, over which he always ambles without his head; and a very special promenade of his is from Beeston, near Sheringham, to Overstrand, *after which his course is uncertain !* Which recalls the old adjuration in the legend of St. Margaret—

> " Still be thou, still,
> Poorest of all, stern one,
> Nor shalt thou, Old Shock,
> Moot with me no more.
> But fly, sorrowful thing,
> Out of mine eyesight,
> And dive thither where thou man
> May damage no more."

---

[1] From the Anglo-Saxon *Scucca*, the early native word for Satan.

A near relation of Shuck must have been the Black Dog of Bungay, which, on Sunday, 4th August 1577, during a fearful storm, appeared in the church of St. Mary at Bungay, "running all along down the body of the church with great swiftnesse and incredible haste among the people, in a visible fourm and shape, passed between two persons, as they were kneeling uppon their knees, and occupied in prayer as it seemed, wrung the necks of them bothe at one instant clene backward, insomuch that even at a moment where they kneeled they strangely dyed." It was said of a hardened sinner that he could no more blush than the Black Dog of Bungay.

Mr. Rider Haggard, writing of his parish of Ditchingham, opposite Bungay, on the Norfolk side of the Waveney, alludes to a vague belief, still current, that the devil, in the shape of the Black Dog of Bungay, may even now be met with thereabouts.

Yarmouth was formerly subject to visits from Old Scarp, who used to frequent Southtown Road, and who, besides the terrors of his saucer eyes, jingled a heavy chain, and if a straw were placed in his path, would rattle his chain menacingly and give forth terrifying howls. Something of the same kind was "Owd Rugusan," a little-known fiend having a limited habitat in a few inland Norfolk villages.

Of phantom coaches several are known to haunt the borders of Broadland, perhaps the most notable being a hearse-like vehicle, drawn by four black headless horses, that once a year carries the hapless Anne Boleyn, with her gory head in her lap, through the main avenue of Blickling Park, while her father, for his share in her decapitation, is compelled to ride in and out over forty county bridges on the Bure and Yare every night. It is also common tradition that the leaden coffin of Sir Thomas and his daughter cannot lie still in their mausoleum, but shift and toss in an agony of unrest at every new burial.

Another family in Norfolk with a similar legend were the Blennerhassetts, who had a house at Norwich, but acquired property at Barsham, near Beccles, by intermarriage, and it is an old tradition at Barsham that "Old Blunderhazard" drives out every Christmas Eve, just before midnight, to visit Hassett's Tower, at Norwich, and to return to Barsham before he may snuff the morning air. Here, too, the horses were headless, but always with fire flashing from their nostrils.

A curious devil story is told about Tunstall, a village over-looking the marshes which occupy a triangle between Reedham, Acle, and Yarmouth. The tower and nave of the church were long ago ruined by fire, and there is a persistent legend that the parson and churchwardens quarrelled for the possession of the bells, which were uninjured. Taking advantage of the preoccupation of the wranglers, the arch-fiend strode off with the booty, but being pursued and overtaken by the indignant parson,—who began to exorcise him in Latin,—took earth to his place below, carrying the bells with him. The site of his descent *in inferos* is now a pool of boggy (not bogey!) water called Hell Hole, while an adjoining clump of alder trees is known as Hell Carr. Bubbles of marsh gas constantly breaking on the surface of the pool amply confirm the tradition that it forms an entrance to the bottomless pit, and that the bells are still falling, and falling for ever!

At Langley, not far off, but on the other side of the Yare, might be seen the Devil's Round House, which, whenever it was built by day, the devil overturned at night. There was also at Langley an abbey of some note, and Langley Cross stood, perhaps for centuries, in the village, exposed to rough usage in later times, so that the dwellers in the Hall time and again thought of removing it into the precincts of the park for protection. There was, however, an ancient prophecy, of quite unknown origin, which declared that upon the same day that the cross was removed there would be a conflagration at the Hall. At length a Lady Beauchamp, setting oracles at defiance, had the cross carefully moved into the park and re-erected. While the villagers witnessed the daring deed, and just as it was completed, a shout of " Fire " was raised, and the whole gathering rushed off to save the Hall, from a turret of which ugly wreaths of smoke were curling. Prompt measures quenched the enemy, and it was satisfactorily proved that no son of the prophet had tried to verify his predictions.

Near Oulton Broad, in the village where George Borrow

lived so long, is Oulton High House, built in the middle of the sixteenth century, long known as the haunted house, whence at midnight a Wild Huntsman and his hounds, and a "White Lady" carrying a poisoned cup, were believed to issue and to go their fiendish rounds. The legend is that in the time of George II. the lady was the wife of a roystering squire, who, returning unexpectedly from a hunting expedition, surprised her toying with an officer, his guest, whose pity for her had developed into guilty love. High words arose, and when the husband struck his wife's paramour, the latter drove his sword through the unhappy squire's heart. The murderer and the lady fled with her jewels and the gold of the murdered man. Years after, her daughter, who had been forgotten in the haste of departure, having grown up into a beautiful woman, was affianced to a young farmer of the neighbourhood. Being on the eve of marriage, she was sitting with him in the old Hall one bleak November night, when a hearse-like carriage, its curtains closely drawn, and with servants dressed in sable liveries, stopped at the door. The masked men rushed in, and carried off the young girl to her unnatural mother, having stabbed the lover, who had endeavoured in vain to rescue her. In a convent cemetery at Norwich was a grave, said to cover the hapless daughter, who had been poisoned by her mother.

The pleasant heath between Lowestoft and Corton is said to be haunted by a mysterious "Lady in White," supposed to be an unhappy nun who came to a tragical end. Her flittings have probably been discontinued with the advance of building operations.

A romantic story attaches to the tower of the church at Caister-next-Yarmouth, a place so celebrated for the heroism of its lifeboatmen. On the top of the tower is, or was, a central ridge which appears above the parapet, marking, according to old tradition, the place of a tomb wherein a maiden was buried. Her lover returning from a long voyage, perished by shipwreck off the coast, and the maiden, dying of grief, directed that her corpse should be entombed on the tower top under a pyramid raised high enough to serve as a sea mark.

Sayings and rhymes about villages are, as a rule, distinctly uncomplimentary, but Potter Heigham, in the middle of the Broad district, fares well in the local saying—

> " Blessed are they that live near Potter Heigham,
> Double blessed are they that live in it." [1]

Of a more common type are the following :—

> " Blickling Flats, Aylsham Fliers,
> Marsham Peewits, and Hevingham Liars ; "

or this, concerning a group of villages between Norwich and Yarmouth—

> " Halvergate Hares and Reedham Rats,
> Southwood Swine and Cantley Cats,
> Acle Asses and Moulton Mules,
> Beighton Bears and Freethorpe Fools."

Other local characterisations are Proud Stalham, Sleepy Ingham, Silly Sutton, Clever Catfield, and Raw Hempstead. Stalham proud because of its central position, " Metropolis of Broadland," as it has been called ; Ingham so sleepy from its isolation, that an old Ingham man once put on his Sunday clothes and went off to church on Monday morning. The Sutton people are credited with the habit of thrusting their hands out of the window to feel if it is daylight; while, on the other hand, if any strange story is agog, the right thing is to proceed to Catfield " to know the truth of it." Hempstead, on the bleak eastern shore, is certainly often raw enough.

A long chapter might be written concerning local compliments of this kind, but many of them can only be appreciated by natives of the district, while others are unrepeatable. We may just say, however, that in some parts of Broadland a stranger may be advised to go to

> " Beccles for a Puritan,
> Bungay for the poor,
> Halesworth for a drunkard,
> And Hilbro' "—

but we have given enough currency to these local libels.

Considering how abundant is the bird life of Broadland, it is not surprising that strange sayings and beliefs

[1] Also see p. 171.

concerning the significance of encountering certain birds should survive. Even the nest-raiding lads of the marshland hamlets believe it to be unlucky to kill wrens and robins or to interfere with their nests. " If you rob a robin of its eggs, you're sure to break your arm," is, says Dr. Emerson, a local rockstaff; consequently the redbreast's eggs need no Protection Act in Broadland. Wrens and robins, however, are unlucky only when interfered with ; the swift or develin— that strange, wild-screaming bird which grows so restless when night approaches—is unlucky to encounter at any time. So too is the cuckoo. " If one flies ahead of you down a road, there will be a death in your family." This bird's first call in spring, however, has a different significance, for, according to Mr. Thistleton Dyer, " in Norfolk it is a widespread super- stition that whatever you are doing when you first hear the cuckoo, that you will do most frequently all the year." That the presence of seagulls in the fields and the crying of plovers overhead at night are signs of stormy weather, not even the least credulous native will deny.

That ill-luck attaches to seeing a black cat many Broad- landers assert; but for all that, all the black kittens born in the district are not drowned. Nor, in spite of the aversion with which they are viewed by many people, are all species of spiders looked upon with equal abhorrence. Indeed, one kind, a small red spider, is called the " money-spinner," and wherever it appears, whether on a fruit bush or the brim of a gardener's hat, it is allowed to remain unmolested. Even the common house spider has had its uses. Formerly, when a child was seized with the whooping - cough, one of these spiders was sewn up in a small muslin bag and hung over the fireplace. As soon as it died the child began to recover. The belief that a diet largely consisting of live snails or slug oil is beneficial to persons with consumptive tendencies, is not wholly abandoned by the unlettered inhabitants of the district. A predominance of yellow frogs on the marshes denotes fine weather, but when brown frogs are more numerous there will soon be rain. Concerning that curious little amphibian, the natterjack or running toad, there is the curious saying that " you can quiet a restive horse with the bone of a running toad." A sure sign of a wet harvest is, the marshmen assured Dr. Emerson, "a field mouse up in the stuff." The belief that an adder's skin will draw thorns is often expressed, but is not confined to Broadland. The old folk-lines—

> " Bat, bat, come under my hat,
> And I'll give you a slice of bacon,"

are often chanted by village children when the " flittermice " are flickering through the dusk ; so, too, is the verse—

> " Bishy, Bishy Barnabee,
> Tell me when my wedding be ;
> If it be to-morrow day,
> Open your wings and fly away."

The reluctance with which the lady - bird beetle (*Coccinella bipunctata*) leaves any object on which it has alighted, had no doubt something to do with the composing of these lines, which usually are repeated when a lady-bird has settled on a child's hand. The lines—

> " Lady-bird, lady-bird, fly away home ;
> Your house is on fire, and your children will burn,"

probably had a like origin.

That entertaining little book, *English Folk-lore*, contains several local superstitions. One of these is that "if a drill go from one end of a field to the other without depositing any seed—an accident which may result from the tubes and coulters clogging with earth — some person connected with the farm will die before the year is out, or before the crop then sown is reaped." Another is that when a boy and girl are to be baptized the boy must come first, otherwise the girl will have a beard. Here, too, we find another cure for whooping - cough. The child is placed with its head bent downwards in a hole dug in a meadow. The sod cut in digging the hole is replaced, and the child kept covered until it coughs. If this cure is practised in the evening, with no one present save the child and its father and mother, its efficacy is almost assured. The belief that dock leaves are good for nettle stings surprises no one who has experienced the soothing effect the cool leaves have on the smarting skin ;

22

but to test the curative qualities of a decoction of boiled garlic-mustard (*Alliaria officinalis*) calls for some courage. It is not so simple a cure as that for scalds and burns, which can be tested at any time and anywhere. All the sufferer has to do is to repeat the lines—

> " An angel came from the North,
>   And he brought cold and frost ;
> An angel came from the South,
>   And he brought heat and fire ;
> The angel come from the North
>   Put out the fire
> In the name of the Father, and of the Son, and of the Holy Ghost."

Those

> " Elves of hills, brooks, standing lakes, and groves
> . . . demi-puppets, that
> By moonshine do the green-sour ringlets make,
> Whereof the ewe not bites,"

are not so much in evidence on the misty marshes as might be expected ; but their charmed circles, the fairy rings, are often pointed out by children in the pastures. Children, too, will tell you that if you pluck the bright blue flowers of the bird's - eye (Germander Speedwell), the birds will come and pick out your eyes. Even their parents believe it to be unlucky to bring into a house a bunch of dodder grass (*Briza media*) ; and their names for some of the familiar riverside, field, and marsh plants suggest that the two or three herbalists who still visit the Broadland hamlets do not lack custom. That a "green Christmas makes a fat churchyard" and "a wet harvest makes a moist loaf," no rustic will deny ; but whether the milkmaids still put two-leaved clovers in their shoes so that they may meet the men who are to be their husbands, is a secret of their own. Certainly they have not abandoned the custom of throwing apple - peels over their shoulders to see what initial letters are formed when the peels fall to the floor, nor do they neglect to assure each other that toothache is a love-pain. That "to help one to salt is to help one to sorrow" is as firmly credited as the belief that good luck attaches to the picking up of pins or cast horse-shoes. To open an umbrella indoors is a sure sign that

some one will soon leave the house for ever.   And speaking
of umbrellas reminds one that the lines—

> " Rain after church,
> Rain all the week,
> Little or much,"

are often repeated during a wet journey home from church.
That for the moon to be " new " on Saturday and " full " on
Sunday is an unfortunate combination of circumstances seems
evident from the saying—

> "Saturday new and Sunday full
> Never was good and never wool (will be)."

Concerning the moon there is an old nonsense rhyme of
doubtful local origin.   It affirms that—

> "The man in the moon
> Came down too soon
>   And asked the way to Norwich ;
> He went to the south,
> And burnt his mouth
>   Through eating cold pea-porridge."

To the survival and practice of witchcraft some reference is
made in another chapter.   Even of late years " wise women "
and " cunning men " have existed in Broadland, and all the
fortune-telling practised in the district is not confined to the
swarthy Romany *chies* who visit the cottagers under pretence
of offering cottons, haircombs, and pegs for sale.   The " wise
women " and " cunning men " of to-day, however, are chiefly
charlatans who live in the back streets of Norwich or in some
Yarmouth " row," where, so long as they are undisturbed by
the police, they impose on the credulity of fishermen and
rustics whom designing or equally credulous persons have
advised to visit them.   For the benefit of such visitors, playing
cards—the " devil's books "—are produced and consulted, and
the good fortune prognosticated is usually commensurate with
the amount of silver deposited in the charlatan's hand.   Police
proceedings against these avaricious impostors have led to
some strange tales being told before the local magistrates ; but
when one considers that in the West End of London there are
charlatans who victimise the educated, and how largely the

oily phrenologist is patronised on the beaches of popular watering-places, it is not surprising that the unsophisticated dweller amid lonesome marshes and in isolated villages is easily gulled. Nor, in view of the support accorded him in various parts of the country, is it to be wondered at that the water-diviner with his wand of witch-hazel is occasionally invited to pay a visit to Broadland: even since the commencement of the present century he has been seen going through his antics in the neighbourhood of Oulton Broad.

When a Broadsman looks out of doors at night and remarks that it is "as black as the hakes," he refers to the blackness of the pot-hook which hangs above the fire in some old-fashioned fireplaces. When he says his affairs are "all up at Harwich," he means they are all in a muddle. If he is not feeling very well, he tells you he "ain't up to a sight"; if you invite him on board your yacht, and he feels out of place there, he says he feels "like num-chance on hoss-back." If he prefers his meat underdone, he says he likes it "in the main," and when he gets enough of it he "lives like old Pamp." Should his daughter, who has been "out to service" in town, attempt to imitate the speech of her mistress, he will remonstrate with her thus: "Lor, mor, don't yow frame like that; yow maake me fare right buzzle-hidded." Should a "gathering" be made at the village inn, with a view to relieving an indigent parishioner, he may not have sixpence in his pocket, but he promises to "be his share" later on. He goes to an entertainment in the village schoolroom and apologises for the clatter his heavy boots make on the boarded floor: "Them highlows o' mine du maake a duller." He agrees that his neighbour's daughter is a "strappen fine mawther," but as for his neighbour's son, he is a "gret hudderen good-for-nowt," and "as lazy as Hall's dorg." Should he be questioned as to the outcome of a meeting with a miserly stranger, he tells you that all he got out of him was "an Aylsham treat"; meaning that he was left to pay for his own beer. Strangers who evince what he considers to be an excessive curiosity are "pakenose lollopers," and "he don't howd wi' sich."[1]

---

[1] Most of these colloquialisms, and many others, are to be found in *Broad Norfolk*, a booklet published by the Norfolk News Company in 1893.

APPENDICES

I

RIVER COURSES AND DISTANCES,
AREA OF BROADS, ETC.

IT is usually stated in guide-books that Broadland consists of the district which would be contained within a triangle having the coast between Pakefield and Happisburgh for its base and Norwich for its apex; but though such a triangle would embrace all the principal Broads, it would not include all the Broadland waterways navigable to cruising yachts. To include all these, a line would have to be drawn from Waxham to North Walsham, continued to Aylsham, Norwich, and Bungay, and brought back to the coast at Pakefield.

The principal rivers in this district are the Yare, Bure, and Waveney, which enter the sea by way of Breydon Water, an estuary extending from Yarmouth to the junction of the Yare and Waveney at Burgh Castle. The Bure has two important tributaries: the Thurne, which, flowing from the north-east, joins it near the village of Thurne, about $3\frac{1}{4}$ miles above Acle Bridge; and the Ant, which, after pursuing a south-easterly course from North Walsham, enters it about 3 miles above the mouth of the Thurne. The Waveney has no naturally navigable tributary, but a wide channel called Oulton Dyke connects Oulton Broad with the river. The Broad is also connected by Lake Lothing with Lowestoft Harbour. A canal, called the New Cut, extending from Herringfleet to Reedham, enables yachts and wherries to sail to and from Norwich and Lowestoft, Beccles and Bungay, without going round by Breydon. The Chet, a small, shallow tributary which enters the Yare at Hardley Cross, is navigable to wherries up to Loddon. Waxham Dyke, a narrow canal entering Horsey Mere on the north side, is navigable to wherries up to Waxham.

There are about fifty Broads, but some of them are inconsiderable pools. Four — Hickling, Rollesby, Ormesby, and Barton — each have an area of over 200 acres; eight others — Filby, Fritton Lake, Heigham Sounds, Horsey Mere, Hoveton Great Broad, Oulton, Ranworth, Wroxham, and Sutton—are each over 100 acres in extent; and there are five others, each over 50 acres. Fritton Lake, Flixton Decoy, Filby, Ormesby, Rollesby, Barnby, Benacre, and Calthorpe Broads, cannot be reached by water. Excluding Breydon, which is not a Broad but an estuary nearly 1300 acres in extent, the total acreage of the principal Broads is rather over 3000 acres.

THE YARE AND ITS BROADS

The Yare rises near Letton Park, and flows by way of Hardingham, Barford, Bawburgh, Colney, Earlham, Cringleford, Keswick, Lakenham, and Bracondale to Trowse, adjoining Norwich, where it is joined by the Wensum. It is navigable to all river craft from Norwich downwards to Yarmouth, a distance of about 25 miles. Below Norwich it receives the waters of a small, narrow tributary, the Chet, which is navigable to wherries and small yachts up to Loddon. At Reedham it is connected with the Waveney by the New Cut, a straight canal 2½ miles long. Its only important Broads are Surlingham (where there is now but little open water) and Rockland (66 acres). The entrances to Surlingham are on the south side of the river, about 5 miles below Norwich. Rockland is connected with the river by several dykes, one of which is navigable to wherries which take in and discharge cargoes at Rockland Staithe. The Broad, however, is very shallow and weed-grown, and yachting parties who visit it should do so in small sailing or rowing boats. The fishing on Rockland is free; on Surlingham it is preserved. Anglers can hire boats at the Yare Hotel, Brundall; Coldham Hall, Surlingham; Buckenham Ferry, Cantley Red House, and Reedham Ferry. The following distances are reckoned from Thorpe Second Bridge: Whitlingham Ferry, ½ mile; Postwick Grove, 1¾ miles; Bramerton Wood's End, 2¾ miles; Surlingham Ferry, 4¼ miles; Brundall, 5¾ miles; Surlingham Broad, 6 miles; Coldham Hall, 6¼ miles; Rockland Broad, 7¾ miles; Buckenham Ferry, 8½ miles; Langley Dyke (leading to Langley Abbey ruins), 10¼ miles; Cantley Red House, 11¼ miles; Hardley Cross and the mouth of the Chet, 13¾ miles; Reedham Ferry, 14¼ miles; Reedham village, 15¼ miles; New Cut, 15½ miles; Berney Arms, 19¼ miles; Yarmouth Haven Bridge, 23½ miles. From Hardley Cross to Loddon, up the Chet, is 4 miles.

THE WAVENEY, FRITTON LAKE, AND OULTON BROAD

The Waveney has its source in a spring at Lopham Gate, in the parish of South Lopham, about 6 miles west-by-north of Diss, and flows by way of Diss, Scole, Hoxne, Syleham, Harleston, Homersfield, and Earsham to Bungay, from which town downwards it is navigable. From Bungay it flows through Ellingham, Shipmeadow, and Geldeston to Beccles, receiving on its way the waters of a very small, unnavigable tributary called Broome Beck, which has its source in a small lake in Ditchingham Park. Below Beccles its course is through marshlands to Aldeby Railway Bridge and Burgh St. Peter. A short distance below the church of the last-named hamlet is Oulton Dyke, a wide channel branching off to the right, leading to Oulton Broad, which is connected with Lowestoft Harbour by a tidal channel known as Lake Lothing. Marshlands border the river from Oulton Dyke to Somerleyton, and on the left to Herringfleet, where, near St. Olave's Bridge, is the entrance to the New Cut, connecting the Waveney with the Yare at Reedham. St. Olave's Bridge is the last which spans the river, which, after flowing through a further stretch of marshes, enters Breydon at Burgh Castle, close beside the mouth of the Yare. Oulton Broad (132 acres) is the only Broad accessible from the river. Barnby Broad (11 acres) and Flixton Decoy (22 acres) are private waters without navigable channels leading to them. Nor is there a navigable channel leading to Fritton Lake (163 acres), which should be visited from St. Olave's, from which it is distant about 1½ miles. A charge of threepence is made for admission to the Old Hall Gardens which border the lake. Rowing boats can then be hired for a cruise on the lake. There is free fishing on Oulton Broad all through the year, and on Fritton Lake from April to September. The following distances are reckoned from Yarmouth Haven Bridge: Burgh Castle, 4¾ miles; St. Olave's Bridge, 9½ miles; entrance to the New Cut, 9¾ miles; Somerleyton Bridge, 12¼ miles; Oulton Dyke, 15 miles; (Oulton Broad, 16½ miles; Mutford Bridge Lock, 17¼ miles; Lowestoft Harbour, 19 miles;) Worlingham Staithe, 20 miles; Aldeby Staithe, 20½ miles; Sayer's Grove, 22 miles; Beccles Bridge, 23 miles; Dawson's Dip House,

24¾ miles; Geldeston Lock, 27 miles; Ellingham Lock, 30 miles; Wainford Lock, 32 miles; Bungay Staithe, 33 miles.

THE BURE AND ITS BROADS

The Bure has its source in the neighbourhood of Melton Constable, and pursues a south-easterly course to the sea, which it enters by way of Breydon, into which it flows not far above Yarmouth Haven Bridge. It is navigable from Aylsham downwards, but between that town and Wroxham Bridge there are three locks and several bridges. The scenery of its upper waters is very charming, and Coltishall, about 6½ miles above Wroxham Bridge, is the most picturesque waterside village in Broadland. Below Coltishall there are no locks, and the river is fairly wide. The distance by river from Yarmouth to Aylsham is about 44 miles. The Bure is considered to be the chief Broadland waterway, because there are a greater number of Broads connected with it than with any other river in the district. The principal Bure Broads, taken in the order in which they are met with during a voyage from Yarmouth to Aylsham, are: South Walsham, 57 acres; Ranworth, about 150 acres; Hoveton Little Broad, 80 acres; Woodbastwick, 64 acres; Salhouse, 33 acres; Salhouse Little Broad; Hoveton Great Broad, 120 acres; Wroxham, 102 acres; Wroxham Bridge Broad, 14 acres; and Belaugh, 12 acres. In addition to these there are several smaller Broads or pools connected with the river or the larger Broads. Most of these are private waters, as are Woodbastwick, Hoveton Great and Little Broads, Belaugh, and part of Ranworth. At Wroxham, Salhouse, Salhouse Little, Ranworth, and South Walsham Broads the fishing and shooting are preserved; but tickets (2s. 6d. per boat a day) for fishing on Wroxham can be obtained from Mr. A. J. Rudd, 54 London Street, Norwich, or the money can be paid to the water-keeper. The entrances to all the Bure Broads which can be visited without special permission are between St. Benet's Abbey and Wroxham Bridge.

Two important tributaries, the Thurne and the Ant, enter the Bure within three miles of each other between Acle and Horning. A three-mile dyke called the Muck Fleet connects Rollesby, Filby, and Ormesby Broads with the Bure, but is quite unnavigable.

The following distances are reckoned from Yarmouth: Three Mile House, 2¾ miles; Runham Swim or Ferry, 5¼ miles; Six Mile House, 6¼ miles; Stokesby Ferry, 9¼ miles; Acle Bridge, 12 miles; Thurne Mouth, 15¼ miles; St. Benet's Abbey, and, opposite, Fleet Dyke, leading to South Walsham Broad, 17¾ miles; Ant Mouth, 18 miles; Ranworth Dyke, leading to Ranworth Broad, 19¼ miles; Horning Church, 20 miles; Horning Ferry, 21 miles; Horning village, 21½ miles; entrance to Salhouse Broad, 24½ miles; entrance to Salhouse Little Broad, 25 miles; entrance to Wroxham Broad, 25½ miles; Wroxham Bridge, 27 miles; Belaugh, 31 miles; Coltishall, 33½ miles; Little Hautbois Bridge, 36 miles; Lammas Lock, 38 miles; Oxnead, 40½ miles; Burgh-next-Aylsham, 42 miles; Aylsham, 44½ miles.

THE ANT AND ITS BROADS

This river, which is navigable as far up its twenty-miles' course as North Walsham, has its source in Antingham Ponds, about 2½ miles from that town. Until the railway came, the wherries carried on a considerable trade with North Walsham, and it is on their account that the river is kept fairly clear of water-weeds and other obstacles to navigation; but in spite of this it is difficult for a yacht drawing much water to make very rapid progress above Wayford Bridge. This bridge has lately been rebuilt and the waterway beneath it widened from 12 feet 6 inches to 14 feet; but the headway to the underside of the steel joists of the new bridge is exactly the same as that of the old one. Ludham Bridge, the first encountered by the cruiser up the river, while admitting of the passage of wherries, has such a small arch that some of the larger of the Broadland pleasure-craft cannot pass through it. Unlike Wayford Bridge, Ludham Bridge is, I believe, the property of the Drainage Commissioners of the district, who, it is to be hoped, will soon recognise the necessity for its being heightened and widened. The only important Broad connected with the Ant is Barton (270 acres), a fine sheet of water, but very shallow except in the post-marked channels. The entrance to this Broad is about 4½ miles from the river mouth and 3½ miles above Ludham Bridge. Sutton Broad, which adjoins a dyke leading from the Ant to Stalham, has little open water and is chiefly a wilderness of sedge, reeds, and rushes. Yachts seldom attempt to go beyond Barton Broad, except to reach Stalham by way of Stalham Dyke. The following distances are reckoned from Ant Mouth, where the river enters the Bure: Ludham Bridge, about 1 mile; Irstead Church, 4 miles; entrance to Barton Broad, 4½ miles; entrance to Stalham Dyke, 6 miles; Stalham Staithe, 7½ miles. A little way up Stalham Dyke the channel divides, the left arm being that which leads to North Walsham. Up this channel, which is the continuation of the Ant, it is about

2 miles to Wayford Bridge, 5 miles to Briggate Lock, 8 miles to North Walsham Flour Mill, and 12½ miles to the source of the river.

THE THURNE AND ITS BROADS

The Thurne or Hundred Stream may be said to have its source in the vast network of dykes in the marshlands between Eccles and Winterton; but the greater part of the water it discharges into the Bure is drawn from Hickling Broad, Heigham Sounds, and Horsey Mere. It is navigable as far up its course as Martham or Somerton Broad (73 acres). Horsey Mere (126 acres) is connected with Heigham Sounds (127 acres) by a 1½ miles' navigable channel called the Old Meadow Dyke, and Hickling Broad (464 acres) is connected with the Sounds by Whiteslea (15 acres), the waters of these four Broads, the last-mentioned three of which may almost be said to form one sheet of water, finding their way into the Thurne by way of a navigable channel called Kendal (locally "Candle") Dyke. On the north side of Horsey Mere is the entrance to Waxham Dyke or the New Cut, which, now that it is cleared out, is navigable for wherries and small yachts as far as Waxham, a village on the seacoast. Potter Heigham, where there are two good inns, is a convenient centre from which the chief Broads in this district can be visited. The fishing and shooting on Hickling, Horsey, and Heigham Sounds are preserved; but permission to fish the Sounds—an excellent place for rudd— can be obtained from George Applegate, Potter Heigham. The following distances are reckoned from Thurne Mouth, where the river enters the Bure: Entrance to Womack Dyke, 1½ miles; Potter Heigham Bridge, 3¾ miles; entrance to Kendal Dyke, 4¼ miles; Martham Broad, 6½ miles; Hickling Staithe, 7 miles; Horsey Mere, 7½ miles.

ORMESBY, FILBY, AND ROLLESBY BROADS

These three Broads, which may be said to form one sheet of water nearly 600 acres in area, lie almost due north of Runham Ferry on the Bure, from which they are distant about three miles. They are connected with the Bure by a three-mile dyke called the Muck Fleet, but this dyke is not navigable. Great Ormesby station, on the Midland and Great Northern Joint Line, is about two miles from the Eel's Foot and Sportsman's Arms, two inns where boats for rowing or fishing on the Broads can be hired. Waggonettes from these inns meet the trains during the summer months (fare, sixpence). Brakes run daily during the holiday season between the Marine Drive at Yarmouth and Ormesby Broad. Rollesby is the largest of the three Broads, its area being about 240 acres; Ormesby is 207 acres in area, and Filby 136 acres. Narrow channels spanned by low-arched bridges connect the three Broads; but these channels are very shallow, and it is often difficult to get even a small rowing boat under the bridges. Except in these channels the water is deep. The fishing is free almost everywhere on the Broads to visitors who hire boats at the inns.

A LIST OF THE BIRDS, MAMMALS, REPTILES, AMPHIBIANS, AND FISHES OF BROADLAND

Birds

IN compiling the following list of the Birds of Broadland, I have, in dealing with the rarer species, relied to a very large extent on such authoritative and invaluable works as the *Birds of Norfolk*, by Henry Stevenson, F.L.S. (third volume completed by Thomas Southwell, F.Z.S.); *A Catalogue of the Birds of Suffolk*, by the Rev. Churchill Babington; Mr. A. Patterson's recently published *Catalogue of the Birds of Great Yarmouth*, and the *Transactions of the Norfolk and Norwich Naturalists' Society*.

A line drawn from Palling to North Walsham, continued to Aylsham, Norwich, and Bungay, and returning to the coast at Pakefield, combined with the seaboard between Palling and Pakefield, would contain the district dealt with.

ABBREVIATIONS.—C., common; F. C., fairly common; N. U., not uncommon; N. C., not common; F., frequent; R. R., rather rare; R., rare; O., occasional; A., accidental. *B. of N.* stands for *Birds of Norfolk; B. of S., Birds of Suffolk; B. of G. Y., Birds of Great Yarmouth; N. N. N. S. Trans., Norfolk and Norwich Naturalists' Society's Transactions;* J. H. G., J. H. Gurney, F.L.S., F.Z.S.; H. M. L., *Rough Notes on Natural History*, by H. M. L.; Paget, *Sketch of the Natural History of Yarmouth*, by C. J. and James Paget.

Raven.—R. Formerly bred in Norfolk. Lubbock states that in his time it was not uncommon in winter.

Rook.—C.

Jackdaw.—C.

Hooded Crow.—C. Great numbers arrive in the district in autumn. Local, "Grey" or "Kentish Crow," also "Danishman."

Carrion Crow.—N. U.

Nutcracker.—R. One shot at Rollesby, 30th October 1844 (*N. N. N. S. Trans.*), another at Somerleyton about 1876 (*B. of S.*).

Magpie.—R. R.

Jay.—N. U. Local, "Cadder."

Starling.—C.

Rose-coloured Starling (*Pastor roseus*).— R. Has occurred several times.

Golden Oriole.—R. Several occurrences are recorded. Said to have nested at Fritton.

Red-winged Starling (*Agelæus phœniceus*).—A. Occurred once, in 1843, at Barton (Yarrell).

Greenfinch.—C. Local, "Green Linnet," "Green-ulf."

Hawfinch.—N. U. Local, "Cobble Bird."

Chaffinch.—C. Local, "Spink."

Brambling.—F. C. Local, "Bramble Finch."

Goldfinch.—N. U. Local, "King Harry," "Draw-water."

Siskin.—C.

Twite.—F. C. Local, "French Linnet."

Linnet.—C.

Mealy Redpoll.—F. C.

Holboell's Redpoll (*Cannabina Holboelli*). Two specimens now in the British Museum were obtained near Norwich (*Birds of Great Britain*, by R. Bowdler Sharpe).

Lesser Redpoll.—C.

House Sparrow.—C.

Tree Sparrow.—F. C. Local, "French Sparrow."

Serin Finch (*Serinus serinus*).—R. Four recorded for Yarmouth (*N. N. N. S. Trans.*).

Crossbill (*Loxia curvirostra*).—F. Irregular winter visitor.

Two-barred Crossbill (*L. bifasciata*).—A. A male shot at Burgh Castle, 1st September 1889 (*N. N. N. S. Trans.*).

Greater Bullfinch (*Pyrrhula pyrrhula*).— A. A male shot on Caister Denes, 22nd January 1893 (*N. N. N. S. Trans.*).

Bullfinch.—N. U. Local, "Blood-ulf."

Pine Finch (*Pinicola enucleator*).—A. Doubtfully recorded for Bungay and Yarmouth.

Reed Bunting.—C. Local, "Reed Sparrow," "Blackcap."

Yellow Bunting.—C. Local, "Yellow Hammer," "Gooler."

Cirl Bunting.—R. Two examples obtained by Mr. E. T. Booth at Hickling in 1875. Two males netted on the Breydon marshes, 29th January 1888 (*N. N. N. S. Trans.*).

Ortolan Bunting.—A. Recorded for Yarmouth twice (*B. of N.*) and Lowestoft once (*B. of S.*).

Corn Bunting.—F. C.

Snow Bunting.—C. Large flocks arrive in winter. Local, "Snow Bird."

Lapland Bunting.—N. U. "Migrants arrive every winter in greater or lesser numbers" (*B. of G. Y.*).

Shore Lark.—Irregular winter visitor.

Skylark.—C.

(Short-toed Lark.—A. "Said to have been shot on Breydon wall in November 1889. Possibly an escape" (*B. of N.*).

Wood Lark.—N. U.

Pied Wagtail.— F. C. Local, "Black Wagtail," "Penny Wagtail."

White Wagtail.—R.

Grey Wagtail.—N. C.

Yellow Wagtail.—C. Local, "Cow Bird."

Blue-headed Wagtail.—R. Said to have nested at Herringfleet.

Tree Pipit.—N. U.

Meadow Pipit.—C. Local, "Titlark."

Richard's Pipit.—R. Several times recorded.

Tawny Pipit.— R. Recorded for Yarmouth and Lowestoft (*N. N. N. S. Trans.*).

Rock Pipit.—F. Frequently seen near Yarmouth in autumn (*B. of G. Y.*).

Scandinavian Rock Pipit (*Anthus rupestris*).—R. One shot at Horsey, March 1871 (*N. N. N. S. Trans.*).

Tree Creeper.—F. C.

Wall Creeper.—A. Recorded for Stratton Strawless in a letter from Robert Marsham to Gilbert White in 1792.

Nuthatch.—R. R. Not uncommon at Fritton (*B. of G. Y.*).

Great Tit.—C. Local, "Ox Eye," "Bee Bird."

Blue Tit.—C. Local, "Pickcheese."

Coal Tit.—F. C.

European Coal Tit (*Parus ater*).—R. Two or three specimens have occurred (J. H. G.).

Marsh Tit.—F. C.

Crested Tit.—A. Mr. A. Patterson believes he saw one on the Caister road, near Yarmouth. Ditchingham (*B. of S.*).

Long-tailed Tit.—F. C. Local, "Bottle Tit."

Bearded Tit.—N. U. Now confined to this district, so far as Great Britain is concerned. Local, "Reed Pheasant."

Gold Crest.—C. Local, "Herring Spink."

Fire Crest. — R. Has been recorded a few times, and is commoner probably than is generally believed.

Lesser Grey Shrike.—R. Twice recorded for Yarmouth.

Pallas's Grey Shrike (*Lanius sibiricus*).—Mr. J. H. Gurney states that this bird is a not infrequent visitor.

Great Grey Shrike.—O.

Red-backed Shrike.—N. U.   Local, " Butcher Bird."

Woodchat Shrike.—R.

Waxwing.—An irregular winter visitor.

Whitethroat.—C.   Local, " Hay Jack."

Lesser Whitethroat.—N. C.

Blackcap.—N. U.

Garden Warbler.—F. C.   " Commoner in Broadland than is
generally supposed " (Dr. Emerson).

Dartford Warbler. — R.   Has occurred twice at Yarmouth
(*B. of N.*), once at Lowestoft (Sir Edward Newton), and
once at Beccles (*B. of S.*).

Wood Warbler.—R. R.

Willow Warbler.—C.

Chiffchaff.—N. U.

Sedge Warbler.—C.   Local, " Reed Bird."

Great Reed Warbler (*Acrocephalus turdoides*).—Dr. Emerson
states that he once saw a pair in the district.

Reed Warbler.—F. C.   Local, " Reed Bird," " Reed Chucker."

Marsh Warbler (*Acrocephalus palustris*).—R.   Three examples
obtained near Yarmouth in June 1869 (J. H. G.).

Grasshopper Warbler.—N. U.   Local, " Razor Grinder."

Savi's Warbler.—First British bird recorded for Broadland,
where it formerly bred.   Only six examples have been
recorded (J. H. G.).

White's Thrush. — A.   A male obtained at Hickling, 10th
October 1871—the only Norfolk specimen.

Blackbird.—C.

Ring Ouzel.—R. R.   " Occurs in the spring ; less rarely in
autumn " (*B. of G. Y.*).   Said to have nested at Lowestoft
about 1804 (*B. of S.*).

Redwing.—C.   Local, " French Mavish."

Song Thrush.—C.   Local, " Mavish."

Mistle Thrush.—F. C.   Local, " Fulfer."

Fieldfare.—C.   Local, " Dow Fulfer," " French Fulfer."

Nightingale.—F. C.

Redbreast.—C.   Local, " Cock Robin."

Arctic Blue-throat.—R.   Several times recorded.

Redstart.—F. C.   Local, " Firetail."

Black Redstart.—R. R.

Wheatear.—F. C.   Local, " Coney Sucker," " Shepherd Bird."

Desert Wheatear (*Saxicola deserti*).—A.   Dr. Emerson records
having seen a pair on the coast.

Whinchat.—F. C.   Local, " Furzechuck."

Stonechat.—F. C.   Local, " Furzechuck."

Hedge Sparrow.—C. Local, "Hatcher."

Alpine Accentor (*Accentor collaris*).—A. One at Oulton in 1824 (Rev. R. Lubbock).

Dipper.—R. One shot on Breydon wall in 1849 (*N. N. N. S. Trans.*), another near Lowestoft in November 1868 (*B. of S.*), and a third at Reedham (J. H. G.).

Black-breasted Dipper.—R. A few have been obtained on the Bure (J. H. G.).

Wren.—C. Local, "Jenny Wren," "Tomtit."

Spotted Flycatcher.—F. C.

Pied Flycatcher.—N. C.

Red-breasted Flycatcher (*Siphia parva*).—A. Immature female shot at Rollesby, 12th December 1896 (*N. N. N. S. Trans.*).

House Martin.—C.

Sand Martin.—F. C. Large flocks seen in the reed-beds in spring and autumn.

Swallow.—C.

Green Woodpecker.—N. U.

Great Spotted Woodpecker.—R. R.

Lesser Spotted Woodpecker.—R. R. Nests at Fritton (*B. of S.*).

Wryneck.—N. U. Local, "Cuckoo's Mate."

Great Spotted Cuckoo (*Coccystes glandarius*).—A. A young male shot on Caister Denes, 18th October 1896.

Cuckoo.—F. C.

Swift.—F. C. Local, "Develin."

Alpine Swift (*Micropus melba*).—A. One shot near Breydon on 4th September 1872 (*B. of N.*). Lubbock records one for Buckenham.

Nightjar.—F. C. Local, "Nighthawk."

Bee Eater.—R. One—possibly two—recorded for Yarmouth (*B. of N.*); Beccles, 1825 (Yarrell).

Hoopoe.—O. Has occurred several times.

Kingfisher.—N. C.

Roller.—R. Has occurred several times. First British example obtained at Crostwick in May 1664; recorded by Sir Thomas Browne.

Eagle Owl.—A. One killed at Somerton; but it may have escaped (J. H. G.).

Scops Owl.—A. One killed at Martham on 1st June 1891. One taken at Lowestoft Lighthouse, date unknown (*B. of G. Y.*).

Snowy Owl.—A. Herringfleet, November 1878 (H. M. L.).

Little Owl.—A. "Two specimens are well authenticated" (Paget). Female shot at Yarmouth (*B. of G. Y.*). One at Oulton, 1877 (*B. of S.*).

Long-eared Owl.—N. U.

Short-eared Owl.—N. U. Local, "Woodcock Owl," "Marsh Owl."

Tawny Owl.—R.

Tengmalm's Owl.—A.

Barn Owl.—N. U.

Osprey.—R. Has occurred on Breydon, at Lowestoft, and elsewhere. Two at Filby, 20th September 1898 (*B. of G. Y.*).

Hen Harrier.—R. R. Formerly bred in the district.

Montagu's Harrier.—R. R. Bred in the district until recently. Local, "Blue Jacket."

Marsh Harrier.—R. R. Last nest found in 1878.

Goshawk.—R. A few records of its occurrence. Adult female at Somerleyton in March 1893 (*B. of G. Y.*).

Sparrow Hawk.—N. U.

Common Buzzard.—R. R. Formerly bred in the district.

Rough-legged Buzzard.—R. R.

Golden Eagle.—A. One shot at Fritton about 1850 (H. M. L.).

White-tailed Eagle.—A. Several occurrences are recorded for various parts of the district. One taken alive in a decoy at Fritton in December 1878 (*B. of G. Y.*).

Kite.—A. Formerly a resident. One killed at Martham in December 1865 (*B. of N.*).

Honey Buzzard.—R. Several times recorded.

Peregrine Falcon.—R. R. Local, "Game Hawk."

Hobby.—R. R. Said to have nested at Worlingham about 1866 or 1867 (*B. of S.*).

Merlin.—N. U. "A fairly regular and not uncommon autumnal immigrant" (*B. of G. Y.*). Local, "Blue Hawk."

Greenland Falcon (*Hierofalco candicans*).—A. One shot on Bungay Common (*B. of S.*).

Kestrel.—C. Local, "Wind-hover."

Kestrel, Red-footed (*Cerchneis vespertina*).—R. One on Breydon and three at Horning in 1832 (Paget). Immature male at Somerleyton, July 1862 (*B. of N.*).

Cormorant.—R. R. It formerly occurred in considerable numbers on Breydon. Sir Thomas Browne states that it nested at Reedham. Nested at Herringfleet and Fritton until about 1825.

Shag.—R.

Gannet.—R. Although often seen off the coast, this bird must be considered rare in Broadland. One was shot on Breydon in 1865.

Grey Lag Goose.—O. Several times recorded. Eighty-four counted on the Haddiscoe marshes in the winter of 1890.

White-fronted Goose.—R. R.

Bean Goose.—"Uncertain winter visitant; in some years none, in others several" (*B. of G. Y.*).

Bernacle Goose.—Very irregular winter visitor.

Pink-footed Goose.—Irregular winter visitor.

Brent Goose.—An irregular winter visitor. Local, "Scotch Goose."

Red-breasted Goose.—A. Paget records one for Yarmouth.

(Egyptian Goose.—This goose has occurred several times, but, as Mr. Bowdler Sharpe says, "it is a species which has long been kept in confinement, and the many examples which have been shot in a wild state are doubtless individuals which have escaped.")

(Canada Goose.—What is said about the Egyptian Goose applies equally to this species.)

Whooper Swan.—F.

Bewick's Swan.—F.

Mute Swan.—A considerable number of semi-domesticated Mute Swans exist on the Broads and rivers.

(Polish Swan (*Cygnus immutabilis*).—R. Examples of this supposed species have been met with.)

Sheld Duck.—F. Local, "Bergander."

Ruddy Sheld Duck.—A. An adult female believed to have been shot near Yarmouth in August 1898 (*N. N. N. S. Trans.*).

Shoveller.—N. U. Increasing as a breeding species. Local, "Shovel Bill."

Mallard.—C.

Gadwall.—N. U.

Wigeon.—C. Local, "Smee."

Teal.—F, C, Breeds in the district. Local, "Half Fowl."

Pintail.—R. R. Occasionally taken in the decoys.

Garganey.—N. U. Nests in the district. Local, "Gargle Teal."

Red-crested Pochard.—A. The first British example was shot on Breydon in 1818. A few occurrences since.

Pochard.—F. C. Local, "Poker," "Dun Bird."

White-eyed Pochard.—R. Several occurrences are recorded.

Tufted Duck.—F. C. Local, "Golden Eye."

Scaup Duck.—F. C. Local, "Hard Fowl."

(Harlequin Duck.—A. There is an example of this species in the Castle Museum at Norwich; but although it is said to have been killed at Yarmouth, Mr. Gurney regards it as a very doubtful Norfolk bird.)

Golden Eye.—F. C. Local, "Rattle Wing."

Buffle-headed Duck.—A. An adult male shot at Yarmouth in 1830. The first for Britain.

Long-tailed Duck.—R. R. Has occurred several times. One taken in a Fritton decoy during the winter of 1899–1900.

Steller's Duck.—A. A male shot on Caister Denes, February 1830 (*N. N. N. S. Trans.*).

Eider Duck.—R. R. Several times recorded.

(King Eider.—Paget's record of a female having been shot on Breydon in July 1813 is doubted by local ornithologists, though the species has occurred elsewhere in the county.)

Common Scoter.—Often abundant off the coast, and has been shot on Breydon. One at Beccles in 1848 (*B. of S.*). Local, " Black Duck," " Mussel Duck."

Velvet Scoter.—Only occurs off the coast.

Smew.—R. R. Occurs chiefly on Breydon, but has been shot at Barton, Herringfleet, Somerleyton, Oulton, and Beccles (*B. of S.*). Local, " Weasel Duck."

(Hooded Merganser.—Paget's record of an example for Yarmouth in 1829 is doubtful.)

Goosander.—N. U. Local, " Sawbill."

Red-breasted Merganser.—R. R. Local, " Sawyer."

Purple Heron.—A. Has occurred a few times.

Common Heron.—C. A large colony exists at Reedham. Local, " Harnser."

Night Heron.—A. Has occurred several times.

Squacco Heron.—A. Recorded for Yarmouth, twice for Ormesby, and once for Oulton.

Little Bittern.—R. Formerly bred in the district.

Common Bittern.—N. U. Formerly bred in the district. Local, " Buttle," " Bottle Bump."

White Stork.—A. Several occurrences are recorded.

Black Stork.—A. " One shot on Breydon on 27th June 1877 " (*B. of G. Y.*).

Glossy Ibis.—A. A few occurrences are recorded, the latest at Ludham in November 1902.

Spoonbill.—N. U. Chiefly seen on Breydon. Local, " Banjo Bill." Formerly bred in the district.

Crane.—A. Believed to have bred in the district until the end of the sixteenth century.

Great Bustard.—A. Two recorded for Horsey : one in 1820, the other in 1867 (*B. of N.*). Formerly bred in Norfolk.

Little Bustard.—A. Recorded for Yarmouth, Bradwell, Waxham (*B. of G. Y.*), Bungay (*B. of S.*), and Caister (11th December 1902).

Stone Curlew.—R. Though rare in Broadland, this species still breeds on some of the Norfolk warrens. Local, "Norfolk Plover."

Pratincole.—A. Three are recorded : a pair for Breydon wall in May 1827 (Paget), and one mentioned by Stevenson (*B. of N.*).

Grey Plover.—F. C.

Golden Plover.—F. C.

Caspian Plover or Asiatic Dotterel.—A. An adult male shot at Yarmouth on 22nd May 1890. Two were seen (*B. of G. Y.*).

Dotterel.—R. R.

Ringed Plover.—C. Local, " Ring Dotterel," " Stone Runner."

Kentish Plover.—N. U. " May be frequent, but is not easily recognisable at a distance from the immature of the Ringed Plover " (*B. of G. Y.*).

Lapwing.—C. Local, " Peeweep," " Hornpie."

Turnstone.—F. C.

Oyster Catcher.—N. U. Local, " Seapie."

Avocet.—R. Used to nest in the district. Local, " Shoehorn."

Black-winged Stilt.—A. A pair shot at Hickling in 1822, another by the Bure in 1824 (Paget). Two or three recorded since (*B. of G. Y.*). Bungay Common, 1875 (*B. of S.*).

Grey Phalarope.—O.

Red-necked Phalarope.—O.

Woodcock.—F. C.

Great Snipe.—R. R.

Common Snipe.—C. Local, " Summer Lamb."

Jack Snipe.—C. Local, " Half Snipe."

Broad-billed Sandpiper (*Limicola platyrhyncha*).—A. Four are recorded for Breydon, including the first British specimen, shot on 25th May 1836.

Dunlin.—C. Local, " Ox Bird."

Knot.—C. Plentiful in autumn on Breydon.

Purple Sandpiper.—F.

Curlew Sandpiper.—F. C. An autumn migrant. Local, " Pigmy Curlew."

Sharp-tailed Pectoral Sandpiper (*Heteropygia acuminata*).—A. One killed near Yarmouth in September 1848; another on Breydon in August 1892. The only examples recorded for Britain.

Pectoral Sandpiper (*H. maculata*).—A. First British example shot on Breydon in October 1830. Several have occurred since.

Little Stint.—F. C. in autumn.

Temminck's Stint.—R. R.

Sanderling.—F. C. Local, "Sand Lark."

Buff-breasted Sandpiper (*Tringites sub-ruficollis*).—A. Three are recorded for Yarmouth (*B. of G. Y.*).

Ruff.—R. Formerly bred in the district. Last nest found in 1888.

Wood Tattler.—R. R. One or two occur yearly, in autumn (*B. of G. Y.*).

Green-shank.—F. C. in autumn.

Common Sandpiper.—F. C. First Norfolk nest found at Hickling on 25th May 1897. Local, "Summer Snipe."

Green Sandpiper.—N. U.

Spotted Redshank.—N. U.

Common Redshank.—F. C. Local, "Red Leg."

Red-breasted Snipe Tattler (*Macrorhamphus griseus*). — A. Three are recorded, the latest for Horsey in October 1845.

Bar-tailed Godwit.—F. C. "Abundant occasionally in May" (*B. of G. Y.*).

Black-tailed Godwit.—R. R. Formerly nested at Horsey.

Curlew.—C. Does not breed in the district.

Whimbrel.—F. C. Local, "Half Curlew," "May Bird."

Black Tern.—N. U. Formerly bred in the district. Local, "Blue Darr."

Whiskered Tern.—A. One shot at Hickling on 17th June 1847.

White-winged Black Tern.—A. First British example shot at Horsey in May 1853. Several have been shot since on Hickling and Breydon.

Gull-billed Tern.—A. Nine are recorded for Breydon (*B. of G. Y.*).

Caspian Tern.—R. Nine are recorded for Yarmouth (*B. of N.*). One on Breydon, 21st July 1901 (A. Patterson).

Common Tern.—C. Local, "Darr."

Arctic Tern.—F. C.

Roseate Tern.—A. Several occurrences are recorded.

Sandwich Tern.—N. U.

Little Tern.—N. U.

Sabine's Gull.—A. Two were shot on Breydon in October 1888; a young male at Hickling, October 1889 (*N. N. N. S. Trans.*).

Little Gull.—R. R. Several have occurred in the district, one at Beccles in 1870 (*B. of S.*).

Mediterranean Black-headed Gull.—A. An adult male shot on Breydon in December 1886. The second recorded for Britain.

Black-headed Gull.—C. Breeds at Hoveton and Somerton. Local, "Scoulton Cob," "Puit," and "Kitty."

Great Black-backed Gull.—C. Large numbers to be seen on Breydon. Local, "Saddle Back."

Lesser Black-backed Gull.—C.

Herring Gull.—C. "Common in late autumn" (*B. of G. Y.*).

Mediterranean Herring Gull.—A. A male shot on Breydon, 4th November 1886 (*N. N. N. S. Trans.*). The first recorded British example.

Common Gull.—F. Local, "Sea Cob."

Glaucous Gull.—O.

Iceland Gull.—R. Five are recorded for the Yarmouth district (*B. of G. Y.*).

Kittiwake Gull.—F. C.

Great Skua.—R. Several are recorded for Lowestoft and Yarmouth, and one for Eccles.

Pomatorhine Skua.—N. U. on the coast. Local, "Boatswain."

Richardson's Skua.—R.

Buffon's Skua.—O. A fine male shot on Breydon, October 1890 (*B. of G. Y.*).

Razorbill.—F. C. Only occurs off the coast.

Common Guillemot.—F. C. Occurs on the coast. Local, "Wilduck."

(Ringed Guillemot.—This doubtfully distinct species has occurred at Yarmouth and Lowestoft.)

Black Guillemot. — A. Two are recorded for the coast (*B. of N.*).

Little Auk.—N. U. Considerable numbers have been blown inland during stormy weather.

Puffin.—R. Occasionally recorded for the coast. Local, "Sea Parrot."

Storm Petrel.—O. Messrs. Paget record that in November 1824 between two and three hundred were shot after a severe gale.

Fork-tailed Petrel.—R. R. Several are recorded for the coast.

Fulmar.—R. Recorded for Yarmouth and Lowestoft.

Great Shearwater.—A. One shot at Lowestoft in November 1898 (*N. N. N. S. Trans.*).

Manx Shearwater.—A. Two are recorded for Breydon (*B. of G. Y.*).

Little Dusky Shearwater (*Puffinus assimilis*).—A. One found dead near Bungay in April 1858.

Great Northern Diver.—R. R. Occasionally seen on the Broads.

White-billed Diver.—A. Mr. E. T. Booth shot one on Hickling Broad in December 1872 (*N. N. N. S. Trans.*).

Black-throated Diver.—R.   Three or four are recorded for Breydon and two for Oulton Broad.

Red-throated Diver.—F.   Frequent on Breydon.   One shot at Oulton in November 1900.   Local, "Sprat Loon."

Great Crested Grebe.—F. C.   Breeds on most of the larger Broads.

Red-necked Grebe.—R.   Several are recorded for the district.

Slavonian Grebe.—N. U.   A fairly regular winter visitor.

Eared Grebe.—R.   Several are recorded.   It is believed to have nested in the district, for Mr. E. T. Booth had an adult bird and two nestlings brought to him by a marshman.

Little Grebe.—F. C.   Breeds in the district.   Local, " Dabchick," " Dobchick."

Water Rail.—F. C.

Land Rail.—F. C.

Little Crake.—R.   Has occurred occasionally.

Spotted Crake.—R. R.

Baillon's Crake.—R.   In June 1886 a nest believed to be of this species was found at Potter Heigham.   Another found near Sutton Broad in May 1889 (*N. N. N. S. Trans.*).

Moor Hen.—C.   Local, " Water Hen."

Coot.—C.

Wood Pigeon.—C.   Local, " Dow," " Ring Dow."

Stock Dove.—F. C.   " Blue Rocker."

Turtle Dove.—F. C.   Nests in the district.

Sand Grouse.—A.   A considerable number of examples of this species were shot in the district in 1863 and in 1888.   A flock seen at Winterton in 1876.

Red-legged Partridge.—C.

Common Partridge.—C.

Quail.—R. R.   Formerly occurred occasionally in some numbers.

Pheasant.—C.

(Green-backed Gallinule (*Porphyrio porphyrio*).—A.   Sixteen have been recorded for the county : six for Barton Broad, the latest record 19th July 1898.   These birds are said to be escapes, but, as Mr. Southwell says in the *Transactions of the Norfolk and Norwich Naturalists' Society*, their repeated occurrence at Barton is very remarkable.)

Allen's Gallinule (*P. alleni*).—A.   An immature bird of this species alighted on a fishing-boat off Hopton on 31st December 1901.   It was identified by Mr. J. H. Gurney, who saw it alive, and believed it to be a genuine migrant.

(Pelican.—Sir Thomas Browne refers to a pelican having been shot on Horsey Fen on 22nd May 1663, but mentions that about that time a bird of this species escaped from the

King's Aviary in St. James's Park. The White Pelican (*Pelicanus onocrotalus*) formerly inhabited England: its bones have been found in the Norfolk Fens.)

Mammals

The Otter.—Although seldom seen by summer visitors, and believed to be decreasing in numbers, otters are not uncommon in Broadland; every year I hear of their being met with in the neighbourhood of the more isolated Broads and river reaches. The "orter," as the Broadsman calls it, is, as Dr. Emerson asserts, the "largest and fiercest wild animal" of the district. Calver, the old water bailiff of the Waveney and Oulton Fisheries Protection Society, has in the course of his life shot or trapped about a dozen otters, the largest weighing $27\frac{1}{2}$ lbs. They are, he says, "wasteful feeders," often biting only one mouthful out of a bream they have seized, and then leaving it dead on the river bank. When trapped they are often difficult to kill by blows, but will feign death until released from the trap, and then sometimes escape. Shallow Broads like Rockland and Barton are their favourite haunts: there they fish nightly. They have been known to take eels off the hooks on eel-lines. Their nests or lairs are variously placed, in alder carrs, among tree roots, or on the hovers by the riverside. Usually there is a hole in the hover near the nest, through which the otters dive if disturbed. Formerly they were frequently found drowned in the bow-nets used for taking pike. Marshmen and Broadsmen seldom allow such "warmint" to escape if they can help it, being glad to earn the few shillings a dead otter is valued at by the taxidermist.

The Polecat is rare, though occasionally encountered in the neighbourhood of rabbit warrens. The Stoat, locally known as the "lobster" or "minifa," is fairly common. It is found not only in game coverts and warrens, but on the marshlands, and may sometimes be seen in the dykes, which it visits for the purpose of getting at the eggs and young of water-hens. It is abundant near the coast warrens of Waxham and Horsey. The Weasel, locally the "mouse-hunter," often makes its nest in holes in the river walls. It is less ready than the stoat to enter water, but does so occasionally in pursuit of young rats and voles. Mice are its favourite prey, for which it often resorts to corn-stacks. On the marshes it finds voles. Lubbock says that "mice and voles compose great part of its diet. Even in spring, when partridges and pheasants are young, in all instances in which I have seen a weasel with prey in its mouth, the booty has turned out to be a mouse. The contrary is generally the case with the stoat, the ravages of which amongst game are very great." The gamekeepers, however, affirm that weasels not only attack young game birds, but young rabbits and leverets. Paget states that the Martin formerly occurred at Herringfleet; and on the same authority we learn that the Badger used to frequent the neighbourhood of the upper Ant.

Rabbits are plentiful in the district, but seldom seen on the marshes, though they sometimes make burrows in loose-soiled river walls near the "hangers" which slope down from the uplands to the marshes. Hares, on the contrary, are as fond of the damp ronds and water-meadows as of the upland fields, and strollers along the walls often disturb them from their forms among the rushes and sedges. Coursing - matches frequently take place on some of the marshes. In the neighbourhood of Cantley the marshmen are never tired of talking about a famous match in which the hare, after running a circular course of four and a half miles, was headed off by a boy and went over the whole ground again. It then dropped exhausted, as did the dogs, the foremost of which was only a few yards from the hare, but had not strength to reach it. Squirrels are found in most of the copses and plantations near the Broads and on the borders of the marshes. I have known one to visit a clump of riverside sallows, to reach which it must have made a mile-and-a-half journey across the marshes.

Hedgehogs occur frequently on the uplands and in the coverts on the borders of the marshes.

Moles are very abundant on the marshes, even on those subject to frequent floods; being able to swim as well as water-rats, they easily escape to dry ground when their runs are invaded by water. Not infrequently they are seen swimming across the dykes; on a stormy June day I saw one crossing the Waveney a little way above Geldeston Lock. Lubbock refers to cream-coloured moles havingbeen found in a certain marsh: these are not uncommon in some localities. Albinos are of frequent occurrence.

Brown Rats are too plentiful about many of the marshland hamlets and farmsteads, as well as around the Broads and in the river banks. According to Dr. Emerson, the farmstead rats are easily distinguished from the waterside rats, the former being rabbit-coloured with a yellow chest, the latter brown verging on red. A third variety, a small reddish rat, is also mentioned by marshmen, who call it the "ships' rat," believing that it was imported by ships. The waterside rats can always be seen by Broadland cruisers, who, besides observing their holes in the river banks, can even trace their overland runs along the dykesides. The Black Rat (*Mus rattus*), which the brown rat has almost exterminated, or at least supplanted, survives in Yarmouth, where it is not uncommon in some old houses in the "rows." From the same town Mr. A. Patterson records the Alexandrine Rat (*Mus alexandrinus*), a variety of *Mus rattus* undoubtedly introduced by some ship from the Mediterranean: it has also occurred in Norwich. Among the Mice of the district the Harvest Mouse (*Mus minutus*), a species of local distribution in this country, seems to be the least common. The Long-tailed Field Mouse (*Mus silvaticus*) is generally distributed over the district. Mr. Trevor-Battye asserts that in the dry summer of 1893 the black-headed gulls breeding at Scoulton frequently brought mice, which were probably of this species, to their nests, and killed them by dropping them from a height. I am not aware that the gulls breeding in Broadland have been observed to do this; but the kestrels, stoats, and weasels which frequent the marshes feed chiefly on mice. The Common Mouse (*Mus musculus*) is, as its name implies, common.

The Water Vole (*Microtus amphibius*) is in Broadland incorrectly called the water rat. It is abundant in the district, the banks of the rivers and dykes being honeycombed in all directions by its tunnels. It is less easily disturbed than the brown rat of the marshes, and can often be watched while feeding on some muddy bank ledge just above water. Osier-growers accuse it of damaging their osiers by nibbling the bark, and occasionally it is said to destroy root crops; but in the marshlands it does little harm, except where its tunnelling weakens a wall or causes a dyke-bank to subside. It swims well, and, according to Mr. Trevor-Battye, makes use of its hind legs alone when not hurried, carrying its fore paws close to its sides. The Common Field Vole (*Microtus agrestis*) is common on both uplands and marshlands; and the Bank Vole (*M. glareolus*) occurs not infrequently in fields and hedgerows. Of the Shrews, the Common Shrew (*Sorex vulgaris*), locally known as the "ranna" or "ranny," is generally distributed over the dry soils, and also occurs on the marshes. On account of its nocturnal habits it is seldom seen; but occasionally a nest of young shrews is discovered in a hedge-bank or among the marsh or meadow grass in summer. The Water Shrew (*Crossopus fodiens*) is found in similar places to the water vole, and, though seldom seen, is probably not so rare as some believe. The Oared Shrew, a dark variety of *Crossopus fodiens*, also occurs.

Of the Bats, the Noctule or Great Bat (*Vesperugo noctula*) is common, and the Pipistrelle or Common Bat (*Vesperugo pipistrellus*) is to be seen almost all through the year. The former is easily distinguished by its size; the latter is generally distributed over the district. The Long-eared Bat (*Plecotus auritus*) is probably not uncommon, as it is said to be plentiful in Norfolk. It has been identified at Yarmouth. The Barbastelle (*Synotus barbastellus*) is recorded for both Norfolk and Suffolk, so may possibly be included as a Broadland species. The Reddish-grey Bat (*Vespertilio nattereri*) has been identified.

Sir Thomas Browne records a Seal killed at Surlingham Ferry. A Grey Seal (*Halichœrus gryphus*) was shot on Breydon in 1882. Porpoises have been seen stranded on the Breydon flats. An Atlantic Right Whale (*Balœna biscayensis*) is said to have been taken near Yarmouth in 1784; the Common Rorqual (*Balœnoptera musculus*) has occurred at Winterton (1857) and Happisburgh (1875); a Lesser Rorqual (*B. rostrata*) was caught in Yarmouth harbour in 1891, and a dead example was stranded at Gorleston in 1896. The Grampus (*Orca gladiator*) is recorded for Yarmouth (1823), and the White-beaked Dolphin (*Delphinus albirostris*) for Yarmouth, Gorleston, and Breydon.

Reptiles

The Common Ringed Snake (*Tropidonotus natrix*) is somewhat rare in Broadland, though it may occasionally visit the marsh dykes in search of frogs, its chief food. I have seen specimens between four and five feet long taken on the Bath Hills, a wooded hanger sloping down to the Waveney near Bungay. The Viper or Adder (*Vipera berus*) is found on the heathlands, marshlands, marsh walls, and sandhills. In the neighbourhood of Hickling, it is, Dr. Gerald Leighton tells me, abundant. Marshmen are sometimes bitten by vipers, but I never heard of a fatal case occurring in the district. The treatment of a viper's bite is simple. A handkerchief or piece of cord should be bound tightly round the bitten limb above the wound—that is, nearer the body—to check circulation. Then the wound should be sucked thoroughly, and the saliva and venom spat out of the mouth. Oil or ammonia should, as soon as possible, be rubbed into the wound; but soft fat is almost equally efficacious if used quickly.

The Common Lizard (*Lacerta vivipara*) is common on the heaths and sandhills, and is also found on the river walls and warm dry banks. The Sand Lizard (*L. agilis*) does not occur in North Norfolk, and it is doubtful if it occurs in Broadland. *L. vivipara* is often mistaken for it. The Blind Worm, Slow Worm, or Deaf Adder (*Anguis fragilis*) seems to be rare, though it occurs occasionally near Lowestoft and in other parts of the district. Some of the country folk still believe it to be venomous.

Amphibians

The Common Toad and the Common Frog are abundant. The Running Toad or Natterjack (*Bufo calamita*), though local in distribution, is plentiful in some parts of the district. On the uplands of Reedham and the heathlands of Fritton and Herringfleet it is very common. It is easily distinguished from the Common Toad by its smaller size, the faint yellow line down its back, and its mode of progression. It never hops, but walks quickly, and sometimes runs like a mouse. The Rev. Theodore Wood found an Edible Frog in a lane at Brunstead. Two varieties of this species occur in Norfolk ; but this is the only instance of its being met with in Broadland I am aware of.

The three British newts, the Smooth Newt (*Molge vulgaris*), the Warty Newt (*M. cristata*), and the Palmate Newt (*M. palmata*), occur in the district. Dr. Gerald Leighton found all three species in a pond near Brunstead Church, the Palmate Newt being as common there as the Smooth and Warty Newts.

Alphabetical List of Fishes

Mr. A. Patterson's " Fishes of the Great Yarmouth District," published in the *Zoologist*, and the late Dr. J. Lowe's county list in the *Victorian History of Norfolk*, have assisted me greatly in compiling this catalogue of the Fishes of Broadland. I am indebted to Mr. Patterson for his kindness in reading and correcting the list, which chiefly owes to him its mention of so many marine species occurring in Breydon.

Angler (*Lophius piscatorius*).—Has occurred in Breydon.
Atherine (*Atherina presbyter*).—Occurs in Breydon and Lake Lothing. Common in Lowestoft harbour.
Bass (*Labrax lupus*).—Occasionally taken on Breydon.
Bib (*Gadus luscus*).—Breydon. " Great numbers on Breydon during September 1897 " (A. Patterson).

Blenny, Viviparous (*Zoarces viviparus*).—Breydon, where it is caught for crab bait.

Bream (*Abramis brama*).—Abundant in rivers and Broads.

Bream, Pomeranian (*A. Buggenhagii*).—Most frequently in the Bure.

Bream, White (*A. blicca*).—Abundant in the rivers, less common in the Broads. Plentiful in Fritton Lake.

Burbolt (*Lota vulgaris*).—Occurs in the Yare, Bure, and Waveney. Lubbock says it "seems to prefer the slow-running rivers to the Broads."

Carp (*Cyprinus carpio*).—Dr. Emerson says that the carp has been seen in Hickling and Barton Broads and in Irstead Shoals, being, from all accounts, commonest in Barton Broad. Mr. Patterson has seen specimens in Breydon, brought down by the ebb tide.

Carp, Crucian (*C. carassius*).—Occurs in one or two Broads and in Fritton Lake. "A solitary specimen has twice been observed in the Yare" (Lubbock). One at Potter Heigham, June 1901 (A. Patterson).

Chub (*Leuciscus cephalus*).—One was taken in the Waveney in 1890, by Mr. Patterson, who thinks it may "occur in some numbers in that river."

Coal Fish (*Gadus virens*).—Has been taken in the Bure and in Breydon.

Cod (*G. morrhua*).—Shoals of small ones visit Breydon in October.

Dab (*Pleuronectes platessa*).—Occasionally hooked on sandy patches in the lower waters of the rivers.

Dace (*Leuciscus vulgaris*).—Occurs in the Broads and rivers, chiefly in the upper waters of the latter.

Doree (*Zeus faber*).—A small specimen left by the ebb tide in a pool beside the Bure in 1879.

Eel (*Anguilla vulgaris*).—Abundant in the rivers, Broads, and dykes, and in Lake Lothing and Breydon.

Father Lasher (*Cottus scorpius*).—Frequent in Breydon.

Flounder (*Pleuronectes flesus*).—Locally called "butt." Abundant in Breydon, where it spawns in January, and is taken by fishermen with butt-darts. Occasionally met with in the rivers.

Garfish (*Belone vulgaris*).—Lubbock states that this fish, which is often caught by the herring and mackerel fishermen, once occurred within five miles of Norwich.

Goby, Little (*Gobius minutus*).—Breydon, often plentiful.

Goby, One-spotted (*G. unipunctatus*).—Frequent in Breydon.

Goby, Yellow-speckled (*G. auratus*).—Common in Breydon.

Gudgeon (*Gobio fluviatilis*).—Upper waters of the rivers; rarely in the Broads, though considerable numbers have been seen in the shallows at Filby.

Gurnard, Red (*Trigla cuculus*).—Has occurred in Breydon.

Gurnard, Grey (*T. gurnardus*).—Occurs in Breydon.

Herring (*Clupea harengus*).—Young herrings occur frequently in Breydon.

Lampern (*Petromyzon fluviatilis*).—Ascends the rivers to spawn. Often seen in stony shallows.

Lampern, Mud (*P. branchialis*).—Freshwater ditches (Dr. Lowe).

Lamprey, Sea (*P. marinus*).—Occasionally netted on Breydon. Two good specimens, said to have been taken in the lock at Geldeston, are preserved by the lock-keeper.

Lamprey, Planer's (*P. planeri*).—Has been found in Breydon (A. Patterson).

Loach (*Nemachilus barbatus*).—Stony shallows of the rivers' upper reaches.

Miller's Thumb (*Cottus gobio*).—Upper waters of the rivers and shallow "becks" and Broads.

Minnow (*Leuciscus phoscinus*).—Upper waters of the rivers.

Mullet, Grey (*Mugil capito*). — Breydon, Lake Lothing, and Oulton Broad.

Mullet, Lesser Grey (*M. chelo*).—A variety known as *M. septentrionalis* taken on Breydon in November 1890. "Without doubt *M. chelo* sometimes occurs" (A. Patterson).

Perch (*Perca fluviatilis*).—In all the rivers and most of the Broads.

Pike (*Esox lucius*).—Broads, rivers, and dykes.

Pipefish (*Syngnathus acus*).—Occasionally found in Breydon.

Pollack (*Gadus pollachius*).—Bure Mouth, Breydon, and Lake Lothing.

Ray, Thorn-back (*Raia clavata*).—Frequent in Breydon.

Ray, Spotted (*R. maculata*).—Small ones frequently found in Breydon.

Roach (*Leuciscus rutilus*).—Rivers and Broads.

Rockling, Five-bearded (*Motella mustela*).—Mr. Patterson has taken it on a hook on Breydon.

Rudd (*Leuciscus erythrophthalmus*).—Chiefly in the Broads, but small fish occur in the rivers. Abundant in Heigham Sounds and Hickling Broad.

Ruff (*Acerina vulgaris*).—Broads and river shallows.

Salmon (*Salmo salar*).—Formerly occurred occasionally in the rivers. One taken on a flooded marsh near Norwich in 1886 (Mr. Southwell).

Sea Snail (*Liparis vulgaris*).—Frequent in Breydon.

Shad, Allis (*Clupea alosa*).—Said by Lubbock to have been taken at Norwich in 1840. Occasionally found in Breydon.

Shad, Twait (*C. finta*).—Mr. Patterson has seen it netted on Breydon.

Smelt (*Osmerus eperlanus*).—Plentiful on Breydon, where it is netted. Also met with in the rivers, especially near Reedham. Occasionally two or three are taken in the Waveney eel-setts.

Sole (*Solea vulgaris*).—Occasionally taken on Breydon.

Sprat (*Clupea sprattus*).—Occasionally occurs in Breydon.

Stickleback, Three-spined (*Gasterosteus aculeatus*).—Abundant in many marsh dykes.

Stickleback, Nine-spined (*G. pungitius*).—Marsh dykes, preferring quite fresh water. " Shuns the society of the preceding species, which bullies it" (A. Patterson).

Stickleback, Fifteen-spined (*G. spinachia*).—Occurs in Breydon.

Sturgeon (*Acipenser sturio*).—Has been taken in the Yare and on Breydon. Lubbock records having seen a picture of one taken high up the Waveney, having the inscription, " This Sturgeon was taken upon the sholes above Beccles Bridge, on the 7th of April 1753." This fish is said to have weighed 11 stones 9 lbs.

Tench (*Tinca vulgaris*).—Broads, ponds, rivers, and ditches. Often seen in the weedy shallows of Barton Broad. " The Golden Tench is believed to have become naturalised, and to have bred sparingly in some of the Broads" (A. Patterson).

Trout (*Salmo fario*).—Upper waters of the Bure and Yare. " At long intervals two or three fine examples have been taken at Acle. Several years ago, the late Rev. C. J. Lucas turned out a number in Filby Broad, whence they had access to Rollesby and Ormesby Broads. Some increased in size, but they soon diminished in numbers" (A. Patterson).

Trout, Salmon (*S. trutta*).—Has occurred in the Yare, Bure, and Waveney, but very rarely.

Weever, Viper (*Trachinus vipera*).—Has occurred in Breydon.

Whiting (*Gadus merlangus*).—Often abundant in Breydon. I have known two to be taken in an eel-sett on the Waveney, twelve and a half miles from the sea.

Yellow Skulpin (*Callionymus lyra*).—Occasionally occurs in Breydon.

THE ROTIFERA OF BROADLAND

By H. E. Hurrell

THE following list of rotifers found in the Broads district is absolutely reliable, each species having been found by the writer and ratified by experts. It is to be regretted that the representative species of one order has yet to be found, namely, *Pedalion mirum*, belonging to the order Scirtopoda; but it is just possible that it has been overlooked on account of its resemblance to a larval form of Cyclops. Hudson and Gosse's order of tabulation has been rigidly adhered to, as being *facile princeps* the most up-to-date arrangement extant :—

ORDER I.—Rotatoria, Rhizota.

Floscularidæ—

Floscularia ornata.
      ,,   campanulata.
Stephanoceros Eichornii.

Melicertadæ—

Melicerta ringens.
Limnias ceratophylli.
Œcistes crystallinus.
Lacinularia socialis.
Megalotrocha albo-flavicans.
Conochilus volvox.
      ,,   unicornis.

ORDER II.—Bdelloida.

Philodinaceæ—

Philodina citrina.
      ,,   roseola.
Rotifer vulgaris.
      ,,   tardus.
Actinurus neptunius.

ORDER III.—Ploima (Il-loricata).

Asplanchnadæ—

    Asplanchna Brightwellii.

Synchætadæ—

    Synchæta pectinata.
            „   tremula.
            „   tavina.
            „   gyrina.
            „   cecilia.
            „   tressilia.

Triarthradæ—

    Triarthra longiseta.
            „   breviseta.
            „   polyarthra platyptera.

Notommatadæ—

    Notommata lacinulata.
            „   parasita.
    Furcularia longiseta.
            „   gibba.
    Diglena grandis (Loricata).

Rattulidæ—

    Mastigocera elongata.

Hydatinadæ—

    Hydatina senta.
    Rhinops vitrea.

Dinocharidæ—

    Dinocharis pocillum.
    Stephanops lamellaris.

Salpinadæ—

    Diaschiza semiaperta.

Euchlanidæ—

    Euchlanis dilatata.

Cathypnadæ—

    Monostyla solidaris.

Pterodinadæ—

    Pterodina patina.
            „   mucronata.
            „   elliptica.
    Pompholyx sulcata.

ORDER III.—Ploima (Il-loricata)—*continued.*

Brachionidæ—

Brachionus pala.
,,   Mülleri.
,,   rubens.
,,   angularis.
,,   urceolaris.
,,   Bakeri.

Anuræadæ—

Anuræa aculeata.
,,   acuminata.
,,   cochlearis.
Notholca longispina.
,,   acuminata.
,,   scapha.
,,   labis.

IV

GLOSSARY OF BROADLAND TERMS AND PROVINCIALISMS

BABBING or Bobbing—eel-catching with a bunch of worsted-threaded worms.

Blade—the leaves of the reeds or sedges.

Bolder—the real bullrush, *Scirpus lacustris*.

Bor—a term of address; probably an abbreviation of "neighbour." "Hallo, bor; how are you?"

Bottom-fye—to clean out, applied to dykes.

Buskin-net—a net formerly used along the borders of reed-beds, from which the fish were driven into it by beating the reeds with long poles.

Buttles—bitterns.

Camping—a game somewhat resembling football, formerly very popular in East Anglia.

Carr—a marshland copse or plantation, usually of alders or sallows.

Colts—young reeds.

Crome—a kind of rake used for cleaning out dykes.

Crome-stick—a stick with a curved or hooked handle, generally used for carrying a "frail."

Deek—dyke.

Denes—dunes. Sandy tracts near or among the coast sand-hills.

Ding—a blow; "full ding"—with full force.

Dodman—snail.

Drawing, dyke-drawing—cleaning out dykes.

Drey—nest; usually applied to a squirrel's.

Drift, driftway—a marsh or drove road along which cattle are driven to the marshes.

Drifter—a boat used for herring or mackerel netting.

Dydle or dydall—a kind of spade used in dyke-cleaning.

Eel-box—a box in which eels are kept alive in the water.

Eel-picking—eel-spearing; eel-pick—an eel-spear.

Eel-sett—a large fixed net used for taking eels.

Elvers—young eels.

Enow—enough.

Fare—appears, seems. " He *fare* to know."

Fared—seemed, appeared.

Fathom—five or six sheaves of reeds.

Flappers—young wild ducks.

Flats—mud-banks, oozy tracts left uncovered by the ebb tide.

Fleet—sometimes a marsh dyke, sometimes a shallow pool.

Frail—a basket made of plaited rushes.

Ganzy—a fisherman's guernsey.

Gin—give.

Gladen—yellow iris or water-flag. Really *Iris fœtidissima*, but in Broadland usually applied to *Iris pseudacorus.*

Groundsels—foundations.

Gun-boat or gun-punt—a boat used by marshmen and Broads-men for gunning, eel-spearing, etc.

Ham—a small bay or inlet of a Broad.

Hard—" on the *hard*" = on the shore, on the bank of a Broad or river.

Haysel—haymaking time.

Holls—upland ditches.

Hornpies—lapwings.

Hovers—boggy ground or floating vegetation by the riverside ; peat.

Hyst—hoist.

Keeler—a kind of tub.

Kentishmen—hooded crows.

Laid (with ice)—covered with a thin coating or layer of ice.

Lantern-men—will-o'-the-wisps, *Ignes fatui.*

Ligger—(1) a kind of trimmer, buoyed by a bunch of rushes, used for catching pike ; (2) a plank footbridge over a dyke.

Mash—marsh.

Meak or meag—an implement used by reed-cutters.

Merrimills—maram hills, sandhills.

Mind—remember.

Nigh—nearly.

Oily—a fisherman's waterproof coat.

Orters—otters.

Pattens—skates.

Picking—spearing.

Pokers—pochards.

Pot or pod—a kind of bow-net forming part of an eel-sett.

Puit—black-headed gull.

Pulk—a small pool or marsh pond.

Quant—a pole used for propelling yachts and wherries.
Quanter—punter.
Red-heads—pochards.
Reed pheasant—the bearded titmouse.
Rodger's blast—a sudden wind-gust or whirlwind.
Roke—fog.
Rokey—foggy.
Rond or rand—the swampy margin of a river or Broad.
    Usually applied to the boggy ground between the water
    and the river wall.
Roudding—spawning.
Saddle-backs—black-backed gulls.
Saltings—salt or meil marshes.
Salts—salt tides.
Scissor-grinder—grasshopper warbler.
Scoulton cobs—black-headed gulls.
Sea-smoke—sea fog.
Sets—willow wands or boughs.
Sharming—making a noise, crying.
Shooves—sheaves.
Shutting-in time—sunset.
Sight—good deal.   " A *sight* more "=a good deal more.
Skep—a kind of basket.
Slads—oozy grounds from which water has receded, or pools
    of flood-water on the marshes.
Slugging—cleaning mud, etc., out of the dykes.
Smee—wigeon.
Smelters—smelt-fishers.
Staithe—a wharf or landing stage.
Stuff, marsh stuff—marsh vegetation.
Thowt—thought.
Tru—through.
Turf—peat.
Wakes—holes or unfrozen places amid ice on a Broad.
Walls or river walls—artificial banks constructed for the pro-
    tection of the marshes from floods.
Wor—was.
Worams—worms.
Wuth—worth.

INDEX

INDEX

25

INDEX